FIGURING AGE

WOMEN,
BODIES,
GENERATIONS

FIGURING AGE: WOMEN, BODIES, GENERATIONS

IS VOLUME 23 IN THE SERIES

THEORIES OF CONTEMPORARY CULTURE

CENTER FOR TWENTIETH CENTURY STUDIES

UNIVERSITY OF WISCONSIN-MILWAUKEE

KATHLEEN WOODWARD, GENERAL EDITOR

FIGURING AGE

WOMEN, BODIES, GENERATIONS

Edited by
Kathleen Woodward

INDIANA UNIVERSITY PRESS BLOOMINGTON & INDIANAPOLIS

This book is a publication of

Indiana University Press
601 North Morton Street
Bloomington, Indiana 47404-3797 USA

www.indiana.edu/~iupress

Telephone orders   800-842-6796
Fax orders   812-855-7931
Orders by e-mail   iuporder@indiana.edu

Manufactured in the United States of America

Library of Congress Cataloging-in-Publication Data

Figuring age : women, bodies, generations /
edited by Kathleen Woodward.
p.   cm. — (Theories of contemporary culture ; v. 23)
Includes index.
ISBN 0-253-33450-0 (cloth : alk. paper). —
ISBN 0-253-21236-7 (pbk. : alk. paper)
1. Aged women—Social conditions. 2. Middle aged women—Social
conditions 3. Aging—Social aspects. 4. Women in mass media.
5. Feminist theory.   I. Woodward, Kathleen M.   II. Series.
HQ1061.F52   1999
305.26—dc21   98-20184

1   2   3   4   5   04   03   02   01   00   99

CONTENTS

WITHDRAWN

Contents

PSYCHOANALYTIC THEORY AND AGING

VISUALIZING AGE, PERFORMING AGE

Contents

FAMILY PORTRAITS

Introduction

Kathleen Woodward

In 1929 Virginia Woolf in *A Room of One's Own* lamented the lack of stories about women's everyday lives. Imagine, she urged her readers, "a very ancient lady crossing the street on the arm of a middle-aged woman, her daughter, perhaps, both so respectably booted and furred that their dressing in the afternoon must be a ritual" (116). About this older woman's life, Woolf complained, we know nothing. The details have vanished, never having been thought worthy of being recorded or imagined in the first place. Today we know infinitely more about the lives of younger women. But we still know precious little about the later years of Woolf's imaginary woman "close on eighty" (116), a woman who in her late seventies would not in fact today be considered "ancient" and would probably not be crossing the street on the arm of her daughter.

In 1986 Barbara Myerhoff, an anthropologist who in the seventies had studied a group of East European elderly Jews in Venice, California, told a story that was similar to but also altogether different from that imagined by Woolf. It is a true story, one that took place outside the Israel Levin Senior Center, the setting for the creation of a vivid, expressive community. This senior center was a space supported on the slenderest of shoestrings where people in their seventies, eighties, and nineties came together to celebrate with each other and to do battle with each other. One day as eighty-six-year-old Anna Gerbner was leaving the storefront center, she was run over by a young man on his bicycle. She was not on the arm of her daughter. She died of her injuries. What was his defense? "I didn't see her," he said (265). For me this small story with its appalling consequence is a parable of generational ignorance and the invisibility of older women in everyday life. Without either portentousness or sentimentality, Myerhoff concludes that Anna Gerbner's death was in fact an instance of *death by invisibility*. Importantly, however, the story does not stop with Gerbner's death. It moves into the arena of activism. The members of the senior center organize to protest Gerbner's death and to press for reforms. They are successful. In the process is created what Myerhoff calls an *arena of visibility*.

Introduction

It is my hope that *Figuring Age: Women, Bodies, Generations* will itself serve as an arena of visibility, one where readers find scholars in cultural and literary studies, artists, and writers addressing the virtually invisible subject of older women. "Figuring age" is meant to invoke the calculations of age, both the omnipresent numerical discourse on aging (is fifty old? sixty? sixty-five? and why?) and the virtually relentless social practice of trying to figure out someone's age (just how old is she? is she passing for a younger age? does she look older than she is? and what would that mean?). Figuring age also refers to the representation and self-representation of older women as well as to the figures that they present on the social stage.

Along with race, gender and age are the most salient markers of social difference. Recent research in cultural studies has been virtually dominated by studies of difference. We have invented courses in colleges and universities that study gender, race, sexual orientation, ethnicity, and class. But not age. Yet age is also clearly a relation of difference. Our culture has assigned different norms of behavior to different ages and has invented terms for different "stages." Like other markers of social difference, age is, in large part, socially constructed. Meanings are attached to the figures of age and aging based on a society's evaluation of aging. As Margaret Morganroth Gullette has astutely put it in *Declining to Decline: Cultural Combat and the Politics of the Midlife*, we are "aged by culture" as surely as our bodies experience biological change and, she argues, more so (6–7). Just as studies in gender and sexuality examine the ways in which sex-gender systems operate in various cultures, so age studies is concerned with understanding how differences are produced by discursive formations, social practices, and material conditions. Just as for feminists, experience has been an important touchstone, so for those of us committed to age studies, the tension between discourses of age and experiences of aging requires exploration. But I must emphasize that it is crucial that we focus on "age studies" and not the "study of aging." While at this point in time it is critical that research in cultural studies and the arts focus on the later years precisely because this time of life has been largely ignored, old age and middle age are part of the larger continuum of a discourse on age itself, a system of age that includes infancy, childhood, adolescence, and young adulthood. Thus I see *Figuring Age* as a contribution to the emerging field of age studies.

Our disregard of age is all the more curious because age—in the sense of *older* age—is the one difference we are all likely to live into.[1] Thus one of our most urgent tasks is to understand why we have kept the subject of aging at arm's length, that is, we must understand ageism itself. The term "ageism," in analogy with sexism and racism, was first coined in the late sixties in the United States by Robert Butler to name widespread discrimination against the elderly based on prejudice rooted in the very fact of being older.[2] Offering a predominantly psychological explanation (although one based in the western cultural tradition), he argued that ageism is rooted largely in people's personal fears of their own aging and death. This repression of aging—the denial of old age—characterizes our culture as a whole. The term "ageism" passed into common currency but the concept of ageism, unlike the concepts of sexism and racism, was not adopted by feminists. A few years later, in 1972, Susan Sontag referred to what she called the double marginality experienced by women who are older. Her thoughts were published in the *Saturday Review*, and it is understandable that her short essay might have been overlooked. But how could Simone de Beauvoir's huge book on aging go unremarked? Some eight hundred pages long, it was published in English in the United States in 1972 and offered a trenchant indictment of western culture for its shameful treatment of the elderly. Her earlier book, *The Second Sex*, had influenced generations of women. But *The Coming of Age*, as it was so inaptly entitled in the United States, was ignored by mainstream readers, feminists, and even scholars of Beauvoir herself. In the 1980s lesbian feminists Barbara Macdonald and Baba Copper wrote forcefully about their experience of invisibility as older women within the women's movement itself; indeed, Copper explained that she felt "shunned" because she was older (14). Their work has also been invisible to academic feminists. My point here is that ageism is entrenched within feminism itself. To some this may come with a shock—if so, hopefully it will be one of recognition. But why should we be so surprised that as women we have ourselves internalized our culture's prejudices against aging and old age?

There are other reasons as well for the fact that aging has been virtually ignored as an issue important to women. During the second wave of feminism, the emphasis was on issues that are associated with the earlier years in the life course, with, for example, reproductive rights, child care, and the right to enter certain domains of work. Within the academy, research in cultural studies has reflected the concerns of younger women. Consider, for example, feminist cultural studies of technology and medicine. The focus has been on reproductive technology, not on the delivery of health care in the later years. Consider as well the influential work in psychoanalysis and feminism in the past twenty years. The stress has been on pre-oedipal models of mother-infant symbiosis and on mother-infant mutual recognition. Only now is the topic of generations beginning to capture people's interest. Moreover, what I call the "address" of the academy is young. Its student population is not only for the most part conceptualized as young, most of its undergraduates *are* young. In the humanities and the arts, aging is a subject that many believe holds little interest or relevance for them.

Whatever the reasons for ageism within feminism and especially within the academy itself, the results of ageism, particularly for women, can be lethal, as Myerhoff's story tells us. Consider as well these words of an eighty-seven-year-old widow who lives with her son and daughter-in-law, words that express the aggressive shaming to which she is subjected for her incontinence. "I'm only allowed to sit on one chair," she reported to the sociologist Candace Clark. "Nobody talks to me all day except to yell at me. I've never been so humiliated in my life. I just want to die" (311). Here we see the pedagogy of mortification at work to teach an older woman to recede into invisibility. It is as if the practice of humiliation by the younger generation produces shame and the corresponding wish to shrink in size.

Virginia Woolf brilliantly remarked in *A Room of One's Own* that for centuries women have functioned as mirrors to men that reflect them back twice their size. Similarly younger people (and older people who deny their own aging) have functioned as mirrors to older women, reflecting them back half their size. Surely the practice of the disregard of older women is one of the reasons why in fact we have so many "little old ladies." Lifelong activist Maggie Kuhn, who worked for years championing older women and older men as a vital and overlooked national resource, recounts this telling story. She was invited to the White House when Gerald Ford was president to watch him sign a pension bill, the first federal law to regulate pension plans. Among the many people who wanted to ask a question or make a statement, Kuhn attracted Ford's attention. "'And what have you to say, young lady?' he asked." She replied, "'Mr. President, I am not a young lady. I'm an old woman.' . . . I just couldn't help reminding him that his words weren't a compliment. Old people are old" (143). By patronizing her, Ford reduces her size to that of a child, and as we know, the link between childhood and old age is, as we say, age-old.

But we also have formidable older women, women whose mirrors are their work and their friends. Consider, for instance, the testimony of American sculptor Louise Nevelson, who in her mid seventies responds, as it were, in her extravagantly theatrical way to Woolf's wish to hear the stories of older women. In a striking series of autobiographical reflections Nevelson insists in a voice that is explosive with declarative energy, "Nothing—friendship, love, or anything—will come to such a harmony or unity as you come to in your work. . . . The work and you are one, the work is a living example, it's just as living as you are. It's your reflection" (43). The life-world of Nevelson's monumental sculpture does not reflect back to her a little old lady but a vitally creative woman who works with wood. And what would she be, Nevelson concludes, if she still lived in the small coastal Maine town where she was brought up? "If I was there now and I was seventy-six years old, I'd be an old lady. . . . So you see," she continues, "it's placement" (7). A woman's "placement," her social context— and thus in great part her sense of herself—can largely determine whether she is seen, and sees herself, as a little old lady (what Nevelson means by "old," a woman who is given no sense of power or potential). Carolyn Heilbrun, literary scholar and author of the Amanda Cross detective stories, writes in her book *The Last Gift of Time: Life beyond Sixty* that for her, work is essential, but friendship is even more so. "Friendship was the key and the great gift of my sixties," she tells us (100). Importantly, Maggie Kuhn believed that the work of older activists should not be only on their own behalf. "We must act as elders of the tribe," she has said, "looking out for the best interests of the future and preserving the precious compact between the generations" (209).

The distasteful metaphor of "over the hill" implies being out of sight, invisible and hence out of mind. The practice of ageism can also be a horrible self-fulfilling prophecy. As younger women turn these very prejudices against women older than themselves, they will in effect be turning against their very future selves as older women. If it is true that older women are more vulnerable than older men to the stigma attached to age and thus suffer more from negative cultural stereotypes, what younger woman counts among her ambitions to be a little old lady or a wicked old witch?

The cultural demographer Patrice Bourdelais has persuasively shown that "the age of old age," as he calls it, has changed over the centuries.[3] Although his research takes gender into account, Bourdelais is interested primarily in old age, and in old age in predominantly biological terms. Sontag, as I mentioned, astutely observed that older women are subject to a double marginality. Women are also subject to what I call "double aging" or "multiple aging." Unlike men, women in mainstream culture in the United States today are struck by aging as it is defined by our culture far earlier than men. This symbolic date with aging occurs when they—we—are around fifty, a date that coincides with the biological marker of menopause, an event (if one can call it that) that in our culture has been viewed negatively. In the West female attractiveness has long been associated with youth, and the older woman has been thought of in disparaging terms as "menopausal" and "post-menopausal."[4] It is thus not an accident that many women around the age of fifty *experience* aging, an experience that does not have the same counterpart in men and thus the same psychological, social, and economic consequences for men. By experiencing aging, I am referring primarily to the internalization of our culture's denial of and distaste for aging, which is understood in terms of decline, not in terms of growth and change. As the late Glenda Laws argued in "Understanding Ageism," in order to understand ageism as a set of social practices with the aging body as its target, we must avoid essentializing the aging body. The experience of growing older is, in other words, profoundly shaped by the meanings which are ascribed to aging.

It may at first seem odd to associate aging with what is understood after all to be midlife. But that is precisely the point. For women, aging casts its shadow earlier than for men. I am here alluding to the words of one of Fannie Hurst's characters, a woman named Bertha who, when trying to find employment in domestic service, was told in one of her last interviews that she was too old. Frantic and perceptive, Bertha thinks to herself: "*You're too old. You're too old. You're too old.* The phrase was so sly. It ran after you like a shadow. It would never let you be" (311). Thus it is critical that we attend to the articulations of women's experience of the shadow of aging cast by our culture at midlife. It is not for nothing that Betty Friedan opens her book *The Fountain of Age* referring to her own dread of aging in her fifties. Or that *Fear of Fifty* is the title of a recent book by Erica Jong. Many of the contributors to *Figuring Age* are also women in their fifties, but if they write of anxiety and ambivalence associated with aging, they also write with surety and self-confidence, even with equanimity. The poet Maxine Kumin, in an interview with Diana Hume George, has said that she first began to feel confident around the age of fifty. Tellingly, both Germaine Greer and Carolyn Heilbrun, among others, have written of the age fifty as a turning point in terms of the invisibility of older women. Both insist that this new phase of life will be different.

But to my mind something peculiar happens in the pages of Greer and Heilbrun. The invisibility of older women is taken up not only as a condition imposed on women by a male- and youth-dominated culture, but as one that can be salutary in and of itself. Greer's book *The Change* bristles with caustic energy. Nonetheless, she insists: "It is quite impossible to explain to younger women that this new invisibility, like calm and indifference, is a desirable condition, at first even the changing woman herself protests against it . . . but sooner or later she will be forced to accept it" (430).[5]

More curious still is the notion of invisibility as a *passage*, as something we must submit ourselves to if we are to emerge later as fully ourselves (Greer) or as authoritative (Heilbrun). Greer wants to invest menopause with the weighty significance of a rite of passage, one she understands as the transition from being reproductive to being reflective—as if all women defined themselves in terms of reproduction before menopause and in asexual terms after menopause. This oddly archaic biological essentialism is, in my view, both retrograde and anachronistic. Greer adopts the age of fifty as her pivot point, assuming that in a woman's life her children have now left home. But today many women at fifty have not had children. Today many women are having children later in the life course precisely as a matter of course. Today many women are as a matter of course serving as the primary caretakers of their grandchildren. And today many are also profoundly involved with the care of their own mothers. We must abandon the older models of age-appropriate behavior and experience (when the birth of children should occur, or marriage, or retirement, for example). We need to imagine a long course of life that will realistically stretch for women into their eighties and nineties and reach to one hundred years.

Heilbrun draws on the trope of the passage through invisibility in the life course as a quest, one beset by the dark emotion of desperation. As she writes in an essay entitled "Coming of Age," "we will watch ourselves grow invisible to youth worshippers, and to the male gaze. Despair is inevitable but must be wrestled with. The hardest initiation lies ahead, an initiation as in a fairy tale, readying one for a quest: To get to that new place, a woman must pass through the stage of invisibility" (58). Although it is true that Heilbrun is reducing female power here to sexual attractiveness, nonetheless the contributors to *Figuring Age* reject the notion that women as they grow older must pass through invisibility, as though we must adopt the veil.

The next date of aging—sixty-five—coincides with our society's setting of sixty-five as an appropriate age of retirement from work (that is, from work outside the home). Both men and women, whether they work or not, are affected by this chronological signpost, one that signifies old age in the United States. Given, however, the dramatic increases in health far into one's seventies and beyond, this symbolic date is no longer linked with biological old age. Indeed the age of old age is now, according to Bourdelais, seventy-five.[6] This would be, then, a third date of aging, one not yet recognized by western culture at large. We need, in other words, to distinguish carefully between biological aging and aging that is produced by culture. We need also to see how peculiar a cultural practice it is to associate certain transitions with a precise chronological age. In her essay included in this volume, literary scholar Teresa Mangum, discussing children's literature of the Victorian period in England, reminds us that the age of old age is historically specific; she traces the very marginalization of older women in part to the cultural invention of social groups on the basis of age—children and the old—and to the legislation that brought these groups into being. We also need to recognize that we are living in the midst of a long revolution that Robert Butler has termed the longevity revolution. It is one of immense demographic proportions that will alter postindustrialized societies in profound ways, a revolution that is affecting women in particular.

In the United States life expectancy has increased by a stunning number of years since 1900—from forty-seven years to eighty-one. This means that growing old has become, as it were, a birthright. Today people in the United States can expect to live into what has long been understood as "old age," with women in fact living on the average eight years longer than men. We have achieved what the philosopher and cultural critic of aging Harry R. Moody has called, to refer to the title of one of his books, *The Abundance of Age*. And yet many fear this newfound abundance of life, assuming that it inevitably brings years of decline when in fact this is not the case. We have, in other words, hardly begun to examine critically what this revolution in longevity means. As the historian of aging Thomas Cole remarked in his introduction to the *Oxford Book of Aging*, we are culturally illiterate about aging.

When in fact someone dies today before their time, as we say, we are shocked into a sense of the unfairness of such an untimely death, as indeed the contributors to this volume were when the talented geographer and cultural critic Glenda Laws, whom many of us had met for the first time in the spring of 1996 at the conference from which the essays in this book are drawn, suddenly died—from a cerebral hemorrhage—only two months later. She was thirty-eight. We miss her—and the prospect of her continuing work in the field of age studies. As the poet Marilyn Hacker writes in "Against Elegies" in *Winter Numbers*, a poem Mary Russo quotes in her essay in this book about the very subject of untimely death, "No one was promised a shapely life / ending in a tutelary vision" (13).

What is also shocking is that if someone dies in their sixties today, often their death is not perceived as untimely. This is wrong. Many will seek to console themselves and others with the notion that they have lived a full life—that is to say, a long life. But the promise of the longevity revolution is that our expectations for what is a full life—an abundant life—should be consonant with life expectancies. Here again we see the evidence that we are culturally illiterate about aging and the meanings of the longevity revolution, a lack of understanding that can have devastating consequences, as when, for example, a woman in her early seventies may not receive adequate medical attention because she is deemed in effect at the end of her life.

In addition to the increase in life expectancy, the number of those who are older proportionate to those who are younger is rising at a rapid rate. The fastest growing age group in the United States today is comprised of those eighty-five and older. We are an aging society, and the vast proportion of those who are older are women. In the future, societies will require the active participation of older people in all levels of the organization of social life. We thus need to invent new ways of thinking about growing older, in particular for the much later years. As Alan Pifer and Lydia Bronte have argued, by the middle of the twenty-first century the impact of this revolution in aging "will have been at least as powerful as that of any of the great economic and social movements of the past" (3), including the women's movement of the past thirty years in the United States. The aging of the population in western countries will have consequences as far-reaching as the massive displacements and migrations of populations that are taking place today around the globe.[7]

The purpose of this book is to help to bring the subject of older women into visibility and to reflect on growing older as women, with our contributions to this project built primarily on the foundation of stories and images, words and visual texts. Many of the essays address the cultural discourses and social practices that construct the meaning of aging for us. Many of the authors, turning to the genre of personal narrative, reflect on how their experience of growing older is inflected by these cultural meanings attached to age. Many turn to recent artwork—in literature, film, photography, and performance—to imagine alternative futures. Bodies and generations constitute two of the major themes of the book. The work of our visual culture itself, which constructs many of our images of both bodies and generations, constitutes a third.

As Glenda Laws so succinctly put it, "demographic landscapes are, of course, part and parcel of consumer landscapes."[8] Given the virtual obsession of western culture with youth and with the appearance of the body, given the very real prospect of frailty in older age, mass culture, which is a consumer culture, seizes on the vast disparities between what it presents as two extremes, producing the older female body as both invisible and hypervisible, envisioning aging as a medical problem to be cured and leaving small explosions of anxiety in its wake. A cleaver-sharp binary between beauty and the so-called ravages of time, between health and disability, figured as old age, is encoded daily in the stories and advertisements in the mass media. In 1995, for example, the cover of *Time* carried the image of two women's hands—one young and the other older—accompanied by these words: "Estrogen: Every Woman's Dilemma." The implication of the image is that the choice is clear. Moreover, this image is in fact only that—an image, the devolution of the body (indeed just parts of the body) into the "catastrophe" of old age. These are not particular women. There is no history, no experience, no subjectivity embodied in the image of the two hands held up to our gaze for ruthless comparison. In this image we have encapsulated as well one of the intractable problems of the discourse of age itself: it pivots on the blunt binary of young and old, as if there were only two states of age. It is surely clear, however, that the meanings of our experience over the long lives that we may live cannot be expressed by the rhetoric of young and old. In feminist theory and in queer theory much recent work has focused on theorizing both sex (female and male) and gender (femininity and masculinity) beyond the number of two. This has been a difficult project. We should also think beyond youth and age, young and old, a project that would seem to be altogether easier.

The first section of *Figuring Age*—"Opening the Subject"—includes essays by Nancy K. Miller, Mary Russo, and Margaret Gullette. Nancy Miller's essay elegantly introduces many of the recurring themes in the book—women witnessing their aging through the mirrors held up to them by the older women in their family, our need at this point in time for what she calls "public" bodies that represent older women otherwise, and the uncanny intersections that can take place between developmental time and historical time (Miller refers to the strange coincidence between midlife aging and what seems today to be a virtual epidemic of breast cancer diagnosed at precisely that point). Mary Russo, who has previously written incisively on the normative and deadening injunction to not make a spectacle of yourself, one which includes "acting your age," also takes up themes central to the book, including the rhetoric of age and the old in a culture of commodification and the shame and abjection that may be a woman's lot in later life. Russo's impulse is to disrupt the orderly developmental model of the stages of a woman's life and she does so in part by reflecting on cross-generational relationships between women (they are not daughter and mother) that take us, I suspect, by surprise—relationships between an "aging" woman in midlife and an older woman who will in all likelihood survive her. The third essay in the opening section is by Margaret Gullette who was, to my knowledge, the first to use the term "age studies" (in analogy with gender studies). Gullette's essay is a superb model of age studies as well as an invitation to others to consider the category of age in analyzing any pervasive cultural practice. Just how we are aged by culture is her specific interest, and in her essay she appraises the crazy and relentless logic of the fashion system, propelled by consumer culture. In teaching us both how to desire something new and to unfeelingly discard the old, the fashion system teaches us as well that growing older is a process of loss and of decline, ultimately one in which we lose our very selfhood.

All of the contributions to this book could be described as inquiries into the formative influences on women's aging, but three of the essays—those that constitute the second section, entitled "Historicizing Age"—explore this question from explicitly historical perspectives. Teresa Mangum discusses the representation of older women in Victorian children's literature and conduct literature, focusing on the link established between children and older women. It was this link, Mangum argues, that forged the destructive view of older age as a second childhood and thus a period of dependency, and established the hegemony of adulthood, which is to say, of the middle-aged. Mangum also explores the connection between the figure of the older woman as marginal and England's imperial colonial mission, showing how the older woman was often represented as deserving of deportation along with criminals and other unworthy figures; here she makes explicit the destructive association between ageism and racism. Like Mangum, Susan Squier also takes up linkage between the first part of life and the latter part of life, but her focus is altogether different. Squier examines the converging discourses of medical science, feminism, and racialization in the early part of the twentieth century in England and the United States. She shows that the projects in reproductive technology and in rejuvenation therapy mirrored one another in interesting ways (as she brilliantly suggests, the neo-nate found its analogue in the neo-mort), in particular how growing older came to be viewed as a medical problem that could be solved by technological intervention. As she points out, the descendant of rejuvenation therapy for women is hormone replacement therapy for the "disease" of menopause. Finally, Stephen Katz, commenting on the disappointing lack of connection between those who do research in women's studies and those who do research in what is called "aging studies" in gerontological circles, returns to the site of Jean Charcot's Salpêtrière in France in the late nineteenth century, a hospital associated for so long in the minds of many with the hysteric female. Surprisingly, what Katz finds there is also a large population of older women, the bodies of whom in fact served as the basis for Charcot's *Clinical Lectures on the Diseases of Old Age*, a landmark if not founding text in geriatrics.

In "Psychoanalytic Theory and Aging," the book's third section, social theorist Teresa Brennan addresses the question of the relation between the social and the physical, drawing on Freudian psychoanalytic theory to explore the means by which we are aged by the very process of "development"—in particular how "rigidity" comes to mark both femininity and age. Brennan compellingly theorizes how over time what she calls a person's "fixed point" or "standpoint" emerges (it is born out of repression), achieved by binding what was once freely circulating energy. The more that we see things from our own fixed point, the stronger our ego, but the less energy—energy that is unbound—we have to resist the inevitable rigidity that accompanies the very formation and persistence of the ego. What can we do to resist this process? We can resist psychically, she suggests, by seeking out experiences—meditation, the fictional worlds provided by literature and drama, and exercise are all examples—that do not mirror ourselves in rigid ways and thus reinforce our self-centeredness, but are free of our selves and thus refresh us, providing new energy. Drawing on a Freudian model of energetics, Brennan also gives it a cultural cast, theorizing how our image culture contributes to canceling energy and thus hastening aging.

My essay takes as its point of departure another model provided by Freudian theory, that of the relations between generations. Based on the model of parent and child, it is limited, I argue, not only because it views relations between generations in terms of the nuclear family (that is, two generations only) but also because it is based on the damaging notion that the younger generation must struggle against and break away from the preceding generation. We expect mothers to care for their children when they are young without reciprocity. But if when we are adults we continue to regard older women as existing in a structural relation to us as mothers or grandmothers, women who served us or frightened us when we were young, what does that mean we will continue to expect of older women—especially women who are not members of our family but rather are friends and colleagues? What will younger women expect of us?

The fourth section of *Figuring Age* is entitled "Visualizing Age, Performing Age." If we live in a culture driven by consumption, we also live in a culture saturated by images. A cluster of these essays address the ways in which our "image culture," as Vivian Sobchack puts it, shapes our view of older women and shows women performing age. Sobchack astutely argues, in fact, that the institution of cinema itself and the technology of digital morphing and digital cleaning are altering our very sense of how our bodies should deflect the passage of time. Cosmetic surgery (a case of which Sobchack recounts) is the analogue of this digital technology on the screen, both of which reveal the dread of middle-aging. This dread is openly declared in the low-budget fantasy films of the late fifties and sixties which Sobchack discusses, films that show middle-aged women as truly scary women.

It is clear that aging is a veritable trauma for many women, as E. Ann Kaplan acutely suggests, especially for women whose work depends on the glamorous gaze of the screen itself and whose value as an image-commodity depends on their youthfulness (this theme is also central to the essay by Jodi Brooks). Marlene Dietrich is for Kaplan a perfect exemplification of this, while Melanie Klein and Marguerite Duras provide different models of how the medium itself in which they chose to work affects and inflects how they experience growing older. How are stars of the screen represented as dealing with the crisis of aging? Brooks considers such films as *Sunset Boulevard* and *Opening Night*, arguing that it is in the stars' charismatic rage and confusion at being dismissed from the scene that they retain for the spectator a galvanizing power. It is in the very performing of the crisis that is aging for women—performing "an excessive visibility," in the words of Brooks—that they resist being aged by culture, slowing down the process of time itself. How does the stage differ from the screen? Anne Basting reflects on her experience as a younger woman watching the spectacle of Carol Channing at the age of seventy-four play what has become over time her signature role of Dolly, a character who is middle-aged and whom Channing herself first played when she was forty-three. In this instance, age is both denied and celebrated; it is both invisible and hypervisible. Channing's performance becomes the performance of age itself.

Basting also explores the relationship between femininity and age in her essay, a subject of other essays as well, including Joanna Frueh's essay on midlife bodybuilders. The aesthetic of the strong and consciously built body serves, Frueh suggests, as a kind of rebuttal—I would say also as a rebuke—to the vapid femininity many women cultivate in midlife, capitulating to a male-dominated set of values. Molded by an aesthetic discipline, this body, importantly, has vast reservoirs of strength and can thus resist the physical weakening that can come with growing older. The built body, often shocking in its hyperarticulation, also serves for Frueh as a rejoinder to the matronly body, one of our culture's models for the older woman, a woman who is outside of the circuit of sexual desire.

What other alternatives can we imagine to our culture's stereotypical models for the midlife woman and the woman older than that? In her essay Nancy Miller refers us to Sheila Solomon's monumental and reassuring sculptures in which we see the body differently, otherwise. Anca Cristofovici refers us to the artwork of several photographers, including Cindy Sherman, Jeff Wall, and Geneviève Cadieux. Paradoxically, Cristofovici's purpose is not so much to recast our culture's view of the body as to see through the body, as it were, to psychic space, a space in which our identity is always composed of what she calls our different "age-selves." Cristofovici thus poses a subtle challenge to the binary of young and old, youth and age, suggesting as well that we see the older body not as what it is not—it is not a youthful body—but as an accomplished shape.

Other contributions to the volume are from artists who work in visual mediums themselves. Rachel Rosenthal, the flamboyant, risk-taking, shape-shifting performance artist who has recently turned seventy, offers thoughts on her experience—on her life as a process of orphaning herself, on her seeing herself suddenly as an old woman at the age of sixty, and on her new work in the theater. A sheaf of Jacqueline Hayden's outsized, stunning photographs of nude older women, work about which Cristofovici writes, is included in *Figuring Age*, as is the libretto of "Not a Jealous Bone," a videotape by Cecelia Condit. The words to "Bone," a magical micro-opera of the struggle between an older woman and a younger woman (the older woman wins the bone), is accompanied by several stills from the piece. Rendering older women visible in dramatic and delicate ways, the images and words of Rosenthal, Hayden, and Condit constitute not "an aesthetic of effacement," to quote Cristofovici, but "an aesthetic of expressivity," an impulse to which this book is dedicated.

The book closes with a section entitled "Family Portraits," composed of personal narratives, each of which return us to the domain of the family, albeit in different ways. For in our culture, permeated as it is with images of youth, we may first *experience* aging through the mirror of the family and through the care given to our older relatives, or we may model our relationships in life through older women in our families. The essays by Marie-Claire Pasquier and Patricia Mellencamp are in fact more than personal narratives—they are hybrids. Pasquier reflects on the prevalence in France of the lesbian couple composed of a younger woman and an older woman, speculating that this choice may not be based, as is often assumed, on a narcissistic model of the mother-daughter relationship but rather on the model of the younger sister–older sister. One of the important contributions of her essay is that she is attentive to the specificity of the major events in the history of France from World War I to today which, she suggests, may have shaped the development of this lesbian couple. Pasquier also filters her reflections through her own personal history, although it is a history which is, I would say, more public than private. Patricia Mellencamp intricately interlaces a story of her personal life (her experiences span four generations of her family), with a disarming tale of her intellectual life, offering a deft reading through Freud and others of how aging has come to be seen as a catastrophe, especially for women. But as Mellencamp suggests, the view of aging as a catastrophe is countered in one of our most pervasive cultural forms—television. In daytime soaps in particular, aging is presented as a process of gradual change, one that takes place within the domain of an extended family that spans many generations. "TV history," she writes, "is mixed up with the comfort and reassurance of personal history and personal memory, which are often generational and familial." Continuity is her theme, including the continuity of one's identity over time even as the body changes. The very emphasis of our culture on the body as key to one's identity is, of course, part of the problem. We must, she suggests, drawing on Freudian terminology, shift our attention away from the body ego.

Like Mellencamp, Joanne M. Braxton, in the four poems included here, also traces a genealogy of women through four generations, whose common story is in part how to survive white America. In the first two poems Braxton writes as a young woman, a student returning in her mind's eye to the women who preceded her. In *Miss Maime*, we read about her grandmother ("*An old Colored woman whose picture / I take out at three o'clock in the morning*"), the woman whose hands "healed" her. Some twenty years later Braxton's focus has shifted. She turns to a woman of her own generation—to the woman who makes love to her and whose childhood she imagines—and to a child who will become a woman, her own daughter, Mycah. Will the genealogy hold? Braxton seems to ask, wondering how her own ancestors will make her daughter their own. In Braxton's work, age and the continuity of generations are both embodied and phantasmatic, figuring hope for the future.

Susan Letzler Cole and Elinor Fuchs both write of their mothers in a mode that is focused more personally. "Missing Alice" is excerpted from a longer piece by Cole in which she finds herself compelled, after her mother's death, to write letters to her. I find this fascinating—in great part because Cole addresses the letters included here not to "Mother," but to "Alice Parson," to the person who, as an adolescent, wrote the diary which her daughter found only after her death. That Cole strives to understand Alice Parson not only in relation to herself, as her mother, but as a young girl whom she never knew is crucial here. This is a family portrait, but a family portrait where, in a very real sense, the dimension of family is partially extruded. Fuchs, in an autobiographical account that is alternately moving and hilarious and often both at the same time, focuses on her relationship to her mother over the years, but particularly during her mother's last years when she suffered from Alzheimer's disease. Fuchs's essay thus also returns us to the experience of the undeniable vicissitudes of aging that may touch our lives and our bodies. For unlike other markers of difference (gender and race, for example), old age cannot be theorized or understood as a social construction only, one that erases the real changes of the body that can come with aging and old age. There is a point at which the social or cultural construction of aging must confront the physical dimensions, if not the very real limits of the body. As social theorists Mike Featherstone and Mike Hepworth have correctly asserted, "we must be careful not to adopt a view of the life course in which culture is granted the overarching power to mold nature in any form it chooses. Human beings share with other species an embodied existence inevitably involving birth, growth, maturation, and death" (147). Thus in recognizing and repudiating our culture's negative and trivializing stereotypes of old age, we must take equal care not to produce a similarly limiting repertoire of "positive" stereotypes that ignore what may be the real physical liabilities of old age.

I see *Figuring Age: Women, Bodies, Generations* as complementing two excellent and important collections of essays on aging that have appeared recently— *Aging and Gender in Literature: Studies in Creativity*, edited by Anne Wyatt-Brown and Janice Rossen, and *Images of Aging: Cultural Representations of Later Life*, edited by Mike Featherstone and Andrew Wernick. *Aging and Gender in Literature* is devoted to the study of how growing older may affect psychological development and creativity in the realm of writing, with an emphasis on how change may begin in middle age. As their starting point the contributors to *Aging and Gender in Literature* draw on literary texts, but biography is central, as is theorizing about fiction and late life. Among other things, *Images of Aging* focuses on the ways in which the images of the older body overdetermine a culture's collective sense of what constitutes aging, especially in late twentieth-century consumer culture which is, I would say, in overdrive.

Introduction

In his essay in *Images of Aging*, the American historian Andrew Achenbaum looks back at an exhibit that he and the art librarian Peg Kusnerz assembled in 1976 to explore the cultural and historical influences that shaped the experiences and meanings of old age in the United States from 1790 on. Although both he and Kusnerz were explicitly concerned with the heterogeneity of aging in the United States, Achenbaum stresses that if they were to re-envision their exhibit they would want to emphasize diversity even more strongly. If I were asked to single out what I find most lacking in *Figuring Age: Women, Bodies, Generations*, it would be the diversity of which Achenbaum writes. It is my hope, then, that *Figuring Age* will serve to invite, if not to incite, others to write about women, bodies, and generations not just in terms of mainstream, middle-class culture, one that is predominately white, but in a myriad of other cultural and subcultural contexts as well.

All of the contributions to *Figuring Age* were initially presented at a conference I organized at the Center for Twentieth Century Studies in April 1996. Over fifty people participated in "Women and Aging: Bodies, Cultures, Generations," and some one hundred fifty people attended. It was for me an exhilarating event. Those who know me personally are well aware that I thrive on conferences, but this particular event was especially important to me. I am enormously grateful to the University of Wisconsin-Milwaukee for the sponsorship of "Women and Aging" which was, to my knowledge, the first international academic conference devoted to the study of women and aging from the perspectives of cultural studies, literary studies, and the arts. I want to thank Marshall Goodman, Dean of the College of Letters and Science, for his energetic support. I want especially to acknowledge here the long-term sponsorship of the Center by the late George Keulks, a man who believed deeply in the value of research and who understood how that strange institution that is the public university works; as the dean of the Graduate School, he had been my colleague ever since I was appointed director of the Center for Twentieth Century Studies. I miss his presence on the second floor of Mitchell Hall.

That the conference took place within the context of an entire year's research at UWM's Center for Twentieth Century Studies devoted to the subject of "Age Studies" provided the three-day event with both intellectual amplitude and depth. My intellectual companions from UWM that year who were fellows at the Center were Cecelia Condit, Dale Jaffe, Susan Heidrich, Sharon Keigher, Patricia Mellencamp, and Robin Pickering-Iazzi. To all of them I owe my thanks for stimulating—and often wild—exchanges in an informal study group that met regularly. Of the many scholars who lectured at the Center that year I would like to mention in particular Thomas Cole and Margaret Lock.

Our conversations at the Center during 1995–96 were immeasurably enhanced by the presence of the first scholars in age studies appointed to be in residence as Rockefeller fellows. In a marvelous coincidence, in fact, four of the people whose work is included between the covers of this book—Elinor Fuchs, Anne Basting, Anca Cristofovici, and Teresa Mangum—have been awarded these Rockefeller fellowships in age studies at the Center. I think of this book, then, as having in great part been underwritten by the Rockefeller Foundation. I am thankful to the Rockefeller Foundation—and especially to Lynn Szwaja who first encouraged me to submit a proposal even though the subject of age and aging was not included in the guidelines—for granting these fellowships in age studies, the first of their kind in the United States. I am pleased that this book can stand as material testimony to the fruitfulness of this three-year sequence of fellowships at the Center. It also gives me pleasure to say that I know that there will be far more research on aging that will be published as a result of the foresight and support of the Rockefeller Foundation.

I want to thank Carol Tennessen, Associate Director of the Center for Twentieth Century Studies, and Nigel Rothfels, Associate Editor of the Center, for their invaluable help both in coordinating the conference and preparing the book for publication. I am fortunate to be able to work with these two wonderful people on a daily basis. My pleasure in everyday life owes much to them. They are in great part responsible for creating the fluent atmosphere in which we all work at the Center, a space in which many other people contributed to this project in one way or another, including Cathy Egan, Patti Sander, Liz Barrett, Clark Lunberry, Joe Milutis, Kelly Mink, Glen Powell, and Ted Wesp.

So much good work was presented at the conference, and it is my regret that a single book could not accommodate it all. I am thinking here of papers by Virginia Blum, the late Glenda Laws, Rebecca Wepsic, Charlotte H. Welman, Elisa Facio, Deborah Owen, Robin Pickering-Iazzi, Bethany Ladimer, Christiane Orcel, Nancy Backes, and Christine T. Lowery. I am also thinking of the video work that was premiered at the conference, including the brilliant "Oh, Rapunzel," by Cecelia Condit, in collaboration with Dick Blau, and the startling "Visualizing Memory" by Ayisha Abraham. One of the most stunning presentations of the conference was a reading by Joanne M. Braxton of a sequence of her poems tracing a genealogy of women in her life and in her family through four generations of women extending from her grandmother to her daughter; some of those poems are included here. Other people whose presence at the conference was enlivening and important in so many ways include Kate Davy, W. Andrew Achenbaum, Ana Zahira Bassit, Mike Featherstone, Hilary Harris, Melinda Heywood, Laura Stempel Mumford, Diane Rothenberg, and Anne Wyatt-Brown. To Anne Wyatt-Brown, who read the entire manuscript of *Figuring Age* and offered astute suggestions, I am especially indebted.

I want to extend my thanks as well to Indiana University Press and especially to Joan Catapano, Assistant Director and Senior Sponsoring Editor, with whom I have been fortunate to collaborate over the years on the Center's book series *Theories of Contemporary Culture*, of which *Figuring Age* marks the twenty-third volume.

NOTES

1. In comparison to the outpouring of research in women's studies from the perspectives of history, literary studies, art history, philosophy, cultural anthropology, and cultural studies, there has been far less research in age studies (in particular older age). But much important and exciting work has been done. In addition to other books cited in the introduction, see, for example, historians W. Andrew Achenbaum's *Old Age in the New Land*, Lois Banner's *In Full Flower: Aging Women, Power, and Sexuality*, Thomas Cole's *The Journey of Life: A Cultural History of Aging in America*, Peter Laslett's *A Fresh Map of Life*, and Terri Premo's *Winter Friends: Growing Old in the New Republic*; anthropologists Lawrence Cohen's *No Aging in India: Alzheimers, Bad Families, and Other Modern Things*, Barbara Myerhoff's *Number Our Days*, and Sharon Kaufman's *The Ageless Self*; anthropological psychologist David Gutmann's *Reclaimed Powers: Toward a New Psychology of Men and Women*; media theorist Patricia Mellencamp's *High Anxiety: Catastrophe, Scandal, Age, and Comedy*; literary critics Margaret Gullette's *Safe at Last in the Middle Years: The Invention of the Midlife Progress Novel*, Carolyn Heilbrun's *Writing a Woman's Life*, Nancy K. Miller's *Betrayal and Bequest: Memoirs of a Parent's Death*, and Barbara Frey Waxman's *From the Hearth to the Open Road: A Feminist Study of Aging in Literature*; and philosophers Joseph Esposito's *The Obsolete Self: Philosophical Dimensions of Aging* and Harry Moody's *Ethics and Aging*. See also the interdisciplinary collections of scholarly essays *Aging and the Elderly: Humanistic Perspectives in Gerontology*, ed. Stuart Spicker, Kathleen Woodward, and David Van Tassel; *Aging, Death, and the Completion of Being*, ed. David Van Tassel; *Handbook of the Humanities and Aging*, ed. Thomas Cole, David Van Tassel, and Robert Kastenbaum; *Memory and Desire: Aging—Literature—Psychoanalysis*, ed. Kathleen Woodward and Murray Schwartz; and *What Does It Mean to Grow Old? Reflections from the Humanities*, ed. Thomas Cole and Sally Gadow.

2. Although theoretically "ageism" can refer to any systematic prejudicial behavior toward or favored treatment of people based on chronological age (teenagers, for example), it has come to be associated with old age.

3. Bourdelais used this phrase in a 1997 lecture entitled "Death and Dying in Two Cultures."

4. See *A Certain Age: Reflecting on Menopause*, ed. Joanna Goldsworthy. Nancy K. Miller and Carolyn G. Heilbrun both contribute forewords to this book.

5. Greer calls on the authority of poets who, as she puts it, "since classical times have celebrated an ideal stage of tranquil thoughtfulness to round off a busy life." "The woman of fifty," she continues, "has even more reason to long for that time . . . when she may be allowed to turn into herself" (45). Astonishingly, this "self" Greer identifies as her pre-adolescent self. It is as if, having only a conventional biologically based model of the life course in mind, Greer can only imagine a return to pre-adolescence as a time when the life of a female was not defined by men or caretaking (in her book *Revolution from Within* Gloria Steinem arrives at the same conclusion). But the age of fifty is far and away simply too early to begin the rounding off of a life—and certainly not into *tranquility*.

6. Bourdelais developed this idea in his 1997 lecture. A shorthand way of thinking about this marker of old age at the chronological age of seventy-five is that

from this point on, a person might expect to live on the average at least ten more years.

7. I decided not to recite any more statistics in the body of my Introduction because the very elaboration of the statistics themselves, as Lawrence Cohen has pointed out in "Old Age: Cultural and Critical Perspectives," creates the impression of a catastrophe, a crisis; indeed, the convention of much writing on aging—especially journalistic writing—is to open with a barrage of statistics. All of these statistics are subject to various critiques and qualifications (for example, while it is true that people born today in the United States are likely to live some thirty years longer than people born in 1900, by far the major proportion of this increase is due to the reduction in death rates for children and young adults). Nonetheless, a few statistics are in order here. In the United States in 1995 there were some 250 women for every 100 men in the age group of eighty-five and older. Three-quarters of the residents in nursing homes are women. Thus old age is a territory populated largely by women, many of whom are poor, if not impoverished, and powerless, invisible and without voice in national policy here and elsewhere. Indeed, Medicare and Medicaid could be called women's programs because the vast majority of their beneficiaries are women. See Robert Butler, "On Behalf of Older Women," for a recent analysis of the relation between women and the programs of Medicare and Medicaid. As Jessie Allen summarizes in *Women on the Front Lines*, "Women are on the front lines of our aging society for three main reasons: first, they are a majority among the elderly; second, they provide most of the care for disabled elderly Americans; and third, they face economic disadvantages at older ages" (1).

8. Laws in "Tabloid Bodies."

WORKS CITED

Achenbaum, W. Andrew. "Images of Old Age in America, 1790–1970: A Vision and a Re-vision." Featherstone and Wernick 19–28.

———. *Old Age in the New Land.* Baltimore: Johns Hopkins UP, 1978.

Allen, Jessie, and Alan Pifer, ed. *Women on the Front Lines: Meeting the Challenge of an Aging America.* Washington: Urban Institute P, 1993.

Banner, Lois. *In Full Flower: Aging Women, Power, and Sexuality.* New York: Knopf, 1992.

Beauvoir, Simone de. *The Coming of Age.* Trans. Patrick O'Brien. New York: Putnam's, 1972.

———. *The Second Sex.* Trans. H. M. Parshley. New York: Knopf, 1953.

Bourdelais, Patrice. "Death and Dying in Two Cultures." Lecture delivered at the conference on A French-American Dialogue on Care Near the End of Life. Reid Hall, Paris, France. 25–27 June 1997.

———. *Le Nouvel âge de la vieillesse: Histoire du vieillissement de la population.* Paris: Odile Jacob, 1993.

Butler, Robert N. "Ageism: Another Form of Bigotry." *The Gerontologist* 9 (1969): 243–46.

———. *The Longevity Revolution.* Ms. in progress.

Introduction

————. "On Behalf of Older Women—Another Reason to Protect Medicare and Medicaid." *The New England Journal of Medicine* (21 March 1996): 794–96.

Clark, Candace. "Emotions and Micropolitics in Everyday Life: Some Patterns and Paradoxes of 'Place.'" *Research Agendas in the Sociology of Emotions*. Ed. Theodore D. Kemper. Albany: SUNY P, 1990. 305–33.

Cohen, Lawrence. *No Aging in India: Alzheimer's, Bad Families, and Other Modern Things*. Berkeley: U of California P, 1998.

————. "Old Age: Cultural and Critical Perspectives." *Annual Review of Anthropology* 1994. 137–58.

Cole, Thomas R. *The Journey of Life: A Cultural History of Aging in America*. New York: Cambridge UP, 1992.

Cole, Thomas R., David D. Van Tassel, and Robert Kastenbaum, eds. *Handbook of the Humanities and Aging*. New York: Springer, 1992.

Cole, Thomas R., and Mary Winkler, eds. *The Oxford Book of Aging*. New York: Oxford UP, 1994.

Cole, Thomas R., and Sally Gadow, eds. *What Does It Mean to Grow Old? Reflections from the Humanities*. Durham: Duke UP, 1986.

Copper, Baba. *Over the Hill: Reflections on Ageism between Women*. Freedom: Crossing P, 1988.

Esposito, Joseph L. *The Obsolete Self: Philosophical Dimensions of Aging*. Berkeley: U of California P, 1987.

"Estrogen: Every Woman's Dilemma." *Time* 26 June 1995.

Featherstone, Mike, and Mike Hepworth. "Ageing and Old Age: Reflections on the Postmodern Life Course." *Being and Becoming Old: Sociological Approaches to Later Life*. Ed. T. Keil Bytheway, P. Allatt, and A. Bryman. Newbury Park: Sage, 1989. 143–57.

Featherstone, Mike, and Andrew Wernick, eds. *Images of Aging: Cultural Representation of Later Life*. New York: Routledge, 1995.

Friedan, Betty. *The Fountain of Age*. New York: Simon, 1993.

Goldworthy, Joanna, ed. *A Certain Age: Reflecting on Menopause*. New York: Columbia UP, 1994.

Greer, Germaine. *The Change: Women, Aging and the Menopause*. New York: Penguin, 1992.

Gullette, Margaret Morganroth. *Declining to Decline: Cultural Combat and the Politics of the Midlife*. Charlottesville: UP of Virginia, 1997.

————. *Safe at Last in the Middle Years: The Invention of the Midlife Progress Novel: Saul Bellow, Margaret Drabble, Anne Tyler, and John Updike*. Berkeley: U of California P, 1988.

Gutmann, David. *Reclaimed Powers: Toward a New Psychology of Men and Women in Later Life*. New York: Basic, 1987.

Hacker, Marilyn. *Winter Numbers*. New York: Norton, 1994.

Heilbrun, Carolyn. "Coming of Age." *New York Woman* Feb. 1991: 56–58.

————. *The Last Gift of Time: Life beyond Sixty*. New York: Dial Press, 1997.

————. *Writing a Woman's Life*. New York: Norton, 1988.

Hume George, Diana. "'Keeping Our Working Distance': Maxine Kumin's Poetry of Loss and Survival." *Aging and Gender in Literature*. Ed. Wyatt-Brown and Rossen. 314–38.

Hurst, Fanny. *Lummox*. New York: Harper, 1923.

Jong, Erica. *Fear of Fifty: A Midlife Memoir*. New York: Harper, 1994.

Kaufman, Sharon R. *The Ageless Self: Sources of Meaning in Later Life*. Madison: U of Wisconsin P, 1986.

Kuhn, Maggie, with Christine Long and Laura Quinn. *No Stone Unturned: The Life and Times of Maggie Kuhn*. New York: Ballantine, 1991.

Laslett, Peter. *A Fresh Map of Life: The Emergence of the Third Age*. London: Weidenfeld, 1989.

Laws, Glenda. "Tabloid Bodies: Aging, Health, and Beauty in Popular Discourses." Paper presented at the conference on Women and Aging: Bodies, Cultures, Generations. Center for Twentieth Century Studies, University of Wisconsin-Milwaukee. 18–20 Apr. 1996.

———. "Understanding Ageism: Lessons from Feminism and Postmodernism." *The Gerontologist* 35.1 (1995): 112–18.

Macdonald, Barbara, and Cynthia Rich. *Look Me in the Eye: Old Women, Aging, and Ageism*. San Francisco: Spinsters Ink, 1983.

Mellencamp, Patricia. *High Anxiety: Catastrophe, Scandal, Age, and Comedy*. Bloomington: Indiana UP, 1986.

Miller, Nancy K. *Bequest and Betrayal: Memoirs of a Parent's Death*. New York: Oxford UP, 1996.

Moody, Harry R. *Abundance of Life: Human Development Policies for an Aging Society*. New York: Columbia UP, 1988.

———. *Ethics and Aging*. Baltimore: Johns Hopkins UP, 1992.

Myerhoff, Barbara G. "'Life Not Death in Venice': Its Second Life." 1986. *Remembered Lives: The Work of Ritual, Storytelling, and Growing Older*. By Myerhoff. Ed. Mark Kaminsky. Ann Arbor: U of Michigan P, 1993. 257–76.

———. *Number Our Days*. New York: Dutton, 1978.

Nevelson, Louise. *Dawns and Dusks: Taped Conversations with Diana Mackown*. New York: Scribner's, 1976.

Pifer, Alan, and Lydia Bronte, eds. *Our Aging Society: Promise and Paradox*. New York: Norton, 1986.

Premo, Terri L. *Winter Friends: Growing Old in the New Republic, 1785–1845*. Urbana: U of Illinois P, 1990.

Russo, Mary. "Female Grotesques: Carnival and Theory." *Feminist Studies/Critical Studies*. Ed. Teresa de Lauretis. Bloomington: Indiana UP, 1986. 213–29.

Sontag, Susan. "The Double Standard of Aging." *Saturday Review* Sept. 1972: 29–38. Rpt. *No Longer Young: The Older Woman in America*. Occasional Papers in Gerontology II. Ann Arbor: Inst. of Gerontology, U of Michigan; Wayne State U, 1975. 31–39.

Spicker, Stuart, Kathleen Woodward, and David D. Van Tassel, eds. *Aging and the Elderly: Humanistic Perspectives in Gerontology*. Atlantic Highlands: Humanities P, 1978.

Steinem, Gloria. *Revolution from Within: A Book of Self-Esteem*. New York: Corgi, 1993.

Van Tassel, David D., ed. *Aging, Death, and the Completion of Being*. Philadelphia: U of Pennsylvania P, 1987.

Waxman, Barbara Frey. *From the Hearth to the Open Road: A Feminist Study of Aging in Contemporary Literature*. New York: Greenwood P, 1990.

Woolf, Virginia. *A Room of One's Own. Three Guineas.* Oxford: Oxford UP, 1992.

Woodward, Kathleen, and Murray Schwartz, eds. *Memory and Desire: Aging—Literature—Psychoanalysis.* Bloomington: Indiana UP, 1986.

Wyatt-Brown, Anne M., and Janice Rossen, eds. *Aging and Gender in Literature: Studies in Creativity.* Charlottesville: UP of Virginia, 1993.

OPENING
THE
SUBJECT

The Marks of Time

Nancy K. Miller

Q. How do you feel about growing older?

A. Any woman who says she doesn't care about aging is lying.

— Catherine Deneuve (1995)

I. MIRROR, MIRROR

What does a woman of a certain age see when she looks at herself in time's mirror?

Four faces, four bronze autoportraits by sculptor Sheila Solomon. (Figure 1.) They belong to an installation called *Time/Pieces*: nineteen sculptures and two

Figure 1. *The four autoportraits. Courtesy of the artist. Photo shot in the foundry. An-My-Lê. (All photographs of Solomon's unless noted otherwise are by An-My-Lê.)*

drawings that engage with the questions of women, change, and time.[1] Solomon conceived the work as an "organic whole with the pieces resonating and amplifying one another. . . . The organization of the works is circular," she writes, "in that it reaches back into my past and extends forward into the future."[2] (The face covered by hands is the last of the series, completed in 1992, although it is not the last piece of the installation.) Between the portrait covered with hands and the uncovered one (1990) exists the task of face work: dealing with one's face as it changes over time. Solomon's heads and figures embody the vision of a woman who looked at herself head on—and from all angles—in midlife for more than a decade. I want to speak here of aging as a project of coming to terms with a face and a body in process—as an emotional effort, an oscillation that moves between the mirrored poles of acceptance and refusal. An emotional project, that like Solomon's never stops, and also an act of the imaginative mind.

Heads bear an intimate and complicated relation to the bodies they crown. Solomon insists that the wood pedestal is integral to the sculpture. Like the aging process in human beings, the appearance of the base evolves. The wood keeps working; it develops cracks. When I first saw these pieces, I caught my breath and thought: this is a woman not afraid of the mirror. As Solomon said later in response to one of my questions about *Time/Pieces*, "my body has been good to me." How we interpret the bodiliness of aging is intimately bound up with the story of seeing ourselves as women in the first place. "I don't think I know a single woman," Barbara Grizzuti Harrison writes in *An Accidental Autobiography*, "who knows what she looks like" (16). For many of us, an archaic but tenacious private shame haunts our vision.

II. REFLECTIONS

In an extended memorial note to the writer Alfred Chester, Cynthia Ozick meditates on time's betrayal: "Passing my reflection in a shopwindow," Ozick writes, "I am taken by surprise at the sight of a striding woman with white hair: she is still wearing the bangs of her late youth, but there are shocking pockets and trenches in her face; she has a preposterous dewlap; she is no one I can recognize." In this portrait of a writer (a contemporary) as a minor literary light—a coming of age story set in postwar New York—Ozick never returns to the question of her own face in the shopwindow (this is the reflection one might have thought to be the referent behind the essay called "Reflections"). But no. The experience of mistaking herself for another (who is that woman looking back at me in the mirror?), someone other than herself—"a woman with white hair" and a "preposterous dewlap"—seems to interest Ozick only metaphorically, as an example of how we can be surprised by time. She calls this discrepancy a "generational pang": the realization that the minds that currently interest her belonged to "little children" when she was learning—precociously —to think and write (79).

In *Aging and Its Discontents* Kathleen Woodward comments on Freud's "shock of recognition" upon encountering his elderly double in the mirror, a "dismaying" experience that he recounts in a note to the essay on "The Uncanny." What Freud sees, Woodward argues, is "the image of the Other, to use Beauvoir's terminology, an image Freud would prefer not to recognize" (65). Following Woodward's rereading of Freud, we can wonder whether the way Ozick dismisses the shock of coming up against her face in the mirror, the alacrity with which the writer immediately moves on to questions of memory, might not also be a form of repression that leaves intact the belief that in her unconscious—like Freud's—she is forever young. Ozick goes on instead to delineate different models of identity. She is not interested in a "fixity of self" but rather "platonic enclosures"—islands, as she puts it, "independent of time, though not of place" (79). It's one of these "platonic islands" that allows her to remember the writer Alfred Chester as he was—when he was young—and she was, too.

III. LOOKING ONE'S AGE

There's a color photograph that captures the style of emotional entanglement between my mother and me in the mid sixties. (Figure 2.) My mother is about the age I am now as I write. In the photograph, two women look at each other across their war. We are alone, fixed in our struggle. My father loved this picture, which he had enlarged from a color slide and framed. It hung in the dinette and presided over meals. It's a good picture, he said.

Figure 2. My mother and me circa 1965. Photo by Louis Kipnis.

Not long after after my mother's death, more than fifteen years ago, my sister and I began fighting over the best way for my father to lead his new life alone. (The building was going co-op, and he needed to decide whether to buy the rent-controlled apartment he'd lived in for fifty years.) My sister turned on me and said bitterly, "You're just like Mommy, you'd kill to get what you want." I'd never thought I was anything like my mother—I identified against her, with my father—but now, in my fifties, I think maybe my sister was right. I can see how I have become my mother. It's not so easy to know who you are like—and sometimes this resemblance changes over time.

Going through my mother's clothes after her death, I found in the pockets of every coat (and she had many, many coats) the traces of her commitment to personal comfort: a crumpled-up kleenex and a wrapped coffee candy. I was struck by the regularity with which these items turned up. Recently, taking some of my (many) coats to the cleaners, I emptied out the pockets and I found in each a crumpled-up kleenex (the same leaky nose) and a box of Ricola mints (the same need to have something in our mouth).

My mother lives in my pockets and also in my face. In the mirror, I silently measure with her the spreading pores, the advancing crepe, lines that crease even earlobes. I think: in fifteen years I, too, could be dead. Of course that doesn't tell me what I need to know. How to live with this face—our face—in the face of death. How to live without that other against whom we think we know who we are.[3]

In the *Elle* interview from which I've drawn my epigraph, Catherine Deneuve responds to a question about cosmetic surgery: "By the number of surgeons in Paris who claim to have operated on me, I should look like the bride of Frankenstein. That said, I find it wonderful to slow down the marks of time—so long as the face matches the rest of the body. You have to look at yourself objectively" (158). What does it mean to have your face match the rest of your body? Should you have your body fixed to match your face? Or is it the other way round? Above all, what would it mean to look at yourself *objectively*? "How is it possible to look at our bodies objectively," Harrison asks, "(and with love)?" (31).

Deneuve's understanding of objectivity is at war with her commitment to delaying the visible signs of the aging process. To an earlier question about turning fifty, and whether she would lie about her age, Deneuve responds, "I never hide my age—it's a question of pride. I'm often struck when people say, 'You're so youthful!'—as if they saw me as an image, not a human being. There are people who don't seem to realize I've been around for quite a while. They must have some idea of my age, but maybe my face doesn't correspond with their notion of what a fifty-year-old woman looks like." But what does fifty look like? People who think that they know what fifty looks like—old, unattractive, a face bearing the marks of time—are surprised by Deneuve's "youthful" face. Deneuve's face in which the marks of time have been "slowed down," maybe even erased, is not a face in which "fifty" has been allowed to appear. But what is "fifty"? Like the famous Steinem remark around the event of her fiftieth birthday—"This is what fifty looks like"—fifty exists in the eye of the beholder.

Carolyn Heilbrun notes in her biography of Steinem, *The Education of a Woman*, that Steinem was in fact repeating the quip first uttered when she turned forty, adding at fifty, the less frequently quoted words: "We've been lying for so long, who would know" (355). In another interview, Deneuve answers the question about plastic surgery and lying about age a little differently: "Of course I've had some face work," she admits. She says this, she adds, so that "other women won't feel demoralized."[4] You confess that you've had some plastic surgery so that other women won't feel bad about looking their age. With a little face work, you too could look like Catherine Deneuve! At sixty, Steinem at least had the grace not to say this is what sixty looks like (great, let me tell you, from eyeballing her across a seminar table); the only face work involved, Heilbrun reports in a rare footnote (377), was having some fat removed from her eyelids so that she could wear her contact lenses early in the morning before television cameras.

The two streaked blond icons—feminine and feminist (though Steinem's appearance is also "feminine") are and aren't talking about the same thing. Aging—in public, visually.[5] I doubt very much that Deneuve enjoys the arrival of age spots on her hands and enjoys their presence, the way Steinem says she does, as the friendly proof of the wonderful experiences she's had over a lifetime. Still, both famously gorgeous women point to the same question for the rest of us mere female mortals: how do you know what you look like over time? How does time produce its own scrim of interpretation, or rather, what resistance can one mount against the narrative of decline? Especially when female icons—Deneuve, Jackie O, like all media-produced images—are carefully adjusted *not to age* over time.[6]

To resist the narrative of decline requires an active, arduous engagement with the general cultural assumption that we are at our most beautiful or desirable at a youthful moment and the rest is downhill. Here is a picture of me at twenty-eight. (Figure 3.) For me this photograph represents one of Ozick's "platonic islands." It was taken at a turning point in my life—my decision, post-1968, to go to graduate school, and the brief fantasy of making my life with an artist, a man who later became a famous sculptor. My father had this photo framed. When he died I brought it home and set it on a sideboard (vintage sixties teak that also came from my parents' apartment) in my study. When students come to see me at home, they unfailingly comment on the picture. "That's you?" they ask, hesitating on the threshold of disbelief. "Yes," I say lightly, "that's me when I was young and gorgeous." Then, evading the invitation to flattery, they say, "you still have that look," the warning in my eyes that says, "cross me at your peril." They've told me that they fear the look that summarizes what one of my students called in the acknowledgments to her dissertation, "my impossibly high standards" (on the other hand, how scared could they be if they *tell* me about it?). Sometimes, too, I think that they are comforted by the contrast between then and now. However unconsciously, they know that they are *young women*—many of them beautiful and sexy as well as smart—and enjoying their

Figure 3. Me post 1968. Photograph by Martin Puryear.

beauty, now. At the same time, I also know that their youthful looks don't mean as much to *them* as they do to me; just as I take my books for granted while theirs are still before them. When I was twenty-eight, I didn't think I was young and gorgeous. . . . I was just twenty-eight and worrying whether I would ever be happy. (Books were not visible on my horizon of expectation.)

At the end of her sixties, Carolyn Heilbrun offers a meditation on the narrative of decline inspired by her discussion of Steinem's fiftieth birthday:

> Turning fifty, both in anticipation and actuality, is a watershed in a woman's life. Nor is this metaphor merely cliché. A watershed marks that place where waters run toward opposite seas. Rivers that once arose from the event of birth become different rivers, moving toward the sea of death. Wallace Stevens has written that "death is the mother of beauty," but certainly in Western culture youth is the prized gift, and aging, the deprivation of youth, is regarded as cruel loss. First comes despair at the aging body, and particularly the aging face, a despair whose alleviation can be sought either by impersonating youth with the aid of drugs, surgery, or makeup, or by abandoning all hope of a youthful appearance and accepting with wry humor the inevitable expanding and sagging. . . . Only recently and gradually has the possibility emerged in female consciousness that something might be gained for women at the cusp of fifty. . . . For the woman turning fifty . . . the reconsideration that surrounds that moment may and often does provide sufficient impetus to reenvision her life. (355–56)

The body, the face, the eyes, the breast. Vulnerable zones for women aging. The breast shows the marks of time but more important becomes—randomly, rampantly—the target of cancer for many women. There's an odd way, as we'll see, in which breast cancer arrives as a crucial part of the aging process for too many women. (Sometimes, of course, it marks the end of the process altogether.) In part as an effect of breast cancer, in part as an effect of therapy, in her early fifties, Steinem set out to reenvision her life; it entailed "looking within." Though readers often find Steinem's new-found interiority naive or sentimental, we might understand more usefully the trope of turning inward, "looking within," as a way of turning away from the mirror (maybe putting your hands over your face), as a resistance to tracking the damage to that face long enough to think about, say, how it is that we came to think we knew what our face—or body—was.

IV. BODY PARTS

How does any woman know what she looks like? How does she learn to recognize what she looks like—from the outside? The look of the look in the mirror. She begins, for most of us, as Adrienne Rich (after Beauvoir) has famously argued, by observing her mother whom she examines by body parts, as though in childhood she had intuited the anatomy of female destiny:

> I saw my own mother's menstrual blood before I saw my own. Hers was the first female body I ever looked at, to know what women were, what I was to be. I remember taking baths with her in the hot summers of early childhood, playing with her in the cool water. As a young child I thought how beautiful she was; a print of Botticelli's Venus on the wall, half-smiling, hair flowing, associated itself in my mind with her. In early adolescence I still glanced slyly at my mother's body, vaguely imagining: I too shall have breasts, full hips, hair between my thighs—whatever that meant to me then, and with all the ambivalence of such a thought. And there were other thoughts: I too shall marry, have children—but *not like her*. I shall find a way of doing it all differently. (219)

There was no getting away from my mother's body. After a bath, she would emerge clothed simply in a towel: a white towel tied around her waist. She would often lie on top of the bed in the towel and read or work the crossword puzzle. When my sister and I were little, we would walk in on her during her bath; even much later, we would come barging in (her word) with a request, since in the tub she was almost always in a good mood. Later, I remember thinking that her body resembled our saddle shoes, two-toned: tanned, freckled arms and legs from playing tennis, pale torso and white, pear-shaped breasts, erect, darkish pink nipples. The body I remember is not the half-submerged body of my childhood memories, though; it is the mother's body seen from my adolescence, the body I saw at twelve and thirteen as I waited for my own body to reveal its secrets.

"Did your breasts always sag like that?" This is not a question I ever admitted asking, though I'm sure it was on my lips as I stared down at my mother's stretched-out form, studying her body. Years later my mother, still walking through the apartment with a towel tied around her waist, would tell that story laughing, as proof of what she had to endure from her hostile daughter, but also with the confidence of a woman proud of her breasts. If I ever grew breasts, what—or whose—would they be like? Both grandmothers were all bosom. Their breasts filled their entire chest (a "C" at least, if not a "D"). My mother edged up to a "B." My sister and I barely made it to an "A." Where did the breasts go? The alphabet in reverse in three generations.

Sometimes it seems as if there is only one body: hers unchanging from age twenty-eight—when she is my new mother—to sixty-eight when she began to die. Her hair has gone from black (blue black, she liked to say) to silver, but the body had kept its form and style. How can that be?

How do you know what you look like as a woman, how you interpret what you see? I turn now to the work of contemporary women artists and photographers, who, like Solomon, have begun to change the inherited gaze of female beauty.

In an interview about her show at the Horodner Romley Gallery (1993), Mira Schor talks about the history behind a series of paintings in which she used punctuation marks to visualize the boundaries between public and private experience. In one of her most pointed paintings, she wrote out P U B (L) I C . . . to evoke the public/pubic boundary so prominent in the Anita Hill/Clarence Thomas affair. "That led," Schor explains, "to painting incarnated punctuation marks: cunts, breasts, and penises framed by quote marks; red commas and semicolons set into pubic hair, embedded in flesh. Gender positions, no matter how gory their physicality, are put into question by the quotation marks. Markers of printed language are sexualized, and text, which had been so dominant over visuality in feminist theory and art in the 80s, is presented for its visual seductivity and bodily contingency."

What does it mean to put your breasts into quotation marks? To see them as "constructed," of which implants are only a literal example? I especially enjoy Schor's *"Breast"*—the fact that this particular style of breasts gets named generically *"Breast"*—not least because it looks like mine. (Figure 4.) (Schor's *"Breast"* might also be read as a quotation of Marcel Duchamp's famous "Prière de toucher" [Please touch].)[7] Looking at your breasts—and what happens to them as unnatural, as political, or ideological—leads to a particular brand of feminist wit. (Figure 5.)

Many years ago, I had an affair with a Frenchman [an art historian, no less] who described my breasts as "deux oeufs sur le plat." The French way of saying flat as a pancake, or literally, two eggs sunny-side up. I thought that was unfair since his language

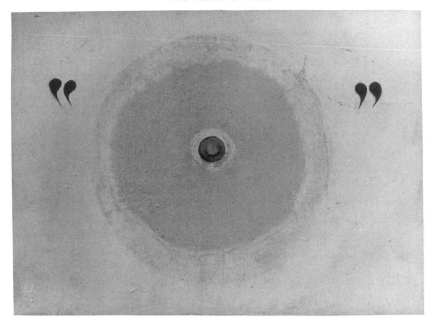

Figure 4. Mira Schor. "Breast." *1993. Oil on linen. 12 × 16". Private collection.*

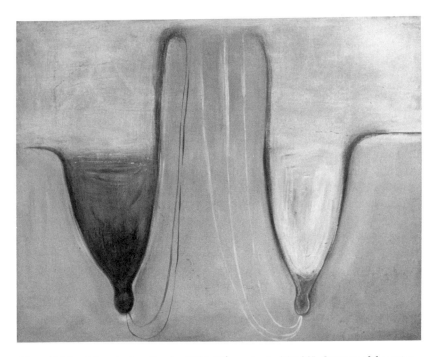

Figure 5. Mira Schor. Against Gravity. *1989. Oil on canvas. 16 × 20". Courtesy of the artist.*

flattened out what were also two nice if little . . . mounds. But I confess that when I saw Mira's painting I thought, well, maybe he had a point. How else would you represent them?

One day last winter I walked into the locker room at my gym and saw a large naked woman with huge breasts (watermelons, to stick with food metaphors, fruits as measurement for breasts and tumors). She had been powdering herself, I guess, or putting lotion on, and was flipping her breasts with her hands (sort of like pizza dough) to make them dry. I stood there mesmerized thinking about what it would mean to have breasts like that. Were we in the same story? What happens to my identification with women when I look at those breasts—in action?

If learning to see oneself—as a woman—aging, can't be separated from how we've learned to see ourselves as women in the first place, part of how to find new ways of perceiving ourselves as aging bodies and faces is to construct a narrative in which these images can be read, otherwise.

One of the boldest explorers of this territory is the British photographer Jo Spence. In her posthumously published book *Cultural Sniping*—a collection of essays dating from the mid seventies to the early nineties—Spence defines her undertaking as an autobiographical project in which she tried to tell—in images—the story of who she was, and how she came to rethink both her work and her place in it. "As soon as I knew I was telling myself a story that made sense to me I felt I had discovered a major structuring absence," Spence writes, "a frame in the middle of my identity. There are no categories for artists who invoke notions of class. . . . Now . . . I see that I am no longer an ugly duckling trying to be a swan but that I belong to a very specific and previously unlabelled group" (161–63). The radical change of view came from having a "body in crisis," Spence's reactions to breast cancer, and the "shame" of ugliness, of having a "deformed and injured body" (158). Spence describes the pictures of herself taken throughout her illness as part of a refusal to be a victim.

The series "Narratives of Dis-Ease" was produced in collaboration with a cancer doctor, Tim Sheard, who was interested in understanding Spence's experience in the hospital as a patient. I want to juxtapose Spence's self-representation with a roughly contemporary picture that caused a sensation on the cover of the Sunday *New York Times Magazine* (1993). This strikingly beautiful woman, a model, posed glamorously, presents another—and equally if quite differently disturbing—way to push the acceptable limits of self-representation. As luck would have it, this image is the first one to represent the nineties in the *New York Times 100th Anniversary* issue. The photograph by the artist Matuschka is a self-portrait: her breast was removed after she developed cancer in 1991. The image drew worldwide attention and won the photographer numerous awards.

Spence makes explicit the bridge from the work she did on her own life and death struggle with cancer to the question of aging women's bodies. "The results were very painful," she writes, "particularly those prints which showed the ways in which my body is not only badly scarred and damaged, but also ageing, overweight and deteriorating." She hopes that in displaying these self-portraits of "an ageing/older woman" the images will be understood as "an act of solidarity" with other women caught in this collective dilemma (140). In a separate essay, Spence describes the purpose of a mask she used to create the "Crone" picture, a mask of advanced aging used to "symbolically reenact" her grandmother's life (178).

The mask was part of a workshop experiment but the notion of the mask also serves as a possible metaphor for self-production over time. Perhaps faces are no more than masks that we put on or peel off—a layering of selves, no single one more authentic than the other, or layers of self-identity. Lucy Grealy writes at the end of *Autobiography of a Face* about the denouement of the story she tells—a girl who grows up with part of her face missing from the effects of cancer. After many operations to arrive at the semblance of a "normal" face, Grealy concludes, "As a child I had expected my liberation to come from getting a new face to put on, but now I saw it came from *shedding something, shedding my image*" (emphasis added; 222). Grealy speaks of shedding the ugly self, lifting up the skin, and pulling it back to make a new image. This sounds a lot like the process of the facelift. But a new face—the lifting of the old—like the treatment of breast cancer—requires a literal cut. What will win out, the figure or the knife?

The last image of *Cultural Sniping*, an untitled photograph, was taken by Spence's collaborator, Terry Dennett. The caption reads: "Jo Spence on a 'good day' shortly before her death, photographing visitors to her room at the Marie Curie hospice, Hampstead" (227). Jo Spence died at the age of fifty-eight. Until the very end, this was a body committed to work, a working body—and a mind unafraid of looking at its face head on. Looking at us and urging us to look, too. To look beyond what we've been taught to see.

Despite her commitment to undermining the ideologies of youthful beauty surrounding the aging female body, Spence struggled, as many of us do, with what's called body image:

> Now that I am moving on to work on ageing, the breast has taken on a completely different set of meanings for me. Last year I had a tragic love affair with a bloke (tragic in that it didn't work out). I was rejected because of my age, because I don't look "beautiful." He didn't want this clapped-out working class woman who has a spirit and an intellect but also a badly scarred breast and is overweight. These other structuring presences of male desire are there, however much you love and respect your body or your class background for having got you to this stage in your life. I still would like to look like a 25-year-old. I feel a bit daft even saying it. (211)

By the time Spence died, she was as thin as she might ever have wanted to be.

Although she was never really fat, my mother had weighed more than she wanted to. After two months of not eating, she had at last melted into the size she longed to be. Despite its obvious frailty, her newly slim body was unnervingly youthful. And her face revealed the bone structure she had always maintained was the source of true beauty. My mother was particularly gratified by the confession of a friend's husband (a doctor who happened to see patients in the hospital where she had her chemo) that he hadn't realized how beautiful she was—until she was dying. So I guess you could say that my mother died finally looking the way she had wished to live: beautiful and thin.

V. MOTHER END

To my great perplexity, my mother used to say, "Inside, I still feel sixteen." I'd look at her and think: you, sixteen! I've begun now to understand this feeling in a new way. On a good day, when I forget who and where I am, and find myself completely absorbed in what I'm doing, if I turn and see myself in the mirror, I often have the shock of misrecognition Ozick describes. Who is that yenta in the mirror, that matron walking down Broadway? It's . . . my mother, but it's also *me*. How did I get there? When did I stop being twenty-eight?

How one gets there is the story Spence wanted to understand. Sheila Solomon, to come full circle now, tells that story as well. *Time/Pieces* begins with a self-portrait of a woman, her arms folded under her breasts; across her slightly rounded belly are etched the words: *Mother End*. (Figure 6.) A woman's life after reproduction.

What follows is in the nature of a fable. Toward the end of her series, Solomon creates *The Guardians*. The eight-foot-tall figures, modeled on Sheila's body and three times its size, are bolted to wood, rough-hewn poplar. They are meant to evoke Roman road markers, Herms—classical male figures which serve as public signposts, sometimes also grave markers. *The Guardians* divide space and provide a sense of boundary, where you enter and exit. They are associated with the idea of journey—personal and mythical. You see them at a crossroads. The figures are identical but to the viewer they seem to be different. The eyes are focused and looking. They see you, even if they don't meet your gaze, reflect you.

One day this winter, wanting to keep my impression of the sculpture fresh, I went to have a look at the Guardians. I also thought I might try and have my picture taken in the garden outside Sheila's studio. I walked over to the middle Guardian to have a closer look and found myself irresistibly leaning into it. (Figure 7.) It was an exceptionally sunny day and I was squinting into the snow after taking off my sunglasses, so I look a little pained. When Sheila saw the picture she was pleased because she'd always wanted a picture that would show the scale of her monumental pieces and because we both realized immediately that this shot would be the mark of our collaboration. I like the idea of leaning into, resting against this large impassive female body, so unafraid of the world, so sublimely indifferent to the passage of time, but marking it nonetheless. I've found myself thinking that this is what we need as we age: the figure of an older female body occupying time and space—a public figure, though, not a private

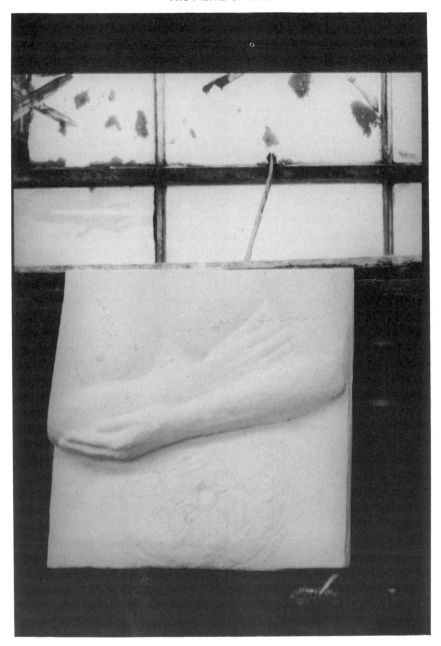

Figure 6. Sheila Solomon. Mother End. *Plaster. Courtesy of the artist.*

Figure 7. Me, leaning against one of the Guardians. *Photograph by Sandy Petrey.*

*Figure 8. Author photo. Makeup by
Fern Feller. Photograph by Kristine Larsen.*

one. The comfort of another form of recognition, outside the family. I see myself in relation to her and she is not me.

I would be lying, as Deneuve declared, if I said I don't care about growing older, that I prefer this picture of me outside Sheila's studio, to my indoor sullen, stony portrait at twenty-eight. But perhaps in time I'll take my hands away from my face and see what's out there to lean on. Other selves like us and different, who've also journeyed in time. That might feel less lonely.

CODA

As I was writing this piece for the conference, I was also getting ready to have a picture taken for my new book. This turned out to be something of a production. A first set of "natural" poses taken by a family member and a budding amateur photographer made me feel suicidal. So I decided to hire a professional photographer. On her advice (but I didn't need much persuading) I decided to have professional makeup done. The day of the shooting I felt sure I had too much makeup on: too much mouth, too dark eyes and eyebrows. I was all for contour to restore my jaw line, and concealer to cover my deep circles, but mascara and all that lipstick—*that* seemed unnatural.[8] The two women conferred. The eyes are the first to go, the makeup woman explained. I put myself in her hands. When the contact sheet came, I tore open the envelope and took out a magnifying glass. Oh, God, it's not me! (Joan Collins minus the boobs). OK, I looked good, but too good. Too much bad stuff had been erased. (Figure 8.) Imagining friends and colleagues seeing my remade face on the cover, fantasizing a book signing, I thought, people will never recognize me. And then I thought, no, no, yes, it's not . . . "me." It's only my author-photo mask, no more "real" than the face of disaster in my young cousin's shots of me, sitting in the park with natural light.

In the end the photo I chose was a face closer to (but still much younger than) my own—closer to what I think I might look like on a very good day. A face that through makeup showed only faint traces of the marks of time. This shot was taken in Tribeca on the photographer's roof. Invisible in the picture but essential to my mood that day is the Woolworth building where at the close of his career my father had rented office space. It felt right that this picture should appear on the jacket of a book largely inspired by his death.

NOTES

I'm especially grateful to Elizabeth Hollow, who shot the images drawn from magazines and books.

1. The installation was featured in (and on the cover of) *Feminist Studies* 21.2. The text includes a poem by Alicia Ostriker, "The Book of Life," and photographs by An-My Lê. See Solomon, "Collaborative."

2. Solomon's description of her work.

3. The passages in italics are excerpted from my *Bequest and Betrayal*, a book that deals with the aging of parents and the implications of family resemblance.

4. I have been unable to relocate this interview but I don't think I've invented her words.

5. In an interview for the *New York Times*, Deneuve talks about the "marks" left by the "passage of the years" and what this means for a movie star: "It's a very visual profession, even if one's career is not based on looks. Cinema is still something people first see and then hear. Beauty is not everything, but it still has a power of attraction" (8).

6. Revising this essay in France, I couldn't help noticing the ubiquity of Deneuve's face on the standard issue postage stamp. Deneuve (and before her Brigitte Bardot) has lent her face to the figure "Marianne," who in turn embodies the French Republic.

7. I discovered and came into possession of this image thanks to Mary Ann Caws.

8. I'm not going to address here the philosophical issue of plastic surgery. The testimony included in Vivian Sobchack's powerful essay does this vividly. In terms of the ephemeral cosmetic makeover, I confess to casuistry. I dye my eyelashes so as not to wear mascara (hell on contact lenses), and though I like to wear lipstick, I'd be embarrassed to draw over my mouth to even out my aging lips (you can see this excess in the picture). It seems especially unfair that (upper) lips go—and so early, too.

I place my hands over my face and for a while stop looking—at me.

WORKS CITED

Deneuve, Catherine. Interview with Sylvie de Chirée. *Elle* Nov. 1995: 156–58.

———. Interview with Alan Riding. *New York Times* 24 Apr. 1996: C1+.

Grealy, Lucy. *The Autobiography of a Face.* Boston: Houghton, 1994.

Harrison, Barbara Grizzuti. *An Accidental Autobiography.* Boston: Houghton, 1996.

Heilbrun, Carolyn G. *The Education of a Woman: The Life of Gloria Steinem.* New York: Dial, 1995.

Miller, Nancy K. *Bequest and Betrayal: Memoirs of a Parent's Death.* New York: Oxford UP, 1996.

Ozick, Cynthia. "Reflections: Alfred Chester's Wig." *New Yorker* 30 Mar. 1992: 79–98.

Rich, Adrienne. *Of Woman Born.* New York: Norton, 1976.

Schor, Mira. Interview with Stuart Horodner. Catalogue for Exhibition. Horodner Gallery. New York, NY. 5 Oct.–6 Nov. 1993. Np.

Sobchack, Vivian. "Scary Women: Cinema, Surgery, and Special Effects." In this volume.

Solomon, Sheila. "Collaborative Portfolio (Art, Photography, Poetry)." *Feminist Studies* 21.2 (Summer 1995): 302–16.

———. Description of her work. Ms.

Spence, Jo. *Cultural Sniping: The Art of Transgression.* London: Routledge, 1995.

———. *Putting Myself in the Picture: A Political, Personal, and Photographic Autobiography.* Seattle: Real Comet, 1988.

Woodward, Kathleen. *Aging and Its Discontents: Freud and Other Fictions.* Bloomington: Indiana UP, 1991.

Aging and the Scandal of Anachronism

Mary Russo

One of the most unforgettable images in twentieth-century critical writing is Walter Benjamin's grand and terrifying portrait of the angel of history. In an allegory of time, the angel faces backwards with his wings outstretched by the violence and the power of an oncoming storm which "irresistibly propels him into the future to which his back is turned" (258). "This storm," writes Benjamin, "is what we call progress" (258). How at odds with this turbulent image is the placidity of some developmental models of aging gracefully, progressing stage by stage, generation by generation, counting the years. I imagine this experience as one of being pushed along slowly and kept in place by some bureaucratic angel, an implacable guardian-functionary who is just doing his job, and, by example, urging us at every stage to just do ours.

Benjamin's critique of progressive, quantifiable, continuous time associated with the failure of the European Left after World War I and with Social Democratic theory reminds us of the high political and cultural stakes which are always involved in changing the experience of time. To change the world is implicitly or explicitly to change time. For Benjamin, true revolutionary change demands a leap out of the "homogeneous, empty time" of modernity and progress into a present time which is filled with urgent possibility (261). The "lifework," the "era," the history of mankind—all these are in Benjamin's evocation of a Jewish Messianic tradition of timeliness in which "every second of time was the straight gate through which the Messiah might enter" (264). The past is not simply received but it is revealed "unexpectedly," as in an emergency. The past flashes up in a moment of danger as a spark of hope. In generational terms, Benjamin deplored the assignment to redeem future generations which was given to the working class by the Left. "This training," he writes harshly, "made the working class forget both its hatred and its spirit of sacrifice, for both are nourished by the image of enslaved ancestors rather than that of liberated grandchildren" (260).[1]

Aging and the Scandal of Anachronism

While the critique of Progress is more often the rule than the exception in contemporary cultural theory, progressivism still dominates the commonsensical notions of a life course, generational difference, and social change. Hope, desire, understanding, and optimism seem ineluctably joined against the forces of the past, the backward, the unenlightened, the old. The trajectory of a lifetime, for instance, is ideologically weighted in favor of a future goal, a going forward into empty time. Sometimes, the models of a life course seem about as varied as the programmed exercise machines at a health club. You choose: the plateau (up to a long middle-age, and then quickly down again); the roller coaster (up-down, up-down, stop); pike's peak (straight up, straight down—exciting, but rather difficult); and my own personal favorite, "random."

In one sense, this essay is a defense of randomness as a way of understanding and assuming the risks of aging. Of course, a more rigorous program of exercise would emphasize physiological repetition and dispense with the story lines. This metaphorical emphasis might suggest a theoretical reconsideration of aging as cultural repetition or performativity, along the lines of Judith Butler's powerful work on performativity and gender.[2] In fact, repetition as a model of bodily discipline and social practice figures prominently in what follows in relation to aging, but my interest and emphasis are somewhat different, partly because my work on the category of the grotesque has attracted my attention to bodies which miss or exceed the age mark in various ways, and are not easily instrumentalized.[3]

In this essay, the interrogation of risk is organized around the concept of anachronism. Anachronism means literally "against time." More, generally, however, it refers to an historical misplacement. Early uses of the word in English, for instance, referred to antedating (placing the birth of Christ too early, for instance) and to retrogression, drawing up the past inappropriately into the present. Nowadays, anachronism is a kind of historical faux pas, involving the projecting of attitudes or ideologies that are contemporary onto a former time. Thus as I understand it, anachronism is a mistake in a normative systemization of time. As such, one *risks* anachronism. In my view, anachronism is a risk which is both necessary and inevitable as *a sign of life*. Given the common placement of women's lives within the symbolic confines of birth, reproduction, and death, the risk of anachronism is scandal. Not acting one's age, for instance, is not only inappropriate but dangerous, exposing the female subject, especially, to ridicule, contempt, pity, and scorn—the scandal of anachronism. Only slightly ironically, the May 9, 1997 television news show *Dateline NBC* recently asked its viewers "how old is too old?" referring to the miniscule number of women in their sixties having babies with help from the new reproductive technologies (it was reported that fifty-seven percent said it is "too old"). Never mind the sixty-year-old new dads or the number of women, in this country at least, who of necessity raise grandchildren and foster children at that age and older. Consider also the May 12, 1997 cover of the *New Yorker*. It shows an old white-haired "granny" contemplating her pregnant belly in front of a mirror, a reference to the sixty-three-year-old Californian woman who gave birth earlier in 1997, topping the record of an Italian woman who was slightly younger. The cover image is a pale version of the Kerch terra-cotta figurines of "senile, pregnant hags" that Mikhail Bakhtin sees as the epitome of grotesque realism as social change and affirmation (25–26).

In contrast to the embarrassment and derision suggested by the *New Yorker's* pregnant crone and her misplaced narcissism, consider the Old Testament figure of Sarah, over ninety when she overhears God's promise to Abraham that she will bear a son: "Now Abraham and Sarah were old and well stricken in age; and it ceased to be with Sarah after the manner of women. Therefore Sarah laughed within herself, saying. After I am waxed old, shall I have pleasure, my Lord being old also" (Genesis 18.12). After she bears a son, Isaac, Sarah laughs again: "And Sarah said, God hath made me to laugh, so that all that hear will laugh with me" (Genesis 21.6). This is risk and anachronism in the ludic mode. In the more melancholy vein that characterizes much of this essay, however, the ultimate example is the risk and anachronism represented by "untimely death." Many modern philosophers, including Nietzsche, Heidegger, Levinas, and of course Benjamin, have contemplated the untimeliness of being in the consciousness of death as a future past. However, no one has caught the poignancy and defiance of this anachronism more boldly, in my view, than the British philosopher Gillian Rose in her last published works. In *Mourning Becomes the Law*, she writes:

> [If]—as we have been encouraged to generalize—"anachronism" may be taken to mean the relation between the time one nominally inhabits and the actuality of any other, then is not *the future* the supreme anachronism?
>
> For the future is the time in which we may not be, and yet we must imagine we will have been. The focus here is not the promiscuous ecstasies of verb-tenses transporting finite being around in time, but *the not*, the time in which we may *not* be. The pathos of syntax, its punctuation, sets time against negation.
>
> I may die before my time.
>
> I may *live* before my time. (125–26)

These last two propositions—chances, really—open the way for the philosophical and amorous risks which frame a life's work. It is negation, the against-time, the ana-chronism which propels the mindful and embodied soul into life. The bracketing of time within this concept of anachronism is less a "time-out" than an intensification of the "time-in" the future past; death and mourning are "not for nothing," as they may appear to be in a progressivist model of development where "there is always a further step ahead of one who stands in the march of progress" (13). The seeming meaninglessness of life is a function of the "progressiveness" which steps over one death and then another.

In the concluding essay of *Mourning Becomes the Law*, Rose turns to Benjamin and his exploration of the baroque in the *Origin of German Tragic Drama* to describe the modern beginnings of unredeemable death and its subsequent manifestation as part of the political philosophy of fascism. In a book published earlier—though written in the same period during the author's terminal illness—Rose's personal relations of her own life become the text against time and progressivism. *Love's Work*, a philosophical memoir written in the full knowledge of probable, imminent death, is, if anything, more adamantly opposed to contemporary views of progressivism and its links to political psychologies of our time. This dark brief against progress is also one against feminism, which Rose sees as bearing the imprint of a seemingly irresistible teleology and its attendant psychology of self-fulfillment.

Unexpectedly, however, *Love's Work* describes some of the most unique and moving relationships between the author and other women in contemporary writing. That these women are old and that they will, nonetheless, belong to a future which will exceed her life course is the guiding anachronism of the book. At the end of my essay I will return to *Love's Work* as the last of three examples of contemporary women's writing, including Marilyn Hacker's *Winter Numbers* and Marleen Gorris's film *Antonia's Line* as well, all of which link the concept of anachronism and thus risk, with a deeply imagined female genealogy, a subject to which I will turn first.

Sarah's miraculous late-life pregnancy notwithstanding, the Bible records that Abraham begets Isaac, who begets Esau, and so on. The male line continues and, with it, the continuity of culture. Feminist writing since the seventies has attempted to counter this patrilinear genealogy with matrilinear stories of cultural genesis and influence. Associated in the United States with "cultural feminism" and new age versions of the "eternal feminine," female genealogy surfaces more in fiction and poetry than in serious academic discourses, except when it is discredited.[4] Of recent interest has been the discussion of female or feminine genealogy in Europe as proposed by Luce Irigaray, Rosi Braidotti, Luisa Muraro, and others as a social and symbolic practice of countermemory and cultural generativity.

The social and political contexts for this reconsideration of female genealogy set it apart from earlier cultural feminisms in the United States. These differences deserve a much more detailed elaboration than can be afforded here, but a useful introduction to female/feminine genealogy and "sexual difference theory" (as it is referred to) is contained in an interview with Rosi Braidotti by Judith Butler in 1994. This exchange, published in *differences*, reminds us of the shifting frames through which theoretical and political debates are received and exchanged. In her introductory remarks, Butler informs the reader that at the time of interview, the two had never met but "appear to be members of the post-topical feminist community" (27), as their theoretically high-stakes conversation materializes at "odd hours" by way of fax machines; Braidotti describes it as taking place in cyberspace. No matter how abstract the conversation and its delivery system over the Atlantic (Butler being based in the US, Braidotti in the Netherlands), there is something familiar, concrete, and open-ended about their discussion of sexual difference theory; it is reminiscent of, or maybe even prefigurative of, a time when feminism was, or will be, less constrained by theoretical statements like the debates over essentialism and anti-essentialism.

I share Braidotti's stake in crossgenerational female bonding as a psychic support and a political necessity in the empowerment of women. Like others, however, I am deeply troubled by the prospect of a maternal symbolic that, in effect, normalizes relations between women by limiting or privileging the difference configured in the mother-daughter dyad. These differences include but are not limited to class, ethnicity, and sexuality. I understand that at a theoretical level the "symbolic order of the mother" is a function in the service of subjectivity rather than a social role or a political agency. Nonetheless, as Butler asserts in the interview with Braidotti, there is a problem if not a confusion in this putative separability of the symbolic and the social, "one which in making a claim to a status beyond the social offers the social one of its most insidious legitimating ruses" (53). Braidotti, of course, denies that this is the case and argues that in sexual difference theory, genealogy, far from reifying the social, offers temporal possibility, a transformed future for different subjects and for different axes of subjectivity.[5] As she writes in *Nomadic Subjects*, "Sexual difference is a political alliance of women in recognition of their respective differences" (207). Genealogies, "as politically informed countermemories," are central to this project; more specifically, feminist genealogy is "a discursive and political exercise in cross-generational female bonding" (207). Braidotti sees the notion of a feminist genealogy as not only a way to cut through the institutionalization of power which separates women hierarchically by virtue of the "trust" (Muraro) given to Philosopher-Woman by her younger disciples. It is also a way to displace feminist philosophy as the privileged site of symbolic transfers of power and knowledge. Thus is the distinction between creative and theoretical texts collapsed, and the aesthetic dimension of thinking and receiving inspiration from the past through poetry, film, anecdote, autobiography, and other genres is fully credited as part of this "social-symbolic" practice.

Lines of difference on one subject may productively converge on another and, as Braidotti points out, these contradictions and convergences are especially evident in creative texts. In attempting to understand and elaborate the usefulness of a female and feminist genealogy, I draw on creative texts but take up a different axis of subjectivity and power: age. Age and aging are insufficiently interrogated in feminist theory perhaps because until recently old age for women exceeded the mirror of reproduction. With the advent of new reproductive technologies and extended life expectancies, age and aging are—inappropriately or not—now part of this picture. I am particularly interested in texts which disrupt the developmental model of a woman's life and emphasize an untimeliness in relations between women, as does, in fact, the use of reproductive technology itself in postmenopausal women. In them, as we'll see, the mother-daughter dyad is not erased so much as it is transformed by the anachronism of thinking backwards toward a future through a cross-generation bonding which outlives the norms of reproduction. Each features an "aging" woman and a very old woman who will probably outlive her. One is older; one is younger, but closer to death.

Despite the dominant fiction of chronological aging, one that plots our lives in continually increasing numbers, it is clear that we experience age in relation to the ages of others (although this is not, of course, the only way we experience age). Before we consider acting or not acting our age, it is necessary to ask: how old are we? I say "we" because these calculations are always social and always about the Other. A friend of mine, for instance, always sees herself as seven years younger than her sister, whose hair is thinning. We often cling to the flimsiest clichés. A woman who lives with a much older partner says that, as a result of this age difference, she always feels young. Walking with another friend recently, we passed an old woman. Her much-younger husband is dying, and my friend remarked that maybe for the old woman, it was "like losing a child." Is it? Are we ever only the age we are?

We know each other in different ages, and we measure ourselves by the aging of everyone—from close relatives to film stars. The uncanniness of our own images of aging—shaped by loss, separation, and death—can fix or blur age boundaries. We all have our own examples. I knew my grandmother only as a very old woman. My sister died when she was eighteen and, given our age difference, I thought of her as an older child. For years, with those ages fixed in mind, I idealized my grandmother's proud endurance and my sister's bright promise. Lately, however, I imagine my grandmother as a teenager, an immi- grant pregnant with her first child, skipping rope in a churchyard with girls her age until she is scolded by the parish nuns for her immature behavior. I suppose my sister could be a grandmother now, or a state senator. Numbers count, of course, but what do they mean?

In *Winter Numbers*, Marilyn Hacker shows how the numbers don't compute in a season of AIDS and cancer:

> Catherine is back in radiotherapy
> Her schoolboy haircut, prematurely gray,
> now frames a face aging with other numbers:
> "stage two," "stage three" mean more than "fifty-one"
> and mean precisely, nothing, which is why
> she stares at nothing: lawn chair, stone,
> bird, leaf; brusquely turns off the news. (12)

And later, apropos of life as progress:

> No one was promised a shapely life
> ending in a tutelary vision. (13)

In the above poem, entitled "Against Elegies," an older generation of sixty-five-year-olds is younger than their children: "splendid, vying with each other in work hours and wit. / . . . But their children are dying" (11). In "Cancer Winter," she blames her small, dense, out-of-sync "breasts like a twenty-five year old" for hiding her cancer (82). After surgery and chemotherapy, she knows that "to survive / my body stops dreaming it's twenty-five" (84). Is that possible?

These breasts, the one taken and the one remaining, constitute a bodily anachronism, an untimeliness which risks fatality. Risk is always about these numbers—twenty-five, sixty-five, fifty-one—and the effort to wrest from them some reasonable cost-benefit analysis, or some odds on survival. These are, after all, reasonable numbers. But they are "winter numbers" all of them, as we read in "Cancer Winter":

> . . . Who's gone?
> The bookseller who died at thirty-nine,
> poet, at fifty-eight, friend, fifty-one
> friend, fifty-five. These numbers do not sing. (88)

In contrast to these numbers, there are two excessive numbers—ninety-nine and 102; they belong to Mme. Mehling, the poet's next-door neighbor, and they indicate more than her survival. She dies at one hundred two, an event as "exceptional and humdrum as the sparrows that she fed on fine days" (92). She herself is an anachronism in the modern world of commodification, scandalously leaving behind her "sexagenarian saucepans" (92). If one hundred is very old for a woman, sixty is off the scale for a saucepan in contemporary consumer societies!

Quantified time circulates between bodies and things, conflating biological longevity and product turn-around in the ideology of age. Kathleen Woodward has elaborated this relationship in her work on technology and aging. A consequence of the ideology of age is the creation of arbitrary contrasts and competitions between generations which, of course, appear natural or self-evident through their very commodification (for example, Generation X and the baby boomers). Much more sophisticated market segmentation is, of course, already in place, but the binary of old and new still dominates advertising and marketing strategies which target women. This is not to deny that there are such things as aging and generational difference. The "new," however, is not the same as the "young," if what we mean by "new" is radical transformation.[6]

Risk, associated as it is with disease, deficit, danger, and abnormality of all kinds, can be understood at a very basic level as the turbulence which exists in every system. The normalization of aging into fixed patterns of tasks and challenges undoubtedly has the advantage of preparing us for what is ahead with thick descriptions of the coming of age, but like other forms of normalization, it insists on keeping us in place and apart from the unsafe populations that are polluted by extremes and excesses. And of course, it is these extremes and excesses that accumulate as so much debris around the taboo category of the old. The rhetoric of the old as the culturally residual, the decrepit, the distorted, and, finally, the alien in the new world to come, permeates discussions of public policy, medicine, education, electoral politics, feminism, and art (where the cliché of the new is by now very tired). Risk, in my view, is not solely a bad thing to be avoided (a dominant view of personal risk), but also a condition of possibility, a kind of error in calculating normality. Ultimately, it is a sign of life. By risk in relation to aging, I mean those effects of aging which are produced by the normalization of the aging body across disciplines in the modern era. Acting one's age, in a certain sense, can be understood as a caution against risk-taking, with higher and higher stakes associated with advanced chronological age until finally, acting one's age means to die. The shame of not accepting this as if it were simply "natural" or a "fact of life" extends to the high-risk population of the elderly, but also as well to their advocates and eventually to those who mourn them.

In a much-cited passage from Simone de Beauvoir's book about her mother, *A Very Easy Death*, we find an explicit—and powerful—example of this:

> The sadness of the old; their banishment: most of them do not think that this age has yet come for them. I too made use of this cliché, and that when I was referring to my mother. I did not understand that one might sincerely weep for a relative, a grandfather aged seventy and more. If I met a woman of fifty overcome with sadness because she had just lost her mother, I thought her neurotic: we are all mortal; at eighty you are quite old enough to be one of the dead . . .
>
> But it is not true. You do not die from being born, nor from having lived, nor from old age. You die from *something*. The knowledge that because of her age my mother's life must soon come to an end did not lessen the horrible surprise: she had sarcoma . . . as violent and unforeseen as an engine stopping in the middle of the sky. . . . There is no such thing as a natural death: nothing that happens to a man is ever natural, since his presence calls the world into question. (122–23)

Beauvoir's surprise and shame associated with her grief might be attributed in part to her particular and much-noted attitude toward the body, but she herself comments on the social pressures of class and intellectual style which mark this death for her. It is important to insist that the prejudices against the very old weigh on the survivors. When I was in a hospice bereavement group with other adults in their thirties, forties, and fifties, this was a persistent theme. Not only were we feeling devastated by the loss of a parent, but most of us expressed a tremendous shame that we were indeed feeling that way—at "our" age and because the death of an elderly parent was "natural." As Kathleen Woodward has pointed out in *Aging and Its Discontents*, aging in the West has not "provided a social arena for the fulfillment or playing out of generational identity" (107). For aging women, loss is too often accompanied by shame and abjection.

In Marleen Gorris's 1995 film *Antonia's Line*, a fable of female generativity and influence, the title character, Antonia—a wonderful, independent, broad-shouldered mother, grandmother, and great-grandmother—dies just when she is supposed to. She gets up one morning and decides that it is her time. This is not a question of accepting fate. Antonia seizes the day—dying just exactly as she had lived (as the viewers will find out because her death is shown at the beginning of the film). Although the film is historically framed, taking place in a Dutch village after World War II, time moves cyclically, following the seasons of agrarian economy and the cycles of biological reproduction. It is a feminist, pastoral fable, idyllic and passionate in its commitments to a different kind of genealogy.

But, to quote Marilyn Hacker's "Against Elegies" again, "No one was promised a shapely life." Even in this idyll, there is abjection and a representation of the extremely old woman as alien. Antonia's mother, whose death is the reason for Antonia's return to her Dutch village, provides an astounding counterpoint to the dream of fulfillment. As opposed to Antonia's death, her mother's death is in every sense untimely. She is supposed to be already dead by the time Antonia and her daughter arrive for the funeral. Instead she is only half-dead. Antonia finds her in her bed, at first rigid and still, then tossing and turning, cursing the sexual indiscretions of her long-dead husband. Her body and her foul language pollute the house and later the church. She is nearly bald, androgynous, and certainly crazed, although we are meant to understand that she was always more or less like this in her self-presentation. A hilarious and moving figure, she exceeds and interrupts Antonia's "line" by sitting up in her coffin in church. Antonia keeps her distance, explaining her mother to her own daughter as if she were a stranger. But she comes to haunt Antonia's artistic, lesbian daughter, who sees everything differently, including motherhood. This "extra mother" insinuates herself between generations at the parameters of time and life itself.[7] Much like Addie in Faulkner's *As I Lay Dying*, she figures the unruly woman *in extremis*, resisting the confines of her coffin and her family position. She is transgressive, repulsive, the archaic mother as taboo.

As a last and very different kind of example of scandal in relation to anachronism and generation, I turn to Gillian Rose's *Love's Work: A Reckoning with Life*. A British philosopher and critical theorist who wrote on the Frankfurt School,

Adorno, and Judaism, Rose wrote this small book in the crisis of a diagnosis of untreatable ovarian cancer. It is a fierce and elegant defense of reason in the face of physical devastation. As the title suggests, it seeks out a new allegory of love in the ruins—in the wreck of and reckoning with life. It is not a cancer journal or even about how Rose feels (except that she feels physically strong, in general, during the course of the book). It is a book about aging and growing old in full knowledge that one probably will not have the opportunity to do so.

Around the central and sustaining theme of the consolation of philosophy and its attendant risks, there are signs of the very positive grotesque. In my view, however, the power of *Love's Work* lies in the negative challenges it poses to much contemporary writing on the body and cultural politics. The negations are many and include a repudiation of feminism and a last question for it.

The book begins with Rose's introduction to Edna in 1991, before learning of her own illness. As she writes, the first meeting is inauspicious. She has come to New York after five years to visit her old friend Jim, who has AIDS. She finds Jim almost unrecognizable. His hair, which she remembers as glossy and black, has grown out in ungainly red patches. This "uneven growth" (4) is evident in his manners as well, linking him with "multitudes like him, the old men in their forties, shrivelled, drained, mumbling across intersections, icons of AIDS" (4–5). Jim introduces her to Gary, a wealthy private scholar who employs Edna as his secretary seven days a week. Gary, who himself has a wasting disease which makes his posture and movements rigid and off-balance, presents Edna, who is going to put Rose up in her apartment during the visit. Rose expects a woman perhaps in her fifties, but Edna is ninety-three at the time of their first meeting and will be alive and ninety-seven when she is last mentioned. By that time, Jim has died, and Rose is, in a sense, older than Edna is. Edna exceeds, in other words, the space and time of the book. The two afflicted men seem harbingers of Rose's illness, like the grotesque figures who proceed Aschenbach's transformation in Thomas Mann's *Death in Venice*. Edna, however, in her vibrancy and social grace, completes and transforms the triangle of affliction which surrounds Gillian Rose at this point. When they are all together, Rose observes the wonderful rapport between Edna and Jim and revels in "the delight that flew between the fading forty-seven-year-old and the one full of ninety-three years" (8).

Edna's appearance, which might have been startling, seems at once both very strange and comfortable. She is a small old woman with an artificial nose, which she sometimes leaves off when she is at home. When they share Edna's apartment, Rose doesn't notice the nose (or more precisely, lack of it) and, in fact, finds the "neat, black, oblong black hole in her face, even more appealing" (7). Edna, whom Rose calls later her "Intelligent Angel," is in retrospect, the very reason she has come to New York: "She is an annunciation, a message, very old and very new" (9–10). She seems to represent a new sociality and a new home, one without the bitterness associated with the familial home.

The theme of loves which are old and new at the same time continues throughout the book. Yvette, who is a lusty sixty-five years old when they first meet, is described as both an affectionate and inventive grandmother and as inexhaustible in her erotic engagements (she has concurrently three lovers). After a reoccurrence of breast cancer, Yvette falls in love with a man thirty years her junior and pursues him mercilessly with phone calls and letters. Yvette was, Rose writes, "monstrous" (32). Nonetheless, the lessons she teaches of facing one's desires and one's losses, of gaining new friends and new loves to the very end of life, place her in the extraordinary company of Jim and Edna, whose lives cross the very real and well-marked boundaries of chronological time to meet up just in time or on the brink of time.

As an allegory of love, *Love's Work* insists upon the conditionality and risk of love and reason joined. Rose, concluding the chapter on her surgery and illness, rejects the languages of clinical diagnostic medicine and of alternative healing. Indeed, her clear and harrowing description of her relation to her altered body after a colostomy earns her the right to rail against the faint-hearted and the pietistic:

> Exceptional, edgeless love effaces the risk of relation: that mix of exposure and reserve, of revelation and reticence. It commands the complete unveiling of the eyes, the transparency of the body. It denies that there is no love without power; that we are at the mercy of others and that we have others in our mercy. Existence is robbed of its weight, its gravity, when it is deprived of its agon. Instead of insinuating that illness may better prepare you for earthly impossibilities, these enchiridions on Faith, Hope, and Love would condemn you to see blissful, deathless, cosmic emptiness—the repose without the revel.
>
> I reach for my favourite whiskey bottle and instruct my valetudinarian well-wishers to imbibe the shark's oil and the aloe vera themselves. (105–06)

Implicitly, Rose indicts any morality of aging and maturity which involves developing into a body without the edginess of pain and opposition. What looks full in the progressivist model of maturation is, to her, emptiness. As she concludes: "Matured by love, practiced in the grief of its interminable exercise, I find myself back at the beginning. Is feminism able to credit that it may be better sometimes, not to get what you want?" (142).

Although I find the renunciation of feminism in *Love's Work* narrow and wounding, hers is nonetheless an interesting and serious question. Perhaps Rose is here like the fictional character Lizzie in Angela Carter's novel *Nights at the Circus*, a small, wizened aerial performer who looks skeptically into the future, as "through a glass darkly" (286)—a useful if painful interlocutor.[8] Rose's question assumes, of course, a feminism that is fully implicated in a discourse of liberation and individual fulfillment, a feminism that never works from yearning, loss, and mourning. Of course, this is at best only partially true, though indeed books have already been published that prescribe a "getting over, getting older" as a feminist style of aging and a version of maturity which for Rose signifies an empty death. I think I understand how this feminism could never have offered Rose any help, as she writes earlier in *Love's Work*, for it fails to comprehend loss and therefore leaves out so much and so many.

At the same time, however, the intensity of Rose's vision, her being-for-death, threatens to overpower the mundane, which is why, I think, she needs Edna and why at the end of the book, she honors Agatha Christie's disarmingly mundane Miss Marple:

> I like to pass unnoticed, which is why I hope that I am not deprived of old age. I aspire to Miss Marple's persona: to be exactly as I am, decrepit nature yet supernature in one, equally alert on the damp ground and in the turbulent air. Perhaps I don't have to wait for old age for that invisible trespass and pedestrian tread, insensible of mortality and desperately mortal.
>
> I will stay in the fray, in the revel of ideas and risk; learning, failing, wooing, grieving, trusting, working, reposing—in this sin of language and lips. (144)

There is a fair distance, of course, between aspiring to the persona of Miss Marple and being Miss Marple. The lives of very old women in western societies are apt to be much lonelier than that of the thrill-seeking, inquisitive, and insinuating detective. Nonetheless, her "invisible trespass and pedestrian tread" suggest a vector at once stealthy and companionable.

Despite her quarrel with feminism as she knew it, Gillian Rose insists on the power of women and counts herself as a woman feminism does not speak of, one who "with the gift of and power of Active Intelligence" gives love and draws it to her, "enabling and difficult" (141). She also understands that the melancholy anachronism of the statement, "I may die before my time," is countered by the defiant statement, "I may live before my time." To live before one's time is to live in a revolutionary present that embraces the risks, injuries, and insults accorded to the new, the unfamiliar, and the very old.

NOTES

1. Hope, for Benjamin, lies with the very old and even with the dead. "Only that historian will have the gift of fanning the spark of hope in the past who is firmly convinced that *even the dead* will not be safe from the enemy if he wins" (255). For Benjamin, the historian must "brush history against the grain" (257), which I take to be a practice of anachronism.

2. See Butler's *Gender Trouble*.

3. See my book, *The Female Grotesque*.

4. The reception of Julia Kristeva's essay "Women's Time," linking gender, generation, and time (though not aging), is both typical and an exception. For a brief

discussion of "Women's Time" in relation to Braidotti's notion of feminist genealogies, see her *Nomadic Subjects* (121).

5. In this interview, Braidotti claims a specifically European political identity to situate the interests vested in "sexual difference" (over or beside "gender equality") in the emerging context of the European union. Obviously, the critique of Eurocentrism which is so important in the United States cultural politics and the formulation of multiculturalism in North America and which followed on the first reception of "sexual difference theory" through "French" feminism or even French feminisms, as opposed to "Anglo-American" feminism (as if these were ever the only choices), is meant to be both claimed and deconstructed in this move toward a new Europe, one characterized by regional differences and multicultural and multiethnic populations. To some extent, this is a Europe yet to be discovered. In the United States, the recognition of western European countries like Italy, for instance, as internally marked by ethnic, regional, and economic differences, has often been blocked by a pattern of importing material and cultural products "made in Italy" and by the residual ideology surrounding the "Italian-American" family. On nationalism and the new Europe, see the book I edited with Beverly Allen, *Revisioning Italy*.

6. See Kathleen Woodward's "From Virtual Cyborgs to Biological Time Bombs: Technocriticism and the Material Body."

7. I am alluding here to Woodward's phrase "extra mother" in *Aging and Its Discontents* (107).

8. As I argue in *The Female Grotesque* in relation to the intergenerational couple of Lizzie and Fevvers (a young performer of impressive proportions), they do not represent generational difference in terms of the mother-daughter dyad. Rather they figure an intergenerational grotesque of the kind evoked by Bakhtin in the terra-cotta figures of pregnant, senile hags that I mentioned earlier. When the older Lizzie first sees that her young companion has wings, she refuses to recognize this as a sign of the "new"; instead she historicizes *herself* and sees in Fevvers, the "Annunciation of my own Menopause" (178). This intergenerational subjectivity means that here the new is not transparently identified with the young. The "new" is included in this bodily configuration as a possibility that already existed, a part of the aging body-in-process, rather than as the property (like virginity) of a discrete and static identity. In the course of the novel, Lizzie retains her skepticism and views time from a standpoint which is analogous to Benjamin's startled and contemplative Angel of History: "'It's going to be more complicated than that,' interpolated Lizzie. 'This old witch see storms ahead, my girl. When I look to the future, I see through a glass darkly. You improve your analysis, girl, and *then we'll discuss it*'" (285–86).

WORKS CITED

Allen, Beverly, and Mary Russo, eds. *Revisioning Italy: National Identity and Global Culture*. Minneapolis: U of Minnesota P, 1997.

Bakhtin, Mikhail. *Rabelais and His World*. Cambridge: MIT P, 1968.

Beauvoir, Simone de. *A Very Easy Death.* Trans. Patrick O'Brien. New York: Putnam's, 1973.

Benjamin, Walter. *Illuminations.* Trans. Harry Zohn. New York: Schocken, 1969.

Braidotti, Rosi. *Nomadic Subjects: Embodiment and Sexual Difference in Contemporary Feminist Theory.* New York: Columbia UP, 1994.

———. "Feminism by Any Other Name: Interview with Judith Butler." *differences* 6.2–3 (1994): 27–61.

Butler, Judith. *Bodies that Matter: On the Discursive Limits of Sex.* New York: Routledge, 1993.

———. *Gender Trouble.* New York: Routledge, 1990.

Carter, Angela. *Nights at the Circus.* New York: Viking, 1986.

Gorris, Marleen, dir. *Antonia's Line.* 1995.

Hacker, Marilyn. *Winter Numbers.* New York: Norton, 1994.

Irigaray, Luce. *Sexes and Genealogies.* Trans. Gillian C. Gill. New York: Columbia UP, 1987.

Kristeva, Julia. "Women's Time." Trans. Alice Jardine and Harry Blake. *Signs* 7.1 (1981): 13–35.

Milan Women's Bookstore Collective. *Sexual Difference: A Theory of Social-Symbolic Practice.* Trans. Patricia Cicogna and Teresa de Lauretis. Bloomington: Indiana UP, 1990.

Muraro, Luisa. *L'ordine simbolico della madre.* Roma: Editori Riuniti, 1991.

Rose, Gillian. *Love's Work: A Reckoning with Life.* New York: Schocken, 1997.

———. *Mourning Becomes the Law: Philosophy and Representation.* Cambridge: Cambridge UP, 1996.

Russo, Mary. *The Female Grotesque: Risk, Excess, and Modernity.* New York: Routledge, 1994.

Woodward, Kathleen. *Aging and Its Discontents: Freud and Other Fictions.* Bloomington: Indiana UP, 1991.

———. "From Virtual Cyborgs to Biological Time Bombs: Technocriticism and the Material Body." *Culture on the Brink: Ideologies of Technology.* Ed. Gretchen Bender and Timothy Druckrey. Seattle: Bay P., 1994. 47–64.

The Other End of the Fashion Cycle
Practicing Loss, Learning Decline

Margaret Morganroth Gullette

I. AGE STUDIES LOOKS AT THE FASHION CYCLE

My mother still buys almost all my clothes. After college, when she might have stopped, she really didn't want to. Even after I married, had a baby, got my first leg up in academe, published my first book . . . even after she retired, she continued to dress us all up at her expense. She likes shopping, has excellent taste, and wants us to be well dressed. I still get most of my clothes when we visit in our respective cities, twice a year. Shopping together, we are two well-dressed women, obviously chromosomally related, getting along, mildly disagreeing about what is in, what is "right for me." When we come out with something useful and desirable, we share a tired satisfied glance; we say, "We did well." Other times of year, surprise packages arrive. If at first as a young, wannabe-independent woman I went along grudgingly, in time I found myself relieved and grateful.

This arrangement is unusual. It has saving touches of excess—the very fact that my mother continued her loving, generous practice into my middle years provided one.[1] That ongoing practice surfeited my level of need at a time of

34

life—early mid-adulthood—when overextended working parents can vaguely feel under-cherished, giving more than they're getting; they may be individuating but they're feeling orphaned. Moreover, my attractive wardrobe comes free. Recognizing the cultural oddity of our whole arrangement helped me wrench the practice of clothes shopping out of the class of thoughtless habits and lift it into the realm of the theorizable. This partial detachment was crucial in enabling me to bring to bear on fashion my work in feminist age studies.

In the long run, I was freed to see involvement in fashion as a practice that demands of the participant not just money to buy new objects, but an experience driven by the object's "life cycle." A chilling metaphor.[2] It's the product, not the human being buying it, whose life is attended to—and only a limited part of the cycle at that. The known life of an object moves from purchase, through consumption (public display of possession), to the "decline" (going out of fashion) necessary to start up the cycle again. Even when the psychology of the human purchaser is in question, the investigators (whether marketeers, sociologists, economists, or cultural critics) use a metaphor that privileges the beginning, "point of purchase." The youth part of the cycle. Youth! Again, yanking this chain of signifiers out into cleaner air, we find decline ideology.

I see the experience of undergoing the cycle—especially the final stage of discarding/decline—as a core experience of consciousness. Analyzing the experience shows, first of all, how emotional self-manipulation and continuing education go on throughout our human life course. Every fashion change you perform, in whatever your zone of alleged expertise, requires new learning, conscious and unconscious. The conscious knowledges (for example, brand names) may become obsolete. Yet there are always millions who master them, and not just once and for all, but after a punctuated interval, again, many times. People become "knowledgeable," "smart shoppers," "educated consumers." (Praise for market learning uses the vocabulary of academic success.) I'm not interested in the *content* of what each individual learns in order to begin the cycle again, but in the unconscious experience, especially the continual unlearning that marks the end of the cycle. "Who loses and who wins; who's in, who's out / . . . packs and sects of great ones, / That ebb and flow by th' moon"—King Lear rightly begins with those who lose (*King Lear* 5.3.15–19).

All our lives long, we—the entire population of the country—do remarkably well at these repeated educational and emotional examinations, including the forgetting required at the ebb. Gaping at the culture, we notice prodigious acquisitions of new knowledge and feelings, and equally precipitous deaccessions. Running up to a war, for example, a nation learns geography, history, current events, the name of the enemy, the issues to be passionate about and those to ignore. Unlearning never comes without emotion; in war, after we learn to feel strongly, we are encouraged to let those feelings go. Most do.

In all fashion, the pattern we learn by going through the entire cycle is freighted with emotion. Purchase involves learning and wanting and spending money; possession involves some affective relationship with the object over time; going out of fashion (the end of one cycle) involves some yet-to-be-measured degree of rejection and loss. Wanting, getting, living with, losing, and—the most important phase, the one that gets omitted—discarding. Going through such a cognitive/emotional cycle unconsciously can be considered a process of socialization. It may seem like a "unique," "individual" experience, but it is structured into everyday life in such a way that participants experience the same cycle, time after time. Social practices can score—scar—the psyche. Feminist theorists like Thorstein Veblen, Sandra Bartky, and Naomi Wolf have shown how dangerous fashion can be in constructing aspects of gender identity: shame and narcissism, "femininity," the sense of being an object of display, a devalued commodity.[3]

But the fashion cycle has never previously been considered a practice through which American culture constructs our *age identity* and our sense of the meaning of "aging."[4] What I propose here is that going through any market cycle affects our experience of the life cycle. The fashion system is one source of emotional resocialization that promotes a specific "knowledge": what befalls the self in time. If purchasing-and-display make troubling demands on the psyche, discarding—in part because it is an unrepresented experience, an untheorized practice—can be far more dangerous. Over time, the routine involves constant relearning and altered emotions about such identity issues as durability versus transitoriness, investment of self versus withdrawal of self, and the most basic question about temporality: whether time can be relied upon to provide us with gain or loss. Discarding teaches us that the self can expect to *lose* from living in time—lose selfhood. And we learn this not just exceptionally but as a routine of everyday life, over and over. Under rubrics like fun and pleasure, people are taught that obeying the cyle is coterminous with life. Ninety is not too old to shop.[5]

The zone of my story is clothing, and my story is dense with specificity—I'm a woman of a certain class, historical era, region, and age, with her own family dynamics, personal psychology, access to theory. Yet, at the outset of this particular feminist age study, written in the nineties, I want to posit some degree of broadly shared vulnerability to the fashion cycle. Why? First, because the market's reach changes constantly. In North America at the turn of the century, the rise of the department store, mass production, and advertising went along with the expansion of consumption-dedicated classes. Theorizing about fashion is based on models appropriate to that modern era. Discussions of psychological internalizations imposed by fashion refer primarily to women—partly because theory focuses on the front end of the cycle, point of purchase and display, where women, especially middle- and upper-class women, were once the designated shoppers. Men too still assume that men are never "docile bodies," never adversely affected by fashion.[6]

Now postmodern capitalism is making those older gender and class binaries anachronistic. The imperializing tendencies of the transnational apparel industry are sweeping up new consumers, male and female, and swooping down the class ladder. Capitalism doesn't care about the gender or color of the dollar. In North America men above the ideal age grow steadily more vulnerable to the cycle because of the growing identification of masculinity and work-related savvy with youth.[7] With "the mass production of cheap smart clothes," George Orwell pointed out during the Great Depression, even the unemployed in First World countries invest in the cycle (88). Now the employed in Third World countries have been lured in. I see this on my trips to postrevolutionary Nicaragua every year. There too fashion is connected, via jeans, donated T-shirts, children's paintbox colors, and TV, with North America/youth/vitality/pleasure. Everywhere higher status tends to mean more intense and repetitious involvement in the front end of the cycle, more rapid and frequent discards. Do people with that experience feel less loss at the end of each cycle? Does that mean they have *less* protection against decline narratives, or more? And what of the increasing number of those who at midlife are downwardly mobile? These correlations are unstudied.

Moreover, fashion-cycling begs for further comparison with all cycles that comprise practices-with-purchased-objects. Perhaps they all make participants more vulnerable to decline narratives. Any semi-durable objects that you later replace may let you in for the basic experience of unwilling enforced loss: music systems, cars, boats. The object need not be made of heavy metal. It can be furniture, houses, or vacation spots. The object can "as easily take the form of a person or a person's time"; as Rachel Bowlby says, "anything at all" can be commodified (qtd. in Williamson 228). Affective relations with the object are the key. Sports are one version of the lifelong experience: there men (now, more and more women) voluntarily learn prominent names, facts, relationships, winners and losers, just the way in the clothing zone people learn the "new" and the "old-fashioned." Politics, film, popular music have also become zones of human discard: the prematurely declining careers of people with whom we have deeply identified teach related emotions. Language is a another powerful zone of loss, as expressions that made us feel "with it" become kitsch or worse. Philosophies go out of fashion, and so do moral ideas. There are attempts to make whole political theories extinct. Through these overlapping zones, some degree of relearning, self-manipulation, and loss can be a part of any life.

Innocently going through normalized routines that appear to concern "things" softens up our psyches to accept other narratives of necessary loss personally and prematurely, more and more rapidly. The fashion cycle is only one of the mysterious ways both men and women learn, early in life in American culture and certainly no later than the middle years, that we are no-longer-young. The totality of these ways of telling our life course constitutes our age identity. I can't speak for anyone but myself, but I speak here *to* all participants in any cycle who are willing to examine the degree to which they have been trained and aged by culture in ways they cannot yet imagine. And whenever a true anti-ageist movement begins, women and men will need to be allies, and the elite too will need to see they have stakes in the outcome.

II. EARLY LEARNING AND LONG LOVES

My mother started taking me shopping with her, to the baroque and gilded discount store, Loehmann's, in Brooklyn's Bedford-Stuyvesant district, not far from Ebbett's Field, when I was only about six years old. Amid the grandeur of Jacobean-style benches and sculpted-figure torchères, I didn't yet care about clothes. The marble lion on the landing up to the first floor served as my mount from which to regard incuriously the "ladies" changing on the floor below. My mother wasn't then working, but she had worked at Macy's as a clerk and was still dreaming of being a buyer. By the time I was ten she had her teaching job and her own checkbook. Even before I left for college she had let me know that shopping was a pleasure for her for many symbolic reasons.

As a teenager, I was driven to Loehmann's by my mother regularly. By then I had moved into the next and ghastliest role in the history of my lifelong involvement with the garment industry. The clothes-horse. My mother had a connoisseur's eye for designer fashion, and where my wardrobe was concerned, a Jeeves-like sensibility for correctness. By my college years, the combination gave me a wardrobe of a small number of perfect garments and a habit of minute attention to details: the cleanliness of cuffs, the absence of loose threads, the evenness of hems—a perfectionist's stance. Away from home, a scholarship student from a family trying to settle permanently in the middle class, I served as my own Jeeves. Bertie Wooster was not more meticulously turned out every day. Before dates, I fretted over matching hats and shoes and gloves. Freshman year I was asked to give a makeup demonstration in the bathroom: girls crowded in, looking at a "New Yorker" applying eyeliner, mascara, eye shadow, blush, powder (never lipstick). That era included French existential fashion associations (the "unforgettable" Juliette Greco)—pallor and doe eyes and some intellectual man like Sartre in the background. My favorite models, Suzy Parker and Dovima, broke through pre-pill restraint with sophisticated sultriness. I'm dropping these names and sense-of-the-era to demonstrate what a good student I was, how effective the training. My husband remembers the heavy boots he wore at that age, borrowed iconographically from Marlon Brando in *The Wild One*. Almost everyone has this kind of recall about their first teenage learning experiences with "fashion." It was so intense, so sexualized, that it laid down the conditions for later-life nostalgia—as well as later-life purchasing habits.

As a college freshman, *nota bene*, I was already not just a student but teaching the lore. My students were prepped to learn (especially the private-school kids, previously sheltered from boys and lore and thrust in timidity and innocence into the college sex and marriage market). I didn't do any more to emphasize the importance of the subject than to appear during orientation week in broad daylight in my green eye shadow and black turtleneck in front of eyes that had been looking at shirtwaists and white blouses and saddle shoes for a decade. In my appearance, foreign and yet tailored, "exotic" (that was Jewishness seen from outside) and meticulous, they may have seen a way of being both sexy and rebellious at relatively low social cost. I don't want to mock me or them. All steps toward rebellion can lead on to more interesting and subversive rebellions.

Retrospection, sharpened by the right questions, can demonstrate the construction of emotions and demystify "experience." I want to emphasize the cognitive/emotional functions of the little rite we were accomplishing in the bathroom of Comstock Hall during the postwar economic boom. Disregard the tiny style differences between us that loomed so large: some would go on buying shirtwaists and a few would buy turtlenecks. Disregard even the vast economic differences: some would go on to buy gemstones and others have modest budgets for clothes and shoes. Whatever style we affected, from the point of view of lifelong learning and emotional baggage, every one of us attended boot camp for American culture, just like the kids who didn't go to college. The commitment to conforming to local norms is never so strong and credulous as in the teen years. In the nineties the learning starts earlier yet, with preschoolers being inducted via toys and sneakers and grade-school pupils getting ads piped into the classroom. Although one's relationship to fashion can and often does become more alienated over time, the process of involvement is "continuing education" in that it goes on outside of formal settings and continues forever. Nothing I say is likely to stop any of these behaviors. But theory can skew the meanings of this activity in slightly subversive ways, to make more conscious resistance possible.

I dislike shopping, even with my mother's help and high spirits. But there were many pleasures in the system my mother set up for turning me out in style. This is important, as no learning goes on without affect, and intense affect makes learning memorable. I shared some of the pleasures she got. Inducted into the fashion system in filial ways, we associate shopping with the way we bonded with the parent investing in us—usually a mother?—who supported the desire for the objects, and provided the guidance and the cash. Even leaving aside the factitious glamor conferred by advertising, in any current practice of cathecting an object can be found, thickly layered from childhood on, pleasure and serious misery, money power and symbolic love, class aspirations, competition in the sexual sweepstakes, "taste," gender identity, and (for women) female bonding. Were my own layers especially thick?

I also loved the clothes. Loving the clothes was so overdetermined and is now so transparent in my case that it strikes me as almost laughable. I had one little black dress (it was long and sleeveless and buttoned from top to bottom with two dozen tiny cloth-covered buttons) that I felt made me look like Audrey Hepburn, who managed to give a slightly foreign and risqué air to looking boneless and cool. We were trained to find a model and try to transform ourselves in that direction. All my clothes were beautifully made: in the colors and textures and lines of clothes, the love of beauty ("esthetics") can find an everyday outlet. Influenced by my mother's admiration for craft, I appreciated the labor that went into them, the ingenuity of the design, the skill that worked the looms, the pains-taking that produced the final material item. When profit margins were lower, even "affordable" clothes were lined, some seams were finished; and in more expensive clothes, fabrics were matched across pockets and openings, and finishing (seams, embroidery, sequins) was done by hand. "We don't see workmanship like that any more"—except in a garment that costs what a Nicaraguan family spends to survive for a year. I won't knock esthetics or appreciation for skill, but that's all the space they'll get here, because from the point of view of continuous education these values ordinarily just give a fillip to learning what "taste" is and demonstrating expensively that you have it, and they provide the subordinate emotions that, added up together, overproduce "loving the objects."

I "loved" the clothes more than we are supposed to. And that was another saving touch of excess—perhaps the crucial one—for the cycle to snag on. My good feelings toward an object take a form fashion must frown on: I go in for long possession. I have clothes for comfort and use and show that I go on wearing year after year. I have a house-painting outfit flecked with as much paint as a Jackson Pollack. I had a bathrobe that I wore to write in every day for years, until it fell into tatters at unrepairable places. Two party dresses, as the second-hand furniture dealers say, "have age on them." The designer trousers are out in the garden, kneeling and weeding.

I harp on this subversive affection because it is relevant to the emotional cycle of fashion. No possession without its levy of emotion. No intense initial relationship with objects, without some perilous aftermath pinned into its side. The bad side of loving the objects now emerges. Leaving them. As long as one is growing physically, discarding is necessary, not optional; it has its own name, "outgrowing." Childhood is (or was) the innocent time of the cycle: relatively little cathexis at the beginning, no coercion to discard, no sorrow at the end. It's after one has outgrown outgrowing—when one realizes that one's adult size is more or less fixed—that people can unconsciously feel coerced when forced to discard. And some enact their resistance.

I keep a drawer full of fabrics, from clothes whose styles or patterns were made obsolete. Fabrics with Renaissance or art-nouveau designs, a scrap of silk velvet I bought a yard of in Paris in the seventies, a cotton piqué dress that I was led to cut too short in one of the recurrent mini phases. I regret many that I didn't—couldn't—save. If that verb sounds human, that's close to how I felt. I look regretfully as each favorite faultlessly becomes "unfashionable." Stubborn but unable to break out of the system, I have my bottom drawer, a small permanent private museum of my sensualities and esthetic tastes and semiotic intentions and economic ambitions that have publicly been made passé. They may be *schmattes*—a Yiddish word for old clothes that nicely combines contempt and affection—but I didn't make them rags. The drawer is a mausoleum, in which are housed the relics of objects I learned to love and then learned to relinquish publicly. I'm not nostalgic about them; I don't yearn to be the self that wore them. By itself my sweet museum of *schmattes* doesn't take us far. But it's telling, a bit of the micropolitics of everyday life, a bit of filial synthesis of parental values. It expresses my originally intuitive resistance to the required second half of the fashion process: the death of the loved object, the making of the current into "the past"—the emotional production of the passé and every other dire outcome that is thus foretold—in short, the shedding of pieces of the self.

III. SOME POSSIBLE SOURCES OF RESISTANCE

Do other people have museums or wear their clothes to rags? How would we know how widespread clinging to old objects is, when next to nothing is spoken or written about this end of the cycle? I was astonished and charmed to find, in Ann Beattie's *Another You*, a midlife woman who also hangs onto her clothes. When she turns embroidered free-flowing dresses into summer nightgowns, she does it as a semi-conscious resister: "maybe . . . it wasn't judiciousness so much as a desire to make the past fit in with the present" (41). Beattie sees how, symbolically, life time is involved when people relinquish something they once learned to love and planned to long possess. Indeed, I like to believe that everyone reading this essay this far has devised some ways in which they resist mandatory obsolescence.[8]

In my own case, the exceptional conditions of my arrangement provided private sources of detachment. To start with, my mother writes the checks. My husband doesn't come on these trips and he invariably likes what I bring home. His kind of non-investment maintains and supports some of my estrangement from the system, the reach of its economic, psychosexual, heterosexist tentacles. For most of my life, most of the time, I have not paid and do not pay much at all for having a relationship to fashion. It's amazing what a difference it makes. Since I buy little on my own and also wear what my mother sends, including hand-me-downs, I wear clothes without any fetishizing of my "unique" taste and choice and semiotic intentions. I can wear something without any delusion that I "love" it or that getting it was the fun part. A garment suffices if it marks me—when a mark is needed—as a just-sufficiently fashionable New England woman of the middle class of an academic/bohemian type who has pretensions to shoulders, legs, et cetera.

Therefore, other explanations are needed for why I am so loathe to relinquish the clothes. Quite consciously but much later, they represented to me my mother's continuing good will, which didn't let me down when I was no longer "young" but follows me through my middle years. They certainly represented her money, which she earned— with pleasure, to be sure, because she enjoyed being a first-grade teacher, an educator, a Deweyite, and, of course, an independent woman. My mother's own complex psychological, feminist, and class relationship to clothes—which I have known since I was a child—is a set of facts material to my narrative of resistance to the cycle. I knew the values of a woman-earned dollar.

And those of a dollar earned by a man. My father, who died in 1974, was a leftist with a lifelong, eloquent, proselytizing, and aggressive allegiance to the working class. A man marked by the Depression, who worked long hours in all weathers, he never forgot how hard it could be to make a living under capitalism. During his forties, from being a working man with skills he turned himself into a small businessman who owned and drove his own truck, and later owned and worked his small parking lot. All this time, the clothes he wore were a kind of uniform: khaki pants over a union suit, heavy plaid work shirts, layered one over the other in the winter so his arms would be free, a watch cap. He never wore a tie; he didn't own a middle-class jacket until many years later. I've known only one person more alienated from the American fashion cycle. (This was my mother's brother, my Uncle Charlie. In adulthood, he never owned more than two pairs of pants. When the other pair was stolen, and my mother expressed sympathy, he shrugged, "One less thing to worry about.") My father bought good tools and saved them and repaired them and over time gave them to me. My shop is not a museum; I use these tools frequently. He repaired things—not just (as a young man) professionally but lifelong as a pleasure and a form of identity. He was not only frugal in practice but anti-bourgeois in theory. My mother and I went shopping; he kept to a different standard. In my teens, I experienced that contrast of personalities and ideologies with pain, but now I see it as part of the excess that saved me.

My mausoleum was a result of already being partly detached from cold-hearted, fickle fashion even before I knew how to theorize it. Later I discovered that capitalism needs to train us all to perform the cycle. Those who can see that they are part of the system feel somewhat degraded by their powerlessness to resist it much, or to exit entirely from it; somewhat sheepish about showing off the latest item they've just purchased even though it proves what they've learned about technology or style or whatever the new lore is; somewhat embarrassed about conspicuous consumption even though their class-situations may require it as condition and reward; and defensive enough to harp on pleasure and appropriation and playfulness. So far, we are vulnerable to these self-criticisms without (even on the Left) having found sufficient justification for inventing collective resistance.

There is a justification. I believe that everyone in the cycle potentially has a grave emotional grievance against it. We are emotionally manipulated by being required to give up allegiances, and deprived when we succumb and do give them up. Muriel Spark has a poem about seeing "one sad shoe" thrown out on the highway. Perhaps the owner kept the other because he was afraid "to hurt its feelings." "That one shoe in the road invokes / my awe and my sad pity" (82).

Like the old shoe, our objects may be trivial in themselves—I'll say here that for my argument they *are* trivial, *pace* my dear, loyal, working-class-identified father, who saw them as equivalents of hard labor. *Pace* my dear, generous, middle-class-identified mother, who sees them as objects of beauty and skill and signs of achieved status. Their points of view are both right, within their contexts. She will forgive me, and he would, once I make my theoretical point clear, because together, jointly and severally, they freed me to learn what I needed in order to make it. As things, clothes are rags and heavy metals are scrap. What counts is how we feel about them—the amount of self we use up in the fashion cycle, and what we are forced to learn by loving and losing, again and again, bits of self. Awe and sad pity can be reserved for ourselves.

Maybe resistance to the fashion cycle is connected with a kind of positive or Kohutian narcissism, the kind of self-preservation that *in extremis* rescues us from thoughts of suicide, that nerves us to survive torture—the power that keeps us from succumbing not only to staggering onslaughts on selfhood like these, but that helps as well against the minute, repetitive, incremental, and invisible onslaughts that culture exposes us to.

IV. THE SCREAM CAME FROM THE DRESSING ROOM

A kind of resistance actually may begin early in the cycle, in the relationship between the fashion we buy and the putative "self" that buys it. This happens at point of purchase, the cynosure of anecdote and theory. Young participants develop the habit ("shopping") of providing moments when they are supposed to cathect an object. Marketeers and economists talk about the point of purchase as the moment of the self's greatest "pleasure," not just to sell goods but also because they have an interest in representing the object as gradually becoming unsatisfactory. Another simple decline narrative. Obviously point of purchase has to be made into an intense moment. Here the culture succeeds one way or another, because intensity can as easily be made out of pain as pleasure. More easily. The fashion side of my age autobiography began with my being driven as an adolescent toward that moment, in order to provide a context in which to analyze all the unpleasures, especially those of the unregarded end.

Everyone who tries on "looks"—whether in clothes or cars or boats or houses or vacation spots—believes to some degree that she/he has a relationship to that look which seems pretty important. "The self chooses its look." In my lifetime, I have moved from a girlhood spent in the working/lower-middle classes to a mid adulthood in the academic/artistic/middle-upper classes, and I have scarcely known a single woman who did not speak as if she had a special relationship with the front end of the cycle—meaning, "her" look. We sidle up close to any "choice" we make and think of it, naively, as an "expression" of self. There's flattery in this marketeers' view: the buyer is made to seem creative and expressive, individual, intentional, potent. When semiotic approaches to fashion privilege "expressivity" and expand discourse about "meanings," they too effectively enhance the intensity of the transactions around the point of purchase.

There's mystification too: it implies free choice, and an original uninfluenced self, and an "infinite" array of looks, provided by the astonishing American "free-market" system, the envy of all the world. But in fact there's only a limited array of looks (rigidly determined by the market despite all the talk of "choices"); the self is strongly influenced to change by the multiple discourses that elaborate the purported differences among looks past and present; and the idea of "selecting" among current looks (perfectly accurate within the most constrained view of the procedure) hides the prior condition of selection, which is money. Most of shopping is not-buying, because you can't afford to. Each time you back away from a purchase you relearn your class standing, as based on disposable income. This most people will not mention, since under capitalism it's humiliating to admit we can't afford something.

Despite knowing at some level that "free" choice is a joke, everyone in the culture who can afford to buy semi-durable, obsolescing goods participates in some part of the mystification that goes with a vocabulary of choosing. *Later*, suppressing any prior misery, we say, "I chose the little black one with buttons," hoping that we will be represented by our fashion well enough.

The self in consumption studies (as in marketing) is the self that wants to buy, gets enjoyment, "appropriates" the object. The self in age studies (as in feminism) can not be considered just a mystified victim; it is also a source of resistance.[9] But neither is it a perfectly free and delighted elector of its pleasures. In its aspect as participant in the fashion cycle, it may even elect to move from delighted consumer to conscious victim to some phase beyond. This complex, self-changing self is a necessary assumption for anti-essentialism—for an age theory that sees the life course both historically and developmentally, as, ideally, an uncoerced narrative of being and becoming.

The simplistic consumption self is belied by pain we know we are having. Say I'm in a dressing room and I shuck off a dress. I've divested myself of a look. I'm still well within the system. I'll try on another, discard that, and so on, maybe for hours; then I get fraught, fret, conclude "nothing looks good on me," leave the store depressed and discouraged and even truly grieving. Many women say this happens to them. Going into the dressing room might always result in an inner scream. For women (and increasingly for younger men), clothing comes with too many competing choices, too many confusing discourses, too much coercion to be in the system at all, too much fear of failure. Moreover, while some looks might be better than others for the majority of the population, we in the majority don't get them. The average American woman is not quite 5' 4" tall and weighs 143 pounds (Gilday). So any look that emphasizes slenderness, or height, or perfect muscle tone—qualities also falsely associated with "youth"—is going to be wrong in the dressing room. Most of the time, then, most women must feel wrong about themselves while trying on clothes, don't want to buy them, and leave the place of defeat in dejection. Feminist theory has provided saving explanations for this phenomenon. The feminist self knows itself always-about-to-be-grieved by fashion.

Maybe all selves are grieved. Economist Albert O. Hirschman, one of the rare analysts of disappointment within the cycle, thinks that "disappointment with oneself" might be the result of "any purchase that requires discrimination on the part of the buyer" (43).[10] With younger men overwhelmingly featured in ads, what protects midlife men in the dressing room? Perhaps disappointment with oneself comes from any purchase that requires more money than you have, or more "taste" (class-based learning) than you think you have, or a different body. In fact, isn't it possible that point of purchase brings about a net lowering of self-esteem one way or another? This must be denied in many ways so that the cycle can go on.

Subjects might want to calculate how much at point of purchase they are avoiding pain, how much denying pain, and how much finding pleasure. One of the compromises a woman often describes conversationally to a friend involves maintaining some unstated continuity with the way she likes to dress. I can always find basic black, one friend wears eccentric belts, another hand-woven cloth. The shopper has succeeded, as my mother and I did in the first paragraph, in buying *something*. In describing this as a success, she hides the scream and reveals her semi-participation in the system, constrained but mildly subversive of the automatism of changed selfhood. No one I know shucks her wardrobe annually; people postpone getting into another new look; they slow down the cycle. At some level, by my age most women are not "seduced" by fashion. If they get a little anticipatory lift when, say, the previews of the fall collection come out, that rather complicated feeling does not actually translate into joy or whole-hearted expectation in the stores. "The triumph of hope over experience" ought to be torn away from its current demeaning locus (second marriage) and put squarely where/wear it belongs: attached to *fashion*, in all its forms.

As a relationship with a chosen object continues, however, it may become genuinely personal—if not necessarily happier—because of the life we lived in it. I remember the evening I first wore that little black dress—the first freshman "mixer"—and the way even though *it* was perfect, I didn't make a hit. I didn't blame the dress. Even now I can think of it and immediately recall the lonely, shy girl who wore it. There was another great dress that the hostile age gaze declared "too young." A wool suit that I felt wonderfully competent in, that I still keep hanging in my closet. A scarf I wore at my father's funeral. However slightly, identity is bound up in some definite way with the events associated with the item, the historical era or time of life. There's a whole range of ways in which we *put* self into a chosen object.

Despite the buyer's feelings of relationship, reserve, and reluctance, she/he eventually goes on to make a replacement purchase. An inexhaustible will-to-believe in the system? As a life of consumption goes on, the misery accrues, and hesitation builds up. I doubt that by midlife many believe the implied promises of the manufacturers (that we'll advance our status or beauty or youth or superiority, or acquire someone else credulous enough to believe in our representation). Middle-ageism too raises doubts about the connection between a delivery and a surge of happiness. That is why the guy of a certain age driving the red convertible seems not just a cliché but an *ingénu*. The will-to-believe is not exactly robust. The tantalizing resources of advertising must be constantly at work so that the no-longer-deluded self can hide from itself its grudging enforced relationship to the system.

If we return to the scene in the dressing room, then, our dejections fit into the fashion cycle. The cycle survives them. It doesn't care one way or another if I go out into the harsh world of observers feeling anxious. But might I buy more if I didn't get dejected? If, say, I yearned to fall in love with the fall line and then the fall line turned out to fit me in some delicious way that actually fed and satisfied some modest fantasy of improved life chances? But then I might keep using the magic garment rather than discarding it. For built-in obsolescence to work, we need to buy not once, but many times. We need not only to fall in love, but to fall out of love. "Dissatisfaction is our most important product." And discarding comes more readily if we actually feel unhappy and unexpectant as early as the first stage of the cycle—like so many women, and now, midlife men. On our way to estimating our deeper grievance against the system, it is worth noting that point-of-purchase dejection—low self-esteem, anxiety, premonition of failure (whatever it is recorded as)—is not incidental to the system but useful. As long as we locate failure in the object and/or in the self, rather than in the cycle, the system remains untouched by our misery.

V. GET RID OF/REJECT/LOSE/GRIEVE

The moment we're not supposed to acknowledge is the moment of getting rid of a now-unfashionable object that we once identified with. In neither marketing nor consumption theory is there a name that matches "point of purchase" to describe the end of the relationship with that object. Call it "the point of losing." We're supposed to get it over with, and get over it, rather silently. The ideological label we learn to apply is that discarding is, once again, free choice. To express this, we are trained to welcome the new enthusiastically and to mock the old. Men look in disbelief at their old ties, narrow pants, tennis sneakers. Women: "How did we ever wear those psychedelic pastels, those shoulder pads, those . . . ?" Such language makes relinquishment seem voluntary. Men boast that they keep clothes long, but the system half-permits men to do that; so keeping things, for men, doesn't by itself prove they exercise more will within the fashion cycle or have more detachment from it. (My father could have provided arguments against "commodified desire" on behalf of the real needs of the world.)

For clothes, structures are provided to assure good riddance. Goodwill, the Sister City project, and now, as the middle class diminishes, the consignment store. Clothes used to go as hand-me-downs to siblings, cousins, or the young of friends. Now they go mostly to strangers. Isn't it lucky for the market that the poor ye shall have always with ye? Rules are provided for knowing when to relinquish. "If that tired old skirt has been in your closet for more than two years, you'll never wear it. Now is the time to get rid of it." (Apparently, many people keep clothes hanging in the closet for *years* after fashion says they can no longer wear them.) Since it is practical and virtuous to give away clothes, this makes any painful feelings we may have about discarding irrational, preventing hostility toward the entire cycle. The concept of recycling validates giving a next life to our once-valued garments, but also enrolls them in the lists along with plastics, green glass, newspapers, and other waste.

The unhappiness involved in change—even when it's upwardly mobile (supposedly desired) change—doesn't often come into print in advanced industrial societies. But in a 1935 novel by Margaret Ayer Barnes, about a successful man whose conspicuous consumption keeps leaping ahead of his submissive wife's, the misery of the wife about changing houses wells up in pages of soft-voiced objection. "I love this house and I love Oakwood Terrace. I like the neighborhood and I like the neighbors and I'm perfectly devoted to Susan and Elmer. . . . If we moved we'd never see them" (233). Her husband devalues these feelings along with the other current satisfactions Edna has: the friends the children have made, the class status they already possess, the love they have shared in that place. He tells a future story he calls progress: headier friends, handsomer goods, higher status. "She raised her head a little to look around the den at the beloved household objects that surrounded them. She could not see them clearly because of the tears in her eyes" (235). She is never happy with their (his) possessions again.

When sorrow about change is given to a character, it's given to someone who isn't quite with the program. Edna has to be represented as not only humanly conservative (which can be read as touching) but also as slow to add new skills, interest, and knowledge. She's affectionate but boring. She's also unfashionably plump and no longer young. The idea of progress that her husband lives has been a model from early in the era of conglomerate capitalism, as Thorstein Veblen explained in *The Theory of the Leisure Class*. People with increasing incomes are led to believe that if you are rich, you're smart; if both, you should readily pick up new social class cues and change your consumption patterns. Early in the century, a term from the clothing industry began to be used to designate *people*. "Back numbers." In F. Scott Fitzgerald's *Tender Is the Night*, a midlife woman thinks young people are saying it of her and her husband, even though they are rich and fashionable.[11] Suddenly people were as discardable as clothes. Visual images of men or women clinging to "past" styles are still a metaphor for not keeping up. These days, back numbers can be the poor, the rural, the elderly, or the dowdy middle-aged middle class. Barbara Ehrenreich said once that the working classes had been "assigned the symbolic burden of [representing] the past" (119). Now anyone in midlife is also liable to carry that load. Those whose being is less important than their ability to carry a product appropriately: this is beginning to look like a majority category.

Given our eyes' reliance on the semiotics of dress and appearance, midlife people who wear older hair or dress styles do look retrograde—even if we know that men can be stupid in Armani suits, and that we ourselves can think just as well in a bathrobe as in a Chanel. Ayer Barnes was writing during the Depression, when people forced into downward mobility did not just know but passionately felt all the flaws in the dogma that we choose our fashions and that our fashions "represent" us. Edna gets to utter one mildly subversive query as she succumbs to her husband's constructed desires. "Oh, dear . . . why not be satisfied?" (235). If being satisfied over the long term with what you already have is constructed in mainstream discourse as something that only the dim-witted or the unsuccessful or the middle-aged feel, then we'll never get people to acknowledge that there are significant human problems at the end of the fashion cycle, as there are at the beginning, not to mention something disturbing about the entire cycle itself.

VI. THE FASHION CYCLE AND THE LIFE COURSE

The fashion cycle constructs our emotions to teach us, unconsciously, a normal pattern of feelings over time, about time. As I have suggested, this begins with some degree of wanting/desiring, and, however qualified, some level of self-identification with our "choice" that could be called (self-)loving. This phase is complexly associated with "youth." Then the middle of our relationship contains some degree of affect (comfort, loyalty, esthetic enjoyment, eventfulness)—a continuity of self-investment. And then comes the need to enter the allegedly more progressive, next cycle: (self-)rejection. Obedience sooner or later follows. As it does, the self learns it will lose the object into which it has genuinely put a part of itself. The part may be tiny—that wouldn't obviate some sense of loss. Compulsory repetition brands the lesson as experience. Over time, the self learns its relationship to passing time: loss from within. The social name given to this biographical movement is "decline." The social name given to the process is "aging." The item in question is "old" and having feeling for it labels you as old.

Roland Barthes has described the workings of fashion in his own emotional, resistant way as "a vengeful present which each year sacrifices the signs of the preceding year." "Each year it reverses entirely and at a single stroke collapses into the nothingness of the past," he writes; fashion "disavows the past with violence." I admire Barthes's vengeful language. But we need to go beyond projecting emotions onto the fashion system, in order to talk phenomenologically about the effects on us—on our sense of self over the life course—of participating in its cycle. It isn't just that, as Barthes writes, "Fashion is systematically unfaithful," but that it makes us unfaithful to parts of ourselves. We don't in fact disavow the past "with violence" or glee, as a rigid system that didn't depend on "agency" and voluntary compliance might ordain. (Sorrow or regret, wry amusement, silent oblivion are also possible.) But we do disavow the past in whatever mode we relinquish the prior object. It's not that the past is shameful, it is we who incur shame if we ally ourselves with the past, the unwanted, the "old."[12]

It is essential to the market system that we be constructed, by consumerism, to live the cycle even though the cycle implicitly devalues our sense of prior selfhood. Into the foreseeable future, then, people will go on learning to downgrade old knowledge, dispraise past objects of affection, discard them, and identify the renewed self with the newly accepted values that despise the old. If a small group were to start explicitly opposing fashion on these philosophical grounds, the system would insist we were just losing competence in another locus of control and trying to hide the loss. Since midlife aging—being not-young—is now almost synonymous with being unfashionable, this would be plausible to many people. They would displace their rage onto what they think of as natural aging, where rage appears to be futile.

In such overdetermined circumstances, it is naive to think that "aging baby boomers" with nothing but financial power are going to be able to re-engineer American culture and save their cohort from middle-ageism. They can't expunge their own internalizations and displacements before they understand the mysterious condition of being (re)socialized into midlife aging.

VII. AGING-AS-LOSS AT MIDLIFE

Of all the emotional learning we endure, the very oddest acquisition in this historical era is an individual's internal acceptance of a lesser identification with an "aging" and "declining" self, occurring long before debility at some unspecified time in the middle years. As male superiority in age identity is being diminished, men as well as women are likely to accept a new self-image as a being who fails on certain already specified and essentially desirable measures. At first these may be read as piecemeal moments of random failure—the soliloquy of age anxiety works to hold on to this idea of randomness. But eventually, the incidents are fit into a master narrative of aging. The middle years can be recognized, although that is far too definite a verb, as the stage when one's worth has suddenly become shaky. We are aged by culture through a process of accepting "Time" as insuring losses to prior achieved identity.

The analysis of the market cycle begins to answer the question of why people accept any of this in midlife (especially when they are otherwise as healthy, well-employed, loved, et cetera, as before). This is a strange phenomenon; let's estrange it. Accepting decline counters the instinct for maintaining self-esteem and for preserving identity. Empirical psychologists tell us (or used to) that people tend to have rather stable traits over the life course, and post-Freudian therapists and theorists speak of developmental processes going on through midlife and beyond, so the notion of midlife decline counters both our own intuitions and some contemporary theories about self. Identity stripping via aging also requires the self to reject or consider inconsequential all the counter-narratives that emphasize aging into wisdom or maturity or any valued progress.[13] True, we don't all read life-course development literature, high or pop, or feminist midlife progress fiction. But we have all been taught from childhood on through everyday practices and celebratory occasions that we relinquish a past self only to come into a same-but-better one. We happily give up the self that carried a blanket and sucked its thumb, that didn't know how to gargle, skip, or read, and in that process we learned to look forward to growing older in order to get better attributes. In other words, in the early crucial decades we learn, without benefit of purchases, one way to see the life course as a progress. Suddenly, not much farther along, through a kind of enforced progress march symbolized by relinquishing objects, we have to begin to unlearn that, and learn that it's a decline.

The specific mechanisms by which this form of masochistic knowledge gets installed—even in those with what I would consider excellent defenses (in their different ways, Alpha males, older feminists, black-empowerment advocates, those emerging into the middle class at midlife)—need to be detailed. The installation involves a long, silent resocialization. Other resocialization processes that sociologists talk about concern incarcerated prisoners getting therapy or immigrants becoming naturalized as citizens—all groups of people in institutional programs that cost someone else real money, that require the subjects to participate consciously and voluntarily and offer positive outcomes as the reward for change. While learning aging, on the other hand, each of us is responsible for our own internalizations. We rarely know it's happening, we don't know what it's costing us, and it hurts. As the sociologist Melvin Fein explains, "Mechanisms similar to those found in the mourning of loved ones must be set in motion, if change is to occur. Since these of necessity involve anguish and fear, resocialization is not tranquil" (ix).[14] But discovering our unconscious pain, buried as it is under signs of status success, may be difficult.

With so much personal pain and even some cognitive dissonance involved, it seems even odder that belief in midlife decline is so entrenched. This happens at a time in history when life expectancy has been extended well into the seventies for men as well as women, when many of us look better and feel healthier than our parents did at the same age, et cetera, and when antiageist thinking is seeping slowly into some subcultures. If the culture must have decline-via-aging, why isn't it getting located ever later in the life course?

Decline is the side of the midlife unconscious that most needs explaining.

VIII. AGE CONSCIOUSNESS AND RESISTANCE

There's no standard theory for how men and women in our culture and era learn around midlife to feel we are losing and to blame ourselves for aging. I'm building narrative and theory here, hoping others will want to continue with the project. My book on contemporary constructions of aging at midlife, *Declining to Decline*, mainly emphasizes the level of discourse, to show how subtly and continually age knowledge is being diffused through culture. Yet people do not become resocialized in mid adulthood simply by being told we're declining. Discourse cannot by itself explain how midlife age-stripping occurs.

If it did, all (all!) we would need do, once united into a pressure group, is reform mainstream culture. We could pressure the mainstream to eliminate the malignant stereotyping of baby boomers, and to present more intelligent and plausible progress narratives, and, for experts on "aging," turn to novelists producing midlife heroines and heroes, to humanistic gerontologists, midlife development specialists, age theorists and critics and historians. We could offer an age-conscious conceptual framework in which to do textual, autobiographical, and social analysis. But putting discourse on the defensive cannot be accomplished as long as only a few people do it. We few can be attacked as querulous, as if we were asking for a special dispensation of the laws of the universe for ourselves. There's not enough creative reinforcement to write the new sentences, not enough conceptual backing. With numbers of people in crucial discursive sites, however, I think we could have some successes at this level of the enterprise, and that they would be important. Chains of age-graded decline metaphors might appear in print not casually, as now, as if they were accepted truths, but as hesitant (declining) opinions that needed to be explicitly defended and reasserted. And because of the lively, persuasive, and frequent repetitions of antiageist ideas, young people might learn *them* by rote but tell them with creative conviction.

My earlier writings were organized to abet these strategies. I not only tried to put decline on the defensive; I also tried to shoehorn a more plausible idea of progress into the unreceptive mainstream, offering readers options for recognizing both the falsities of the narrative of decline and the compulsory optimism of positive aging—to free themselves to renarrate their age autobiographies.[15] People have let me see them working personally through these ideas.

But such reasoned invitations and examples might prove inadequate in an atmosphere so toxic. Even if we were to change discourse considerably, we could still find ourselves stymied. Decline feels true to many people because it *enacts* itself. *Practices* constrain us to translate "messages" into feelings, meanings, and habits. The important fact about practices, in Ian Hunter's terms, is "that the use of such and such a procedure becomes compulsory: that a particular technique has been installed, that . . . individuals master a particular technology for identifying colors or confessing their sins or finding their conscience reflected in literary characters, and so on" (193). My discussion of the fashion cycle suggests that as we master a technology of remaining fashionable, within the current economic and discursive climate, we practice identity-stripping and learn decline unconsciously.

The fashion cycle teaches losing as fate through its own cumulative emotional effects, but other practices, cyclings, and stories of losing deepen the unconscious lesson: discontinuities in work life (where your "old" skills or knowledge become useless, or your "old" job disappears). Bodybuilding, whether through aerobics or weight-training, is another practice that teaches its participants "constant effort without redemption," "a continuous awareness of the shortfall," a kind of "'slow death.'"[16] Like the fashion cycle, bodybuilding promises a staving-off of decline but no exit from the cycle. There must be other sources of invisible, insidious practices of learning the shortfall. Resocialization-into-midlife-decline is bound to have a curious, thick, overdetermined story. My analysis here of a particular practice, added to other analyses of specific midlife discourses, can help us comprehend how little of midlife pain is natural; how much it depends on reiterated stresses and patterns. Age studies is vitally interested in these issues and in encouraging the other cultural studies to address them.

In the current culture, it would be pointless to instruct numbed participants to stop shopping, give up aerobics, never look in mirrors. As early anti-fashion feminists realized, the answer cannot be to end harmful practices mechanically. But it might snap shoppers into mindfulness to warn them that they buy their own disempowerment when they get into the cycle.

In general, once we recognize our location in a cultural war centered on age, we need to experience ourselves consciously as both targets and resisters. "The contradictions . . . must be intensified," as Sandra Bartky reminds us in a related context (43). If "aging practices" happen, so can creative alternatives. If you can't wait to find out what would happen to your relationship to shopping under this regime of wariness, good, try it. (And let us know.) With practice and collective reinforcement, just like anti-racism, anti-sexism, anti-homophobia, age consciousness becomes automatic, permanent, freed from the cycle. It becomes a piece of self you need never lose.

NOTES

This essay is reprinted with some changes from my book *Declining to Decline: Cultural Combat and the Politics of the Midlife*. The catalyst for the essay was an innovative course, "The Construction of Economic Desire," created and taught by David Gullette and Daphne Kenyon at Simmons College. Michael Brown's detailed comments and queries enabled me to improve the final version immensely. I benefitted from the readings of Alix Kates Shulman, Penelope Sales Cordish, Sarah

LeVine, and from discussions with Ellen Rosen and those at the Center for Twentieth Century Studies in April 1996 that led to this book.

1. My mother sees nothing marvelous about our arrangement. She believes parents who can afford to should continue to give gifts to their adult children. A number of my friends have followed her example.

2. George B. Sproles is given credit for identifying the fashion "life cycle" (McCracken 43). Its phases span a product's existence "from invention to decline" (Simon-Miller 71). Stuart Hall and Richard Johnson appropriated the metaphor for "the passage of cultural forms through the moments of production—circulation—consumption," according to Sean Nixon ("Looking for the Holy Grail" 466).

3. Veblen and Bartky do not write about age. Wolf has index entries on age and several of her examples of the way the beauty myth works are of practices that can be reread as affecting women's age identity (35, 83).

4. See my *Declining to Decline*, esp. chs. 1 and 12, for discussion of age identity.

5. A *New York Times Magazine* fashion spread for Sunday, September 12, 1993, featured models over ninety, men as well as women.

6. Middle-ageism and modern patterns of consumption emerged simultaneously at the turn of the century, I will argue in a work in progress called *Midlife Fictions*. For "saturated" markets, "more efficient factory techniques," and the rise of advertising, see Jennifer Wicke (*Advertising Fictions* 104). On prior history, see Fred Davis, *Fashion, Culture, and Identity*: "The fashion cycle [is] exclusively a product of Western civilization" (16n8). On the nineteenth-century origins of the "presumed connection of women and shopping," see Rachel Bowlby's "Modes of Modern Shopping." "Docile bodies," comes from Monique Deveaux, who provides a useful typology of post-Foucaultian feminist work on subjectivity and empowerment. Claudia Kidwell and Valerie Steele assume that men are docile, but argue that they are satisfied; see their *Men and Women, Dressing the Part*.

7. See my *Declining to Decline*, esp. part three, "Men. All Together Now?"

8. For "saturated" markets, "more efficient factory techniques" and advertising, see Wicke 104. Many current ways of writing about consumption minimize the profit orientation of the market system. Business people themselves have no interest in denying that they are profit-driven. Another view of fashion, identifying itself as "postmodern," distracts attention from the profit-orientation by emphasizing the "fun" or "carnivalesque" elements of markets and describes criticism as "moralistic dismissals of the 'degraded pleasures and commodified desires' of a left cultural pessimism" (Nixon, "Have You Got the Look" 150, quoting Fredric Jameson). The people in postmodern cultural studies who write this way about fashion need to consider the psychic effects of silencing the sorrowful elements of the fashion cycle, not to mention the political, economic, and social.

9. On "age studies," see Gullette, "Age/Aging" and *Declining to Decline*. For the first use of "age studies," see Gullette, "Creativity," and Anne Wyatt-Brown's introduction to *Aging and Gender in Literature* 5.

10. Hirschman's typology, based on the products (durables, semi-durables, et cetera), however, implies that the pain derives from the nature of the product. Once again, an analyst is found starting from the product, not from the human subject.

11. *Tender Is the Night*, book 3, chapter 7, the water-skiing scene.

12. See Barthes 289, 286n10, and 289n17.

13. On post-Freudian developmentalism, see John Oldham and Robert Liebert's edited collection, *The Middle Years*. On identity stripping, see Gullette, *Declining to Decline*, esp. chs. 1 and 9.

14. Feminists more than others are conscious of this kind of resocialization. Sociologist Ellen Rosen (private communication) suggests that what Carol Gilligan discovered about eleven-year-old girls losing their self-confidence could be considered a study of resocialization in my sense.

15. See Gullette, *Safe at Last*, esp. ch. 7, "Declining to Decline," and *Declining to Decline* 11–12, 68, 175–77.

16. Morse 34, quoting Baudrillard.

WORKS CITED

Barnes, Margaret Ayer. *Edna His Wife*. London: Houghton, 1935.

Barthes, Roland. *The Fashion System*. Trans. Matthew Ward and Richard Howard. New York: Hill, 1983.

Bartky, Sandra Lee. *Femininity and Domination: Studies in the Phenomenology of Oppression*. New York: Routledge, 1990.

Beattie, Ann. *Another You*. New York: Knopf, 1995.

Bowlby, Rachel. "Modes of Modern Shopping: Mallarmé at the *Bon Marché*." *The Ideology of Conduct: Essays on Literature and the History of Sexuality*. Ed. Nancy Armstong and Leonard Tennenhouse. New York: Methuen, 1987. 185–205.

Davis, Fred. *Fashion, Culture, and Identity*. Chicago: U of Chicago P, 1992.

Deveaux, Monique. "Feminism and Empowerment: A Cultural Reading of Foucault." *Feminist Studies* 20.2 (1994): 223–24.

Ehrenreich, Barbara. *Fear of Falling: The Inner Life of the Middle Class*. New York: Harper, 1990.

Fein, Melvyn. *Role Change: A Resocialization Perspective*. New York: Praeger, 1990.

Gilday, Katherine. *The Famine Within* (video). 1990.

Gordon, Steven L. "Social Structural Effects on Emotions." *Research Agendas in the Sociology of Emotions*. Ed. Theodore Kemper. Albany: State U of New York P, 1990. 145–79.

Gullette, Margaret Morganroth. "Age/Aging." *Encyclopedia of Feminist Literary Theory*. Ed. Elizabeth Kowaleski-Wallace. New York: Garland, 1996.

———. "Creativity, Aging, Gender: A Study of Their Intersections 1910–1935." Wyatt-Brown and Rossen 19–48.

———. *Declining to Decline: Cultural Combat and the Politics of the Midlife*. Charlottesville: U of Virginia P, 1997.

———. "Declining to Decline." *Women's Review of Books* Sept. 1996: 1, 3–4.

———. *Safe at Last in the Middle Years: The Invention of the Midlife Progress Novel*. Berkeley: U of California P, 1988.

Hirschman, Albert O. *Shifting Involvements: Private Interest and Public Action*. Princeton: Princeton UP, 1979.

Hunter, Ian. "After Representation: Recent Discussions of the Relation Between Language and Literature." *Ideological Representation and Power in Social Relations: Literary and Social Theory*. Ed. Mike Gane. London: Routledge, 1993. 167–97.

Kidwell, Claudia Brush, and Valerie Steele, eds. *Men and Women, Dressing the Part*. Washington: Smithsonian Institution P, 1989.

McCracken, Grant D. "The Trickle-Down Theory Rehabilitated." Solomon 39–53.

Morse, Margaret. "Artemis Aging: Exercise and the Female Body on Video." *Discourse* 10.1 (1987–88): 20–53.

Nixon, Sean. "Have You Got the Look? Masculinities and Shopping Spectacle." Shields 149–69.

———. "Looking for the Holy Grail: Publishing and Advertising Strategies and Contemporary Men's Magazines." *Cultural Studies* 7.3 (1993): 466–92.

Oldham, John, and Robert S. Liebert, eds. *The Middle Years: New Psychoanalytic Perspectives*. New Haven: Yale UP, 1989.

Orwell, George. *Road to Wigan Pier*. New York: Harcourt, 1958.

Schweickart, Patrocinio. "In Defense of Femininity: Commentary on Sandra Bartky's *Femininity*." *Hypatia* 8.1 (1993): 178–91.

Shields, Rob, ed. *Lifestyle Shopping: The Subject of Consumption*. New York: Routledge, 1992.

Simon-Miller, Françoise. "Commentary: Signs and Cycles in the Fashion System." Solomon 71–81.

Spark, Muriel. "That Lonely Shoe Lying on the Road." *New Yorker* 20 Sept. 1993: 80.

Solomon, Michael R., ed. *The Psychology of Fashion*. Lexington: Lexington Books, 1985.

Wicke, Jennifer. *Advertising Fictions: Literature, Advertisement and Social Reading*. New York: Columbia UP, 1988.

Williamson, Janice. "Notes from Storyville North." Shields 216–32.

Wolf, Naomi. *The Beauty Myth: How Images of Beauty Are Used against Women*. New York: Morrow, 1991.

Wyatt-Brown, Anne M. Introduction: Aging, Gender, and Creativity. Wyatt-Brown and Rossen 1–15.

Wyatt-Brown, Anne M., and Janice Rossen, eds. *Aging and Gender in Literature: Studies in Creativity*. Charlottesville: UP of Virginia, 1993.

HISTORICIZING AGE

Little Women
The Aging Female Character in Nineteenth-Century British Children's Literature

Teresa Mangum

Most of you who have turned to this page have been "readers" since childhood. I put the word "readers" in quotation marks because reading doesn't precisely describe how we absorb books in early childhood. As an adult reads aloud, the child's eyes fasten on the illustration accompanying the text. At times the child picks up the book to "read" alone, remembering or inventing a narrative to explain what must seem a disjointed series of pictures on page after page. What is fascinating to me is that the reading process begun in childhood continues even after we learn to read for ourselves. As adults interpreting the narratives we live, we consciously consider people and plots in light of those remembered childhood stories, "reading" the world in part through the texts and images of childhood. If this literature has such a hold on the conscious mind, how powerful must be its place in the fabric of memory, feeling, and fears that we call the unconscious.

In this essay, I want to speculate about the place of British children's fiction of the last century in the expression and shaping of a culture's perspective on the figure of the aging woman. My speculations are guided by several questions. First, I take seriously the phrase "second childhood," so popular in Victorian conduct literature that advised readers how to perform their old age with propriety, and ask how and why it was that at the same time children found so many old women in their books, old women so often found themselves leagued with and described as children. Second, I consider the special speaking power of text in relation to illustration, now a hallmark of literature for young children but historically a form of expression that came into its own in the late eighteenth century with the creation of presses and book series devoted exclusively to literature for children. Third, although I began my adult journey into both the past of children's books of the last century and my past of fondly remembered words and images with foolish confidence that I would find only a few types of old women characters, I have been startled by the myriad representations of old women in books for Victorian children. Because I have found these characters variously enlightening, amusing, horrifying, intellectually exciting, and, in a few instances, truly instructive as I reflect on how I want to live and be old myself, I try here to suggest the diversity of these figures—conventional, unconventional, and often in contradiction with one another—as they appear in several of the most popular genres of children's Victorian literature.[1]

But before turning to the pictures addressed to children, I want to examine briefly the place of old women and young children in pictures addressed to adults—the popular narrative paintings which filled exhibition halls with middle-class, middle-brow viewers of all ages. British nineteenth-century paintings tended to push children and those women marked by stooped shoulders, fallen faces, and unruly gray hair to the margins of family groups, thereby oddly linking as-yet-undeveloped youth to newly undeserving elders. Again and again, the youthful or middle-aged heterosexual couple occupies the center of the canvas, while the elderly woman is relegated to the frame with her child counterparts, as in George Elgar Hicks's *Changing Homes* (1863). (Figure 1.) In this painting, a long white dress and veil illuminate the bride, who stands at the center of a cavernous Victorian drawing room, framed by her groom on one side and bridesmaids on the other. Far to the viewer's left sits the kindly, smiling grandmother, positioned lower than the bride and shadowed by the dark clothes of proper old age; two young girls are displaying a basket of wedding flowers to her. In another bridal painting, Luke Fildes's "The Village Wedding" (1883), the bride also draws the eye. Wearing clothes that suggest she is a lower-middle-class or well-off working woman, she, along with her groom, promenades down a village street. Young people and curious children of the village trail after her. Here, behind the small army of children, the figure most likely to be the grandmother follows cheerfully at the rear of the procession. In Thomas Webster's "The Return from the Fair" (1823), young village children display their souvenirs from a local fair to their grandmother who, raising her hands in mock amazement, sits in a comfortable low chair, leaning into the audience of children whose pleasure she enters wholeheartedly. But, once again, the youthful parents occupy the center of the painting, the mother's light dress drawing attention to her figure.

The connection between older women and younger children makes a certain sense, of course. Grandmothers and elderly nurses often act as caregivers to children. Moreover, in *When the Grass Was Taller: Autobiography and the Experience of Childhood*, Richard Coe argues that autobiographical narratives recalling memories of childhood foreground the grandparent as "the major influence for evil or for good" to the extent that writers who incorporate versions of their childhood into fiction tend to exaggerate the role of the grandparent (140). Coe

Figure 1. James Elgar Hicks. Changing Homes. *1863.*

offers several explanations for the centrality of grandparents to childhood. Because the grandparent is associated with the past, only this relationship remains "static" and whole in memory, providing "a point of rest, against which the unceasing movement of the remainder of the Childhood can be *measured*," a connection distinct from vacillating relations with parents, siblings, and friends. In addition, he argues that the grandparent's association with the past allows the autobiographer to write indirectly about "the self-as-a-child." As Coe explains, "the grandparent-figure is invaluable, since it usually incarnates that vision [of the self-as-a-child] uniquely, to the total exclusion of the later self" (158–59). Nostalgia, the past, and perhaps in particular one's own past seem especially likely to embed themselves in the figure of the old woman—the once young girl whom marriage and children passed by, the mother now aged into grandmother, the demanding or doddering teacher, the suffering poor woman, the angry harridan, or the dignified matriarch.

This interplay of past and present, of available image and nostalgia, of age and youth are nowhere more richly displayed than in the easily overlooked universe of Victorian children's literature. The social relations in play around the bodies of the aging women in the paintings I referred to above coalesce into narratives in the Victorian nursery. Whether postmenopausal mothers, grandmothers, aunts, nannies, servants, governesses, fairy godmothers, or, in Britain, queens, aging female characters enter the child's world through poetry, alphabet books, moral tales, fairy tales, fantasy, and adventure novels for boys. In addition, children's literature of this period draws attention to the way "old age" resisted specific definition. The term "old age" signaled only a general and shifting category in England until the passage of the 1908 pension bill forced members of Parliament to attach old age to a specific chronological age. Historian Janet Roebuck points out that earlier in the century it was function rather than chronology that determined when one became "old." "The old were those who were infirm, frail, and suffering incapacities of body or mind to the extent that they could no longer fully support or take care of themselves, *and who also* gave the appearance of being old," she concludes. "The assumption was that people could be advancing in years, or they could be incapable of supporting themselves, but it was only when the two conditions came together in one person that the person was considered 'old' by authorities" (417). This suggests why those people labeled as old came to be seen as childlike or to be described as living a second childhood. As the representation of the very old and very young in painting as well as in children's literature suggests, the figures of both are marked by similar codes of appearance and function. The old and the young alike are small, dependent, and slower to comprehend their circumstances than their mutual authorities, the middle-aged. In middle-class homes, both elders and children were typically relegated to the margins of domestic activity.

Both were understood to be unequal to the crucial work of life, especially since childhood and old age were simultaneously being defined with new specificity. This shift can be traced in the passage of labor laws beginning in the 1840s, which controlled the hours children could work; in mandatory education laws culminating in the Education Act of 1870, which established free, compulsory elementary education; in age of consent laws which determined when a girl could legally have intercourse (late into the century the age was twelve); and in social welfare laws beginning with the New Poor Law of 1834 and followed by other welfare laws, which regulated old age, especially for the poor. Moreover, the bodies of children and "the aged" were both distinguished as other to the same normative bodies, those of young to middle-aged adults, the population who then—and now—perceives itself to be the appropriate governor of economic, social, political, and domestic authority. As social anthropologists Jenny Hockey and Allison James explain in an illuminating essay on the cultural formation of "second childhood," it is by linking childhood and old age that "the hegemony of adulthood remains unchallenged" (138).

During the nineteenth century, then, the designation of childhood as a social and cultural space belonging to a clearly demarcated life stage prompted a corresponding social and cultural space of old age. This is not to say that before the nineteenth century, one could not speak of a child or an old person. The Victorians, however, came to imagine "childhood" and "old age" as abstract realms with material consequences. A wealth of conduct literature as well as other popular representations, such as the paintings I've described and the children's stories I discuss in the rest of this essay, ushered children and people considered old into their appropriate social and psychological realms. Hockey and James argue that once "the child" became a relatively fixed conception, at least for the middle classes, the figure of the child then began to act as an organizing image which attributed a limited set of qualities to all children: dependence, the right to be cared for but not to be self-sufficient, smallness and weakness, and the character of being a nuisance but also a responsibility. These qualities in turn required that children be consigned to separate spaces, such as schools and nurseries. Discussing the tendency of twentieth-century caregivers to interpret older people through the constellation of images commonly called "second childhood," Hockey and Allison warn of the self-serving motivation of the middle-aged person who uses the label and the devastating consequences to the people so objectified. "Through metaphoric recourse to the positively perceived 'limitations' of the child's body adults shield themselves from the approaching vision of illegitimate social dependency in old age," they write. "In doing so, however, the basis for the denial of elderly personhood is formed. At its most extreme this can lead to the social death of those who are merely growing old" (143).

Just such a projection of the features of a second and ultimately condemnatory "childhood" onto older characters in Victorian children's literature signals a similar cultural constitution of "the aged." The aged, like the "undeserving poor," thus become a category of people both in need of the care the middle classes were being urged to lavish upon children and unworthy of it. Because children's books are essentially an adult conception of the psychodynamics of a child's world rather than any direct picture of "childhood," they offer insight into the process by which members of a culture come to accept institutional or social categories that justify the trivialization, marginalization, domination, even exploitation of groups deemed weak. The mundane sociological, biological, and psychological processes we call aging are refashioned into spectacles of old age which ultimately justify family and state "managing" of the elderly comparable to the generally unquestioned managing of children.

From another point of view, the ongoing struggles of the Victorians to define what old age meant and the curious connections between youth and age that were in part made possible by the very vagueness of the definitions of youth and old age confound the desires of twentieth-century readers (or at least myself) for simple categorizations of old age in children's literature. Indeed, the inexactitude of age complicates the very designation "children's literature." As scholars of books for young readers frequently remind themselves, their subject is literature written by adults about all ages and kinds of beings for children but clearly also for adults. To return to Coe's characterization of the adult autobiographer writing about the grandparents of childhood, the self of later life reaches through the elderly figure for the "self-as-a-child" in order to speak about that self to other adult readers.

The relationship of female readers who ranged in age from young girls to middle-aged women to the plots and pictures of the old women who inhabited their childhood books must have been particularly complex, given the ways that fantasies about gender intersect with fantasies about aging in so many of these books. Unlike many of the male figures in these books, female characters who age beyond their reproductive years find themselves eclipsed by the master social narrative of the nineteenth century—the belief in separate spheres. This belief system and the social practices it supported structured the gender roles available to middle-class women and influenced working-class women who were pressured by religious workers, philanthropists, and employers to emulate their "betters." Advocates for the division between public life and a protected domestic space for women and children promised that by trading financial autonomy, economic productivity, and political rights for reproductive work and child care, middle-class women would accrue endless if ineffable moral and spiritual powers. Ironically, those women who cooperated were most likely to then be viewed as childlike if not childish. Children's literature, a body of work addressed to the denizens of the domestic sphere, dramatizes both the implausibility of such a rigidly bifurcated world and the collapse of the reward system for women who stand apart from or age beyond their crucial role as producers of children under the culture's arrangement of separate spheres. In children's literature as in the popular genre of narrative painting, images of older women (helplessly dependent old women, excluded old women, bitter old women, but also passively content older women) inadvertently expose the false promises of the contract of separate spheres. In addition, children's literature offers a welcome alternative cast of assertive elderly female characters who talk back to the culture so eager to abandon them to chimney-corners, workhouses, and nurseries—or to caretakers who treat them like children. This leads us to the literature itself, to the pictures and books which carry adult conceptions of the figure of the old woman into the world of the child. I should confess that while I cite a number of children's books in which the elderly female characters are conventional and colorless, my impulse has been to focus upon those images which seem to present a challenge to the conduct writers and legislators who would leave the old woman in her chimney-corner, bereft of financial independence and domestic authority, as well as to medical commentators who would deny old women desire or sexual identity.

Before older people became the frequent subject of periodicals and pension plans, they populated eighteenth-century chapbooks, which were among the first books to be marketed explicitly to children. Such chapbooks had long served to instruct adults as well as children who were learning to read. In the late eighteenth century, however, John Newberry, Elizabeth Newberry, and later William Darton[2] began to print books expressly for child readers. Throughout the nineteenth century, as schools were established for working-class children by religious and philanthropic groups and as middle-class education became more formalized and more widely available to girls as well as boys, an immense market developed for school books, gift books, books that served as "prizes,"

and, increasingly, books to read for pleasure alone for this growing national audience of children. In the early-nineteenth-century alphabet books and simple illustrated tales of village life, both old male and female characters are usually seen at work. Female characters often appear in rural settings as apple gatherers (indeed as agricultural workers of all kinds), seamstresses, teachers in village dame schools, and sellers of various wares. These older figures seem fully incorporated into a larger social milieu. As laborers, they also generally appear to be "respectable" working-class characters, though they are pictured in a romanticized agrarian past, one before class emerged as a politicized, conflictual organizing system.

Even in these early years, however, certain elderly female figures, represented as at odds with the social roles dictated by age in tandem with class and gender, break ranks. In *Dr. Goldsmith's Celebrated Elegy on that Glory of Her Sex, Mrs. Mary Blaize* (1808), written by Oliver Goldsmith and probably illustrated by William Mulready, the appropriately named Mrs. Blaize overdresses with glee, wearing a bonnet that resembles the hoops and cloth of a covered wagon, and flirts outrageously:

> Her love was sought I do aver,
> By twenty Beaux and more;
> The king himself has followed her,
> When she has walk'd before. (Tuer 105–06)

As one turns a page on which the rhyme promises she "never followed wicked ways—" (Tuer 101) the reader is met by a drawing of Mrs. Blaize in her gown and night cap. She eats supper alone, her hand firmly grasping a bottle prominently marked "gin" as she smiles knowingly at the viewer over the caption that finishes the line from the previous page, "Unless when she was sinning" (Tuer 102). (Figure 2.) Rather than submitting to the dictates of separate spheres or to later prescriptions for appropriate aging, Mrs. Blaize uses her independence as a middle-class old woman of means to pursue her pleasures and wins only praise—in fact, an elegy. The book was popular enough to have been reissued with new illustrations by Randolph Caldecott in his "Toy-Book Series" in 1885.

Two beloved children's chapbooks from the first decades of the nineteenth century, *The Moving Adventures of Old Dame Trot and Her Comical Cat* (circa 1807) and *Dame Wiggins of Lee and Her Seven Wonderful Cats* (1823), draw upon earlier traditions that associated assertive, eccentric, or unusually intelligent old women with witchcraft. While these two books in no way openly resist conventional characterizations of old age, they do revise the script which would treat a lonely old woman who has only her pet for company as pathetic. In these marvelous, witty tales of what seem almost alternative family narratives, these female characters have the elongated and whiskered chins, the broomsticks, and, of course, the cats that are the usual trappings of witches. But they and their cats have been domesticated and rendered comic; they seem free of the

Unless when she was sinning.

Figure 2. William Mulready. Dr. Goldsmith's Celebrated Elegy on that Glory of Her Sex, Mrs. Mary Blaize. *1808.*

larger community that would have ostracized witches in the past or trivialized old women in the present. (Figure 3.) *Dame Wiggins of Lee* is especially intriguing in that the title page claims it was "Written Principally by a Lady of Ninety." Andrew Tuer speculates the books shared the same printing blocks and that the elderly author was a Mrs. Pearson, assisted by writer R. S. Sharpe.

A second genre that prominently features elderly female characters, a genre that gained great popularity despite its didactic detractors, is the fairy tale. Translations of German and French fairy tales circulated in Britain throughout the century. However, in the first several decades, religious authorities, educational philosophers, and writers of children's literature such as Maria Edge-

Figure 3. Dame Wiggins of Lee and Her Seven Wonderful Cats.
Written principally by a lady of 90. 1823; John Ruskin, 1885.

worth, Sarah Trimmer, and Mary Sherwood harshly dismissed such imaginative literature as dangerous to children, and they largely controlled the children's literature presses.[3] By 1840, however, the stories of Charles Perrault, Hans Christian Andersen, and Jacob and Wilhelm Grimm began to appear in new translations and with new illustrations. In addition, Victorian writers produced a rich array of their own fairy tales.[4] Charles Dickens, John Ruskin, and William Thackeray all wrote successful fairy tales as did a number of less well-known men and women of the period. These fairy stories offer a gallery of elderly characters ranging from wicked stepmothers, tyrannical kings and queens, and unpredictable witches, to fairy godmothers and kindly (but usually ineffectual) grandmothers and grandfathers. Though many of the older female characters are innocuous grandmothers and old nurses or unmitigatedly evil fairies, the burst of publication in this form of fantasy permitted greater scope for the expression of feelings toward old women. In these stories we find more complex qualities attributed to imaginary old women, and more varied and textured alternatives to conventional representations of women in old age than in the earlier texts. Victorian fairy tale writers, and women writers in particular, often address the social assumptions about old women through what I call the "pragmatic fairy tale," a clever, self-reflexive, de-mystifying rewrite of a well-known story or of conventional fairy tale types.

This parodic impulse motivates Charles Dickens's "The Magic Fishbone" (1868), which he attributed to a Miss Alice Rainbird. The tale focuses on the relationship between the young princess Alicia and her fairy godmother Grandmarina. In Dickens's tale, the princess's father rules a kingdom that operates like a small, disorganized, near-bankrupt business. He lives for his quarterly raise and barely manages to feed his enormous family. Grandmarina gives the king a fishbone which he must entrust to Alicia, who will decide when its use is absolutely necessary. Alicia infuriates her father and delights her fairy godmother by using common sense, imagination, and hard work to solve a series of problems before resorting to the wishbone. The pattern of deflating the romance and magic of fairy tales shapes Dickens's fairy godmother as well as the plot. She abuses adults, especially the central authority figure, the king, and sides instead with the young Alicia. When the king questions the effectiveness of a mere bone, she chastises him: "'Don't be impatient, sir,' returned the Fairy Grandmarina, scolding him severely. 'Don't catch people short, before they have done speaking. Just the way with you grown-up persons. You're always doing it'" (Zipes 92). When he again interrupts, she becomes "absolutely furious," replying, "'The reason for this, and the reason for that, indeed! You are always wanting the reason. No reason. There! Hoity toity me! I am sick of your grown-up reason'" (92). No doubt her quick dismissal of adult inquisition delighted child readers; Alicia, for example, echoes Grandmarina's annoyance when she later whispers to her doll, "'They think we children never have a reason or a meaning!'" (94). But the story also casts the older woman as both childlike and anti-adult so that she simultaneously enacts and challenges "second childhood."

Anne Isabella Richie explicitly rewrote "Cinderella," even giving it the same title in her 1868 version. Her narrative completely explains away the element of magic so that the fairy godmother becomes a prosaic older woman who serves as a guide to a young girl. In Richie's witty version, set in contemporary Victorian culture, the poor stepsister "Ella" is befriended by a wealthy woman who is renting Ella's stepmother a house in London for the season. When the stepmother excludes Ella from a trip to the Crystal Palace and doesn't allow her to go to a ball, Lady Jane Peppercorne, whose name suggests her sprightliness and the annoyances of aging, intervenes. The narrator describes her as "old" and "very kind as well as flighty" (Zipes 112). She is a fascinating fantasy projection of the young girl's desire: she has wealth, authority, a coach, social savvy. Most importantly, her authority intimidates the unwilling stepmother. After all, she's the landlord. Unlike the "properly" aged older woman, she exists to serve her own pleasure, which is also the child's: "She really *had* been going to Sydenham; but I think if she had not, she would have set off instantly, if she thought she would make anybody happy by so doing" (Zipes 117). Lady Jane Peppercorne also dissolves the dilemmas that structure the conventional fairy tale by offering not magical but matter-of-fact solutions to them. When Ella loses her diamond shoe buckle (Richie's replacement for the glass slipper), the narrator notes: "This little diamond buckle might, perhaps, have led to her identification if young Richardson had not taken the precaution of ascertaining from old Lady Jane Ella's name and address" (Zipes 123). The tale celebrates Lady Jane's action, determination, wit, and authority as well as her identification with (Cinder)Ella. It also insists again and again that Lady Jane is "old."

In another wonderful rewriting of a classic fairy tale, Harriet Louisa Childe-Pemberton's "All My Doing; or Red Riding-Hood Over Again" (1882), the older woman is also cast as a wealthy guardian. Here, however, she is remarkable for her indulgence to herself, which is in direct contradiction to the urging of conduct literature that the old should sacrifice material comforts to the young. This story involves a unique interplay and overlap of generations. The story is narrated by Pussy, an elderly spinster, to her niece. However, the action is set in Pussy's own childhood and draws upon her relationship with her grandmother and middle-aged, unmarried aunt. This grandmother resists the attempts of her middle-aged daughter to organize and moderate her life; the narrator recalls that her grandmother "quietly declined to be made the victim of Aunt Rosa's restless energy" (Zipes 226). As Roderick McGillis points out in his Lacanian reading of the story, the grandmother "lacks a husband, but this lack is hardly a lack" (133). Childlike, she delights in avoiding responsibility and in living for pleasure—comfort, food, and parties. Here is a description of this engaging character: "She was a large, handsome, good-natured woman, who liked everything about her to be handsome and on a large scale; she habitually wore good silk dresses, and had her rooms filled with choice flowers; her cook was good, and her carriage and horses always smartly turned out. . . . Yet she was hardly to be called an epicure, was my grandmother; she only liked to be comfortable and have nice things about her" (Zipes 225).

But once again the uncanny shrinks to the pragmatic. In this story the granddaughter unwittingly destroys her grandmother's life of pleasure (and her own romantic future) by allowing a human "wolf," a con man posing as a tourist, into the house to see its architecture. Later, he returns and, throwing the narrator's red cape over his head, robs the grandmother of her valuables. More importantly, he causes her to have a severe attack when she sees his terrifying face beneath her granddaughter's hood. The burglar also shoots the narrator's young suitor, who gives her up because of his injury. Ultimately, the old grandmother pays dearly for her "indulgent, take-it-easy ways" (225). Just as the granddaughter suffers for impulsively usurping domestic authority, the grandmother suffers for her gentle decadence. After the robbery, she ages "properly." The narrator bemoans "the sight of my poor old granny lying helpless and listless, white and aged and shrunken. . . . Those cheeks were wasted now, and those eyes dull, all her comeliness was gone, and from having looked hardly more than middle-aged, she had suddenly withered into an old woman!" (245). Significantly, daughter Rosa steps into the breach, caring for and claiming authority over both the fallen old woman and guilty child.

While the grandmother is "properly" socialized by the tale, the narrative structure of this version of "Little Red Riding Hood" collapses the role of the child and the old woman. As I noted, the narrator is herself an elderly single woman when she tells this story about herself-as-child and her grandmother to a young niece. The lesson is a warning to heed the advice of adults, which the narrator had failed to do in opening the house to a stranger. In this sense she serves as elderly mentor to her niece, as a kind of fairy godmother who offers experience rather than magic. Not only has Pussy destroyed her grandmother's life, she has also left her suitor a "lame old bachelor" and herself a lonely old maid. Her gift is to use her own old age and her grandmother's to guarantee her young niece a happy old age.

As a final example of the collapsing of first and second childhoods permitted by the fairy tale, consider George MacDonald's "Little Daylight" (1864). A "true" fairy tale in the sense that actual fairies appear, the story tells of the birth of a young princess to a king and queen who invite the kingdom, including local good fairies, to a birth celebration. However, they neglect one fairy who is described as a witch but who sounds remarkably like the stereotypical characterization of an irritable old woman: "A wicked old thing she was, always concealing her power, and being as disagreeable as she could, in order to tempt people to give her offense, that she might have the pleasure of taking vengeance upon them" (Mark 103). Her revenge in this case is to make the princess sleep all day long. When a good fairy tries to deflect the curse by guaranteeing that the princess will awaken during the night, the first fairy, the "wicked old thing," retaliates by decreeing that the princess will "wax and wane" with the moon. Not surprisingly, the hope of salvation for the princess depends upon the intervention of some young man.

During the dark phases of the moon, the curse takes the form of aging. At new moon, the princess looks "like an old woman exhausted with suffering. This was the more painful that her appearance was unnatural; for her hair and eyes did not change. Her wan face was both drawn and wrinkled, and had an eager hungry look. Her skinny hands moved as if wishing, but unable, to lay hold of something. Her shoulders were bent forward, her chest went in, and she stooped as if she were eighty years old" (Mark 106). The wonder is that she is indeed saved when a young man, pitying "the worn decrepit creature" for her "gray, wrinkled cheeks," kisses her "on the withered lips," turning her face "bright as the never-ageing Dawn" (Mark 116–17). Here aging fulfills a curse even though it depends upon the "natural" cycles of the moon. Whereas the grandmother in Childe-Pemberton's rewriting of "Little Red Riding Hood" is disciplined for refusing the responsibilities and disabilities of old age and the child pays for overstepping bounds, the young girl in "Little Daylight" literally takes on her own aging, embodying it in punishment for her parents' incivility.

Here, an unusually affirming reading of the fusion of youth and age is available. Rather than waking a beautiful princess from sleep, as does Prince Charming in "Sleeping Beauty," the hero of this tale embraces what the beautiful young princess will become when he spontaneously kisses her "withered lips." MacDonald may be drawing upon medieval tales of "loathely ladies." In these early tales, a man seeking a wife is persuaded by an aged, harsh-featured crone to marry. After he marries her, whatever enchantment she was under dissolves and he finds himself rewarded with a wife who is wise as well as beautiful.[5] In any case, "Little Daylight" offers one of the most generous responses to the decrepitude of age I have seen in Victorian fairy tales. The character, Daylight, is liberated from her night life and her vacillating body and delivered to daylight, romance, family, and a more gradual experience of aging. Even as it sends the message that age is a curse, the story depicts love and compassion redeeming that curse.

The most extravagant and hostile attitudes toward aging in Victorian children's literature appear in the two genres that permit the greatest excesses generally—fantasy and adventure fiction. In these genres, children's literature reveals increasing fascination yet impatience with old age over time. Particularly in the verbal and visual representations of fantasy literature, a genre free of the imagined constraints of "realistic" representation, readers find competing impulses regarding aging characters. At one extreme, magical powers are attributed to women who have passed beyond their reproductive years. At the other extreme, the suffering associated with an aging body is trivialized, and aging characters are infantilized, thus casting old age into a marginalized cultural space inhabited by beings who have returned to a second and unsanctioned childhood.

The dangers posed by what the Victorians considered inappropriate aging—a refusal on the part of older people to succumb to either decrepitude or the middle-aged—are played in comic colors in two of the best-known of Victorian fantasy texts, Lewis Carroll's *The Adventures of Alice in Wonderland* (1864) and Edward Lear's various editions of *Nonsense Books*. While the books of both Carroll and Lear were published at mid century, they reached the peak of their popularity in the last twenty years of the century. In the case of Carroll's *Alice*, the verbal narrative has become almost inseparable from John Tenniel's illustrations. The novel repeatedly raises the specter of aging as a perverse feature of Wonderland. Young Alice's chief antagonist in Wonderland is an aging queen. The Queen and Duchess feature most prominently as irascible and dangerous abusers of the authority that comes both from the State and their age. Like brattish children, they refuse to play social or political games by the rules. Rendered as a short, squat, rigid, grotesque foil to Alice's slender, youthful, supremely flexible body, the Queen in particular energizes the text with mad passion, jealousy, vindictiveness, and the compulsion to subdue her younger minions, as heard in her repeated cry: "Off with their heads."

The representation of aging in *Alice* echoes Carroll's larger preoccupations with the unmanageable, growing, aging female body.[6] Carroll's drawings of Alice, which guided John Tenniel's illustrations, obsessively and exaggeratedly document the unruly body of the pre-adolescent Alice: in response to the unpredictable food and drink of the underworld, Alice's body elongates, expands, shrinks, and compacts. Less well-known than the illustrations are Carroll's photographs of young girls, including Alice Liddell, the inspiration for the novel. These photographs trouble modern viewers in part because they seem to age children inappropriately and in far more unnerving ways than in "Little Daylight," perhaps because we know we are looking at photographic images, however posed the figure or innocent the subject. In a photo of circa 1872, for example, a child named Julia Arnold lounges provocatively upon a daybed. In a photo from circa 1879, a child named Evelyn Hatch also lies on a bed, eyeing the camera deliberately; with her hands behind her head, she imitates the pose of an adult seductress. While there is no evidence to suggest that Carroll molested the many young girls whom he befriended in his lifetime, these photographs, along with biographical accounts of his preference for the company of prepubescent girls, certainly signal his discomfort with the sexually mature woman and her body. Carroll's preoccupation with the aging female body, then, seems embedded in more generalized anxieties regarding the processes of female development and maturity as well as the decrepitude associated with the body of an old woman.[7]

If we rely on the verbal text alone, the Queen is merely a voice, and hers is the voice of raw anger and energy. She roars, thunders, screams; once the narrative notes that she turns purple with rage. From her first appearance when she unleashes her fury upon her deck of knaves for trying to paint roses the wrong color to her insistence in court that the sentence should come first and the verdict later, the Queen provokes Alice's irritation and the other characters' terror. The principal work of constituting such a tiny terror is performed by the voice as embodied by Tenniel's grotesque drawings. The Carroll/Tenniel casting of such an infelicitous elder as the Queen is particularly curious because the book risked insulting the real Queen. Ironically, Victoria became a great fan. A recent obsessive study of the novel by the Continental Historical Society, a group based in California, even argues that the novel is a coded version of Queen Victoria's own personal notebooks which she and Carroll colluded to publish under his name. This Queen appears to have been a recognizable type. In the conduct essay "The Art of Growing Old" published in *The Argosy* in 1866, the writer berates the aging woman who clings to the powers of middle age, calling her a "queen":

> A domestic queen, she rules omnipotently. Confident in herself, she cannot bear the rude shock of having advice from her married daughter; nor can she

resign the reins, now too heavy for her feeble hands, to a child who, though middle-aged, has never been married, and governed a house of her own. She must interfere; she is rather weak and fancies domestic mishaps are hidden from her; she is irritable and won't be treated like a child. Her memory fails her, and failure is attributed to those around her, and not to her own waning faculties. This state is a pitiable one. Rarely does the intellect prove sufficiently strong to battle with the growing sense of infirmity. It is accepted as a boon by those around her,—the melancholy crisis of *second childhood*. (Emphasis added; 41)

While Carroll's Queen has a larger domain, she childishly treats Alice and her other subjects like just such upstart children. She serves as a reminder, however, that the child of second childhood might be an *enfant terrible*.

The unreasonable, aggressive qualities of the Queen are exaggerated and queerly sexualized in the perverse maternity of her royal companion and competitor, the Duchess. Alice first encounters the Duchess in her home, torn between a screaming match with her cook and abuse of the child she holds in her arms. The child promptly turns into a pig and flees, suggesting that the aged woman who has passed her reproductive prime can only produce a monster. When the Duchess later reappears at the Queen's croquet game, Alice is repulsed by her wrinkled visage and what, stripped of grotesquerie, might have been represented as an older person's longing for attachment and affection. The Duchess tries to engage Alice in conversation and to embrace her. What is Alice's reaction? "Alice did not much like her keeping so close to her: first, because the Duchess was *very* ugly; and secondly, because she was exactly the right height to rest her chin on Alice's shoulder, and it was an uncomfortably sharp chin" (79). After a series of inappropriate aphorisms such as "'tis love, 'tis love, that makes the world go round" (80), the Duchess sidles closer in a grotesque performance of female pedophilia: "'I dare say you're wondering why I don't put my arm round your waist,' the Duchess said, after a pause: 'the reason is, that I'm doubtful about the temper of your flamingo. Shall I try the experiment?'" (80). Alice resents the overtures. However, motivated by a fear of being rude (rather than compassion), Alice engages in a maddening, thoroughly Carrollian conversation. The Duchess's tendencies—her inability to hear clearly or to follow conversation rather than leading it into associational detours—parody traits frequently ascribed to old age. Here, though, these tendencies lend her curious conversational clout. Until the greater tyrant, the Queen, appears, the Duchess burdens Alice with her words as well as her body.[8]

Alice hurriedly withdraws from the fury of the Queen and the threatened lasciviousness of the Duchess. Contributing to the view that she is irrational and impotent, the Queen's commands are surreptitiously overridden by the King. The Duchess's eroticism is presented as pathetic. In the harshness of the illustrations as well as through the narrative triumph of the vapid Alice, these two aging female characters are rendered excessive, absurd, repugnant. Although the novel treats Alice's escape from Wonderland with the same odd detachment that characterizes the entire narrative, the juxtaposition of Alice and the Queen in Tenniel's illustrations suggests the same dynamic Mike Featherstone discusses in the introduction to the important anthology, *Images of Aging*. He describes the effects of imposing "second childhood" on old people by means of an example from a care facility: "this long-standing image in our culture is still with us, bolstered by a range of representations such as the elderly wearing Donald Duck hats for tea-parties in old people's homes." The visual consequence, he astutely concludes, is that the bodies of the "frail elderly" are "often dwarfed by the bodily presence of a young nurse or attendant" (7). In both the verbal and visual texts of Alice, it is only the body of Alice—under the influence of mushrooms and drink—that wildly expands and contracts, permitting her to dwarf the other characters in moments when she feels threatened.

The distrust of such quite literally "grand" motherliness in older women who hang onto authority becomes even more pronounced when put into a larger context. In a series of sermons on children's education written in 1783 but still influential throughout the Victorian period, John Wesley pauses in his lengthy discussion of the difficulties of subduing a child's "will" to point a finger at grandmothers. Like servants, he asserts, grandmothers' "improper" relations with their grandchildren threaten to undermine all the tedious labor of disciplining parents:

> Possibly you may have another difficulty to encounter, and one of a still more trying nature. Your mother, or your husband's mother, may live with you: and you will do well to shew her all possible respect. But let her on no account have the least share in the management of your children. She would undo all that you have done; she would give them their own will in all things. She would humour them to the destruction of their soul, if not their bodies too. In four-score years I have not met with one woman that knew how to manage grand-children. My own mother, who governed her children so well, could never govern one grand-child. In every point obey your mother. Give up your will to hers. But with regard to the management of your children, steadily keep the reins in your own hands. (64)

Over a century later, one of the essayists who offers advice about how to age properly chastises just such old women. In the 1887 essay "The Conduct of Age," published in *The Spectator*, the writer claims that men "and often women, are far too tenacious of all the practical rights which they gain in middle life, and which, whatever they may say to the contrary, they evidently never dream of relaxing their hold upon, while they live." Explaining this impulse, the writer continues: "The dregs of a carnal hankering after controlling force, which age now so often leaves behind, is the legacy not of years merely, but of a jealous and unchastened middle life" (286). From the point of view of the child reader, who is left to assert proper authority over the world but the child?

Certainly, kindly grandmother figures can be found in popular children's literature of the period. George MacDonald's novels form a continuum of grandmothers from the character who personifies natural powers in *At the Back of the North Wind* (1871) to the gracious and powerful "Old Irene" of both *The Princess and the Goblin* (1872) and *The Princess and Curdie* (1877), a great-great-great-grandmotherly guardian angel who conveniently disappears when she is not needed and whose powers include the occasional ability to appear as a young woman. Edith Honig describes these figures as "magical women," a fusion of wise women and witches, whom she sees as powerful alternatives to the figure of the mother, arguing that to invest actual mothers with magical powers would have been too threatening given the constraints of the cultural belief in separate spheres for women and men. More tamely, Juliana Ewing's popular *The Remembrances of Mrs. Overtheway* (1894) describes a pink-cheeked, rosebush-growing, cookie-baking, story-telling elderly neighbor who comes to the rescue of the lonely daughter of a long-lost sailor. However, Carroll's old women amply display the problems Wesley and conduct writers envisaged. In the enormously popular *Alice*, neither the Queen, the mother of the State, nor the Duchess, the royal mother of a "pig," can manage her family, her retinue, or Alice. Ultimately, Alice must use the hyperbolically oscillating, flexible body of youth to tower over the shrinking bodies of old age as she soars over the courtroom, shouting down the Queen just before awakening into the un-wonderland of her own drawing room.

Children's fantasy poetry as well as prose demonstrates this preoccupation with the childishly unruly old woman. Lear's *Nonsense* books probably owe a debt to an earlier collection of illustrated limericks, *The History of Sixteen Wonderful Old Women, Illustrated by as Many Engravings Exhibiting Their Principal Eccentricities and Amusements* (1821). Many of these "eccentricities" depend on the illustrated old woman's inappropriate appearance or behavior, given her years. In the most explicit, a woman is pictured rolling a hoop, which she pushes with a stick as a child might. Her body is in motion and looks youthful and graceful. Only her long nose and cap indicate her age:

> There was an Old Woman of Croydon
> To look young she affected the Hoyden
>   And would jump and would skip
>   Till she put out her hip;
> Alas! poor Old Woman of Croydon.

Here nature punishes her with injury while society disciplines her with the comically insulting label "hoyden," a term suggesting not merely the impropriety of age but also of gender. A second limerick pictures a plump, seemingly bald woman before her looking-glass, an odd mop atop her head:

> There was an old Woman of Gosport
> And she was one of the cross sort,
>   When she dressed for the Ball
>   Her wig was too small,
> Which enrag'd this Old Woman of Gosport.

The "eccentricity" in this case appears to be vanity. Although the "old woman" looks at the viewer, not the mirror, she is ridiculous for wanting to "go" and to "sport" herself, striving to compete for attention at a ball, the realm properly ruled by the young woman.[9] The "youthful" behavior of such characters is attacked by the writer of the previously noted conduct piece, "The Art of Growing Old" (1866), who warns: "Time is so remorseless with beauty, yellowing the fair skin, wrinkling the brown ones. . . . No blue ribbon will now light up the iron grey hair, or hide the bald ragged untidiness of the remains of matchless curls. . . . And if joined to these attempts there is a youthful effort at gaiety and giggly, how mournful, how painful is the sight!" (41–42). Given that the essay is a diatribe against elders who cling to domestic, economic, or political power, this "pain" must be the middle-aged spectators' annoyance with older people who refuse to recede into "the graceful but unexacting dependence which is quite willing to owe much to others, but is fully aware of the conditions under which alone it is possible to owe much to others without being a heavy burden upon them" (286). If the old would not voluntarily become ridiculous, writers were often quite willing to make them so.

In Lear's case, older men as well as women are pinioned when their desires, demeanor, attitudes, and behaviors do not conform to the general expectation that the old should "moderate" their ambitions, a change that inevitably benefits the middle-aged. Because Lear's male older characters are often rendered absurd precisely by being feminized, much of what can be said about the female figures also applies to his elderly male figures.

Lear, like Carroll, tends to ridicule strong female figures for their energy and irrationality. Elderly characters' frustrations with the physical and social constraints placed upon their aging bodies are trivialized through diminution: anger shrinks to irritation, demand shrivels to petulance and complaint. Absurdity, redundancy, and abuse seem to be the fate of most of Lear's female characters. (Figure 4.) Several of his limericks recount abuses that the old heap upon the young—and the consequences. In this well-known piece, the old person simply won't leave:

> There was an old person of Loo
> Who said, "What on earth shall I do?"
> When they said, "Go away!" she continued to stay,
> That vexatious old person of Loo. (310)

Her confusion and sense of displacement are presented as vexatious rather than pitiful. In another limerick, an old woman refuses to move to the margins of the domestic sphere where the paintings I have discussed would prefer to place her. Her refusal translates into a parodic depiction of irritability and unreasonableness:

There was an old person of Stroud,
Who was horribly jammed in a crowd;
Some she slew with a kick, some she scrunched with a stick,
That impulsive old person of Stroud.

Figure 4. Edward Lear limerick.

> There was an old person of Pisa,
> Whose daughters did nothing to please her;
> She dressed them in grey, and banged them all day,
> Round the walls of the city of Pisa. (312)

Like the "domestic queen" vilified in "The Art of Growing Old," this old woman resists encroachments of the young. Here, Lear wittily portrays her as retaliating by forcing her daughters to dress in the somber hues of old age rather than the whites and pastels "appropriate" to youth. Thus, she forces them into her own social position and then torments them in a comic reversal of generations.

Finally, in a third example, irritation escalates into puny malevolence, a characteristic not only of the unsexed "old person" presented in the following limerick but also of many of the male characters in Lear's verse. It is as if old age neuters in addition to threatening class standing and citizenship itself (as we saw in the previous limericks, the old person is turned into a foolish foreigner from real and imagined countries):

> There was an old person of Stroud,
> Who was horribly jammed in a crowd;
> Some she slew with a kick, some she scrunched with a stick,
> That impulsive old person of Stroud. (336)

This anomalous "old person" is featured in numerous Lear limericks. At times only the accompanying illustration designates gender. The point is that Lear draws on a common assumption about the elderly: when representing bodies that have aged, he dispenses with sexual distinctions, casting them into gender neutrality. The consequence is that Lear's figures are all the *same*. Their actions can therefore be treated as having a simple, constant meaning. Mike Feather-stone and Mike Hepworth have written of the limited vocabulary available to describe how old age *feels* in all its complexity and specificity. In Lear's limericks (and in most comic representations of older women in Victorian children's literature), the available vocabulary derives from the ways old people's appearance and behavior *look*, especially in implicit comparison with that of children. As a result, the comic vocabulary of these limericks narrates old people's actions as vexatious and impulsive—appropriate expressions only of the annoyance middle-aged adults feel toward those children and old people who resist their authority.

In these as well as other nonsense limericks by Lear, aggressive behavior on the part of older characters is quickly quelled, even violently punished, usually by children. A psychoanalytic reading might suggest that Lear was attuned to the aggression the child reader must feel. As a small being whose will is constantly not just resisted but also systematically destroyed by parents following the dictates of such authorities on child-rearing as John Locke or John Wesley (as opposed to those of Jean-Jacques Rousseau), the child can be imagined as a bundle of repressed anger. Recall Jane Eyre's startling rebellion against her Aunt Reed and the Calvinist Reverend Brocklehurst in Charlotte Bronte's *Jane Eyre* (1847), followed by Jane's near psychological devastation as her anger burns out in the terrifying death chamber, the Red Room. Yet the comic release of petty revenge upon the old certainly prompts amusement from the adult reader as well. The fantastical foreignness of Lear's characters, the diminutive quality of their assaults, and the pettiness of their complaints infantilize and thus undermine the "aged" as a culturally imagined group just at the moment that group becomes a more forbidding national and civic responsibility.

The tenor of verbal and visual illustrations grew more shrill as the public increasingly began to perceive the elderly as a needy group almost as distinctively set apart from the young as the working classes were from the middle classes. In the last group of children's books I will discuss, England's imperial mission joins with adventure books for boys to produce a fantasy of exclusion of the old.[10] The project of colonization was fueled not only by the desire to bring the material wealth of other nations home but also by the desire to exile England's undesirables—criminals, single women, orphans, and the old. Older people began to seem less like innocent children and more like children of nature—Darwinian throwbacks or degenerates whose difference from working, self-supporting middle-class adults required discipline, even deportation. This view must have been fueled by Charles Booth's studies of poverty in the 1880s and 1890s, which revealed the extent to which the poor *were* the elderly. Even before Booth published his findings, however, older people were being characterized as burdens to society. One *Punch* magazine cartoon of 1854 titled *How to Get Rid of an Old Woman* provides an iconographic bridge from the marginalized grandmother and de-classed older woman to the elderly as *émigré*, a new kind of colonial subject. (Figure 5.) Bearing the hallmarks of aging femininity (the shawl, umbrella, heavy bag, and dated bonnet), the masculinized figure, who looks oddly like Carroll's Queen and Duchess, waits to board a steamer headed for some outpost of the empire, where she will join transported convicts and unwanted children shipped overseas by overburdened orphanages.[11]

While Helen Bannerman's *Little Black Sambo* (1899) has a long, controversial history, her lesser-known illustrated book *Little Black Mingo* (1902) bears even more directly on this colonial connection. The book demonizes the mad, bad grandmother figure by locating another Duchess-like character in an African landscape. The illustrations have a childlike roundness and roughness, a cartoon quality that invests this grandmother with the appearance of an ill-tempered child. Here the element of the grotesque specifically translates the bodily idioms of old age into the racialized features that signified black and African in turn-of-the-century British popular culture. (Figure 6.) The African grandmother's tools of abuse are alligators rather than flamingo mallets or the guillotine, and thus, interestingly enough, the transportation of the grandmother to the space of empire preserves rather than disrupts the unruliness of inappropriate aging. Bannerman's novel illustrates the intersections of age and race that had already escalated into gothic horror in boy's adventure fiction of the 1880s and 1890s.

The most vicious example of this fusion is certainly the blood-thirsty African witch Gagool in H. Rider Haggard's *King Solomon's Mines* (1885). Gagool appears to have magically defied time for centuries. She is described as merciless and mad, as monkey-like and savage in a terrifying reversal of Darwinian evolution in which a human paradoxically ages into the worst sort of racist stereotype—primitive, bestial infancy. Gagool threatens not only the middle-aged white male protagonists but also African youth, particularly the young men who lay claim to tribal authority. Like Carroll's Queen, she is also hostile to young women, especially those of special beauty. Gagool's first appearance deserves to be recounted in detail:

> It crept on all fours, but when it reached the place where the king sat, it rose upon its feet, and throwing the furry covering off its face, revealed a most extraordinary and weird countenance. It was (apparently) that of a woman of great age, so shrunken that in size it was no larger than that of a year-old child, and was made up of a collection of deep yellow wrinkles. . . . [T]he whole

HOW TO GET RID OF AN OLD WOMAN.

Figure 5. *Artist unknown*. How to Get Rid of an Old Woman. *From Punch. 1854.*

Figure 6. From Helen Bannerman. The Story of Little Black Mingo. *1902.*

countenance might have been taken for that of a sun-dried corpse had it not been for a pair of large black eyes, still full of fire and intelligence, which gleamed and played under the snow-white eyebrows, and the projecting parchment-coloured skull, like jewels in a charnel-house. As for the skull itself, it was perfectly bare, and yellow in hue, while its wrinkled scalp moved and contracted like the hood of a cobra. (147)

A host of stereotypes coalesce in the witch's features. Both animal and child, she has devolved into bestiality, both snake and monkey (a comparison repeatedly alluded to in descriptions of her). More terrifying, she seems death alive. Even her skin color—yellow—sets her apart from both black and white characters and (in the color scheme of the novel) leaves her in the terrifying cultural and biological space of in-betweenness. Clinging to life and glutted with centuries of accumulated knowledge, Gagool fuses old age and childlikeness into the stuff of nightmares.

The novel, which has been made into at least four film versions, is the story of two upper-class white men, a white hunter, and a regal black African (picture Paul Robeson, the actor who played him in one of the film versions) who trace the prodigal brother of the expedition's leader to African mountains that hide the diamond mines built by King Solomon centuries before. The mines are now a religious shrine of the Kukuana, a tribe of beautiful women and larger-than-life warriors. While the tribe is ruled by a tyrannical king, the true power behind the throne is the old *anusi*, or witch, Gagool, who uses her age and knowledge to dominate king after king over time. As she slyly explains to the current leader, "I have done the bidding of many kings, Infadoos, till in the end they did mine" (261). In *King Solomon's Mines* (and in Haggard's other famous novel *She*), the power to age endlessly without dying gives its possessor terrifying knowledge and control, contrary to the weakness and fragility usually associated with deep old age. Thus, the up-and-coming king finds it impossible to displace Gagool, though he threatens her (in the oddly archaic English that signaled an African language in the codes of adventure fiction for boys): "mother of evil, thou art so old thou canst no longer love thy life. What can life be to such a hag as thee, who hast no shape, nor form, nor hair, nor teeth—hast naught, save wickedness and evil eyes?" Gagool insightfully explains the source of her power, the distance from human feeling and connection consequent to old age: "accursed fool, thinkst thou that life is sweet only to the young? . . . To the young, indeed, death is sometimes welcome, for the young can feel. They love and suffer, and it wrings them to see their beloved pass to the land of shadows. . . . All [the old] love is life, the warm, warm sun, and the sweet, sweet air" (252). In a book about the determination of boys (and men) to pursue their passions across the globe unchecked, Gagool's hunger for life is assimilated in the novel to the hungers of late Victorian culture. She craves military force; she hordes resources; she practices violence and deceit to satiate herself with power. A grand, grand, grand, grandmother, the terrible "infant" Gagool may be the most monstrous representation of perverse aging in all of children's literature.

Kate Greenaway's demure poetry of this period portrays aging women "[w]aiting patiently and still for the end to come, / Looking—with what wistful eyes!—for the last long home."[12] Old women unwilling to sit like these elderly women met with violence in proposals about what to do with them. Consider a scientific version of the *Punch* cartoon *How to Get Rid of an Old Woman*. In an article entitled "Why Grow Old?" that was published in 1893, Dr. N. E. York-Davies draws on strands of social Darwinism and medical theories of aging as cellular deterioration, concluding that "[t]he law of the survival of the fittest may, in some instances, be a cruel one; but it is a beneficent one, for it does not seem right that those entering the world should be handicapped with the weaknesses of their ancestors" (228–29). While York-Davies takes the eugenic line that "hereditary weakness" should not be passed on to future generations, his argument, like that of many late-century eugenics supporters, draws no clear lines between physical, social, or moral qualities that must be restrained. Thus the African grandmother in Bannerman's *Little Black Mingo* is first devoured by an alligator and then destroyed when the alligator explodes. Rider Haggard's Gagool dies a grisly, spectacular death when she is held fast under tons of falling rock by the young beauty she had earlier attempted to murder as a sacrifice to the mountains known as "The Ancient Ones."

During the nineteenth century, images of the figure of the aging woman proliferated and circulated through a host of popular children's genres, from alphabet books and chapbooks to limericks and adolescent imperial romances. By the end of the century, the message was clear: James Barrie's famous character Peter Pan trills a version of this message with irritating frequency in the plays and novels that made Peter famous: "I don't want to grow up!" As the jaundiced author of "The Art of Growing Old" observes, "'Old Age,' in theory, demands respect, veneration, and even admiration. 'Old Age,' in reality, suffers contempt, ridicule, and neglect" (39). By the end of the century, living a long life was less and less likely to win an elderly woman respect, authority, love, or status, whether social or familial. Public discourse had become so saturated with rationalizations for—and the feared consequences of—both class antagonism and the potential for reverse colonization that other real and imagined power relations came to be characterized in these very terms. This cultural shift recast both "the aged" and the feminine, and especially the aging woman, as an other and an outcast. Peter Pan's hostility to growing up suggests that an adult like Barrie, at least, would be content only with the first childhood—one of memory, imagination, and resistance to the inevitability of old age.

And yet children's fiction does permit certain elderly female characters to talk back to the culture that projected such vast economic, social, and national fears onto its weaker members. I close with one of the most explicit addresses on old age I have found in Victorian children's books. As I mentioned above in passing, George MacDonald wrote a series of children's novels in which a ghost-like grandmother, Old Irene, serves as a spiritual counselor to several children. Irene's physical marks of age vacillate, depending on the energy she draws from the presence and point of view of the person to whom she speaks. Unlike so many of the figures I've discussed, this character has the power to appear as her younger self, but she also possesses a clear belief in pleasures particular to old age. Kathleen Woodward has discussed the crucial nature of the mirror—the eyes that look upon the older person—in shaping the older person's feelings about her age.[13] It is this psychological and social dynamic that determines the age of this protean character, who yet sustains a source of power and strength at the core of her imagined identity. Cast in simple language, Old Irene's lecture in *The Princess and the Goblin* (1872) is as necessary and as hopeful a reminder today as it was over a century ago. She explains to the princess, one in a long line of granddaughters: "'I am very old indeed. It is so silly of people—I don't mean you, for you are such a tiny, and couldn't know better—but it *is* so silly of people to fancy that old age means crookedness and witheredness and feebleness and sticks and spectacles and rheumatism and forgetfulness! It is so silly! Old age has nothing whatever to do with all that. The right old age means strength and beauty and mirth and courage and clear eyes and strong painless limbs'" (86).[14]

NOTES

1. I have tried to focus on stories that are still in circulation so that readers like myself who are always looking for interesting representations of aging that they can use in the classroom will find many of these stories in print. Susan Tamke's essay, "Human Values and Aging: The Perspective of the Victorian Nursery," is an excellent companion piece. Focusing on three "models of the elderly"—wise, moral, but passive characters; foolish or malevolent characters; and those who are "neither good nor bad but simply old" (64)—she examines a wide range of long-lost children's stories, songs, and poems.

2. Darton is still one of the best places to begin the study of early children's literature, but also see Peter Hunt's beautifully illustrated *Children's Literature* and a fine earlier reference work, *Illustrators of Children's Books*.

3. See Jackson for a discussion of the debates over religious versus fantasy children's literature.

4. Extensive scholarly work exists on the fairy tale, but I am especially indebted to Jack Zipes's *Fairy Tales and the Art of Subversion: The Classical Genre for Children and the Process of Civilization* and Maria Tatar's *Off With Their Heads! Fairy Tales and the Culture of Childhood*.

5. I am indebted to Liz Corsun, who drew my attention to these preternaturally aged female characters in medieval literature.

6. The translation of general fears of the maturing female body into specific revulsion toward the aged female and her body is a phenomenon that crosses gender and time lines. In her essay "Simone de Beauvoir: Aging and Its Discontents," Kathleen Woodward traces Beauvoir's childhood horror of swelling breasts and coming menses as it transforms into early, exaggerated loathing of her "old" (at forty) body and those of others deemed old.

7. Carol Mavor offers a fascinating analysis of these photographs in *Pleasures Taken: Performance of Sexuality and Loss in Victorian Photographs*. You can see additional examples of Carroll's photographs in Helmut Gernsheim's *Lewis Carroll, Victorian Photographer*. The pictures are also discussed by Morton Cohen in his recent *Lewis Carroll: A Biography* and in his *Lewis Carroll's Photographs of Children*.

8. The Duchess's appearance and actions are even more viciously gerontophobic if Michael Hancher and others are correct in surmising that Tenniel may have used one of several paintings or engravings of a twelfth-century Tyrolese woman (possibly named Duchess Margaret), who gained renown for being, as a 1920s journalist put it, "The Ugliest Woman in History." One version of the painting, titled "A Grotesque Old Woman" (it has been attributed to various painters), is a hyperrealistic half-portrait of a heavy, bald, strongly masculine older woman with large ears, deep wrinkles, and a sagging mouth which earned her the cruel nickname "Maultasche," or "pocket-mouthed." More disturbingly, in all four portraits of the Duchess reproduced in Hancher's book, her square low-cut dress barely conceals, in fact pushes up and out toward the viewer, her heavy, deeply wrinkled breasts. This aspect of the portrait alludes to the Duchess's reputation for lavish sexual exploits, which several centuries of critics have treated as perverse because she is a woman, "ugly," and old. Hancher surveys the evidence that Tenniel may have known one or more of these portraits and the legends attached to them, and indeed

the Duchess of the novel bears remarkable resemblance to this randy ancestor. The article is cited in Hancher (written by William A. Baillie-Grohman, it appeared in *The Illustrated London News*, 25 Dec. 1920: 1080–81).

9. Tamke provides further evidence of this phenomenon—the embarrassingly girlish old woman—in her analysis of a child's book that teaches readers proper attitudes toward other classes, old ages, and so on by fictional example, *A Visit to the Bazaar* (1820).

10. Martin Green has written two excellent studies on adventure fiction—*Dreams of Adventure, Deeds of Empire* and *Seven Types of Adventure Tale: The Etiology of a Major Genre.* Jeffrey Richards's anthology *Imperialism and Juvenile Literature* convincingly demonstrates how embedded in the process of colonialism these novels are.

11. I am indebted to Susan Casteras's book *Images of Victorian Womanhood in English Art* for drawing my attention to this cartoon (66).

12. Kate Greenaway's *Birthday Book* (1880) is a much more conventional representation of the older woman from the same decade. Her delicate drawing of a pitiful old woman accompanies the poetry I quote: "Sitting by the fireside, thinking of the past, / Of the time, long faded now, far too bright to last; / Waiting patiently and still for the end to come, / Looking—with what wistful eyes!—for the last long home" (13). Another entry implores child readers: "Dear children, always pity show / To those who're poor and old" (9).

13. See Woodward's "Instant Repulsion: Decrepitude, the Mirror Stage, and the Literary Imagination." This essay also includes a fascinating discussion of aging in H. Rider Haggard's novel *She*.

14. Perhaps the uniqueness of such optimism about aging is reflected in the fact that Edith Honig and Susan Tamke also quote this passage in full as a rare expression of the gifts of old age. Tamke, however, argues that the passage has little larger significance because it belongs to fantastic rather than realistic literature.

WORKS CITED

"The Art of Growing Old." *The Argosy* 3 (Dec. 1866): 39–44.

Bannerman, Helen. *The Story of Little Black Mingo.* New York: Stokes, 1902.

Barrie, James. *Peter Pan in Kensington Gardens and Peter and Wendy.* 1906 and 1911. New York: Oxford UP, 1991.

Booth, Charles. *The Aged Poor in England and Wales.* 1894. New York: Garland, 1980.

Carroll, Lewis. *Alice's Adventures in Wonderland and Through the Looking-Glass.* 1865. New York: Oxford UP, 1992.

Casteras, Susan. *Images of Victorian Womanhood in English Art.* Rutherford: Fairleigh Dickinson UP, 1987.

Childe-Pemberton, Harriet Louisa. "All My Doing or Red-Riding Hood Over Again." 1882. Rpt. in Zipes, 1991. 209–48.

Coe, Richard. *When the Grass Was Taller: Autobiography and the Experience of Childhood.* New Haven: Yale UP, 1982.

Cohen, Morton. *Lewis Carroll's Photographs of Children*. Philadelphia: Rosenbach Foundation, 1978.

———. *Lewis Carroll: A Biography*. New York: Knopf, 1995.

"The Conduct of Age." *The Spectator* 60 (26 Feb. 1887): 285–86.

Continental Historical Society. *Queen Victoria's Alice in Wonderland* (formerly entitled *Queen Victoria's Secret Diaries*). San Francisco: Continental Historical Society, 1984.

Dame Wiggins of Lee and Her Seven Wonderful Cats. Written Principally by a Lady of 90. 1823. John Ruskin, 1885.

Darton, F. J. Harvey. *Children's Books in England: Five Centuries of Social Life*. Cambridge: Cambridge UP, 1958.

Dickens, Charles. "The Magic Fishbone." 1868. Rpt. in Zipes, 1991. 89–99.

Ewing, Juliana. *Mrs. Overtheway's Remembrances*. Illus. A. Pasquier and J. Wolf. London: Bell, 1894.

Featherstone, Mike, and Andrew Wernick, eds. *Images of Aging: Cultural Representations of Later Life*. New York: Routledge, 1995.

Featherstone, Mike, and Mike Hepworth. "The Mask of Ageing and the Postmodern Life Course." *The Body: Social Process and Cultural Theory*. Ed. Mike Featherstone, Mike Hepworth, and Bryan S. Turner. London: Sage, 1990. 371–89.

Gernsheim, Helmut. *Lewis Carroll: Victorian Photographer*. London: Thames, 1980.

Goldsmith, Dr. *Dr. Goldsmith's Celebrated Elegy on that Glory of Her Sex, Mrs. Mary Blaize*. Illus. William Mulready. 1808. Illus. Randolph Caldecott. London: Warne, 1885.

Green, Martin. *Dreams of Adventure, Deeds of Empire*. New York: Basic, 1979.

———. *Seven Types of Adventure Tale: The Etiology of a Major Genre*. University Park: Pennsylvania State UP, 1991.

Greenaway, Kate. *Kate Greenaway's Birthday Book for Children*. London: Evans, 1880.

Haggard, H. Rider. *King Solomon's Mines*. New York: Oxford UP, 1991.

Hancher, Michael. *The Tenniel Illustrations to the "Alice" Books*. Athens: Ohio State UP, 1985.

"Happy Old Age." *Chambers's Journal* 6th ser. 5 (1901–02): 197–99.

The History of Sixteen Wonderful Old Women, Illustrated by as Many Engravings Exhibiting their Principal Eccentricities and Amusements. London: Harris, 1821.

Hockey, Jenny, and Allison James. "Back to Our Futures: Imaging Second Childhood." Featherstone and Wernick. 135–48.

Honig, Edith Lazaros. *Breaking the Angelic Image: Woman Power in Victorian Children's Fantasy*. New York: Greenwood, 1988.

Hunt, Peter. *Children's Literature: An Illustrated History*. Oxford: Oxford UP, 1995.

Illustrators of Children's Books, 1744–1945. Comp. Bertha E. Miller, Louise Payson Latimer, and Beulah Folmsbee. Boston: Horn Book, 1947.

Jackson, Mary. *Engines of Instruction, Mischief, and Magic: Children's Literature in England from Its Beginnings to 1839*. Lincoln: U of Nebraska P, 1989.

Lear, Edward. *The Complete Nonsense Book of Edward Lear*. Ed. Lady Strachey. Edison: Castle, 1994.

MacDonald, George. "Little Daylight." 1864. Rpt. in Mark 102–17.

———. *The Princess and the Goblin and The Princess and the Curdie*. 1872 and 1877. New York: Oxford UP, 1990.

Mark, Jan, ed. *The Oxford Book of Children's Stories*. New York: Oxford UP, 1994.

Mavor, Carol. *Pleasures Taken: Performance of Sexuality and Loss in Victorian Photographs*. Durham: Duke UP, 1995.

McGillis, Roderick. "Lame Old Bachelor, Lonely Old Maid: Harriet Childe-Pemberton's 'All My Doing; or Red Riding Hood Over Again.'" *Aspects and Issues in the History of Children's Literature*. Ed. Maria Nikolajeva. Westport: Greenwood, 1995. 127–38.

The Moving Adventures of Old Dame Trot and Her Comical Cat. Circa 1807. London: Otley, 1875.

Prickett, Stephen. *Victorian Fantasy*. Bloomington: Indiana UP, 1979.

Richards, Jeffrey, ed. *Imperialism and Juvenile Literature*. New York: St. Martin's, 1989.

Ritchie, Anne Isabella. "Cinderella." 1868. Rpt. in Zipes, 1991. 101–26.

Roebuck, Janet. "When Does Old Age Begin? The Evolution of the English Definition." *Journal of Social History* 12 (1979): 416–28.

Tamke, Susan S. "Human Values and Aging: The Perspective of the Victorian Nursery." *Aging and the Elderly: Humanistic Perspectives in Gerontology*. Ed. Stuart F. Spicker, Kathleen M. Woodward, and David D. Van Tassel. Atlantic Highlands: Humanities, 1978. 63–81.

Tatar, Maria. *Off With Their Heads! Fairy Tales and the Culture of Childhood*. Princeton: Princeton UP, 1992.

Tuer, Andrew W. *Stories from Old-Fashioned Children's Books*. New York: Scribner's, 1899–1900.

Wesley, John. Sermon 6. Rpt. in *Child-Rearing Concepts, 1628–1861: Historical Sources*. Itasca: Peacock, 1973.

Woodward, Kathleen. "Instant Repulsion: Decrepitude, the Mirror Stage, and the Literary Imagination." *Kenyon Review* 5 (Fall 1988): 43–66.

———. "Simone de Beauvoir: Aging and Its Discontents." *The Private Self: Theory and Practice of Women's Autobiographical Writings*. Ed. Shari Benstock. Chapel Hill: U of North Carolina P, 1988. 90–113.

Yorke-Davies, Dr. N. E. "Why Grow Old." *Popular Science Monthly* 43 (May-Oct. 1893): 227.

Zipes, Jack. *Fairy Tales and the Art of Subversion: The Classical Genre for Children and the Process of Civilization*. New York: Methuen, 1983.

———, ed. *Victorian Fairy Tales: The Revolt of the Fairies and Elves*. New York: Routledge, 1991.

Incubabies and Rejuvenates
The Traffic between Technologies of Reproduction and Age-Extension

Susan Squier

On August 16, 1926, *Time* magazine carried the following story:

> Physiologists convening in Stockholm all but forgot other topics in a furore
> created by Dr. Serge Voronoff, famed gland-grafter. . . . To his Swedish hosts
> he revealed that he had grafted within Nora, a mature female chimpanzee, the
> sex organs of a human female. Then, with assistance from Dr. Elie Ivanoff of
> Moscow, he had artificially impregnated Nora with human sperms. She was
> to bear her baby in January and it would be, biologically, a human child.
> ("Ape-Child" 16) (Figure 1.)

DR. VORONOFF
Nora is going to have a baby ?
(See Ape-Child)

Voronoff's pregnant chimpanzee joins a long
list of experimental subjects leading to the
birth in 1978 of Louise Brown, the first in
vitro fertilization baby, and to the late-twen-
tieth-century innovation of surrogate birth.
This medical news item also interweaves
modern literary and social history, for Nora
is a whimsical echo of Ibsen's Nora; her
name an ironic (perhaps even vengeful?)
response to the feminist, suffragist agitations
of the early twentieth century. Moreover, her
"Ape-Child" invokes preoccupations with
degeneration and racialization that gripped
Britain in the years before World War II
(Young). Yet while the tale of Nora the chimpanzee embodies the converging discourses
of medical science, feminism, and racialization in the project of reshaping *reproduction*,

it also embodies another preoccupation of early-twentieth-century science and culture: the project of scientific rejuvenation. In what follows, I will excavate some of the links between those two projects—now more familiar to us as reproductive technology and age-extension strategies—and I will suggest what we might learn from that forgotten history about our approach as a culture and society to the liminal human moments at both ends of the life span.

The "Nora experiment" was actually part of a far larger project of gland-grafting carried out in the 1920s and 1930s by the French-Russian scientist Dr. Serge Voronoff. Its overall goal was not to induce pregnancy, but rather to mitigate the painful symptoms of aging (Voronoff, *Sources* 111). While Nora shared with the rest of the graft recipients the condition of being postmeno-pausal, the rest of the recipients were human women, who had chimpanzee ovaries grafted into them as a rejuvenation treatment. This gland-grafting for women was conceptualized as a medical intervention designed not only to ward off aging, but also to enhance "normal" familial ties, social relations, and gender roles. Like the other scientific and para-scientific therapies for rejuvena-tion carried out between the 1860s and the 1930s, Voronoff's gland-grafts were motivated by a surge of cultural interest in rejuvenation in Great Britain, Europe, and the United States. Beginning before the turn of the century when Charles-Edouard Brown-Sequard injected himself with the extract of canine testicles, rejuvenation experimentation continued in the first three decades of the twentieth century with Voronoff's so-called "monkey-gland grafts"; Vien-nese physiologist-endocrinologist Eugen Steinach's experiments with vasolig-ature (tying off the sperm ducts) and X-raying the ovaries; the "reactivation" treatments of New York physician Harry Benjamin that added "diathermy" or electrical current treatment to the surgical, radiological, and hormonal treat-ments already in existence; and the cellular treatments (injections of prepared fetal sheep cells) of Swiss glandular surgeon Paul Niehans.[1] Frequently repre-sented through such mythic tropes as the elixir of life, the fountain of youth, or the holy grail, these "rejuvenation therapies" were situated at the lively intersec-tion of fact and miracle, of science and culture.[2] They generated controversy in the popular press, became the focus of best sellers, canonical novels, and science fiction short stories, provided the theme for a smash Hollywood movie, and exercised a shaping impact on our attitudes toward aging that persists to the present day.

I've begun with the story of Voronoff's Nora because it suggests that early-twentieth-century rejuvenation therapy was closer than we have previously realized to that other major twentieth-century intervention in human life: the set of techniques for scientifically shaping conception, gestation, and birth we would ultimately know as reproductive technology. Both projects bore the stamp of several closely linked discourses emerging or achieving prominence in the first three decades of the twentieth century: the eugenics movement, the new fields of chemical embryology and "sex endocrinology," the sexology movement, and the life-span reconceptualization fundamental to the emergence of gerontology (Achenbaum). That these new fields would intertwine, influencing the range of ways medical science intervened in the beginnings and endings of human life as the century went on, is not really surprising. Despite their different foci, they all shared an interest in improving the bodily bases of human life, in the male and female human life course, and in the efficacies of surgical and chemical intervention. What interests me is the way these scientific and technical strategies for reshaping the human *body* functioned in consort with cultural and social conditions shaping the human *subject*. In what follows, I will turn to the kinds of cultural work—on the body, on the subject, and on social relations—performed by rejuvenation therapy and reproductive technology. But first we must consider their debt to the new—or newly consolidating—discourses circulating in the early decades of the twentieth century. We can then move on to explore the fantasies that fueled (and continue to fuel) these linked projects of body (re)construction, as articulated through their representation in fiction and popular culture.

I. EUGENICS

From the founding in 1907 of the Eugenics Education Society, the eugenics movement was a point of convergence for medical practitioners, scientists, and social reformers interested in improving the human species by enabling "the more suitable races or strains of blood a better chance of prevailing speedily over the less suitable," in the words of the Society's Honorary President, Francis Galton (qtd. in Kevles ix). The saga of the eugenics movement, from its origins in Francis Galton's and Karl Pearson's statistical analyses of heredity, through its widespread albeit contested popularity in Britain and the United States as a movement housing both emancipatory and notoriously racist social projects, to its disappearance in the late 1930s with the revelations of Nazi eugenics, is too complex to detail here. In fact, the saga does not end in the 1930s, as Daniel Kevles and others have observed; while the eugenics movement went underground during World War II, it reemerged in the 1950s as human genetics. In 1954, the principal publication of the Galton laboratory at University College, London, changed its name from the *Annals of Eugenics* to the *Annals of Human Genetics*, and a new field of genetic counseling emerged, to carry on the reform eugenics ideal under a kinder, gentler name.[3]

Two specific aspects of early-twentieth-century eugenics are worth highlighting, because they influenced the linked projects of reproductive technology and rejuvenation therapy. First, since eugenics addressed the improvement of the human species through negative and positive means, *the point of intervention was the beginning of a human life: the processes of conception, gestation, and birth.* Eugenicists were willing both to discourage, or even forbid, reproduction that they understood as disadvantageous to the human species as a whole (negative eugenics), and to provide incentives for reproduction that they deemed advantageous (positive eugenics). Of course the very concept of what was "disadvantageous" was profoundly subject to ideological influence. Thus, my second point: when eugenicists weighed desirable traits, longevity was frequently included. Although few scholars of the eugenics movement emphasize this point, *the eugenics writers of the 1920s and 1930s included the timing and nature of the end of life in their assessment of the eugenically desirable and/or the "dysgenic."*[4] So for eugenicists, the process of embryological development and the process of aging were both crucial to their project of improving the species: they took as a prominent goal the greatest possible deferral of the latter, and they took as their strategy intervention in the former.

II. CHEMICAL EMBRYOLOGY AND ENDOCRINOLOGY

From its nineteenth-century emphasis on morphology, or the structural development of the embryo, embryology began to shift, with the opening of the twentieth century, to an interest in the chemical processes that triggered embryological development. At the turn of the century, embryologists took a mechanical and experimental approach to the problem of how embryos developed: in the words of medical historian J. A. Witkowski, "variously compressing, constricting, and centrifuging eggs, and killing or separating the cells of early embryos, all directed to finding out at what stage cells become committed to specific pathways of differentiation" (258). Hans Spemann pursued this approach later, using transplants and grafts. Continuing this emphasis on experimentation, not naturalist observation, a group of scientists at Cambridge University, led by Joseph Needham and including Dorothy Needham and colleagues C. H. Waddington, J. D. Bernal, Dorothy Wrinch, and Joseph Woodger, began in 1920 to explore the "biochemical basis of embryonic development" (Witkowski 247). From Spemann's turn-of-the-century work to the Cambridge Group's work in the early 1930s, interest in the chemical basis of embryological development led experimenters to investigate the effects of dividing embryos at early stages of growth and, later, of implanting centrifuged embryonic cells onto host embryos.

This interest in the chemical basis of embryological development was paralleled by a new interest in the chemical basis of sexual development. As Nelly Oudshoorn has documented, the discovery of sex hormones in the first decade of the twentieth century led to an explosion of experimental laboratory endocrinology. In a series of experiments remarkably parallel to the work in embryology, scientists turned to the surgical removal and transplantation of gonads to investigate the chemical substances present in the sex glands. "In this surgical approach," Oudshoorn explains, "scientists removed ovaries and testes from animals like rabbits and guinea-pigs, cut them into fragments, and reimplanted them into the same individuals at locations other than their normal positions in the body. With these experiments scientists tested the concept of hormones as agents having control over physical processes without the mediation of nervous tissue" (*Beyond the Natural Body* 20–21). Organotherapy, as this procedure was called, was also used on human subjects, although as Dr. H. Lisser observed in 1925, "It is curious that far less interest has been manifested in ovarian implantations than the corresponding procedure in the male sex, despite the fact the ovarian castrations are infinitely more common than testicular castrations" (14).

Early-twentieth-century endocrinology anticipated to a considerable degree the issues that would be raised by the nascent field of reproductive technology, as is apparent in a "remarkable" case of ovarian grafting reported by Lisser in the journal *Endocrinology* in 1925:

> In this case amenorrhoea had set in after labor and symptoms of absence [*sic*] developed. The small cystic ovaries were removed and a foreign ovary implanted. The woman again menstruated four months after the operation, and four years after the operation she conceived and bore a normal child. This case was earnestly discussed before the Edinburgh Obstetrical Society, and can not well be denied. There is, indeed, in this case no doubt that if there has been no error of observation, this woman bore the child of another woman. Serious objections might be raised against such procedures on ethical and forensic grounds. (14)

The surgical approach—with its manifest complications—was superseded once the so-called "sex hormones" were chemically isolated and identified in the 1930s: now rather than surgically transplanting gonads containing hormones, the chemical isolates themselves could be administered.

The developmental courses of embryology and sex endocrinology have been traced by a number of scholars, most notably Jane Oppenheimer, Evelyn Fox Keller, and Oudshoorn, and I do not have space enough to rehearse their findings here. Rather, let me briefly delineate the shaping impact of these two fields on the linked RTs. Having begun with a grossly surgical approach, both embryology and sex endocrinology moved in the early years of the twentieth century to a chemical approach, searching for the chemical properties that explained development, whether of the embryo in the former case, or of the sex organs and sexual characteristics of the individual in the latter case.

III. SEXOLOGY

To the surgical and chemical approaches to developmental and social/behavioral questions, the new field of sexology added psychological and psychoanalytic approaches as well. Catalyzed by the work of a number of German physicians, sexology achieved its first public presence in 1908 with the appearance of the *Journal of Sexual Science*, founded by psychiatrist Dr. Magnus Hirschfeld. The field attained institutional consolidation with the establishment of the Institute for Sexual Science in Berlin in 1919, and with the Second and Third International Congresses of the World League for Sexual Reform in Copenhagen (1928) and London (1929) (Wolff; see also Tiefer). Concerned with a range of issues including "sexual biology, sexual pathology, sexual ethnology and sexual sociology," the sexology movement taxonomized sexual behaviors (particularly homosexuality and the psycho-physiological condition sexologists designated "intersexuality"), considered surgical and hormonal solutions to sexual difficulties, and helped to set the stage for medical scientific interventions in birth and aging (Hirshfeld xii; see also Squier, *Babies in Bottles* 102–05). Some of these interventions were given prominence in *Sexual Reform Congress*, the volume compiled after the Third International Congress and published in 1929. In addition to articles on eugenic sterilization, abortion, and contraception, the volume included two essays specifically on age-extension: Dr. Harry Benjamin's "The Reactivation of Women," reporting on the range of "reactivation," or rejuvenation therapies, in current clinical use with female patients, and Dr. Peter Schmidt's "Six Hundred Rejuvenation Operations: A Nine Years' Survey," providing his clinical assessment of the more than 700 vasoligature cases he had performed in the nine years since the publication of Eugen Steinach's *Rejuvenation*. An interdisciplinary or multidisciplinary field itself, sexology lent to the parallel and successor projects of rejuvenation therapy and reproductive technology a characteristically modern technoscientific optimism and reliance on a broad arsenal of medical scientific treatments for biosocial difficulties, as well as a proto-postmodern skepticism about normalizing categories.

IV. GERONTOLOGY

Zoologist Elie Metchnikoff coined the term "gerontology" in 1903, and in a career mingling embryology and experimental medicine, he went on to lay the foundation for that new multidisciplinary field, "the scientific study of old age."[5] Personally motivated to understand aging by an encounter with serious illness at the age of fifty-three, Metchnikoff modeled in his own life the convergence of disciplinary involvements—in embryology, zoology, and immunology—that would characterize all of these emerging fields of study. The story of gerontology's emergence as a (multi-)discipline from Metchnikoff's pioneering work onward has been compellingly told by W. Andrew Achenbaum and, more recently, Stephen Katz. But there is one specific point about the relationship between gerontology and the dual projects of reproductive technology and rejuvenation therapy that merits emphasis. Preparatory to the emergence of gerontology in the twentieth century, a shift occurred in the construction of the human life span that provided the crucial context for a renewed interest in the perennial project of retarding age or regaining youth. As Stephen Katz has shown, before the mid nineteenth century, Enlightenment-based views of the life span mingled science and the supernatural to construct it as an infinitely extendable period capped by old age as a philosophically significant but natural part of the life-continuum. By the mid nineteenth century, in contrast, a new modern construction of the life span reflected the taxonomizing, quantifying, and hierarchical impulse of modernity, positioning old age as a discrete, separate, medically classifiable, and finite developmental stage (Katz, "Imagining the Life-Span"). Hitherto the boundary between miracle and fact had been blurred—so that accounts of marvelous longevity mingled with Baconian-influenced treatises on life-prolongation through proper diet, exercise, and avoidance of harmful emotions. But with the emergence of modern medicine, as Katz has argued, "medical, demographic and insurantial investigations proved the life span to be fixed, thus disbanding premodern images of excessive longevity as fanciful"; the telling result is that old age was constructed not as a site of miraculous possibilities, but rather as a medical problem ("Imagining" 62).[6] These gerontologically motivated changes in the construction of the life span both reflected and catalyzed the modern impulse to tinker with the life course scientifically, the impulse that—I am arguing—undergirds both reproductive technology and rejuvenation therapy.

V. SHARED TRAITS OF THE TWO RTs

25. Steinach injecting cow with female sex hormone.

The discourses of eugenics, embryology, endocrinology, sexology, and gerontology left the following imprints on reproductive technology and rejuvenation therapy, or what I am calling the two forms of RT: 1) the scientific and social focus on a liminal subject (the embryo or fetus, and the aging person or neo-mort); 2) the use of other species as research reservoirs (as in Voronoff's use of Nora the chimpanzee and Steinach's experimentation with hormone injections in cattle, and the more recent use of hamster sperm and mouse ova as crucial aspects of the development of in vitro fertilization[7] [Figure 2.]); 3) the rationalization and Taylorization of human bodies and of medical-scientific interventions into bodily processes (beginning with the separation of sexuality from reproduction, foundational to both reproductive technology and rejuvenation therapy); 4) the reliance on visualization technologies, from the endoscope and microscope to the cinematic apparatus, as both a measurement tool and a rhetorical device (ranging from the use of laparoscopy in the development of in vitro fertilization to before-and-after films of rejuvenation subjects and a hit motion picture made from a novel about rejuvenation); 5) the existence of national rivalries for scientific and medical "discoveries" (as representatives of different nations vie for control of the new rejuvenation techniques, just as different nations vie to be "first" in certain reproductive technologies); 6) a linkage to the broader modern agenda of exercising medical/scientific control over the body (as a decline in religious certainties and a breakdown of community, accompanied by an increasing medicalization of the body, have led people to take refuge in viewing the body as a project);[8] 7) a gender-asymmetrical social "uptake" of the medical scientific innovations (as women's bodies become the primary focus of scientific and medical interventions in western society since the eighteenth century, as fleshly objects, subjects of anatomical dissection, and gendered skeletons, and the primary source for research materials) (Shilling 44).[9] Finally, and most significant for my purposes, both forms of RT are the subject of a phantasmatic investment whose dimensions and implications can be gauged by looking at their representation in imaginative literature.[10] These phantasmatic investments are played out in the production of bodies, subjects and societies, as I traced in the case of reproductive technology in my study *Babies in Bottles*, and as I will go on to detail here in the case of rejuvenation therapy.

VI. FICTIONS OF REJUVENATION

Two novels which explore the personal and social impact of successful rejuvenation therapy and had very different cultural trajectories give me my point of entry to some of these issues, particularly to the desire to participate, in phantasy, in techniques for warding off or rolling back the onset of aging. Gertrude Atherton's 1923 *Black Oxen*, a story about a woman who has received the Steinach treatment, displaced Sinclair Lewis's *Babbitt* on the best-seller list in the United States, while C. P. Snow's 1932 *New Lives for Old*, about the discovery of a technique for rejuvenation through hormone injection, was published anonymously and to little fanfare in Britain in 1932 (McClure 98). Taken together, these novels reveal the contestation over the terms on which rejuvenation therapy was practiced, the meaning that it would have in the cultural imaginary, and how those meanings were inflected by the gendered project of modernity.

Rejuvenation therapy was big news in 1923, the year *Black Oxen* appeared. If we trace the networks extending from the different methods of rejuvenation therapy, as evidenced by the coverage in the *New York Times* and *Time* magazine for that year, we see they reach from cities to small towns, join nations around the world, connect disciplinary colleagues from different countries, and even involve members of different species.[11] Thus when a visit to the United States by Eugen Steinach was impending, the *New York Times Magazine* enthused: "New men for old! Within a few months the name of the Professor of Biology at the University of Vienna has become the talk of cities and has penetrated to the furthest hamlets."[12] Scientific, aesthetic, civic, and personal contexts converged in this new interest in rejuvenation. On July 21, 1923, Serge Voronoff was reported to have galvanized "700 of the world's leading surgeons" at the International Congress of Surgeons in London when he spoke on "the success of his work in the 'rejuvenation' of old men," relying on film both to document his scientific successes and to persuade his audience:

> At London, Voronoff presented moving pictures showing the transference of monkey glands to human beings, with "before-and-after" effects on three specimen cases—men aged 65, 74 and 77 respectively, in more or less advanced stages of decrepitude. Within periods of four to 20 months after the operations, the films showed them as hale and active, apparently in middle age, riding horseback, rowing and doing other athletic feats.[13] ("Voronoff and Steinach" 19–20)

On October 13, the *Times* reported that Voronoff had so impressed his fellow physicians at the French Surgical Congress that he was scheduled to perform his gland-graft operations on eight of them right after the congress adjourned. The new frenzy for gland operations had even enhanced the international value of the chimpanzee, Voronoff's preferred graft source, resulting in new government regulations and international collaborations. As the *Times* reported, "So scarce have chimpanzees become that the Governor of French West Africa has issued an ordinance protecting them and the Pasteur Institute has sent Dr. Vulbert to Africa to establish a farm to raise them" ("Doctors" 15). As the year wound to a close, and the *Times* continued its frequent reports on rejuvenation-related items, even the rare bit of negative press was embedded in a modernist discourse of instrumentality, mechanism, and Taylorized bodies. In a two-hour address to the International Congress of Comparative Pathology in Rome, a Chicago surgeon attacked rejuvenation therapy, but claimed that "further developments in surgical science would make it possible to patch up all human maladies by the use of spare parts, just as one did with a motor car" ("Declares" 6).

This was the climate, then, in which Gertrude Atherton's *Black Oxen* appeared. While clearly inspired by newspaper coverage, the novel had the extra impetus of Atherton's *own* Steinach treatment in 1922, and it took its title from the work of another Steinach patient, W. B. Yeats, who wrote in "Countess Cathleen": "The years, like Great Black Oxen, tread the world, / And God, the herdsman, goads them on behind."[14] An "instantaneous best-seller," *Black Oxen* was also instantaneously controversial. By October 1923, the Mayor of Rochester, New York, had ordered every copy of Atherton's novel "removed from the city's public libraries" on the grounds that the novel was "unfit for young minds" ("Censorship" 22). Prohibition proved a spice to sales, and by the following year *Black Oxen* had become a hit movie, produced by Frank Lloyd and starring Corinne Griffith, Conway Tearle, and Clara Bow.

The novel's plot can be summarized fairly quickly: Mary Ogden Zattiany, a legendary beauty, undergoes Steinach's treatments shortly after World War I and is dramatically rejuvenated: fifty-eight, she now looks a young thirty. When she returns incognito to New York City in order to settle her financial affairs and raise money for her Vienna Fund for Austrian war orphans, she provokes curiosity and confusion in her friends (who think she is her own daughter), resentment once her secret is out (from her age cohort *and* from women a generation younger who are competing for male suitors), and finally love in the thirty-four-year-old aspiring playwright Lee Clavering. In short, the news of her rejuvenation treatment provokes a social and scientific tempest:

> although she would not consent to be interviewed, there were double-page stories in the Sunday issues, embellished with snapshots and a photograph of the Mary Ogden of the eighties: a photographer who had had the honor to "take" her was still in existence and had exhumed the plates. Doctors, biologists, endocrinologists were interviewed. . . . When it was discovered that New York actually held a practicing physician who had studied with the great endocrinologists of Vienna, the street in front of his house looked as if some ambitious hostess were holding a continual reception.[15] (214–15)

Yet if Mary's recaptured youthful beauty caused a younger man to love her, that does not mean that she can unproblematically return his love. Atherton's novel is explicit that rejuvenation therapy has an asymmetrical meaning for the two sexes. Women are sterile, even if rejuvenated, and social constraints limit their enjoyment of even non-reproductive sexuality: "That is where men have the supreme advantage of women. . . . And if these [rejuvenated] men indulge occasionally in the pleasures of youth, or even marry young wives, the world will not be interested. But with women, who renew their youth and return to its follies, it will be quite another matter. If they are not made the theme of obscene lampoons they may count themselves as fortunate" (325–26). No doubt in response to this social reality, but also in response to Mary's experience as a nurse at the front during World War I, the novel's conclusion retrospectively constructs Mary's motivation for undergoing rejuvenation—and thus, the motivation of all women—not as a desire for youth, sex, and love, but rather as an attempt to achieve agency.[16] Mary decides *not* to marry the young man she loves. Rather, she accepts the proposal of an older suitor, who is soon to be the Chancellor of Austria, because he will provide her with the position she needs to help the orphaned children of Vienna recover from the ravages of World War I.

C. P. Snow's *New Lives for Old* shares with *Black Oxen* the sense that men and women will have a range of different reasons for being rejuvenated (which they can gratify to a greater or lesser extent depending on social conventions). However, it differs in the relation of the protagonist to rejuvenation treatment, as well as in the *kind* of treatment it represents. While Atherton wrote her novel from the perspective of the *object* of medical scientific intervention (since she had actually undergone the Steinach treatment), Snow wrote his novel from the perspective of a *subject* of science. A celebrated participant in the traffic between science and literature, and author of the well-known study *The Two Cultures*, C. P. Snow took a Ph.D. in physical chemistry at Cambridge University, and *New Lives for Old* reflects the excitement of that scientific involvement. But in its initial anonymous publication, the novel also reflects Snow's experience of the more troubling side of science, reparatively returning to "the biggest embarrassment of [his] young scientific career," when he and his research partner Philip Bowden mistakenly announced that they had successfully synthesized Vitamin A, and their work was sharply criticized by two senior scientists, leaders in the field of vitamin chemistry (de la Mothe 132–36). Snow's autobiographically tinged protagonists, Billy Pilgrim, Professor of Biophysics in King's College, London, and his junior research partner David Callan, are successful where Snow and Bowden failed. They synthesize a human sex hormone, collophage, which can prevent the physical atrophy of the body associated with aging. As Billy Pilgrim explains:

> The machinery of the body could go on for years and years after old age begins . . . except that with the years less and less collophage is being made, and somehow the body dries up and dies before its time. . . . And if you provide collophage artificially, you prevent this decay happening for a long time. . . . [T]o-night is nothing more nor less than the beginning of the science of rejuvenation. (19)

When Pilgrim informs the Prime Minister of their accomplishment, he attempts to block the public announcement of the discovery on the grounds that it may be too destabilizing. But when Pilgrim threatens to release the news first to the Russians, Britain implements rejuvenation therapy. The consequences aren't wholly surprising—even at the moment of discovery, the two scientists found themselves in a bitter quarrel over whether their new substance should be offered to the public—but Snow documents them extensively. They include: the creation of two classes of people (those who are biologically or economically able to be rejuvenated and those who are not); the disruption of the structure of employment (as older workers fail to retire and younger workers are unable to advance); the dislocation of the family and of the generational system on which it is founded (as rejuvenated wives leave unrejuvenated husbands for younger lovers and rejuvenated mothers compete sexually with their daughters); competition over access to rejuvenation therapy (as classes and nations vie for access, resulting in misapplication and needless deaths); overpopulation (as rejuvenated men continue to father children with young women); and the creation of new economic markets among the rejuvenated (for art, for cosmetics, and for cosmetic surgery).[17] While Atherton's novel stressed the intimate personal benefits and costs of rejuvenation to one woman, Snow has given us a balance sheet of its implications for a whole society—both men and women. He paints a dire picture for his privileged protagonists: what began as a scientific discovery ends as a revolution when the poor—unable to afford the costly rejuvenation treatment so widely used by the rich—riot and seize power in Great Britain.

In contrast to Snow's predictions that rejuvenation therapy would have drastic, indeed revolutionary consequences, as it has played out in fact rather than fiction, the medical practices developing from rejuvenation therapy seem to have been constructed as anything but revolutionary. Instead, between 1935 and 1985 society has quietly assimilated hormone replacement therapy for women into normal medicine, framed less as a *rejuvenation* strategy than as a "treatment" for the female menopause, while there has been significantly less publicity given to male hormone treatment, whether as therapy *or* as a rejuvenation strategy.[18]

This developmental trajectory from rejuvenation treatment to hormone therapy for the "disease" of menopause reflects changes in the new discipline of endocrinology as well as the traffic between popular culture and science, as I understand it. Several factors funneled the development of sex endocrinology, and thus hormone therapy, to a predominately female population in the 1920s and 1930s. First, as we have already seen, the identification and classification of the sex hormones in the 1920s led to a shift from a focus on the gonads as agents of sexual difference to a stress on a chemical approach to sex endocrinology, and on hormones as keys to both human sexuality and human health. Then, the existence of disciplinary sites for intervention in women's bodies (the gynecological and obstetric clinic) narrowed the global focus on glands from a symmetrical focus on both "male" and "female" sex hormones to an asymmetrical concentration of scientific, medical, and pharmacological attention on ovaries, on "female" sex hormones and on women as the site of intervention.[19] A smaller market existed for male sex hormone therapy, reflecting the much smaller number of intake sites—or medical occasions—for men to be treated, whether by "organotherapy" or hormone injection. Urological problems did not bring men into clinics as regularly as gynecology and obstetrics did women, and to reiterate Dr. Lisser's point in 1925, "ovarian castrations are infinitely more common than testicular castrations" (14). Finally, a recoil away from the therapeutic uses of male hormones occurred in response to the exaggerated claims made in the popular press for their uses in rejuvenation therapy. Popular culture thus collaborated with the disciplinary structures of clinical and research medicine to focus hormone therapies on the female body and to shape medical claims away from overt talk of rejuvenation. A similar recoil from exaggerated popular press claims for rejuvenation powers shaped gerontology, according to Andrew Achenbaum. Reflecting this, a feature in 1945 in the very first issue of the *Journal of Gerontology* took pains to distinguish the work of responsible, scientific gerontologists from "alchemists, charlatans, conartists [*sic*], or uninformed adventurers. 'What kind of fountain of youth are we seeking: a fountain that will miraculously erase the wrinkles of age, or a fountain that will make the later years of life a health [*sic*] and intellectually occupied period?'" (qtd. in Achenbaum 128).

When we consider these novels in relation to their era, one in which gerontology and endocrinology were struggling for scientific legitimation against the backdrop of a rejuvenation-mad popular press, what we make of the whole will depend, to some extent, on our position. Those of us committed to understanding the drive to "fix" aging, as if it were a disease rather than a naturally occurring process, may be struck by the movement from external to internal fixes, from the "macro" to the "micro," from grafting to gland therapy, to injections, and finally now—with the recent discovery of the gene for Werner's syndrome of premature aging—to genetic manipulation (Altman).[20] Those of us interested in the intersection between popular culture and scientific culture may notice the powerful influence that negative popular press can have on medical scientific development, as well as the enhancing impact of positive press.[21] Those of us interested in literary representations of aging will focus on the differing ways that the plots of the two novels present the meaning of rejuvenation, demonstrating that the discourse of rejuvenation therapy is as fissured and contested as that of reproductive technology.[22]

Finally, for those of us interested in the interplay between science and culture, Atherton's *Black Oxen* and Snow's *New Lives for Old* register a change of direction not only in early-twentieth-century endocrinology, but in the culture at large as well, in their representation of different methods of rejuvenation therapy.[23] If Snow's *New Lives for Old* portrays a class-based rejuvenation revolution, that may be because a prior, sex-based revolution had already been squelched: the potential revolution embodied by Mary Zattiany's choice of rejuvenation not for sex or love but for agency and power. Through a combination of structural, ideological, and cultural forces, both within and beyond the field of medical science, the nascent field of rejuvenation therapy was being redirected: from the feminist goal of providing aging women with a vigorous life free from the entanglements of (hetero)sexuality and reproduction, to the scientific goal of (re)shaping aging women's bodies to the standard of male delectation, so they stay visually pleasing and reproductively functional.

VII. SYNTHETIC WOMEN

Another short story from the same era, also expressing the fantasy of constructing a woman wholly for male delectation, can return us from a single-minded concentration on rejuvenation therapy to attention to its interplay with reproductive technology in the twentieth century. Jeb Powell's 1940 science fiction story, "The Synthetic Woman," concerns not rejuvenation, but synthetic conception and gestation: reproductive technology, in short. Yet exemplifying

the intertwined nature of these two life-span interventions, Powell's story of reproductive technology also explores some of the central issues raised by rejuvenation therapy: discrepancy between age and generational positioning, disturbance of the life course, divergence between physiological and psychological aging, and the problem of the ethical, forensic, or ideological implications of technoscientific interventions in the life span. The tale concerns Vivian, an "incubaby" formed by the combination of chemicals and ectogenetically gestated, whose aging process has been accelerated by the injection of a growth-enhancing substance, "oxydyne," so that at chronological age eight she has all the physiological appearance of a "beautiful, full-blown bud of womanhood" (117, 102). (Figure 3.) A technoscientific anomaly, legally underage yet the result of scientifically accelerated development, Vivian wants to marry the wealthy young man who has kissed her in the laboratory, although she fails to understand the first thing about marriage, gender differences, or sexuality. Yet her creator, the pseudomystical Dr. Shaiman (the pun is clearly intended), is saving Vivian for another: the racially and intellectually devolved, hirsute and remarkably "dark" incubaby Bruno, who has been damaged in (artificial) utero by an excessively large application of testosterone. Of course, since this is mass-market science fiction, the tale ends happily. Vivian is saved from the devolved Bruno, marries her wealthy suitor, and has a "naturally born" son, catalyzing a dispute between Dr. Shaiman and the attorney-narrator as to who is the rightful grandfather (124). Yet, as is so often the case with mass-market science fiction, the romance plot and the optimistic conclusion are shadowed by some troubling questions about the social implications of science:

> Could she, after all, marry Daniel Laird? What was her legal age? Would the law hold her to her calendar age, or would it recognize her biological age? Was she a legal entity at all? . . . What would be the legal interpretation of "born"? . . . Surely Vivian looked, and acted, and seemed like a normal person. But, in following out the very letter of the law, must she be labeled a "processed person," a synthetic? The thought was ghastly. (108)

"The Synthetic Woman" draws on the embryological and endocrinological experiments of the first three decades of the twentieth century to imagine a woman whose sexuality is out of synchrony with her chronological age, troubling her legal and social status, and indeed her very identity. Nearly forty years before the birth of the first test-tube baby, this tale of Vivian the "incubaby" forecasts the profound socio-legal and psychological disturbances that would result from scientific interventions in reproduction and aging. The story attempts to recontain the threat of these interventions in its concluding chapter, "All's Well," where we learn of the birth of Vivian's baby. "'Born naturally,' Shaiman cackled triumphantly. 'And I'm a grandfather!' 'You?' I snorted. '*I'm* the grandfather. Didn't I adopt her legally?'" (124). Destabilized by technoscientific interventions, biological and generational relations can only be sutured, now, by another form of expert intervention: the legal process. Now that birth and aging are subject to (re)construction, a cultural shift has occurred that requires the full force of law and medicine to remedy.

DR. VORONOFF
"Nora has had no baby."

The true story of Voronoff's Nora, a decade and more before the publication of "The Synthetic Woman," registered an early tremor in the large cultural shift Powell's science fiction story predicted. Some months after Voronoff announced her impregnation with "human sperms," the chimpanzee was found not to be pregnant after all. (Figure 4.) The experiment in surrogate mothering in a postmenopausal female subjected to hormone-induced rejuvenation had failed, and scientists would have to work for another sixty-plus years before they succeeded. Finally, in 1993–94, the western world saw a sudden rash of postmenopausal pregnancies following hormone treatment and the implantation of embryos (from donor ova). From the project of gland-grafting into a chimpanzee that gave us the (falsely pregnant) Nora through the fiction of a synthetically created baby subjected to rapid aging by hormone injections, to the actual hormone treatments and ovum transfer that gave us the (successfully pregnant) sixty-one-year-old Rossana Dalla Corte, we have arrived at a troubling new situation for women.[24] A convergence of the two major technologies to be exerted on women's bodies in the twentieth century—reproductive technology and what used to be known as rejuvenation therapy—is being exploited to produce a drastic narrowing of woman's site of agency, from the world of political and social relations to her own body.

My point is not that either of these two technologies is *inherently* constructed to limit women's options; at earlier moments each could have been shaped to be emancipatory. Now, however, they risk being deployed to reinforce each other, making each a matter of coercion rather than choice, technoscientific intervention rather than personal action.[25] Synthetic woman, indeed. Yet to conclude in the mode of modernist paranoia, satisfying as it is, neglects the more complex tail end of this story. If in its popular cultural image, between 1935 and 1985, hormone therapy seemed to cling to the asymmetrical control project of modernity, focused more on the female patient to be "normalized" or synthesized by a male medical profession, still a subterranean discourse of male rejuvenation through hormone therapy has always also existed, practiced out of the public eye, in exclusive Harley Street surgeries, Manhattan clinics, or Swiss spas.[26] And the last decade has seen signs in mainstream medicine of a more postmodern and complex attitude toward both hormone treatment and the nature of maleness and femaleness. The new medical speciality, andrology, has come into being, its presence marked by a new medical publication, the *Journal of Andrology* (Oodshorn, "A Natural Order of Things" 129; see also Niemi). A study by the University of Pittsburgh Medical School is assessing the medical impact of a scrotal testosterone patch; other studies by the National Institute on Aging, the Medical College of Wisconsin, and the University of Pennsylvania School of Medicine have been looking at the replacement of growth hormone, testosterone, and other less well-known hormones (Brody, "Restoring," "Growth"). Having begun with the technoscientific notion of linear progress in improving the human "product," rejuvenation therapy and reproductive technology may have shifted to a postmodern construction of the human life course. Dedicated to blurring its constitutive categories (the fixed biological life stages of parenthood and generationality), both projects may now serve a new construction of birth and aging, as exemplified in the notion of the postmenopausal mother.[27] These conjoined narratives—of Nora and Rossana Dalla Corte, of reproductive technology and rejuvenation therapy, of *Black Oxen* and *New Lives for Old*, of synthetic women and postmenopausal mothers—suggest five questions that we should ask about the ways we approach (theoretically and personally) the experiences of giving birth and of aging.

1. I have argued elsewhere that reproductive technology has shifted our perspective on reproduction, so that problems with conception, gestation, or birth are now viewed not as occasional natural occurrences, but as unnatural events that must be policed medically. This shift may have a parallel in our treatment of the aging process. To adapt a question from Dr. Peter Snyder of the Pittsburgh study of male hormone replacement therapy, we might wonder: "whether these bodily changes [infertility/aging] represent a condition in need of treatment or whether the changes are physiologically normal aspects of [life] that men [and women] just have to accept" (qtd. in Brody, "Hormone").

2. If we "fight" aging through what I am calling rejuvenation therapy as we "fight" infertility through reproductive technology, for whom or what are we doing so? For love? Or, like Mary Zattiany, for agency? Do we even want to accept that either/or? If it is agency, where is that agency located? Only in our bodies, or in the world?

3. What can bodies or babies be, if they are not our products?

4. What collective responsibility are we overlooking when we conceptualize

both sorts of RT—rejuvenation therapy as well as reproductive technology—as individual choices?

5. How will we negotiate the boundaries of identity and subjectivity as both the beginnings and the ends of life become increasingly characterized by technoscientific collaborations with the human?

Not only do these intertwined narratives raise questions about the medical interventions into women's bodies that characterize modernity and postmodernity, but they also suggest some of the forces that come into play when a new medical field is struggling for legitimation. Between the falsely pregnant chimpanzee Nora and the successfully pregnant Rossana Dalla Corte, rejuvenation therapy and reproductive technology have emerged as asymmetrically situated in medical practice and research. Reproductive technology has forged a solid and profitable interdisciplinary home for itself in contemporary medical practice. In contrast, "rejuvenation therapy" has moved from a central position in the work of Voronoff, Benjamin, and Steinach in the early years of the twentieth century to a marginal position at present. It lingers mainly as an unacknowledged goal or a welcome by-product of more legitimate medical endeavors (from hormone therapy to dermatological uses of Retin-A) and as the continuing recipient of a strong phantasmatic investment expressed in mass-market tabloids and popular books on how to "stop the clock" and "beat aging" forever. Yet powerful cultural linkages still exist between reproductive technology and rejuvenation therapy, between fantasies of incubabies and of rejuvenates. We would do well to remain alert for those fantasies as they circulate through our experiences of orthodox medical practice.

NOTES

I thank Paul Brodwin and Stephen Katz for their comments on an earlier version of this essay.

1. The *New York Times* for 1923 has extensive coverage of the controversy around gland-grafting, particularly of the work of Voronoff and his colleague Heckel. For a sample of the *Times* coverage, see "Paris Doctors Lift Ban on Voronoff," *New York Times* 11 Jan. 1923: 44; "Surgeon Revivifies Col. E.H.R. Green," 30 Mar. 1923: 1; "Gland Treatment Spreads in America," 8 Apr. 1923: 2; "American Surgeons Active at Conference," 21 July 1923: 6; "Graft Gland on Horse," 30 July 1923: 13; "Rejuvenation Is Filmed," 9 Oct. 1923: 17; "Doctors Who Scoffed Now Hail Voronoff," 13 Oct. 1923: 15; "Declares Glands Do Not Rejuvenate," 14 Oct. 1923: 6; "New Blood for the Aged," 23 Nov. 1923: 3; "Old Timers Race in Prison: Show Up Well, Following Gland Transplanting Operations," 30 Nov. 1923: 2; and, in the *New York Times Magazine*, M. B. Levick, "Pursuit of the Elixir of Life: Dr. Steinach's Predecessors Had Recipes for Changing Old Men into Young in 1600 B.C.," 9 Sept. 1923: 9. For a wide-ranging popular discussion of these rejuvenation and age-

extension therapies, see McGrady and Langone. See also Lambert; Voronoff, *La Conquête*; Steinach; and Benjamin.

2. Julian Huxley's survey of rejuvenation therapies, which appeared in 1922 in the *Century Magazine*, was entitled "Searching for the Elixir of Life." In her survey of endocrine treatments, Ruth F. Wadsworth, M.D., assessed the rejuvenating effects of gland transplantation under the heading "The Fountain of Youth" with this dismissive conclusion: "In the present state of our knowledge, operations for rejuvenation are only pitiful. Ponce de Leon found more in Florida than we can find in the operating-room" (48). The tropes extend to the present day, too. A newspaper story on the discovery of the gene that causes Werner's syndrome, a disease of premature aging, quoted the principal investigator, Gerard Schellenberg of the Seattle Veterans Affairs Medical Center: "A kind of Holy Grail of aging research has been to find this gene" (Neergaard 1).

3. Kevles 251–68; and Nelkin and Lindee. See also Spanier 102–03.

4. For example, Frances Seymour, M.D., Medical Director of the National Research Foundation for Eugenic Alleviation of Sterility, Inc., enumerated the "dysgenic" traits that led her to rule out what she called "cross-artificial insemination" (or donor insemination) for infertile couples: "We refuse to aide [*sic*] a couple where the wife has an I.Q. less than 120 . . . or has any physical inheritable stigmata, any family history of inheritable disease or a short life expectancy." When she sent this letter to C. P. Blacker, General Secretary of the British Eugenics Society, he wrote Lord Horder, President of the Eugenics Society, recommending against Seymour's scheme for artificially inseminating European women with semen from American donors: "the central project [is] . . . impracticable, uncalled for, and intrinsically absurd." Note that Blacker does not quarrel with her definition of dysgenic traits, only with her scheme for post-war repopulation through international donor insemination.

5. Metchnikoff, whose brother was the subject of Tolstoy's *The Death of Ivan Ilych*, first used the term "gerontology" in *The Nature of Man* (Achenbaum 23–25).

6. These miraculous accounts include the accounts of supposed centenarian Luigi Cornaro or Englishman Thomas Parr, who allegedly lived to 152 years (Katz, "Imagining the Life-Span"). The miraculous, I would argue, did not so much disappear as transmute itself. With the advent of modernist age-extension and rejuvenation technologies, the impulse fueling these early-nineteenth-century tales of the miraculous was redirected to a more acceptably modern, scientific venue: science fiction. So what once produced tales of miraculous births, phenomenal longevity, and the fantasy of a marvelous eradication of death, now produced stories of scientific wonders, like the novels and stories of H. G. Wells and the flood of science fiction tales appearing in such magazines as *Amazing Stories*.

7. See Squier, *Babies in Bottles* 160, and "Interspecies Reproduction."

8. Thus "self-identity and the body become 'reflexively organized projects' which have to be sculpted from the complex plurality of choices offered by high modernity without moral guidance as to which should be selected" (Shilling 181). As Brian Turner elaborates it, "that is, the notion that the self has a history with trajectories, with self-conscious lifestyles, with modes of operation and development: in this context therefore, the self is not to be taken for granted, not a fact of the person as it were" (255).

9. By the middle of the nineteenth century, this focus on women's bodies was less

a sign of ideological unanimity than the reverse. Thus Mary Poovey argues that "the representation of woman was also a site of cultural contestation during the middle of the nineteenth century. These contests reveal . . . the extent to which any image that is important to a culture constitutes an arena of ideological construction rather than simple consolidation" (9). See also Jordanova; and Schiebinger. As I will discuss at greater length later, Nelly Oudshoorn has documented how doctors found easier access to a female than a male population pool, due largely to the increasing medicalization of childbirth and the social acceptability of viewing the incarcerated female body as a research reservoir (Oudshoorn, *Beyond the Natural Body* 80).

10. For Freud, there seems to have been something scientistic about the very workings of phantasy. Removed from the life course, it nonetheless was a distillate of the very essence of psychic life, not unlike Alexis Carrel's 1930s experiments with tissue-culturing that were so prominent a part of both reproductive technological and rejuvenation therapy discourse. As Jean Laplanche and J.-B. Pontalis write, "Freud presents phantasy as a unique *focal point* where it is possible to observe the process of *transition* between the different psychical systems *in vitro* . . ." (316). The association of old age with childhood, in visual and verbal imagery, is a prominent characteristic of western culture, as Jenny Hockey and Allison James have demonstrated. They argue that we choose to link the aged person metaphorically with the acceptably dependent child in order to "shield [ourselves] from the approaching vision of illegitimate social dependency in old age" (143). A similar link between child and aged person at times even functions as an uninterrogated trope in aging studies itself, as in the following passage: "Today there is a social construction of human lives which consists of the mild morning mist of childhood, the stage of education or training, the parallel stages of work and leisure, the stage of active retirement, and the dusk of old age" (Dahrendorf 92, qtd. in Conrad 68). My particular interest, however, is in the way that control of embryological and fetal development is constructed as parallel to control of the aging process, because beginning-of-life and end-of-life changes are understood in relation to each other. Rejuvenation therapies—as the attempt to exert medical scientific control over the aging process—thus represents the other, untold, half of the story that I told in my recent book, *Babies in Bottles*.

11. I draw my methodological model here from Bruno Latour.

12. Levick continues, "Whatever the validity of his claims, whatever the truth of criticism raised by the conservatives of the medical world against Steinach and against the gland transplantations of Dr. Serge Voronoff, the idea which they have brought forth in scientific terms has seeped into the popular mind like water into sand. For the mind of man has thirsted for this secret for untold centuries, has evolved from it legends, myths, heroes, whole religious systems, creating in manifold form the hope that is built on the desire to become as immortal as the sun" (9).

13. Although Cartwright doesn't explore it extensively, an additional ingredient in this filmic mix was modern nationalism. This impulse was apparent on October 9, 1923, when the *New York Times* reported the inaugural screening of "a motion picture film of the scientific work of Dr. Eugen Steinach of Vienna" made at the urging of none other than Dr. Hainisch, President of the Austrian Republic.

14. The title comes from Yeats's "Countess Cathleen" (Bodeen 224–25). As Alasdair D. F. Macrae reports: "In 1934 [Yeats] was sufficiently worried about a diminu-

tion of vigour, including sexual, that he arranged to undergo a surgical operation. The Steinach operation was widely rumoured to transplant glands from monkeys into the patient (hence the Dublin joke about Yeats as the Gland old Man!); in fact, what he had was a vasoligature and vasectomy of some sort. Whatever the sort, he immediately felt a surge of physical and psychological energy" (118).

15. The passage continues: "'Why isn't your head turned?' Clavering asked her one day when the sensation was about a month old. . . . 'You are the most famous woman in America and the pioneer of a revolution that may have lasting and momentous consequences on which we can only speculate vaguely today'" (215–16).

16. I disagree here with Lois Banner's reading of *Black Oxen*, which unaccountably sees it as depicting "the emotional damage caused by . . . the inevitable failure of" Mary's affair with a younger man ("The Meaning of Menopause" 15).

17. Snow's optimism on this last point anticipates his argument in *The Two Cultures* that there should be more traffic between science and literature, for it implicitly constructs both disciplines as working by accumulation; science, by an accumulation of experimental data, and literature, by accumulated insight. As Pilgrim and Callan agree, science "simply . . . must get better. It's the only organised human activity . . . and so it's bound to get more complete, whoever does it. So long as someone does it" (319). And literature improves because "consciousness is growing every day. It's growing by leaps and bounds since the discovery. That is the real effect of rejuvenation" (321).

18. I want to stress the surprising nature of both aspects of this phenomenon: the focus on women in the medical applications of hormone therapy, *and* the reframing of this not as *rejuvenation* but as health maintenance. Not only does it contradict Snow's stress on male rejuvenation, but it diverges from what social historian Lois Banner has characterized as "the constant leitmotif that aging men, as well as women, experience a climacteric." As she observes, "the notion of a 'grand climacteric' as a dangerous stage of life for men (occurring around the age of sixty-three) had been current for centuries, dating to Renaissance theorizations about life cycle development . . ." ("The Meaning of Menopause" 7).

19. As Oudshoorn observes in *Beyond the Natural Body*, "In the 1920s and 1930s, the female body became the major object for hormone therapy. Female sex hormones became applied as universal drugs for a wide array of diseases in women. In this manner, sex endocrinologists constructed the image of the hormonal woman: it was the female body that became increasingly subjected to hormonal treatment. Compared to women, the introduction of sex hormones had rather minor consequences for men. Although endocrinologists created a market for male sex hormones, male sex hormone therapy was introduced for only a relatively small number of medical indications" (110).

20. Francis Ford Coppola's *Jack*, appearing in summer 1996, capitalized on the surge of interest in the hormonal bases of aging that accompanied the discovery of this gene, giving the public the story of "a 10-year-old with a disease that makes his body age four times as fast as his mind" (Hewitt 15c).

21. Arguably, the popular press's romanticization of the plight of infertile women has made it possible for a wide range of research activities, from embryo experimentation to fetal tissue culturing, to garner funding and support under the aegis of "reproductive" technology, while the press hoopla around unsubstantiated claims of rejuvenation and the resistance to notions of extending a woman's non-repro-

ductive sexuality have made it necessary for endocrinology and gerontology to drastically de-emphasize the rejuvenation aspects of their project in order to maintain scientific status.

22. For a discussion of the debates between feminists about reproductive technology, see the introduction to my book *Babies in Bottles*.

23. As Oudshoorn points out, "It was only after 1929 that scientists could assess the identity of sex hormones with chemical methods, thanks to developments in organic chemistry in the area of steroid and lipoid compounds. Sex hormones—classified as steroids—could now be chemically identified and isolated (Long Hall 1975). Female sex hormones were first chemically isolated from the urine of horses and pregnant women in 1929. In 1932, English and German chemists classified female sex hormones as steroid substances, and a calorimetric test was developed to detect the presence of female sex hormone in organisms (Walsh 1985). Male sex hormones were first isolated from men's urine in 1931 and were classified two years later in the same group of chemical substances as female sex hormones: the steroids" (*Beyond the Natural Body* 29).

24. Schmidt, "Birth to a 59-Year-Old Raises British Ethical Storm," *New York Times* 29 Dec. 1993: A1+; "Why She's 61 and Pregnant," *Newsday* 29 Dec. 1993: 6; "Modern Maternity," *New York Times* 3 Jan. 1994: A22.

25. Those of us interested in the medical treatment of aging may be moved to repeat a question first posed in 1993, after the rash of postmenopausal pregnancies. We could even dedicate this question to Nora the chimpanzee, gland-graft recipient, and potential postmenopausal mother: "if women can have ovarian transplants, will it be even less acceptable for them to grow old without fighting it through medical intervention?" This question was first raised by Dr. Susan Sherwin, professor of Philosophy and Women's Studies at Dalhousie University in Nova Scotia. As Dr. Sherwin has observed, "An enormous industry has grown up in recent years to postpone or prevent menopause through hormone replacement therapy; now reproductive life can also be prolonged. There are questions of what we value in women" (qtd. in Kolata C12).

26. I am grateful to Phyllis Mansfield for this information.

27. My thanks to Stephen Katz for this suggestion.

WORKS CITED

Achenbaum, W. Andrew. *Crossing Frontiers: Gerontology Emerges as a Science*. Cambridge: Cambridge UP, 1995.

Altman, Lawrence K. "Studying Rare Disorder, Scientists Find Gene Affecting Aging." *New York Times* 12 Apr. 1996: A27.

"Ape-Child?" *Time* 16 Aug. 1926: 16.

Atherton, Gertrude. *Black Oxen*. New York: Boni, 1923.

Banner, Lois. "The Meaning of Menopause: Aging and Its Historical Contexts in the Twentieth Century." Working Paper No. 3, Fall-Winter 1989–90. Center for Twentieth Century Studies. University of Wisconsin-Milwaukee.

———. *In Full Flower: Aging Women, Power, and Sexuality*. New York: Knopf, 1992.

Benjamin, Harry. "The Reactivation of Women." Haire 564–73.

Blacker, C. P. Letter to Lord Horder, 2nd November, 1943. Eugenics Society Papers, D.6, Contemporary Medical Archives Center, the Wellcome Institute for the History of Medicine, London, England.

Bodeen, DeWitt. "Black Oxen." *Magill's Survey of Cinema Silent Films*. Ed. Frank N. Magill. Vol. 1. Englewood Cliffs: Salem, 1982. 223–25.

Brody, Jane E. "Restoring Ebbing Hormones May Slow Aging." *New York Times* 18 July 1995: C1, C3.

———. "Growth Hormone Fails to Reverse Effects of Aging, Researchers Say." *New York Times* 15 Apr. 1996: A13.

———. "Hormone Replacement for Men: When Does It Help?" *New York Times* 30 Aug. 1995: C8.

"Censorship Up in Far Monroe." *New York Times* 4 Oct. 1923: 22.

Conrad, Christoph. "Old Age in the Modern and Postmodern Western World." *Handbook of the Humanities and Aging*. Ed. Thomas R. Cole, David D. Van Tassel, and Robert Kastenbaum. New York: Springer, 1992. 62–95.

Dahrendorf, Ralf. *Life Chances: Approaches to Social and Political Theory*. Chicago: U of Chicago P, 1979.

de la Mothe, John. *C. P. Snow and the Struggle of Modernity*. Austin: U of Texas P, 1992.

"Declares Glands Do Not Rejuvenate." *New York Times* 14 Oct. 1923: 6.

"Doctors Who Scorned Now Hail Voronoff." *New York Times* 13 Oct. 1923: 15.

Featherstone, Mike, and Andrew Wernick, eds. *Images of Aging: Cultural Representations of Later Life*. New York: Routledge, 1995.

Haire, Norman, ed. *Sexual Reform Congress*. London: Kegan, 1930.

Hewitt, Chris. "*Jack*, Coppola a Movie Mismatch." *Centre Daily Times* 9 Aug. 1996: 15c.

Hirschfeld, Magnus. "Presidential Address: The Development and Scope of Sexology." Haire xi–xv.

Hockey, Jenny, and Allison James. "Back to Our Futures: Imaging a Second Childhood." Featherstone and Wernick 135–48.

Huxley, Julian. "Searching for the Elixir of Life." *Century Magazine* Feb. 1922: 621–29.

Jordanova, Ludmilla. *Sexual Visions: Images of Gender in Science and Medicine between the Eighteenth and Twentieth Centuries*. New York: Harvester, 1989.

Katz, Stephen. *Disciplining Old Age: The Formation of Gerontological Knowledge*. Charlottesville: UP of Virginia, 1996.

———. "Imagining the Life-Span: From Premodern Miracles to Postmodern Fantasies." Featherstone and Wernick 61–75.

Keller, Evelyn Fox. *Refiguring Life: Metaphors of Twentieth-Century Biology*. New York: Columbia UP, 1995.

Kevles, Daniel. *In the Name of Eugenics: Genetics and the Uses of Human Heredity*. Berkeley: U of California P, 1985.

Kolata, Gina. "Reproductive Revolution Is Jolting Old Views." *New York Times* 11 Jan. 1994: A1+.

Lambert, Gilles. *Conquest of Age: The Extraordinary Story of Dr. Paul Niehans*. New York: Rinehart, 1959.

Langone, John. *Long Life: What We Know and Are Learning about the Aging Process*. Boston: Little, 1978.

Laplanche, Jean, and J. B. Pontalis. *The Language of Psychoanalysis*. Trans. Donald Nicholson-Smith. New York: Norton, 1973.

Latour, Bruno. *Science in Action: How to Follow Scientists and Engineers through Society*. Cambridge: Harvard UP, 1987.

Levick, M. B. "Pursuit of the Elixir of Life: Dr. Steinach's Predecessors Had Recipes for Changing Old Men into Young in 1600 B.C." *New York Times Magazine* 9 Sept. 1923: 9.

Lisser, H. "Organotherapy, Present Achievements and Future Prospects." *Endocrinology: The Bulletin of the Association for the Study of Internal Secretions* 9 (Jan.-Feb. 1925): 1–20.

Macrae, Alasdair D. F. *W. B. Yeats: A Literary Life*. New York: St. Martin's, 1995.

McClure, Charlotte S. *Gertrude Atherton*. Boston: Twayne, 1979.

McGrady, Patrick M., Jr. *The Youth Doctors*. New York: Coward, 1968.

Metchnikoff, Elie. *The Nature of Man: Studies in Optimistic Philosophy*. New York: Putnam's, 1908.

"Modern Maternity." *New York Times* 3 Jan. 1994: A22.

Neergaard, Lauran. "Scientists Discover Gene Linked to Aging." *Centre Daily Times* 12 Apr. 1996: 1.

Nelkin, Dorothy, and M. Susan Lindee. *The DNA Mystique: The Gene as a Cultural Icon*. New York: Freeman, 1995.

Niemi, S. "Andrology as a Speciality: Its Origin." *Journal of Andrology* 8 (1987): 201–03.

Oppenheimer, Jane M. "Present Embryology." *Essays in the History of Embryology*. Cambridge: MIT P, 1967. 1–61.

Oudshoorn, Nelly. *Beyond the Natural Body: An Archaeology of Sex Hormones*. New York: Routledge, 1994.

———. "A Natural Order of Things? Reproductive Sciences and the Politics of Othering." *Future Natural: Nature, Science, Culture*. Ed. George Robertson, et al. London: Routledge, 1996. 122–32.

Poovey, Mary. *Uneven Developments: The Ideological Work of Gender in Mid-Victorian England*. Chicago: U of Chicago P, 1988.

Powell, Jeb. "The Synthetic Woman." *Amazing Stories* 14.7 (1940): 100–24.

Schiebinger, Londa. *The Mind Has No Sex? Women in the Origins of Modern Science*. Cambridge: Harvard UP, 1989.

Schmidt, Peter. "Six Hundred Rejuvenation Experiments." Haire 574–81.

Schmidt, William E. "Birth to a 59-Year-Old Raises British Ethical Storm." *New York Times* 29 Dec. 1993: A1+.

Seymour, Frances. "Artificial Insemination, Gynecology, Eugenics and Their Relation to the Post-World War II Rehabilitation Plan." Eugenics Society Papers, D.6, Contemporary Medical Archives Center, the Wellcome Institute for the History of Medicine, London, England.

Shilling, Chris. *The Body and Social Theory*. London: Sage, 1993.

Snow, C. P. *The Two Cultures and the Scientific Revolution*. New York: Cambridge UP, 1959.

———. *New Lives for Old*. London: Camelot, 1933.

Spanier, Bonnie. *Im/partial Science: Gender Ideology in Molecular Biology*. Bloomington: Indiana UP, 1995.

Squier, Susan. *Babies in Bottles: Twentieth-Century Visions of Reproductive Technology*. New Brunswick: Rutgers UP, 1994.

———. "Fetal Subjects and Maternal Objects. Reproductive Technology and the New Fetal/Maternal Relation." *The Journal of Medicine and Philosophy* 21 (1996): 515–35.

———. "Interspecies Reproduction: Xenogenic Desire and the Feminist Implications for Health." *Cultural Studies*, forthcoming.

Steinach, Eugen. *Sex and Life: Forty Years of Biological and Medical Experiments*. New York: Viking, 1940.

Tiefer, Leonore. "A Feminist Perspective on Sexology and Sexuality." *Feminist Thought and the Structure of Knowledge*. Ed. Mary McCanney Gergen. New York: New York UP, 1988. 16–26.

Turner, Brian. "Aging and Identity: Some Reflections on the Somatization of the Self." Featherstone and Wernick 245–60.

Voronoff, Serge. *La Conquête de la vie*. Paris: Bibliothèque-Charpentier, 1928.

———. *The Sources of Life*. Boston: Humphreys, 1943.

"Voronoff and Steinach." *Time* 30 July 1923: 19–20.

Wadsworth, Ruth F. "Ain't Nature Gland!" *Colliers* 7 Dec. 1929: 22+.

"Why She's 61 and Pregnant." *Newsday* 29 Dec. 1993: 6.

Witkowski, J. A. "Optimistic Analysis—Chemical Embryology in Cambridge 1920–1942." *Medical History* 31 (1987): 247–68.

Wolff, Charlotte. *Magnus Hirschfeld: A Portrait of a Pioneer in Sexology*. London: Quartet, 1986.

Young, Robert. *Colonial Desire: Hybridity in Theory, Culture, and Race*. London: Routledge, 1995.

Charcot's Older Women
Bodies of Knowledge at the Interface of Aging Studies and Women's Studies

Stephen Katz

On the one hand, it seems that gerontology has been a haven for women scholars and practitioners, and for the interests of older women. Even a cursory glance at the development of the field in North America reveals the important contributions made by women in the United States such as Ruth Cavan, Carroll Estes, Meredith Minkler, Bernice Neugarten, Matilda White Riley, and Ethel Shanas.[1] In Canada, women such as Neena Chappell, Anne Martin-Matthews, Sheila Neysmith, and Blossom Wigdor, among many others, have inspired much of Canadian gerontology's major theoretical interventions and academic achievements. As well, gender issues have surfaced significantly within gerontology, especially in studies of care giving, retirement, intergenerational relations, and health services. Much recent work on women and aging, including collections of essays and special issues of journals, attests to the strength of this development.[2] And on a popular level, the fact that celebrated feminists such as Betty Friedan, Germaine Greer, and Gloria Steinem have turned their attention to aging and written personal accounts of the subject, also reveals that the link between age and gender is a crucial one. In fact, as Julie McMullin reminds us, aging studies in general has made it quite obvious that one simply doesn't study old people, but older women and older men (37).

On the other hand, both women's studies and aging studies have accused each of ignoring the other. In 1993 Beth Hess, in her afterword to the special issue of the *Journal of Aging Studies* on socialist feminism, observed that it was easier to bring women into gerontological professional associations, such as the Gerontological Society, than it was, and is, to "bring new perspectives into the research agenda and dominant paradigms of academic gerontology, even though the majority of elderly in modern societies are female, and even though as a relatively new and low-status field, gerontology was more welcoming to women than other fields" (195). Further, it has been pointed out that gerontological considerations of gender, however widespread, often suffer from the "gender-as-variable" or the "add-and-stir" dilemma, that is, that gender is not developed as a politically sophisticated and theoretically innovative impetus for rethinking the diversity of older women's lives, but rather is "added" in an empirical fashion to an already constituted gerontological vision of social relations. As an example we might consider the distinction advanced by Sheila Neysmith between "caring for" and "caring about." According to Neysmith, "caring for" is based on enumerating the "specification of tasks associated with the activities of daily living," while "caring about" involves the often invisible "emotional and mental labour" behind such tasks, the understanding of which would require historical critiques of gender as a social construction and caring-practices as social problems (115).

In their introduction to the collection *Connecting Gender and Ageing: A Sociological Approach*, editors Sara Arber and Jay Ginn offer another reason why gender is reduced to a variable. The quantitative and policy-driven imperatives of mainstream gerontology, they conclude, are at methodological variance with the qualitative and theory-driven mandates of feminist scholarship. In the end, according to Julie McMullin, gender-as-variable approaches result either in "gender ageing theory," where gender is added to sociological approaches to aging, or "feminist ageing theory," where age relations are added to feminist theory—and neither approach is adequate to the task of integrating gender and age (31).

While women's studies have reproached gender-blind and theory-poor work in gerontology, they have also come under parallel criticism from gerontologists and researchers in associated aging studies. Beginning perhaps with Myrna Lewis and Robert Butler's 1972 charged essay "Why Is Women's Lib Ignoring Old Women?" and Donna Beeson's 1975 "Women in Studies of Aging," a series of articles and books have followed that have targeted feminisms and feminists for not taking the extra step and bridging anti-sexism with anti-ageism, women abuse with elder abuse, and women's liberation with elder liberation in both heterosexual and lesbian dimensions.[3] Some of the reasons for such neglect have been attributed to the young age of most feminist scholars and, as Shulamit Reinharz rightly observes, because "feminists, just as everybody else, have been socialized in our aging-phobic and geronto-phobic culture" (507). More profoundly, as Kathleen Woodward suggests, the insistence that "anatomy is not destiny" has led feminists to disregard how, in old age, anatomy is —unavoidably—destiny, and that "we cannot detach the body in decline from the meanings we attach to old age" (19).

Given their entangled connections, where then might women's studies and aging studies join together to enliven scholarly exploration and theoretical critique and transform the various inequities foisted upon human difference in our society? One important area is empowerment, Meredith Minkler suggests. Another is making explicit the link between sexism and ageism so that, in the words of Reinharz, "the major contribution that the issue of aging can make to feminism is the mandate to re-examine all feminist theory in light of this dimension. And the major contribution that feminism can make for those concerned with aging is to provide a model and some of the personnel of a successful social movement" (512). Jon Hendricks and Sheila Neysmith both urge that aging studies re-examine its foundational premises by taking into consideration feminist revampings of biased scientific objectivity and the emotional conditions of qualitative research. Attention to the rhetoric of age studies is also critical. Innovations in language and critical scrutiny of metaphors can shake up and feminize gerontological conventions. Sarah F. Pearlman's coining of "Late Mid-Life Astonishment" as a new developmental transition for women between the ages of fifty and sixty is just such a case in print.

To contribute to this project of connecting women's studies and aging studies, I want here to turn to the rise of gerontological knowledge itself, especially to the epistemological centrality of bodies, both gendered and aged, to the formation of gerontological knowledge.[4] How have bodies of knowledge and knowledge of bodies co-constituted each other? While my recent book *Disciplining Old Age* runs off after this question in the direction of Foucault's work, gender is not its main focus. This essay, then, is about missing bodies—specifically, the missing bodies of older women in the history of gerontological literature inspired by the great nineteenth-century French clinician, Jean-Martin Charcot, doyen of Paris's Salpêtrière Hospital for women. My specific focus is Charcot's *Clinical Lectures on the Diseases of Old Age*, originally published in France in 1867, with a second edition in 1874. In 1881 two English translations appeared: the first by William Tuke for the New Sydenham Society in London, and the second an American edition promoted by physician Alfred Loomis who added his own essays and lectures (the American edition is the source material for this essay). In *Disciplining Old Age* I, like other cultural gerontologists, position Charcot's text as the point of departure for a critique of the founders of gerontology and geriatrics such as Elie Metchnikoff who coined the term "gerontology," Ignatz Nascher who invented geriatrics, and G. Stanley Hall who brought old age into the purview of psychology. I find myself now struck less by the book's reputation as a founding scientific text that sparked the medicalization of old age, than by the basis of its subject material: the women stuck in Paris's immense Salpêtrière Hospital. While most histories on gerontology, aging, and old age accent the canonical power of Charcot's text, few of them comment on the bodies and identities of these women who formed gerontology's first institutionalized population of aged subjects. As far as I know, the feminist literature has also evaded them. Thus Charcot's text not only stands at the contested interface between the practices of scientific culture, technologies of difference, and the corporeal worlds of older women, but also discloses the absence of the critical traffic that should be passing between aging studies and women's studies. As well, it signals the barrier between the sociology of the body and the history of medicine. Thus here I explore the ways in which Charcot's work, the disciplinary imperatives of the human sciences, and the sexual politics of the Salpêtrière Hospital—all so crucial to feminist and cultural histories of hysteria—came together in the late nineteenth century to inaugurate a distinct knowledge about old age and a problematization of its subjects.

I. CHARCOT AND THE SALPÊTRIÈRE

The name Salpêtrière comes from "saltpeter," the Paris hospital having originally been part of a sixteenth-century arsenal. By the mid 1600s it had become a public hospital for destitute women and prostitutes; later it also became a women's prison. According to Christopher Goetz, in the seventeenth and eighteenth centuries the Salpêtrière was the largest asylum in Europe, holding between 5000 and 8000 persons at a time when the entire population of Paris was only 500,000. "Part asylum, part prison, part old people's home," in the words of Mark Micale, "this remarkable hybrid institution housed for over two centuries every imaginable form of social and medical 'misfit' from the lowliest sectors of Parisian life" ("The Salpêtrière in the Age of Charcot" 707). Its reputation as a terrible and terrifying place of confinement on the edge of the city, what Yannick Ripa refers to as the "capital of female suffering" in mid nineteenth-century Paris (9), did not prevent it from becoming a popular and frequently visited site where its unfortunate inmates were subjected to the humiliation of public display and exhibition.

The first medical facility appeared at the Salpêtrière in the early 1780s, over 130 years after its founding. Philippe Pinel (1745–1826), the celebrated liberal reformer of the early nineteenth century, transformed the Salpêtrière through such changes as improved nutrition, the removal of chains, and the demolition of the old basement cells. In turn, these changes opened the Salpêtrière to a new generation of medical researchers for by 1850 the Salpêtrière "offered an untapped and incomparable variety of patient material" (Goetz xxiii). It was into this space of untapped and incomparable patient material, the majority of it female and much of it elderly, that Jean-Martin Charcot stepped, first as an intern between 1848–52 and later, after passing his exams in 1862, as an attending physician, professor, and chief medical officer. Charcot stayed at the Salpêtrière until his death in 1893, remaking the hospital into a world-renowned site of medical authority and a cultural center for the innovation of photographic techniques, the perfection of the art of public lectures, and the demonstration of fascinating new therapies based on hypnosis and electric shock.

With its 5000 patients, the late-nineteenth-century Salpêtrière provided Charcot with the opportunity to enlarge through his own authority the stature of the medical profession in Parisian culture. Inside the hospital Charcot reclassified patients, amassed data, oversaw new scientific facilities, and added a publications press to handle the outpouring of published material. By 1886 the Salpêtrière had over 100 buildings on fifty-one hectares of land. Often compared to Napoleon, Charcot was indeed the emperor of a countersite or "heterotopia" in the sense that Foucault gave to the term: the Salpêtrière was "a kind of effectively enacted utopia in which the real sites, all the other real sites that can be found within the culture, are simultaneously represented, contested, and inverted" (24). According to Jan Goldstein, outside the hospital Charcot entertained Paris's medical, literary, and political elites at the Tuesday soirées at his sumptuous residence which was outfitted with, among other things, Asian antiques and Gobelins tapestries. In the year after Charcot's death in 1893, a street in Paris bore his name as did a number of diseases, disorders, and medical techniques which he discovered.

The force that articulated the inside and the outside of this world of the Salpêtrière was the Charcot lectures. First held in regular wards and later in a new amphitheatre, his lectures were well-publicized, precisely prepared and memorized, and delivered with dramatic panache. An American physician visiting the Salpêtrière reported, for example, that Charcot's lectures "left on the mind of the student a series of mental pictures of patients and of lessons which no amount of private study could possibly produce" (qtd. in Goetz xxx). Charcot's orchestration of medical theatrics involved props, diagrams, photographs, pharmaceutical gadgetry, and most importantly, the patients; or better, the patients' bodies: the silenced, material resources manipulated by Charcot to ground his theories and astonish his audiences. Because it was the Salpêtrière, these bodies were female, a crucial fact that I will elaborate in a moment. The point to be emphasized here, however, is that Charcot, his lectures, and the bodies of his female patients intersected at angles that disciplined medical knowledge as the showpiece of Parisian modernity and scientific progress. At the center of this intersection was Charcot's recreation of hysteria as a predominant pathology. The important, rich feminist and critical histories of hysteria have argued persuasively that much of the success of the Charcotian enterprise depended on its construction of hysteria as a proliferative, positivist, and performative science.[5] Building on this work, I raise a further question: why have scholars paid such little attention to the senilization of women's bodies in light of their sophisticated analysis of hysteria?

According to Jan Goldstein, hysteria was a way of proliferating and widening a zone of nervous diseases intermediate between sanity and insanity, the normal and the pathological, and the physical and the psychological. Under Charcot's reign the physicians and psychiatrists at the Salpêtrière, especially those eager to be acknowledged by him, happened to discover more women suffering from hysteria and classified more kinds of observations and problems as hysterical than did their counterparts at other institutions. Photographs documenting case histories of hysterical women were collected in three volumes of *Iconogra-*

phie photographique de la Salpêtrière (1876–77, 1878, 1879–80) (see Didi-Huberman). In fact the establishment of photography studios at the hospital was inspired by the disciplinary will to represent, circulate, and codify this new horizon of female suffering. Between 1882 and 1893 Charcot, according to Daphne de Marneffe, devoted over one-third of his lectures to the subject of hysteria, some of which Freud heard when he studied at the Salpêtrière between October 1885 and February 1886 and whose influence would remain with him back in Vienna. Thus, hysteria was a proliferative discursive machine whose parts—texts, bodies, photographs, lectures, case studies, careers, and rhetorics—produced a knowledge of femininity that eclipsed all the alternatives. This leads to a second point, which is that the science of hysteria was an intensely positivist one.

Charcot's medical beliefs in the evidential powers of observation, the scrupulous keeping of records, the pathologizing mapping of patients' bodies and, above all, the disavowal of religious or premodern perspectives—all point to his faith in positivism. As he says in the introduction to his lectures on old age: "The new physiology absolutely refuses to look upon life as a mysterious and supernatural influence which acts as its caprice dictates, freeing itself from its law. . . . It purposes to bring all the vital manifestations of a complex organism to workings of certain apparatuses, and the action of the latter to the properties of certain tissues of certain well-defined elements. It does not seek to find out the essence or the *why* of things" (12). In terms of hysteria, Charcot's positivism was a challenge to previously held religious or mystical ideas about demonic possession, witchcraft, and miracle cures. Positivism was also at the core of Charcot's methodology, based as it was on a mechanics of seeing and describing patients rather than of listening or responding to them. In his obituary to Charcot, Freud aptly describes him as "a *visuel*, a man who sees" (qtd. in Marneffe 93).

Critics have also pointed out that Charcot's positivist attempts to territorialize hysteria with such exactitude disclose the arbitrary, biased, and constructed nature of his theories and conclusions. Sander Gilman, for example, has explored the connection between Charcot's work on hysteria and contemporary racist and anti-Semitic discourses on heredity and degeneration.[6] Daphne de Marneffe has argued convincingly that "Charcot's and his colleagues' firm belief in their own objectivity itself constituted a threat to that very objectivity: first, by making them unable to question their own role in constructing the picture of the disease; and second, through their inability to see their own participation in recreating the pathogenic conditions of their patients' lives— neglect, lack of empathy, and exploitation" (106). Marneffe's focus on the lives of the patients brings us to the third and final point about Charcot's hysteria, which is that beneath its intellectual capital as a lofty human science, however discredited it was later to become, lay the realities of the outcast women of the Salpêtrière and their enactments of hysteria.

In 1870, the Salpêtrière restructured its wards so that women diagnosed with epilepsy and hysteria were put together. Charcot was in charge of both. Several commentators maintain that many of the women who exhibited uncontrollable movements and fits during Charcot's lectures on hysteria were in fact acting, even simulating and imitating the seizures of their epileptic ward-mates. Further, the medical authorities actually encouraged such stigmatizing chicanery with the result that a group of favorite hysterics became celebrated through the theatrics of Charcot's lectures. As Elaine Showalter has put it, the *grande hystérie* convulsive seizure was the showstopping "specialty of the house at the Salpêtrière" (150). Charcot was himself aware of this problem, but claimed that such dramatic manifestations were part of the disease.[7] Women diagnosed as hysterical may or may not have performed hysteria, but hysteria was a type of performance nevertheless: spectacular bodies did fantastical things, often under hypnotic conditions, in front of amused audiences under the watchful directorship of Charcot or one of his associates.

Thus, Charcot's hysteria, with its technical and institutional apparatuses and casts of patients, was a proliferative, positivist, and performative science. It invented an ontological depth to femininity with a stunning display of surfaces. An expansive literature from women's studies, cultural history, and psychiatry attests to hysteria's importance as a symbol of the raw sexualization of everyday life in western society.[8] With these insights in mind, I turn to explore Charcot's work on old age.

II. CHARCOT'S *CLINICAL LECTURES ON THE DISEASES OF OLD AGE*

Charcot's *Clinical Lectures on the Diseases of Old Age* consists of twenty-one lectures; in the 1881 American edition Alfred Loomis adds ten more of his own. In his introduction Charcot outlines clearly his intentions as a medical researcher and the institutional connection between the Salpêtrière and its elderly female population. Besides the "lunatics, idiots, and epileptics," he writes, the "remainder of the population of this asylum consists of about twenty-five hundred females, who, with some few exceptions, belong to the least-favored portion of society." He divides these women into two categories, the first of which is explicitly comprised of older women:

> The first is composed of women who are, in general, over seventy years of age—for the administrative statutes have so decided it—but who, in all respects, enjoy an habitual good health, although misery or desertion has put them under the protection of public aid. Here, gentlemen, is where we shall find the materials which will serve us in making a clinical history of the affections of the senile period of life.
>
> The second category comprises women of every age—smitten, for the

most part, with chronic, and, by repute, incurable diseases, which have reduced them to a condition of permanent infirmity. (17)

It is this first class of women—elderly, destitute, confined, but generally healthy—who, for Charcot, provided the cases and bodies for the advancement of geriatric research. The constitution of these women as clinical subjects also offered the opportunity for longitudinal study since, as Charcot notes, "we are here permitted to follow the patients through a long period of their existence, instead of being present only at a single episode of their history" (18).

Although Charcot elaborates his project to identify the pathologies of old age, given the limits of nineteenth-century positivist medical science we are left wondering how this project was realized in relation to the daily lives of the Salpêtrière's twenty-five hundred women. In certain cases Charcot does show how an individual case study contributes to the advancement of gerontological knowledge. An example is his discussion of a woman who is 103 years old and "in excellent health." Taking her temperature demonstrates that the body's temperature in old age is not lower than in the young, as previously believed; more importantly, Charcot insists that "rigorous observation shows us that, in certain respects, the organs of the aged perform their tasks with quite as much energy as those of adults" (24).

In other lectures Charcot's diagnoses raise pertinent questions about the relationships between class, poverty, and health in these women. For instance, in his lecture on rheumatism, Charcot observes that the disease is "one of the most common infirmities of females, at least those of the poorer classes," afflicting eight out of one hundred women at the Salpêtrière (38). Later he adds that about three-fourths of the women attacked with nodular rheumatism "ascribe it to the prolonged influence of damp cold" (151). Charcot raises important medical issues of family and generational relations in a related case, commenting: "there is now in the Salpêtrière a woman that has nodular rheumatism, whose *daughter* and *grand-daughter* are already suffering pains in the smaller joints. Here are three generations successively attacked with the same disease" (original emphasis; 149). This interesting statement suggests the fascinating possibility that perhaps there were generations of women associated with the Salpêtrière. In another passage on rheumatism Charcot concludes that "uterine functions" such as menopause and pregnancy influence the disease (153). How he actually learned this is a perplexity.

In spite of the occasional specific case, the lived world of Charcot's elderly women appears so very distant in his lectures, precisely in part because of his scientific and sexist biases, which also plague his work on hysteria. Notwithstanding the preponderance of women in the Salpêtrière, statistical standards and norms, for example, are often posed in male terms. In the introduction Charcot lists the attributes of the "external appearance of an old man" (such as dry and loose skin, gray hair, a toothless mouth, and stooped posture) as signs of "a general atrophy of the individual" (20–21). More egregiously, in discussing fevers and febrility in old age, Charcot compares the aged to children and adults, but here the pathological aged figure is female and the normal adult figure is male; here we also see that the category of the adult and the category of the aged are understood to be mutually exclusive (32–33). Masculine pronouns pepper the text. For instance, although he has been citing evidence from cases of female patients, Charcot concludes that "the patient suffers spontaneous pains, quite vague in character, which pass off as he walks" (145). Here we find a clear instance of how medical studies have generally identified the male body as the human body, even when the bodies on which such knowledge was built were female. In this instance too we see how, at the same time, the pathology of the bodily aging is associated with the female body. As feminist critics have argued, nineteenth- and early-twentieth-century representations of women's bodies and experiences often portrayed them as incoherent, biologically fouled misadventures. Here, in a microcosm, we see the confusing imbrication of the pathologies associated with aging with the politics of gender and youth. The old man is, as it were, feminized, and old age for both men and women is divorced from adulthood, thus implicitly infantilizing the older person.

The bodies of women, then, were at the site of the birth of geriatrics. But it is difficult to recover both their behavior and the texture of their lives not only because of Charcot's scientific and sexist biases but also because outside of his introductory remarks, he was not obliged by his nineteenth-century audience to talk about them.[9] This obligation belongs to us, however, and presents us with an exciting opportunity to see how the problematization of women and of old age emerged in tandem. Looking critically at what has been and can be made of this opportunity forms the last part of this paper.

III. CHARCOT'S OLDER WOMEN, AGING STUDIES, AND WOMEN'S STUDIES

Gerontologists and historians of old age rightfully acknowledge Charcot's *Clinical Lectures* as a landmark text. Widely circulated, highly regarded, and often quoted, Charcot's work became a model text exemplifying how clinical research on the senile pathology of old age should be done. According to Joseph Freeman, *Clinical Lectures on the Diseases of Old Age* provided the "measuring stick" for geriatrics (*Aging: Its History and Literature* 46; see also "A Centenary Essay"). Indeed for many years Charcot's *Lectures* "remained," in the words of Trevor Howell, "the only serious textbook of Geriatrics" (62). Interestingly enough, W. Andrew Achenbaum has pointed out that one of the reasons why the *Lectures* was "the most influential work of the period" is that the timing of the translations gave it "an importance as a model for future research in the United States far beyond its actual merits" because it corresponded to the advances being made in American medicine at the time.[10]

When it comes to discussing the women behind the science, work in aging studies has been far less discerning, however. The fact that Charcot's research was carried out in a poorhouse for women is usually raised but then left unelaborated. Cultural historian Thomas Cole points out that "Charcot's *Clinical Lectures* rarely gave much thought to the class or gender of the population on which they were based" and that "Charcot viewed these women as exemplars of physiological old age" (201) but does not explore the question further. Jean-Pierre Bois includes only a short discussion of the Salpêtrière in his history of old age in France. Even Simone de Beauvoir, who asserts that "the Salpêtrière may be looked upon as the nucleus of the first geriatric establishment" (26), fails to go the extra step and speak about its women.

A more prominent exception to the trend is the work of Peter Stearns who, in his research on aging in France, insists that the old women of the Salpêtrière, rather than the old men of the Bicêtre, attracted more geriatric research because of the pervasive negative cultural attitudes toward older women. As he concludes in "Old Women: Some Historical Observations," "The available empirical evidence was combined with the judgement on menopause to cast postmenopausal women generally into limbo, with aesthetic contempt added to the whole unsavory brew" (45). Furthermore, as he writes in *Old Age in European Society*, the women, "being poor, often female and, above all, always old," were "open to any manipulative feelings a researcher might have in any event" (85). For Stearns, the distorted vision of female sexuality in part created the discursive background to the development of geriatric medicine. Stearns also astutely concludes as early as 1980 that one of the reasons why "older women have received relatively little attention from historians" is that "attention has been riveted on problems preoccupying other age groups, particularly those groups coinciding with the ages of a student audience and of the new generation of women's historians" (44).

Marjorie Feinson, in her essay "Where Are the Women in the History of Aging?" published five years later, cites Stearns's statement to buoy her contention that, despite the "proliferation of feminist scholarship, the historical experiences of *aging women* have not been examined systematically by either historians of aging, family historians, or feminist historians" (436). She proposes to remedy the situation by recovering from the past "shards of evidence," an apt archaeological metaphor that signals the scattered, unarticulated state of women's studies of aging at the time.[11] For Feinson these shards would include evidence from witch-hunting and demographic history.

Feinson's dilemma is similar to the ones I've been proposing with regard to Charcot's older women. On the one hand, we are witnessing a creative explosion of aging studies, women's studies, the sociology of the body and of medicine, and the cultural critique of modernity and its somber institutions; and on the other hand, such important research seems to be missing some of the key material sites where women, aging, and the production of knowledge were co-disciplined. Thus, Charcot and the older women of the Salpêtrière represent an important puzzle whose shards or pieces await rejoining. One piece is the wider recognition of Charcot as a founding geriatrician and his lectures as disciplinary practices. As Brian Livesley has observed, "Charcot has not been identified previously as a Geriatrician and this aspect of his medical practice and expertise has been overlooked because of the great importance attached to his reputation as a Neurologist" (26). Another piece is treating critical hysteria studies and the acuity of its research on women's bodies and professional discourses as a model for the historical study of aging and women. Was geriatrics, like hysteria, a proliferative, positivist, and performative science? Were theatrics and silenced patients as integral to Charcot's lectures on old age as they were to the lectures on hysteria? What relationship held between the sexual politics of old age and hysteria at the Salpêtrière? A third piece of the puzzle might be the representation of women in the gerontological texts that followed *Clinical Lectures on the Diseases of Old Age* whose authors commend Charcot and take up his positivist zeal to discover the secrets of the aged body.

Finally, there is a crucial piece of the puzzle lodged in the dilemma of silence on Charcot's older women; a dilemma that invites future research. Here I am thinking of interdisciplinary research on women and bodies such as, for example, the recent excellent collection *Deviant Bodies: Critical Perspectives on Difference in Science and Popular Culture*, edited by Jennifer Terry and Jacqueline Urla. *Deviant Bodies* does not include discussions of aging bodies (or more specifically of Charcot or the Salpêtrière), but nonetheless it does provoke thought about them. The "generic human body" in the West embodies the binarisms of western culture in its "more oppressive forms," the editors state, a binarism that I would argue includes that of young and old (4). Hopefully we can look forward to this kind of critical work, one represented also by essays in this volume, alighting on Charcot's older women and drawing the connections between aging studies and women's studies a step closer together.

In their short professional histories, gerontology and geriatrics have attempted to shore up their disciplinary status by canonizing a set of nineteenth-century and early-twentieth-century scientific texts. The male authors of these texts, most of them medical researchers, attempted to define the bodily, psychological, and demographic characteristics of aging and old age. In so doing, they tended to misrepresent women or neglect them altogether. Charcot's *Clinical Lectures on the Diseases of Old Age* is an important case in point. In spite of his ultimately narrow and negative portrayals of the aging process, his text is regarded as a pioneering articulation of clinical research and professional ingenuity, even by his critics. Importantly, his *Lectures* were based on a relatively unknown but very large group of elderly women confined to the Salpêtrière Hospital who provided the subjects, cases, and bodies for his research.

Charcot is well known within feminist cultural studies and psychoanalytic theory for his work with the hysterical bodies of women, bodies that we have come to assume were all young and, through Freud, were expressing in their theatricalized display a repressed sexuality, a desire that also has a long tradition of being associated with young women, not older women. Given that Charcot based his research on the "senile period of life" of women, it is ironic that gerontological knowledge as it has developed throughout the first three-quarters of the century in particular has worked to silence, regulate, and negate women's bodies. At the same time, however, Charcot's Salpêtrière was, as I have suggested, a heterotopia. It is crucial to remember that not only was Charcot studying old age but he was studying it by virtue of the bodies of older women, most of whom were over seventy and enjoyed, as he put it, "an habitual good health." Concealed in the *Clinical Lectures*, in other words, is the model of late life as characterized by a preponderance of health, one embodied in women. Thus Charcot's Salpêtrière also animated and articulated the capacities, self-images, and energies of women in subject-constituting ways, ways which, I hope, we will learn more about in future research on the older women of this celebrated site.

NOTES

This is a revised and expanded version of a paper that was delivered at the conference on "Women and Aging: Bodies, Cultures, Generations" and published in the *Journal of Women and Aging* 9.4 (1997): 73–87. I am also grateful to the members of the Institute of Gerontology at the University of Michigan, in particular to W. Andrew Achenbaum, for their comments.

1. Neugarten, in fact, states: "I do not recall a single instance in which the fact that I was a woman worked to my disadvantage, or to my advantage, in my education or in my research career. I had encouragement all the way" (98).

2. See, for example, Leonard and Nichols; Baines et al.; and the following special issues of journals geared to interests of women: *The Gerontologist* 19.3 (1979), *Educational Gerontology* 17.2 (1991), and the *Journal of Aging Studies* 7.2 (1993). See also the *Journal of Women and Aging*.

3. Examples are Macdonald and Rich; Copper and Rice; Rosenthal; and Pearsall. As Corinne T. Field notes in her illuminating dissertation research, early American feminists such as Elizabeth Cady Stanton (1815–1902), while well-recognized for their struggles for women's rights, are overlooked for their contributions to new ideals around female aging and the life course. Field's question is a valuable one: have the feminist chroniclers of the women's movement sidelined the women's movement's innovations in age studies?

4. See Laws; and Oberg.

5. See, for example, Beizer; Smith-Rosenberg; and the many essays by Mark Micale on hysteria, both male and female, as well as his book *Approaching Hysteria*.

6. On Charcot's hereditarian ideas, see Dowgibbin; and Pick for a fuller account of the nineteenth- and early-twentieth-century European preoccupation with questions of heredity and degeneration.

7. See McCarren's "'The Symptomatic Act' Circa 1900" in which she underscores the performative politics of Charcotian medicine by revisiting hysteria from the perspective of modern dance and staging. See also Owen. Sigmund Freud, in a letter to his future wife on November 24, 1885 describing Charcot's lectures as engrossing and exhausting, also emphasizes the importance of performance to Charcot's lectures: my "brain is sated as after an evening in the theatre" (qtd. in Major 388).

8. In "Hysteria Male/Hysteria Female," Mark Micale outlines the development of Charcot's work on male hysteria. Although Charcot's model of hysteria was based on his observation of women, he published case histories of over sixty male hysterics and treated many others. In 1882, at his request, the Salpêtrière opened a new *Service des hommes*, a twenty-person infirmary for males suffering from nervous disorders. For Charcot, women "fall ill due to their vulnerable emotional natures and an inability to control their feelings. In contrast, men get sick from working, drinking, fighting, and fornicating too much. However, in members of both sexes, it should be noted, hysteria typically resulted from an *excess* of prescribed gender behaviours" (208).

9. Loomis's lectures seem to use mostly male examples though they also intermix women and men as if they constituted one—neuter—patient of old age. Loomis's lectures close the book, ending with one on "senile hypertrophy of the prostate gland," an obvious male condition. Loomis, a New York City physician and professor of pathology, delivered his lectures at New York's Bellevue Hospital.

10. The first quotation is from Achenbaum's *Crossing Frontiers* (37); the second from his *Old Age in the New Land* (43). Other scholars point to Charcot's influential role in medicalizing old age. See Cole; Haber; and Kirk.

11. In addition to the work mentioned above which is critical of women's studies for its neglect of old age and explores the relation between feminism and aging studies, see Arber and Ginn; Davis et al.; and the issues of *Journal of Women and Aging*. Historical studies on women and old age include Jalland and Hooper; Premo; and Gratton and Haber.

WORKS CITED

Achenbaum, W. Andrew. *Crossing Frontiers: Gerontology Emerges as a Science*. New York: Cambridge UP, 1995.

———. *Old Age in the New Land: The American Experience since 1790*. Baltimore: Johns Hopkins UP, 1978.

Arber, Sara, and Jay Ginn. "'Only Connect': Gender Relations and Ageing." *Connecting Gender and Ageing: A Sociological Approach*. Ed. Sara Arber and Jay Ginn. Buckingham: Open UP, 1995. 1–14.

———. "The Invisibility of Age: Gender and Class in Later Life." *Sociological Review* 39.2 (1991): 260–91.

Baines, Carol, Patricia Evans, and Sheila Neysmith, eds. *Women's Caring: Feminist Perspectives on Social Welfare*. Toronto: McClelland & Stewart, 1991.

Beauvoir, Simone de. *Old Age*. Trans. Patrick O'Brian. Middlesex: Penguin, 1972.

Beeson, Donna. "Women in Studies of Aging: A Critique and Suggestion." *Social Problems* 23 (1975): 52–59.

Beizer, Janet. *Ventriloquized Bodies: Narratives of Hysteria in Nineteenth-Century France*. Ithaca: Cornell UP, 1994.

Bois, Jean-Pierre. *Les Vieux de Montaigne aux premières retraites*. Paris: Librairie Arthème Fayard, 1989.

Charcot, Jean-Martin, and Alfred L. Loomis. *Clinical Lectures on the Diseases of Old Age*. Trans. Leigh H. Hunt. New York: William Wood, 1881.

Cole, Thomas R. *The Journey of Life: A Cultural History of Aging in America*. New York: Cambridge UP, 1992.

Copper, Baba. *Over the Hill: Reflections on Ageism between Women*. Freedom: Crossing P, 1988.

Davis, Nancy D., Ellen Cole, and Esther D. Rothblum, eds. *Faces of Women and Aging*. New York: Harrington Park, 1993.

Didi-Huberman, George. *Invention de l'hystérie: Charcot et l'iconographie de la Salpêtrière*. Paris: Macula, 1982.

Dowgibbin, Ian R. *Inheriting Madness: Professionalization and Psychiatric Knowledge in Nineteenth-Century France*. Berkeley: U of California P, 1991.

Feinson, Marjorie Chary. "Where Are the Women in the History of Aging?" *Social Science History* 9.4 (1985): 429–52.

Field, Corrine T. "Age and Gender in the U.S. Women's Rights Movement: Elizabeth Cady Stanton's 'Development Ideal,' 1848–1902." Paper presented at the conference on Agehood and Childhood. Odense University, Denmark. 7–9 Apr. 1997.

Foucault, Michel. "Of Other Spaces." Trans. Jay Miskowiec. *Diacritics* 16.1 (1986): 22–27.

Freeman, Joseph T. "A Centenary Essay: Charcot's Book." *The Gerontologist* 7.4 (1967): 286–90.

———. *Aging: Its History and Literature*. New York: Human Sciences P, 1979.

Gilman, Sander. *Disease and Representation: Images of Illness from Madness to AIDS*. Ithaca: Cornell UP, 1988.

———. *The Jew's Body*. New York: Routledge, 1991.

Goetz, Christopher G., trans. and ed. *Charcot the Clinician: The Tuesday Lectures*. New York: Raven, 1987.

Goldstein, Jan. *Console and Classify: The French Psychiatric Profession in the Nineteenth Century*. New York: Cambridge UP, 1987.

Gratton, Brian, and Carole Haber. "In Search of 'Intimacy at a Distance': Family History from the Perspective of Elderly Women." *Journal of Aging Studies* 7.2 (1993): 183–94.

Haber, Carole. *Beyond Sixty-Five: The Dilemma of Old Age in America's Past*. New York: Cambridge UP, 1983.

Hendricks, Jon. "Recognizing the Relativity of Gender in Aging Research." *Journal of Aging Studies* 7.2 (1993): 111–16.

Hess, Beth B. "Afterward: A Personal Reflection." *Journal of Aging Studies* 7.2 (1993): 195–96.

Howell, Tevor H. "Charcot's Lectures on Senile Diseases." *Age and Ageing* 17 (1988): 61–62.

Jalland, Patricia, and John Hooper, eds. *Women from Birth to Death: The Female Life Cycle in Britain 1830–1914.* Atlantic Highlands: Humanities P, 1986.

Katz, Stephen. *Disciplining Old Age: The Formation of Gerontological Knowledge.* Charlottesville: UP of Virginia, 1996.

Kirk, Henning. "Geriatric Medicine and the Categorisation of Old Age—The Historical Linkage." *Ageing and Society* 12.4 (1992): 483–97.

Laws, Glenda. "Understanding Ageism: Lessons from Feminism and Postmodernism." *The Gerontologist* 35.1 (1995): 112–18.

Leonard, Peter, and Barbara Nichols, eds. *Gender, Aging and the State.* Montreal: Black Rose, 1994.

Lewis, Myrna I., and Robert N. Butler. "Why Is Women's Lib Ignoring Old Women?" *International Journal of Aging and Human Development* 3 (1972): 223–31.

Livesley, Brian. "The Osler Lecture of 1975: Galen, George III and Geriatrics." London: Society of Apothecaries, 1975.

Macdonald, Barbara, and Cynthia Rich. *Look Me in the Eye: Old Women, Aging and Ageism.* San Francisco: Spinsters Ink, 1984.

Major, René. "The Revolution of Hysteria." *International Journal of Psycho-Analysis* 55 (1974): 385–92.

Marneffe, Daphne de. "Looking and Listening: The Construction of Clinical Knowledge in Charcot and Freud." *Signs: Journal of Women and Culture* 17.1 (1991): 71–111.

McCarren, Felicia. "The 'Symptomatic Act' Circa 1900: Hysteria, Hypnosis, Electricity, Dance." *Critical Inquiry* 21.4 (1995): 748–74.

McMullin, Julie. "Theorizing Age and Gender Relations." *Connecting Gender and Ageing: A Sociological Approach.* Ed. Sara Arber and Jay Ginn. Buckingham: Open UP, 1995. 30–41.

Micale, Mark S. *Approaching Hysteria: Disease and Its Interpretation.* Princeton: Princeton UP, 1995.

———. "Hysteria and Its Historiography: A Review of Past and Present Writings I, II." *History of Science* 27 (1989): 223–61, 319–51.

———. "Hysteria Male/Hysteria Female: Reflections on Comparative Gender Construction in Nineteenth-Century France and Britain." *Science and Sensibility: Gender and Scientific Enquiry, 1780–1945.* Ed. Marina Benjamin. Oxford: Basil Blackwell, 1991. 200–39.

———. "The Salpêtrière in the Age of Charcot: An Institutional Perspective on Medical History in the Late Nineteenth Century." *Journal of Contemporary History* 20.4 (1985): 703–31.

Minkler, Meredith. "Critical Perspectives on Ageing: New Challenges for Gerontology." *Ageing and Society* 16.4 (1996): 467–87.

Neugarten, Bernice L. "The Aging Society and My Academic Life." *Sociological Lives.* Ed. Matilda White Riley. Newbury Park: Sage, 1988. 91–106.

Neysmith, Sheila M. "Feminist Methodologies: A Consideration of Principles and Practice for Research in Gerontology." *Canadian Journal on Aging* 14.1 (1995): 100–18.

Oberg, Peter. "The Absent Body—A Social Gerontological Paradox." *Ageing and Society* 16.6 (1996): 701–19.

Owen, A. R. G. *Hysteria, Hypnosis and Healing: The Work of J.-M. Charcot.* London: Garrett, 1971.

Pearlman, Sarah F. "Late Mid-Life Astonishment: Disruptions to Identity and Self-Esteem." *Faces of Women and Aging.* Ed. Nancy D. Davis, Ellen Cole, and Esther D. Rothblum. New York: Harrington Park, 1993. 1–12.

Pearsall, Marilyn, ed. *The Other within Us: Feminist Explorations of Women and Aging.* Boulder: Westview, 1997.

Pick, Daniel. *Faces of Degeneration: A European Disorder, 1848–1918.* Cambridge: Cambridge UP, 1989.

Premo, Terri L. *Winter Friends: Women Growing Old in the New Republic, 1785–1835.* Urbana: U of Illinois P, 1990.

Reinharz, Shulamit. "Friends of Foes: Gerontological and Feminist Theory." *Women's Studies International Forum* 9.5 (1986): 503–14.

Ripa, Yannick. *Women and Madness: The Incarceration of Women in Nineteenth-Century France.* Trans. C. du P. Menagé. Oxford: Polity, 1990.

Rosenthal, Evelyn R., ed. *Women, Aging and Ageism.* New York: Harrington Park, 1990.

Showalter, Elaine. *The Female Malady: Women, Madness, and English Culture, 1830–1980.* New York: Pantheon, 1985.

Smith-Rosenberg, Carroll. "The Hysterical Woman: Sex Roles and Role Conflict in Nineteenth-Century America." *Disorderly Conduct: Visions of Gender in Victorian America.* By Smith-Rosenberg. New York: Oxford UP, 1985. 197–216.

Stearns, Peter N. *Old Age in European Society: The Case of France.* London: Croom Helm, 1977.

———. "Old Women: Some Historical Observations." *Journal of Family History* 5.1 (1980): 44–57.

Terry, Jennifer, and Jacqueline Urla, eds. *Deviant Bodies: Critical Perspectives on Difference in Science and Popular Culture.* Bloomington: Indiana UP, 1995.

Woodward, Kathleen. *Aging and Its Discontents: Freud and Other Fictions.* Bloomington: Indiana UP, 1991.

PSYCHOANALYTIC THEORY AND AGING

Social Physics
Inertia, Energy, and Aging

Teresa Brennan

I. PREAMBLE

It has become habitual to think of the social as immaterial or unphysical, as something which does not enter into or physically affect the body. Despite the strong evidence of psychosomatic disorders, or the logical deductions that follow from the fact that words and images are physical entities as well as conveyors of meaning, social theory continues to think the relation between the physical and the social in terms where either the biological may (some claim) or may not determine the social, but where the social does not have material effects on the body. In other words, the only alternative to sociobiology,[1] which misconceives and reduces the relation at issue to one of biological determination, appears to be a "social" without physical materiality.

The theory of social physicality I have developed[2] is premised on the notion that the opposition between the social and the "biological" is itself misconceived to the extent that it conjures up an idea of the social as immaterial, as lacking matter and/or energy.[3] The opposition between the social and the biological was inbuilt to sociology's foundations: Durkheim, for instance, as Giddens has it, tried to identify the social as something specific and independent of biology and psychology (Giddens 86). But while I agree that the social is specific to itself and independent of biology, and that it also exists independently of *individual* psychology, the social as I will define it here is nonetheless physical. There is no such thing as an immaterial social factor. Moreover it is not that the biological determines the social. It is rather that the physicality of the social enters into and even determines biology, and for that matter, the environment. It follows that human organisms will have physical differences consequent on their different "socializations."[4]

In this essay I will elaborate on the theory of social physicality in relation to aging. We are all familiar with the discrepancies between those who age "well" and those who do not, between an apparent retardation of aging and its untimely acceleration. Such discrepancies suggest that a social level impinges on the biological level. At the same time, the fact of aging seems to legitimate the distinction between the social and the biological for the very reason that while some of us age poorly and some well, we all ultimately age. The thing that varies (how we age) is not the same as the thing that is varied (the fact of aging). The fact of aging is presented to us as a biological fact. But my point will be that the social variations or accelerations and retardations in how we age, while biological in their effects, have to have a material existence that involves something more than somatic biology. To say the same thing, the "social" that affects the body can be understood in terms of physics (this is what social physicality is about); the body of course is understood in terms of biology. So it would be more correct to say not that the social is biological, but that it is physical, a force that interacts with and affects the biological body.

The distinction between the physical and the biological, while frequently collapsed in the humanities and social sciences, is long-standing. But the distinction is needed. Apart from its use in explaining changes in the organism that are not solely consequent on biological developments, the distinction is necessary if one is to resolve a paradox: as Tim Ingold points out, "biology" is meant to be about the increasing differentiation of forms, and how organisms grow in distinctiveness (214).[5] I add that socialization by contrast is about how these organisms conform to common modes of behavior and interaction. If human organisms are subject to socialization, they should become more alike, and if socialization is physical, they should become more physically alike. The people of different epochs do seem to conform to a physical visual type (the medieval type, the modern type, and so on), and this would be something that would demand an explanation if its existence could be shown to extend beyond the eye of the artist. But the stronger point here is that any similarity between people, the very existence of types, is at odds to some degree with what makes them living beings. Increasing differentiation belongs to the living: biology is precisely the life science. If socialization is about similarity, it is, on the face of it, closer to death. Differentiation does not belong to death, which reduces all living organisms, no matter how distinctive they are, to a largely identical rubble. After the lapse of a little time, it is difficult and eventually impossible to identify a body: the process of decomposition is a process of homogenization of form.

It would be too much to say, too quickly, that sharing a tendency to homogenization tells us anything new about death, or about the social. Yet we may approach that conclusion more slowly through an argument that the social, by virtue of its physicality, constitutes a force that overlays and determines the extent to which we age "poorly."

The first step in this argument will be a brief return to Freud's psychophysics. The reason is that, while I have tried to show elsewhere that Freud provides us with some of the raw materials for understanding physicality, I want to develop those raw materials here in relation to aging. What is more, in taking psychophysics as the prototype for social physicality, I shall be able to draw a distinction between the phenomenon of aging and the phenomenon of being aged.[6] This will lead to the issue of the relation between social inertia, physics, and aging.

II. FREUD AND PSYCHOPHYSICS

In Freud's work, the terms "inertia," "entropy," and "rigidity" are keys to his notion of the psychophysical level, and of the singular nature of its materiality. It is no accident that Kathleen Woodward signposts each of these terms in her discussion of Freud and aging. Woodward notes first that "in *The Ego and the Id* Freud explicitly argues that as we mature biologically, we deflect the death instincts away from ourselves by virtue of the very strength of our bodies—by the development of 'the muscular apparatus.' We are invited to wonder what can happen when the body slows down in old age and can no longer, as it were, deflect the death instincts away from itself" (49). There is a connection here, Woodward argues, with a letter of Freud's to Lou Andreas-Salomé, in which he had said that he no longer wanted *to keep going ardently enough*. "The distinction is implicitly between *movement* and *rest*," Woodward concludes. "In terms of aging, then, we could link the life instincts with movement, and the death instincts with rest" (49).

Now this, in fact, is exactly the link Freud makes. Indeed, he sees the death instinct as an urge to restore an earlier state of things and as such "the expression of the inertia inherent in organic life" (*Beyond the Pleasure Principle* 68). Thus he links life with movement, and death with lack of motion, in a mistaken application of Newton's theory of inertia. It is mistaken because Newton's first and second laws do not mean that an inert state is necessarily still or without motion. Newton meant that a body will seek to return to the state of motion that is natural to it, and this seeking constitutes its inertia. The natural state of motion itself could vary from rapid to infinitesimal movement.

While Freud is mistaken about Newton, the mistake is productive because it bequeaths us a theory of how physical inertia is psychically constructed (even though Freud was unaware of this).[7] As I have indicated, its legacy also includes a prototype for understanding socially constructed inertia. Before elaborating on why and how this is so, let us turn to rigidity and entropy: both, as we shall see, are consequences of "inertia."

Rigidity is evoked by Woodward when she notes that Freud, again in a letter to Andreas-Salomé, described aging as the experience of "a crust of indifference creeping up . . . a way of beginning to grow inorganic" (48). "Psychical rigidity" is also what afflicts women long before it afflicts men. Men are still youthful at thirty; women are "rigid" and exhausted by the difficult development to femininity (Freud, "Femininity" 134–35). Elsewhere, Freud will tell us that rigidity is also associated with age ("Analysis Terminable and Interminable" 242). Later analysts will take him seriously, and advise against analysis for those over forty, on the grounds that the psyche is too set in its paths. And yet, the very process by which rigidity is produced means that its strength will vary in intensity, regardless of biological age. Some may be too rigid at forty. Others may not. It remains to see why.

Psychical rigidity (Freud's texts imply) comes about through an increase in "bound" as compared with "freely mobile" energy. If we inquire as to what freely mobile energy is, the only reply is that it is the state of energy before it is bound, and that energy has to be bound in order to learn from experience. Each experience creates a neuronal pathway, based on the memory of doing it right or wrong the first time. These pathways give us guidelines on how to respond the next time. It is the binding of energy, it seems, that gives the pathway its stability. In other words, the binding of energy and the corresponding creation of pathways are testaments to lessons. But they are also, once established, hard to give up, even when they stand in the way of new lessons, as we shall see. In infancy, the lessons which lead to pathways begin with the first hallucination.

A hallucination is the manifestation of a wish.[8] It presents whatever we want as if it were here and now, but the hallucination's agreeability in these respects is countermanded if we believe it to be real. We do not act, because we believe our need has been met, and yet that very need is frustrated. To preempt this unpromising outcome, hallucinations are superseded by another psychical process. Freud later refers to it as the secondary process, or sometimes, simply, as the work of the ego. The ego's work is not to dream, but to act on reality. It diverts "the excitation arising from the need" (for instance, for food) and fixes it on screaming or crying loudly for attention from another, who is, in fact, able to attend to one's needs (*Interpretation of Dreams* 599).

But in infancy, and often in later life (depending on the wish), no action in the real world is an alternative. In which case, the only thing to do with hallucinations, whether they occur in infancy or in dreams, is to repress them. There is also a negative inducement to this repression, a quantitative build up of excitation accompanying the expectation of satisfaction, to borrow from Freud's terminology. This is true for any organism, including human organisms. An organism expecting to be fed or loved (or, one might add, flattered or given money) gears itself up, it puts all systems on go, and then when it is not satisfied, it is left with the amassed excitement and no release for it. It is profoundly frustrated, for what else is frustration other than a buildup of expectant energy without an outlet? It is worse off than it was when the hallucination was first called forth.

Thus human organisms learned that the hallucination was ultimately productive of more unpleasure than pleasure, and learning this, we repressed it. But repression always involves a "persistent expenditure of force" ("Repression" 151). One does not just put the matter to one side. Keeping it to one side and outside of consciousness requires a continuous exercise of force, which Freud is quite clear disables us because the energy used is not available for other pursuits. Repression is also a restriction on future mobility. It makes us less of actors in the world than we would otherwise be, because it leaves us out of sync with the movement of the freely mobile energy into which we are born.

Overall the repression of hallucination and the related binding of energy is the first step in creating an alternative psychophysical world. This has to be so: if energy bound in repression leaves people less mobile, it leaves them in a world with different energetic coordinates. The second step is the binding of energy in pathways.[9] Not every bound pathway, every lesson of experience, requires a repression, but it does require a binding of energy. On the one hand, this binding is supremely useful in that it saves one from endlessly repeating the same mistake. And yet, on the other hand, it should also mean that the greater one's experience, the more energy is bound in pathways, and the less is one's access to freely mobile energy, and hence presumably the less one's ability to adapt. This situation would create an alternate psychophysical world because it would lead to rigidity, a rigidity which was a response to psychical rather than genetic dictates. It would also lead to entropy, insofar as this too Freud associates with aging. He explicitly equates rigidity with "a kind of psychical entropy," and both rigidity and entropy with loss of plasticity ("Analysis Terminable and Interminable" 241–42).[10]

Why then, would anyone seek to make and inhabit this slower, repressed, entropic world? Freud's own answer to the question, a question he phrased himself in terms of the organism's tendency to "inertia" (misunderstood by him as the final rest of Nirvana), was that while this inert trend was the physical disposition of the organism, "biology" came to the rescue. The organism kept going because it was not bound only by the laws of physics. This is an unsatisfactory recourse, and I discuss it below. Freud might also mention the notion of the unpleasure caused by hallucinations in this connection, and reiterate, as in fact he did, that pathways based on experience were also a considerable psychical gain. But the question invites another answer.

The answer is that this newly created psychophysical world, and this world alone, guarantees a self which sees things from its own standpoint. Or rather, it can be used to explain how a self-centered standpoint comes into existence. Moreover, it is because this new self-centered being sees things from its own standpoint that it ages, and ages poorly rather than well. The rudiments for analyzing how this self comes into being have already been laid out. I will now elucidate them, and in doing so, develop the idea that the new psychophysical world is a slower one, which lags behind the freely mobile energy of the world we have lost.

Given how thoroughly modern physics attests to the indissoluble connections between energy distribution and space-time, the alternative energy distribution contingent on repression and bound pathways should result in different spatio-temporal coordinates. And, indeed, time and space feature directly in hallucinatory activity and its repression. Hallucination is about instant gratification: the denial of, or other means of overcoming, time and space. It is a response to the delay between the perception of a need or a wish and its fulfillment. But hallucination, as we have seen, only leads to more unpleasure because satisfaction is not forthcoming. It leads in this sense to pain.

Richard Wollheim has suggested that it is the projection of pain that establishes the ego's first concept of inside and outside. The Kleinian explanation—for it is this that Wollheim develops—of what Freud regarded as an especially primitive form of defense is that projection is an attempt at locating pain outside the self.[11] In projecting its pain outside itself, in establishing an "outside," the infant is also establishing a spatial sense. However, it can only do this if it has a fixed point from which to project. How this fixed point originates has not really been addressed in the psychoanalytic literature. But by my argument, a fixed point has to be born of the repression of the first hallucination, precisely because this repression binds energy by turning it *back* against other psychical activity. Indeed I would submit that primal repression and the formation of a fixed point, and with it the nascent ego, are the same thing.[12] There are other reasons for thinking this is so.

When the organism decides to repress an hallucination, to follow in the future one pathway rather than another, it is per force deciding to remember. Its memory, the condition of its having a sense of its own history, begins with that first fixed point. The fixed point henceforth functions both as a condition of the sense of history, and because of its fixity, as a sense of causality, or time (how one thing comes before and leads to another). Paradoxically, while repression keeps something in place and out of the time of freely mobile energy, it simultaneously creates a sense of time geared to the subject's own standpoint. The fixed point is thus the factor that sets the organism's sense of direction (from its own standpoint) through time (or to say the same thing, its projection of itself in space). Without a fixed point, there can be no direction. A little reflection makes this plain. To go somewhere, anywhere, there must be a point of departure, as well as a destination.[13] Durkheim himself said exactly this, when arguing that the social was the origin for the apparently pre-given Kantian categories of space and time (10). The account I am giving here may explain how those same categories are matched or internalized psychologically.

After establishing that first fixed point, a person will continue to repress and to erect bound pathways to deal with experience. But these subsequent repressions and pathways, as should now be plain, emanate from a fixed point which makes a person central to himself, or herself. It remains to be understood why it is that seeing the world from one's own standpoint intensifies the aging process (and ultimately the loss of form, which means that whatever form is, is it not the same as the ego).[14] I will introduce the discussion here by noting first that Freud associated anxiety with the death drive. And the death drive, as we have seen, is meant to be at work in the aging process. Yet Freud also, well before he posited the death drive, associated anxiety with a threat to the bound pathways which, by this analysis, constitute the self. It is the threat to the self involved in overturning these pathways, even when overturning them is beneficial, which causes stress.

The stress factor is plain enough in an example Freud provides of how the reluctance to enter upon a new pathway is strengthened by anxiety. He tells a story of how he installed a telephone to cope with emergencies. Then, "under the impact of a great anxiety," he forgot about the telephone and consequently did a great deal of needless scurrying. He forgot because the anxiety caused him to fall back on the familiar pathways he used to cope with emergencies, even though he had deliberately outmoded them (*Project for a Scientific Psychology* 357).

Anxiety is possibly the most complicated affect in psychological and physiological theory, as Walter Cannon long ago argued. It is meant to be the signal for when one's actual bodily survival is at stake. In the psychoanalytic literature anxiety also signals jeopardized vanity (it is a response to humiliation or the fear of humiliation), and as we have just seen, it also results from jeopardized familiarity. Anxiety, it would follow, is the ego's response to anything that threatens its established existence. This means its life; but it also means its established life, the world it knows, and the world in which it would like to be central, and where it is at least more centrally located than it may become in the world it knows not. In other words, from the foregoing analysis, we should feel anxiety not only when we doubt that we will go on living, but when we doubt or know that we will cease to live in the same way. Anxiety is felt when the self that has been lovingly crafted, the known self, is threatened with change. Of course reasoning this way, one must conclude that the ego and the death drive are intrinsically related. This idea is resisted in the psychoanalytic literature, where the ego is meant to be on the side of the life drive, if not equivalent to it.[15] But provided we allow that the ego is not all there is to the subject, that there is more to us than the collection of fixed points and pathways that constitute the ego, then the evident alliance between the ego and the drive toward death comes into focus. The argument brooks no other conclusion: the more we see things from our own fixed point, the stronger the ego. But the more we do this, the more sedimented our pathways become. The more sedimented they become, the less freely mobile energy we have, thus the more we age, and the closer we come to death.[16] Hence the "inorganic crust" that Freud felt growing about him as he aged. Hence too "psychical entropy" and inertia.

From this it should follow that an organism need not be subject to inertia and rigidity, to the "crust" of age, if it managed to retain its access to the freely mobile energy that was so abundant in its youth. One can resist psychically by keeping access to freely mobile energy, and this can be done (depending on class position) by any process from physical exercise and meditation to viewing an opera or play, all processes which cathect to that refreshing consciousness which is free of the self. Again, Freud, of course, does not put the matter this way. What he does is to doubt the inevitability of aging as a biological process, as Woodward notes, noting too that this makes no sense (46). Freud's arguments are indeed not very sensible on the face of it. He records how senescence can be postponed or dispensed with altogether in certain animalcula. As he writes in *Beyond the Pleasure Principle*, "If two of the animalculae, at the same moment before they show signs of senescence, are able to coalesce with each other, that is to 'conjugate' (soon after which they once more separate), they are saved from growing old and become 'rejuvenated'" (48). What is of interest in these animalcula is that their moment of coalescence involves merging with another. An organism that merges with another necessarily breaks down its own boundaries, or "crust" perhaps, as it does so.

How could this come about at the human level, and what would be at stake if it did? In general, Freud's appeals to biology are a problem. I indicated above that while Freud's model can be adapted to explain inertia intrapsychically, it leaves the problem of how we move at all, of how we overcome inertia as "a problem for biology" (see *Project for a Scientific Psychology*). That is to say, after Freud explained the tendency to psychical inertia in the terms discussed here, he explained it too well. When it came to accounting for tendencies that ran contrary to this inertia, he postulated that biology would one day fill the lacunae. But rather than invoking a nebulous biology, especially when it is meant to counter a physical trend, we might be better placed to answer questions about how organisms move and live despite their trend to inertia, and how they break down their "crusts" through interaction with others, by stepping outside the one-body psychology in which Freud framed his psychophysical explanations, and into territory where energy is understood in social terms. This will account for how it is that another can break down the "crust." It will also account for the phenomenon of "being aged."

III. SOCIAL INERTIA OR THE PHENOMENON OF "BEING AGED"

So far we have a theory of aging "from the inside." The problem with it is that it is unable as it stands to explain the all too evident exceptions. There are the self-centered people who gleam and flourish in middle age. By the same token, there is that most generous of creatures, Iris Murdoch's "mother of a very large family" whose goodness lies in her utter lack of selfishness, and who is often worn out before her time. To account for the overwhelming number of exceptions, the social ramifications of this theory need to be developed. This development is also necessary to provide an alternative to Freud's fallback to biology as a way to explain overcoming inertia.

In fact, the inadequacy of that biological fallback might be the best place to begin. It is a fallback that presupposes that biology is in actuality a domain entirely apart from physics, when it is not. The soma too is subject to laws of physics, to entropy and dissolution, to the gradual wear and tear of aging which can be explained so well by an extension of Freud's psychophysics. Nonetheless, there must be, as Freud surmised, some counterforce which combats the effects of inertia, even for only three score years and ten. This counterforce, I surmise, can either be intrinsic to the organism, a given supply of energy which runs out over time, or it can be energy from without, from beyond the fixed lines and confines the organism erects in order to experience itself as separate, while robbing itself of its real distinction. I do not know if the organism is born with its "own" supply of energy, although it is evidently born with access to such a supply: "freely mobile energy" after all is the material used in the construction of bound pathways and fixed points. Leaving that to one side: there is no doubt that growth is enhanced from without by the care and nurturance of others.

The living attention of another is an excellent candidate for the supply of energy which is drawn on in combating inertia. Living attention, as I have argued, is energy (*Interpretation of the Flesh* 83ff). This attentive energy facilitates; it enables one both to divert energy along the pathways that construct a self-concept, and to have energy available with which to grow, and later, not to age. At any level of life it is an expansive energy. But if energy from another can enhance, it can also diminish. To see why, let us begin again with rigidity, the rigidity that is meant to mark femininity, as well as age.

Freud explained feminine rigidity as a convoluted psychical response to the rigors of the transition to femininity from masculinity. But the rigidity of femininity can also be explained by the notion that the sedimentation of fixed points and pathways is somehow intensified. This intensification can be seen as an overlay, a projection by the masculine other of all the rigidity he wants to dispose of in himself (or herself) (*Interpretation of the Flesh* 83ff). He wants to dispose of it, but he does not in doing so wish to lose the fixed point that is the core of his (or her) separate identity. He can have his cake and eat it too if another becomes that point of fixity for him, and in doing so carries the rigidity to which fixity leads. This is what the feminine party does for the masculine, and in doing it, she also directs her attentive energy toward him. The masculine party benefits then in two ways: he is able to dispose of fixity by projecting it outwards, a process that is otherwise known as projecting the death drive externally; at the same time he receives a facilitating, attentive energy from the party he restricts while guaranteeing his own identity.

All this happens at an interactive level. This interaction is social but in a limited sense: it takes place between two bodies. It is an interaction that works well enough for explaining how an older man might "break down his crust" through the agency of a younger woman, an interaction which involves femininity as well as age.[17] But there are two other levels of the social which come into this explanation. The first is the level of the image. The second is the level of social inertia.

The image of age in this culture is a powerful force in itself, one which exists and which is conveyed independently of particular interpersonal encounters. The image mainly involves dictates about what the not-young are no longer capable of doing or being. Notions of this capacity are of course skewed in favor of men, perhaps because women of a certain age no longer put out the same supply of attentive energy; women too, as they age, increase the fixed points and pathways that extend the ego's compass. But while masculine beings of either sex might stave off aging by an unconscious parasitical process, men and women alike are subject to the greater cruelty, to the pervading negative images of incapacity, enforced economically by imperatives ranging from compulsory retirement to a not-so-tactful exemption from service. Whether the not-young are or are not capable, they are certainly going to be less capable after receiving an image telling them that this is the case. It is an image which increases anxiety at the most basic level of bodily survival, and because of this, it actually contributes to incapacity. For anxiety, as we have seen, abets forgetfulness. The greater the anxiety, the less the capacity to form and follow new pathways. The greater the forgetfulness, the more likely one is to appear fundamentally old, even senile.[18]

The power of the image is not independent of energy; it is not, as we saw at the outset, immaterial. When the masculine party projects that in himself which is rigid and entropic, by definition he projects that which is anxiety-ridden and confusing, the excess of emotions that interfere with his capability. He projects them into another, who then carries these affects for him, and as he does so he conveys a negative image of the feminine party's capacity. Indeed the image he gives cannot be separated from the affects in its train. But the process of "being aged" is not something that happens in all dyadic relations: it is not—at least in the main—something the child projects onto the parent. The source of the negative image of aging is rather a plural event, a compound of images scattered throughout the culture. But just as the negative image intensifies rigidity in femininity, so it does in aging; it is why we can speak of "being aged," in that the recipient of the image is passive. Those who receive the image are not only dealing with the sedimentation and fixity engendered by their own points and pathways; they are also, like the feminine beings, dealing with the refuse engendered by the striving of others, with an overlay formed out of projected rigidity and entropy.

But where, in the case of those who are aged, does this refuse come from? I may have been overly hasty in concluding that "being aged" is not produced by a projection in a dyadic relation, as with the projection of the masculine party's anxiety and aggression onto the feminine. Adolescence is precisely a time of

denigrating the capabilities of parents, and of fierce insistence that the preceding generation is passé and accordingly limited. And yet, for all its fierceness,
there is something about the adolescent declamatory mode that lacks real force,
in the physical sense in which I use that term. That declamatory mode has more
sound than bite, and more the sense of a resistance to something that was or is
projected onto it. There is also the plain empirical fact that the aging of the
preceding generation is out of sync, as a rule, with the onslaught of adolescence. (While I am qualifying claims about dyadic aging, it may be time to add
that in earlier work, I failed to stress or even note the way in which plural social
events also contribute to feminine rigidity. There is, of course, no doubt that the
compound of negative images of the feminine diminishes the capacity of any
being who is styled feminine, insofar as the image is not fully resisted—and
resistance expends its own energy. Having said that, I see no reason to retract
the broader claim that feminization is primarily a projection from a masculine
other, a masculine other who, of course, may be of either sex.)

The origin of the refuse projected in "being aged" remains to be explained.
This brings us to a third level of the social, the level of social inertia. It cannot
be fully distinguished from the social level of the image, because the image is an
energetic event. The work of David Bohm demonstrates that this is so not only
on the basis of a deduction from psychoanalytic material. As K. H. Pribram
explains, Bohm's research on holographic phenomena shows how the image
and the energy are inseparable. In a hologram, the whole is implicated or
enfolded in each part. Even the smallest particle will contain the space-time
image of a given whole. Moreover, the very prevalence of images in modernity,
the fact that late western culture is image-ridden and that this, as the philosopher Zygmunt Bauman might put it, undermines its ethics, may owe something
to the trend of objectification that is indubitably part of social inertia.

Objectification, in the most literal sense, involves making something or
someone into an object. Objectification, by this account, is tied to social inertia
because inertia is tied to the proliferation of objects. Objects in the form of
commodities have proliferated over the past three centuries, following the shift
to a mode of production which fosters objectification in the form of commodification (although the objectification of this epoch extends beyond commodification: to give peoples a fixed image of who and what they are is, of course, to
objectify them). We may speak of *social* inertia because the construction of
"fixed points" and pathways that produce psychical inertia are paralleled in the
social by the construction of objects, as commodities or artifacts which bind the
energy of nature in the same way that freely mobile energy is bound psychically.[19] When energy is bound in the form of an object, meaning a commodity
that cannot reproduce itself, it is unable to reenter the generative cycles of
nature. It is out of time with those cycles, just as bound energy constitutes a
different time, a time at odds with the freely mobile energy into which the
subject is born. The new social realm, through its proliferation of commodities,
creates entropy, rigidity, and an inertia which slows the world down.

It is critical to remember here that in discussing the psyche, we were speaking of a *constructed* inertia rather than the tendency to the natural state of rest that constitutes the inertia of Newtonian physics. Just as the constructed inertia of the psyche leads to a slowing down of the organism, in that more energy is bound in fixed points and pathways, so can the same process be observed in the social. When commodities are constructed as objects or artifacts which cannot reproduce themselves, they constitute an accumulation of fixed points which are inert, in the sense of unmoved, and thus slower *relative to the generative cycles of nature*. They can not reenter natural reproduction, unless they are biodegradable, and even then they take much longer to "catch up." These commodities are also constructed in relations of production which demand new and extensive pathways of acquisition: means of transport and communication to bring the raw materials of production and the labor that transforms them to increasingly centralized points of construction (cities). These pathways parallel those of the psyche to an extent. They are rigid because the more they are used, the more they are depended upon: take away the roadways and the cars and you incapacitate the average citizen. But there is a difference between the rigid pathways and inert points of the social and those of the psyche: the former are spatial pathways; those of the psyche are historical, in that they are based on memory. In the social, the spatial pathways embody the history of the region, but only to the extent that they are not consumed in the construction of new spatial pathways of extended acquisition. There are few Italies, where the Via Appia has been the main pathway from Rome to Naples for nearly three thousand years.

While the new pathways appear to speed things up (as production, consumption, and geographical mobility geared to both gets faster and faster), they actually slow things down because they retard the pace at which nature overall reproduces itself. However, the idea that the world is getting slower (and perhaps, like the rigid psyche, less intelligent) is profoundly counterintuitive when everything appears to be daily speedier. This is so much the case that we need to address what the new speed is composed of. By this account, the new speed is written out of the accumulation of fixed points or objects: these constitute a sequence that registers as a temporal sense. They do so in this way. As with the psyche, each fixed point that needs to be formed involves an event and causality. Fixity is both a response to a cause and gives rise to a causal sense, and thus to a sense of direction. We are able to think in terms of A leading to B if and only if the position of A is secure. But the more secure it is, and the more fixed points we have established, the stronger the sense of causality. Moreover, without the fixed points there would be nothing that constituted the direction necessary to the passing of time, that is to say, linear time as we know it. Accordingly, the sense of the passing of linear time increases as fixed points and pathways increase.[20]

IV. SOCIAL INERTIA: PHYSICS AND AGING

The next question obviously should concern the energetic effects on space-time concepts of this new extrusion, this constructed inertia, onto the earth, if not the cosmos. But at this point it becomes difficult to pursue this enquiry further, because the questions to which it gives rise have as yet no analogue in the armory of physics. Bohm pointed out that "conceptualizations in physics had for centuries been based on the use of lenses which objectify (indeed the lenses of telescopes and microscopes are called objectives). Lenses make objects, particles."[21] But what if the objects themselves change the physical continuum, so that the physicist who perceives the world in terms of objects is perceiving the present social reality correctly, while remaining oblivious to its historical contingency? If the physical reality becomes more objective, by virtue of becoming detached from the "implicate order" (Bohm's term for the intricate unity of thought and matter), it would appear that sight is the sense most involved in the shift to social objectivism: sight, more than any other sense, perceives in terms of objects, and a proliferation of objects accordingly feeds the culture of images.

This returns us to the question of the refuse to which social inertia gives rise. Simply put, there should be refuse from the proliferation of objects precisely because they are excerpted from the natural world, and the transformations they undergo as they become commodities do not use all that is excerpted; there is a necessary debris. Just as its bound energy weighs heavily on the psyche, so too must socially constructed fixities be felt as a pressure, and not just in the sense that they are pollutants. Their very existence means there is less that is living in the atmosphere. This new dead weight must be felt as a pressure because any presence which cannot escape, which is confined by its inability to reenter the flow, is felt as a pressure. Pressure is when a force builds up because it is has no discharge. If the organism is sensitive to the presence of living things, so too must it have a response to deadly fixities. And if the death drive directed from one subject to another ages them, either because its burden is accepted or because the resistance to it also extracts a toll, then it is as well to remember here that the death drive by this argument is nothing more than the accumulation of fixed points and sedimented pathways: it is the pressure of bound energy. The energy bound in socially constructed fixities should also generate a death drive. Obviously it is not directed against specific subjects (unless there is some law whereby the more vibrant exercise a fatal attraction for the relatively mortified). But the refuse of social inertia should, by this logic, nonetheless accelerate the process of being aged. Not that the refuse which ages is distributed fairly, no more than are the bought forms of resistance to it (everything from a massage to a sunny retirement, which loosen and lighten up the old fixed points). The point rather is that pressure seeks release from its containment. While the bound energy of dead things has lost the forms that connected them with the flow of life, it will nonetheless be drawn to the living, and seek entry there by whatever door is open.

All this, of course, is completely hypothetical, and as I mentioned above, any concretization is handicapped by the utter lack of relevant enquiries in the physical and social sciences alike. But I would like to pursue this hypothetical direction a little further before reining it in. The reason is that this direction is yielding a concept of social pressure which is at least consistent with the connection made by various social theorists, most notably Max Weber and Hannah Arendt, between the rise of the social and industrialization. By my reasoning so far, the extent to which social pressure is produced, and with it the relative force of social inertia, will vary according to the balance between technology and nature in any given territory. Not for nothing, then, has Arendt described the social as a phenomenon born of the last three centuries, for this is the period over which the pressure increases, the pressure in the most literal sense of that word. However, we can now give a precise content to the "social," seeing it as a force and a pressure with definite determinants. The most social of environments, the one in which the social matters most, is the one with the most intense concentration of history and technology, and with the least geographical relief in the form of living things and free space, in which maximum pressure is generated in consequence. The rise and spread of this social is the most significant object for study by sociology, and it can never be studied independently of the territories it extrudes upon, like an unavoidable gaseous emission.

If I am right and social pressure is a physically tangible force contingent on industrialization, then we are in a position to buttress Durkheim's remarkable argument in *The Elementary Forms of Religious Life* that "it is far from true that the more individualized we are, the more elementary we are" (274).[22] He is making the point that our social being is inseparable from our individual being, and for this reason it may not have anything individual about it. Our social being, by my account, involves a loss of distinctness, a loss of personal form, the stronger the social is as a force in a given environment: this is foreshadowed by the alliance between fixity, aging, and death, and the notion of social pressure as embodying the force of accumulated fixities. Durkheim himself remained on the border of offering an energetic explanation, and taking his distance from it, as social science has done since.

As with the overlay in the case of the ego, the overlay that sediments and rigidifies, that prevents one seeing clearly and hearing distinctly, is it too much to hazard that the overlay of the social will also impair the capacity to take on broad fresh ideas and the new energy that accompanies them? In the same vein, we might then wonder if this is why on the coast of the unspoilt sea, or in the Highlands, one might find eyesight improving, or the reception of fresh ideas more free, for no other reason than that the social weighs less heavily there: there is less of the pressure whose intensity will vary according to the proliferation of fixed points in a given locale, together with the history that connects them in pathways that are familiar. Yet, these familiar pathways also constitute a form of organization, which is better by far than a mindless proliferation of technological fixed points, superseded or outmoded so rapidly that there is no time to assimilate the debris in the bound paths of history, or even the spatial pathways of extended acquisition. It is when the pathways become paths to nowhere that the social becomes senile. It becomes pure sociality without space or grace or meaning, where memories float back up from the past for a quick nostalgic charge, memories that are divorced from the energy that once made them cohere, and thus as quickly lost as they came.

NOTES

1. There is an excellent critique of sociobiology in Ingold.

2. See my *The Interpretation of the Flesh* and *History after Lacan*.

3. This physicality is unhappily disguised by one of those dichotomies that characterize the attempt to define a separate space for sociology, namely, the opposition between the social and the biological. By this argument, that dichotomy is as unreal as that between economics and society. On the function of these dichotomies, see Strathern and Leach. Ingold's outstanding article is also addressed to the relation between biology and anthropology (although it could as well be addressed to social science overall).

4. On the significance of the term "organism," see Ingold.

5. Hence, incidentally, the impossibility of "sociobiology," which argues that biology will make human beings act in the same way socially!

6. In addition, while Freud has been criticized by social and feminist theorists for his biologism to the point of tedium, meaning that he has been criticized for reductive explanation (he did say, "following Napoleon," that "anatomy is destiny"), Freud himself distinguished his biological accounts from his psychophysical theories. The term "psychophysics" is a nineteenth-century one, associated above all with the name of Fechner. Freud was deeply indebted by his own account to Fechner's physics of the psyche ("An Autobiographical Study" 59), in which intensities of physical energy are preeminent, and which influenced his early attempts to explain the mechanism of hysteria. See, for instance, the *Project for a Scientific Psychology*, where Freud refers to "Fechner's Law" on the mathematical relation between the intensity of stimulation and the resultant sensation. While Freud felt he could not make these early attempts work, so that the *Project*, the most notable of them, failed to explain repression in terms of quantities of energy and laws of motion, as Freud hoped it would, the force of physicalist approaches continued to make itself felt throughout his life: *Beyond the Pleasure Principle* is the main example. Freud's concern with the physical left as its legacy the impossible concept of psychic energy. The concept is impossible because it cannot, according to Robert Shope's excellent study of the topic, be the same thing as physical energy. Shope concen-

trates on the relation between psychical and physical energy, arguing that the two cannot be coterminous. But he, like Freud, operates with a "one-body" psychology, which I will question later in my essay. Fechner's influence on Freud has been discussed by Jones, Ellenberger, and Sulloway, with Sulloway arguing that Freud's debt to Fechner is greater than his debt to the so-called "Helmholtz School" with whose "mechanic materialism" Freud had to struggle (65ff).

7. For an extended discussion of this point, see my *Interpretation of the Flesh* (107ff).

8. Freud defines a wish as a current of excitation, starting from unpleasure and aiming at pleasure, where the first wishing "seems to have been a hallucinatory cathecting of the memory of satisfaction" (*Interpretation of Dreams* 604, 598). He adds that a second psychical system (later known as the ego) comes into being in order to prevent the memory of the cathexis from reaching perception, as the memory cathexis would then "bind" the psychical forces. The result of this binding would be to make the hallucination appear real. It would be perceived as if it were present.

9. The steps in binding energy are only logically separate; temporally, they coincide.

10. If this is so, there is a paradox involved. Bound energy is energy organized in certain pathways, while entropy is meant to be synonymous with disorganization. We will return to this.

11. In Kleinian terms, pain is projected via the configuration of "bad objects," agents that cause pain and distress.

12. The hallucination is not the ego, because the ego is a response to the hallucination. It sees the hallucination, and represses it.

13. This is not my first attempt at exploring the difference between the psychophysical time of the subject and another time, a faster time, which has to exist insofar as a field of energy exists which is not bound by repression. I argued in *The Interpretation of the Flesh* that the delay between the perception of a need and its fulfillment contrasted with a prior state in which there was virtually no delay between that perception and the appropriate response, and suggested that intrauterine existence met the requirements for this prior state. That is to say, we can postulate that in utero, the gap between need and fulfilment is not felt in the way it is after birth. Now we can add that another dimension meets the same requirement. This is the contrast between bound and freely mobile energy, which is also a contrast between more rapid energy and the fixity of bondage. The intrauterine experience remains a fleshly memory, but the contrast between bound and freely mobile energy is an ongoing one. We live with it daily.

14. This idea will be developed in my book, *Consciousness and Social Consciousness*, of which this essay is part.

15. See the discussion of the life drive and death drive in my *History after Lacan* 105–09.

16. Incidentally, this would also explain the notorious conservatism of the aging process. The tendency to inertia is conservative in the physical sense by definition. The notion that pathways have an ideational content, committed to sustaining certain ideas and identifications (which also take the form of fixed points, see my *Interpretation of the Flesh* 114ff), means we can understand conservatism in an additional social sense.

17. It may however be small comfort for the man who ages rapidly vis-à-vis his partner to know that his nature is fundamentally non-exploitative, or that his sense of justice is lodged securely at the core of his being.

18. It would be interesting to investigate senility crossculturally by comparing the greater or lesser cultural prevalence of anxiety (from whatever source) to which the aging are subject.

19. I have tried to show this at length in *The Interpretation of the Flesh* and here am including only the briefest of summaries of that argument in order to be able to extend it.

20. In another context, one could explore how this is also a processual issue for the psyche, in terms of the amount of information that has to be taken on board, leading to internal fixities as well as external ones, and hence to an internal sense of rapid time.

21. Pribram 366. Pribram continues, "Should one look through gratings rather than lenses, one might see a holographic-like order which Bohm called implicate, enfolded (*implicare*, Latin to fold in)" (366).

22. Translation mine. Karen Fields's exemplary new translation includes many sentences that were unaccountably omitted from Swaine's original 1916 translation into English. However I have preferred here my own translation.

WORKS CITED

Arendt, Hannah. *The Human Condition*. Chicago: U of Chicago P, 1958.

Baumaun, Zygmunt. *Postmodern Ethics*. Cambridge: Blackwell, 1993.

Brennan, Teresa. *The Interpretation of the Flesh*. New York: Routledge, 1992.

———. *History after Lacan*. New York: Routledge, 1993.

Cannon, Walter B. *Bodily Changes in Pain, Hunger, Fear and Rage: An Account of Recent Researches into the Function of Emotional Excitement*. New York: Appleton, 1922.

Durkheim, Emile. *Les Formes élémentaires de la vie religieuse: Le Système totemique en Australie*. Paris: PUF, 1968.

———. *The Elementary Forms of Religious Life*. Trans. Karen E. Fields. New York: Free Press, 1995.

Ellenberger, Henri F. *The Discovery of the Unconscious: The History and Evolution of Dynamic Psychiatry*. London: Allen Lane, 1970.

Freud, Sigmund. *The Standard Edition of the Complete Psychological Works of Sigmund Freud*. Trans. and ed. James Strachey. London: Hogarth and the Inst. of Psycho-Analysis, 1953–74. 24 vols.

———. "Analysis Terminable and Interminable." 1937. SE 23: 211–53.

———. "An Autobiographical Study." 1925. SE 20: 7–74.

———. *Beyond the Pleasure Principle*. 1920. SE 18: 3–64.

———. "Femininity." 1933. SE 22: 112–35.

———. *The Interpretation of Dreams*. 1900. SE 4–5: xi–338, 339–627.

———. *Project for a Scientific Psychology*. 1950. SE 1: 283–397.

———. "Repression." 1915. SE 14: 143–58.

Giddens, Anthony. *Capitalism and Modern Social Theory: An Analysis of the Writings of Marx, Durkheim, and Max Weber*. Cambridge: Cambridge UP, 1971.

Ingold, Tim. "An Anthropologist Looks at Biology." *Man* 25.2 (1990): 208–29.

Jones, Ernest. *Sigmund Freud: Life and Work*. Vol. 1. London: Hogarth, 1953.

Leach, Edmund. *Pul Eliya: A Village in Ceylon*. Cambridge: Cambridge UP, 1961.

Murdoch, Iris. *The Sovereignty of Good over Other Concepts*. Cambridge: Cambridge UP, 1967.

Pribram, K. H. "The Implicate Brain." *Quantum Implications: Essays in Honor of David Bohm*. Ed. B. J. Hiley and F. David Peat. London: Routledge, 1987. 365–71.

Shope, Robert. "Physical and Psychical Energy." *Philosophy of Science* 38 (1971): 1–11.

Strathern, Marilyn. "Presentation for the Motion." *The Concept of Society Is Theoretically Obsolete*. Ed. Tim Ingold. Manchester: Group for Debates in Anthropological Theory, 1990.

Sulloway, Frank. *Freud, Biologist of the Mind: Beyond the Psychoanalytic Legend*. London: Burnett, 1979.

Wollheim, Richard. "The Bodily Ego." *Philosophical Essays on Freud*. Ed. Richard Wollheim and James Hopkins. Cambridge: Cambridge UP, 1982. 124–38.

Woodward, Kathleen. *Aging and Its Discontents: Freud and Other Fictions*. Bloomington: Indiana UP, 1991.

Inventing Generational Models
Psychoanalysis, Feminism, Literature

Kathleen Woodward

When I was a little girl I would often stay overnight on Saturday with my grandparents who lived in the one-bedroom apartment just above ours in Chicago. In the morning my grandfather would get up early, and my grandmother and I would stay in the bedroom, she firmly settled in her high twin bed while I explored the contents of the bottom drawer of her chest of drawers, fingering objects that seemed to me fragile and exotic while she embellished them further with stories—tiny seed pearls from oysters, a small book of drawings of birds, a miniature bronze pineapple from Cuba where she and my grandfather had lived after they had gotten married. It was the objects that enchanted me then. It is the scene of the two of us together that holds a theoretical lure for me now. For it is a scene of a young girl and an older woman, a figure missing in Freudian psychoanalysis. In terms of age we were separated by more than fifty years and a generation, but I did not feel either then or now that we were divided by generations. Rather I felt connected by them. This scene for me thus represents attachment—an emotional attunement and mutual recognition that stretched across a continuity established by three generations. Our mood was one of a convivial ease and fluent companionship marked by a meditative rhythm and laughter too. Missing were the stormy emotions of envy, fear, hostility, guilt, and jealousy intrinsic to the nuclear family of Freudian psychoanalysis (although I do have to confess that my mother would complain after I came down on Sunday that I had been spoiled while I was up there).

Consider the difference between this convivial ease and the mood of a late piece by Freud, his letter to Romain Rolland published under the enigmatic title of "A Disturbance of Memory on the Acropolis" in 1936. When Freud was eighty years old, suffering from feelings of depression and gloom, of discontent and irresolution, his mind turned to his memory of a vacation he had taken to Greece some thirty years before with his brother, a vacation that had been ruined with similar feelings of gloom, the memory itself being, as he put it "the expression of a pessimism" (SE 22: 242). What was the reason for these disturbing feelings of his, both earlier and later? Analyzing this memory, Freud concluded that these feelings were the sign of filial guilt. In his ambition and in the spirit of competition he had surpassed his father (in going to Greece he had literally traveled further than his father ever had and he had achieved far more than his father had professionally). And he was being punished for this. His very depression, his pessimism, was itself that punishment, exacted by his superego. Thus Freud's disturbing feelings of foreboding were not only the precipitants of the memory of an earlier event but also the signs of the expectation of an event, the Freudian fear of castration, of punishment. At the end of his life, then, we find Freud still thick in the world of two generations, after all these years still tragically bound to his now long-dead father, fastened tight by the cord of the Oedipus complex, and ruled by its dynamic of desire and prohibition, guilt and punishment.

I know that these two scenes are asymmetrical in many respects, perhaps most importantly in terms of point of view. I am telling the story of an older woman and her granddaughter not from the point of view of the older woman —she is no longer here to tell the story—but from mine, while Freud in fact speaks out of his own old age. But my very purpose in the first part of this essay will be to sketch how theoretically we might find our way out of this Freudian world limited to two generations, one from which older women are missing.[1] In psychoanalysis a woman beyond childbearing age is considered old. For Freud a woman of fifty was "elderly," dysfunctional in reproductive (sexual) terms and therefore virtually unrepresentable—sexually invisible.[2] In Freudian psychoanalysis it is as if at the biological time bomb of menopause, the point when a woman's increasing age and her diminishing fertility intersect, female sexuality explodes, leaving only gender behind. But since Freudian psychoanalysis cannot contain the concept of gender as distinct from sexuality, the inevitable conclusion is that the postmenopausal woman is dismissed from the world as posthistorical. In the second part of this essay I will turn to models of crossgenerational identification provided in work and writing by women, work that for me ultimately serves as a way of allowing us to invent our own future as older women, anticipating the future not as a punishment, as did Freud, but as one of possibility.

I.

The developmental politics of Freudian psychoanalysis is twofold. The constitution of male and female sexuality, established within the nuclear family, is understood to be achieved simultaneously with the rigid separation of the two generations, the generation of the parent from the generation of the child. Both the two sexes and the two generations are ever after to remain unequal in power. The triangular geometry of this nuclear family is established through the threat of force, which entails for the child the emotions of guilt over the desire for the parent of the opposite sex, fear of punishment, and jealousy of the parent of the same sex. Classically the father is cast as the third term that intervenes in the mother-child dyad.

In her essays "Place Names" and "Motherhood According to Giovanni Bellini," both published in the mid 1970s, Julia Kristeva rewrites this developmental process, introducing into the equation the mother of the mother. In the process of giving birth to a child, a woman, now becoming a mother herself, "enters into contact with her own mother," writes Kristeva in "Motherhood" (239); the two mothers become "the same continuity differentiating itself" (239). For Kristeva it is the very experience of becoming a mother that fosters this psychic identification of the younger mother with the older mother, an identification that for Kristeva must ultimately be broken, an identification that is in fact finally ruptured by the child itself. Even though Kristeva does not speculate on the subjectivity of the older mother (what is she feeling?), what is at this point important for my purposes is that Kristeva's model, unlike that of Freud, is composed of three generations—and it is one that will more than half of the time take the form of three generations of women.

Who is this child and what is the child playing with? In "Femininity," published in 1933, Freud admits that the pre-oedipal attachment of a little girl to her mother is much more powerful and richer than he had before believed. He comes to this conclusion in part by calling attention to the little girl's practice of playing with dolls which is, he concludes, an expression of her "affectionate" attachment to her mother, of her "identification with her mother," the mother who is in the little girl's eyes the phallic mother (SE 22: 128). (The mother is "phallic" because the little girl does not yet understand that in Freud's psychological universe the mother is indeed castrated.) Interestingly, the little girl plays the role of the mother while the doll represents herself. What is exciting to me here is that Freud theorizes through play and performance the possibility of psychically inhabiting different generations simultaneously, practicing another generation, as it were, teaching oneself generational difference through continuity.

But we may also read this scene as representing not two but three generations. The little girl plays her mother, yes, but the doll may represent not just herself—and thus her own generation—but also an infant of a younger generation altogether. Here the infant does not ultimately separate the mother from her own mother. Instead the infant connects them in a lineage of generational continuity, one composed of the linking of generations through the care of one generation for another, care modeled on what one has received from the previous generation. The dominant model here is not the Freudian triangle composed of two generations, with the parental generation holding the power, but rather one of three generations that establish a line, a heritage based not on struggle for domination but on pleasurable interaction (play) and care.

Lending support to this model of generational continuity is the provocative and persuasive research of Earnest Abelin on pre-oedipal triangulation during what Margaret Mahler has identified as the rapprochement subphase (it occurs around eighteen months). Abelin insists that core gender identity for little girls and little boys is profoundly different, based on different articulations of different terms altogether. For little girls the three key terms are "mother," "self," and "baby," and as a result the little girl establishes her core gender identity based on generational continuity. "Generational identity," Abelin concludes, "establishes the self 'between' two objects, along one linear dimension. 'I am smaller than mother, but bigger than baby,' . . . 'I wish to be taken care of by mother and I wish to take care of baby'" (158). For little boys, by contrast, core gender identity is based on the three familiar Freudian terms of "father," "mother," and "self," and thus core gender identity for little boys is based on sexual difference (the dichotomy of male and female), on a model of two generations in competition with one another as opposed to a model of three generations linked to each other through a heritage of care for the next generation.[3]

One of my purposes in elaborating this model of generational continuity is to insist that there are alternatives to the Freudian model of oedipal struggle between generations, one that has been reproduced by feminists in the academy—and to our disadvantage. For in feminist psychoanalytic and cultural criticism over the past twenty years the older woman of the third generation and the fourth generation has not found a place. In much of this work a woman is often implicitly theorized or represented as a mother to young children. To be sure she may appear in the guise of a woman juggling work of her own with the demands and pleasures of motherhood, but at her oldest she tends to be cast as on the young side of middle age (I think here of the surprised, almost shocked tone with which I have heard some of my only slightly younger colleagues refer to an older woman as—of all the impossible things—a *grandmother!*).

Or if age is explicitly analyzed, what we find is the Freudian plot of a struggle for power between two close but emotionally and intellectually distant "generations": the mother and daughter have gotten older but they don't seem to have learned much—or they have learned only too well how to jockey for power. Consider two texts published in 1989. Literary critic Marianne Hirsch, writing candidly in her book *The Mother/Daughter Plot* of her experience as a fellow at the Bunting Institute, eloquently acknowledges the "painful set of divisions which emerged between the discourse of mothers and that of daughters"; "the sympathy we could muster for ourselves and each other *as mother*, we could not quite transfer to our own mothers. This inability, this tragic asymmetry between our own two voices, was so pervasive as to be extremely difficult to discuss. It revealed the depth and the extent of the 'matrophobia' that exists not only in the culture at large but also within feminism, and within women who are mothers" (26). In a similar vein Alice Jardine describes the relationship between the two successive post-1968 groups of feminists in the academy in the United States as thoroughly oedipal. She does not want to "succumb" to this paradigm, but in fact she does—and for good reasons: the oedipal paradigm does accurately describe the struggle she has witnessed between two generations in the institution of the academy. As she puts it, "I would like to avoid the mother/daughter paradigm here (so as not to succumb simply to miming the traditional father/son, master/disciple model), but it is difficult to avoid being positioned by the institution as mothers and daughters" (77). My point is that if we use a different model to analyze our situation in the academy, we may in fact find different relationships at work. And we must stretch our model to include more than two generations not only for salutary theoretical and pragmatic reasons, but because in fact in the academy itself are represented more than two or even three generations at this moment in time.

Consider as well a conversation in 1994 between Jane Gallop, a distinguished professor who teaches feminist theory at the University of Wisconsin-Milwaukee, and Elizabeth Francis, who was then a graduate student at Brown University finishing up her dissertation in American civilization on modernism and women and their relation to feminism. The title of the piece—"Talking Across"—explicitly refers to talking across generations, specifically academic generations. What especially interests me is that both of them perceive members of the other generation as on the attack—and that this comes as a surprise to Gallop, the senior academic. As she says, "I had never heard anyone who was junior or new in the profession talk about senior people attacking junior people," which, she realizes, mirrors her own discourse with her colleagues and peers "about how graduate students will just attack whatever we say" (112–13). For Gallop the graduate student as "terrorist" is "always a feminist" and "always a she," and the metaphor they both use to describe the relationship of these parallel generational worlds (that of the senior scholar, that of the graduate student) is that of the parent and child (118). Although the tone of their conversation is probing and evenly analytical (it reads to me as though it were a "good" conversation, one in which they did manage to talk across generations, learning something in the process), still what is replicated is the structure of there being only two generations: the younger generation and the senior generation. I might add too that, interestingly enough, Gallop associates the production of new knowledge with the figure of the graduate student. "For me," she says, "the construction of the graduate student as terrorist is very close to another construction I have which is the graduate student as totally attractive figure, full of energy, youth, and vitality, who is going to do something new" (124). New and old are thus also put into conversation as a binary structure, with all of the conventional associations between young as good and old as, well, less interesting. My question is: would the terms of the conversation have shifted if in fact, say, a woman, or two, from other academic generations had been present? Would the conversation have been substantially different if the metaphor of the Freudian family had been explicitly proscribed from usage?

In a provocative essay entitled "Generational Difficulties, or the Fear of a Barren History," Judith Roof challenges the use of the word "generation" itself in feminist work in the United States, suggesting that it carries the connotations of a "reproductive narrative" with its oedipal familial logic of struggle and recrimination. Roof entered the academy later than some women and thus writes from the position of seeing herself, I think, as both an older woman and a younger academic simultaneously, a position that may make her particularly sensitive to age relations in the academy, and especially to feminists senior to her.[4] Her view of this widespread generational model is that it privileges and protects older feminists, based as it is on "the metaphor of the patriarchal family in the throes of its illusory battle against mortality" (85). As she writes, the generational narrative "does less to enlighten the trajectory of feminist intellectual history than it does to superimpose assumptions about property, propriety, and precedence that attempt to assure that feminism's offspring remember their mothers and in so remembering reproduce their mothers' gains, while honoring their mothers appropriately. Thinking in generational terms contributes— and might even produce—the sometimes torturous relations among women in academe" (71). Clearly this bothers Roof. I would respond, one absolutely should honor the good work that came before, yes, but there is no need to think of older professional women as mothers.[5] And with this latter point Roof would clearly agree. What really bothers her is the metaphor of the family which subtends, in her view, the metaphor of generations.

Although the metaphor of the family underlies both the psychoanalytic models of oedipal struggle and of generational continuity, as I have sketched the latter here, the trope of the family, which casts all of our relations into the net of relatives—brothers, sisters, mothers, fathers, grandmothers, grandfathers— need not be the base for generational models, where older women are figures of knowledge and vitality. Finally, then, consider an essay by Nancy Chodorow, one I greatly admire, in which she reports on a series of interviews with women psychoanalysts who had trained in the 1920s, 1930s, and 1940s. In "Seventies Questions for Thirties Women," Chodorow seeks to understand why these women were apparently gender-blind in our sense of the term, coming to conclude not only that they had a different sense of gender-consciousness then but that in our historical moment we are hyper-sensitive to questions of gender. Chodorow does not figure these women as mothers, grandmothers, or great-grandmothers, but as professional women of other generations. One of the lessons of her essay, with its tone of deep respect, is that we have no right to expect the answers we would give to the questions we ask of generational others. It is a vain and immature enterprise to wish either to be mirrored at our age or to enter automatically into struggle as if we were adolescents, following the widespread model of revolt against parental control and authority in order to gain a sense of identity. Psychoanalysis accents the formative identifications we make when we are young. But such identifications do not cease with childhood, and many identifications allow us to entertain new ways of thinking and of living. But perhaps, as we will see, the very notion of identification is not what we require in this moment of time.

II.

We need to create for ourselves cultural models of older women as a way of generating alternative futures for ourselves as we live into lives longer than we had imagined for ourselves, if we had even previously thought consciously about aging at all—and many of us have not. Under the concrete pressure of the demographic revolution in longevity, we need new models. What form could they take?

I am acutely conscious as I write that I am speaking for myself, perhaps about myself, as a woman in her early fifties and as a person who has been thinking about these questions for quite some time now. Thus I want to begin by reflecting briefly on models that I found especially valuable in the past but no longer contain the same resonance for me, which will lead to the question of why some models may prove to be so suggestive at certain moments—at certain historical moments and at certain moments in our individual lives. I will then turn to several literary texts that seem more suggestive to me now in modeling older women. But perhaps the word "model" is too schematic, abstract, or grandiose for what I mean. For I am, after all, referring to bits and pieces of paragraphs I've read and literally underlined, words to which I've returned in my mind's eye. I'm referring to phrases and sometimes to single words. These bits and pieces I've culled from here and there, but notwithstanding the somewhat random nature of this search (although I have looked, it seems, everywhere for writing on aging in the human sciences), they have assumed for me the status of "evocative objects," in the sense that the psychoanalyst Christopher Bollas gives to the term.[6] They are objects to which I have found myself attached (or to which I have attached myself), fictive kin,[7] as it were, that have populated my life and to some of which I have granted the lofty rank of theoretical object—that is, it is through them as virtual talismans that I have thought through growing older into the future (the scene which opens this essay functions in such a way). Just when and why such objects cease to be "evocative objects" are themselves productive questions.

I will mention four texts which served me as touchstones for many years, two of which represent major contributions to research on aging and two of which are single passages from autobiographies. All were published in the 1970s. None holds the same force for me now.

In her book *The Coming of Age* Simone de Beauvoir offers in her opening pages one such model: "If we do not know what we are going to be, we cannot know who we are: let us recognize ourselves in this old man or that old woman.

It must be done if we are to take upon ourselves the entirety of our human state. And when it is done we will no longer acquiesce in the misery of the oldest age; we will no longer be indifferent, because we shall feel concerned, as indeed we are" (14). I first read *The Coming of Age* some twenty years ago, and these words provided me with a moving model of imagining old age. I want to stress the word "moving" because Beauvoir herself, known for her stirring analysis of patriarchy in *The Second Sex*, here took a more sentimental stance. It is a model that in fact I now reject as being based on the identification of a younger person with an unnamed older person who, representing all older people, is cast as an object of pity, one miserable in all senses of the word (impoverished, alone, frail), one who ultimately represents the fatality of the human condition. Here identification is in part projective identification in Melanie Klein's sense—the projection of Beauvoir's own fear of aging onto older people as a class. Equally as invidious is that Beauvoir's model assumes a leveling of individuality to sameness. The reality is quite different. As the gerontologist George Maddox has put it, "Older people do not become more alike by becoming old. In many areas, they become more varied" (qtd. in Friedan 117).

Nonetheless, this paradigm was productive in past decades. Beauvoir's ambitious manifesto, a compendium of research across cultures and histories, was the first I read that attempted to do so much. That Beauvoir asked her readers, implicitly figured as younger readers, to entertain the question of aging in terms of imagining a subjectivity and position different from theirs was a fruitful strategy. But it is altogether clear to me that it does us a disservice now. Beauvoir's analysis was based on two primary and intertwined assumptions, which also served her as analytic tools and conclusions—the existential revulsion of the condition of being old and the powerlessness of the elderly as an economic class. Imagine the difficulty of identification with what you hold repugnant, as Beauvoir did aging; her view of old age as being associated with disgust is itself a blatant example of ageism. In addition, economic circumstances have changed dramatically. I will only pause to note here that in the United States people over sixty-five *as a group* have indeed accumulated considerable purchasing power over the last two decades. What is required is an analysis differentiating levels of economic strength and weakness.

Second, consider the deceptively simple declaration by the anthropologist Margaret Mead who in her memoir of her childhood, *Blackberry Winter*, writes that her grandmother was "the most decisive influence in my life" (45). For feminists concerned with the subject of aging, the figure of the grandmother requires sustained analysis. Over twenty years ago Adrienne Rich observed that the relationship between the mother and the daughter had received little attention. Since then, we have witnessed an outpouring of work on mothers and daughters. As I suggested in the first part of this essay, we need to turn our attention to older women; we need also to understand how we have "used" that figure. Elinor Fuchs has told me in conversation that in her informal survey of scholars in the humanities who have done research on aging, a grandparent has figured prominently and positively in their lives, and I would be, it is true, no exception to her speculative rule. Does this mean that we "rejected" our parents? (This would not be my case.) Does this mean that we idealized and romanticized older figures and had little real knowledge of their subjectivity? (This would be my case, I think.) What, then, would be the consequences for our analysis of aging?

In the case of Mead—and of myself—our grandmothers were important in our early years before we had any truly nuanced conscious notion or understanding of what it was to be an adult, never mind a truly older woman.[8] While these women may have been critical to our lives, it may be profoundly childish of us to continue to use them—or the very word "grandmother"—as a talisman to imagine our future as older women, particularly since in all likelihood they stood in relation to us as nurturers. As Barbara Macdonald has written, "like all who serve, the older woman soon becomes invisible" (40). Baba Copper, in *Over the Hill: Reflections on Ageism between Women*, is virulent about the traditional role of the grandmother as supplemental nurturer, calling it one of the "horrors" of old age, railing against "the humiliation and self-sacrifice built into the role of grandmother" (6). While I find it difficult to accept what I see as exaggerated contempt for this social role, Copper's analysis is astute. "We aren't usually angry at grandmothers so we seldom trash them. Like mothers they serve us," she writes. "We may feel superior to them because they were less well educated or were old fashioned (we like that, as well); often we are taught not to take them seriously. So now when they are safely out of our lives, we use the memory of them to evoke nostalgia—less assimilated ethnicity, less complicated times, the security of ascribed relationships" (10).[9]

Nostalgia, however, is not at the base of all such relationships. Consider, for instance, Francine du Plessix Gray's account of growing up: "my oldest childhood mentors had not been parents of reproductive age but two bewitching female relatives, a maternal great-grandmother and a paternal aunt, who were already well past midlife when I was growing up. From infancy on, I had been in awe of their freedom and power—qualities that, I sensed even then, could be achieved only in what the French call the Third Age" (186). Surely, too, as we have grown older, our sense of the possibilities of adulthood has been shaped by more than the early figures of childhood, by others drawn from outside the family circle. At the same time, I might add that today in the United States many grandmothers are in fact performing the role of mother. They are not supplemental, but rather the critical givers of care to their grandchildren. The orderly progression of roles that many imagine in a traditional conception of the life course is undergoing immense change.

Third, consider a moment in the autobiography of the physical anthropologist Loren Eiseley, who, the last time he sees his mother—she was nearly eighty—foresees both of their deaths by old age.

"Why," she said, surprised, running a finger down the blue vein of her forearm, "I believe I'm getting old." Again the bright sparrow's eye looked up at me, escaping as always. "Do you think that's it?" she repeated doubtfully. "Old age?"

I shook my head wordlessly and turned away, raising my hand in a combined gesture of despair and farewell. The last I saw was the blue vein creeping down her arm as she repeated in a voice that seemed to emanate from another dimension, "I'm old, I think I'm old."

The thought was contagious. I extended my own arm later on the airfield, while waiting in the blistering sun. By the powers of heredity a blue worm was beginning to inch its way in a precisely similar fashion down my arm. The culmination was still some years away. (222)

I have been fascinated for years by this scene—the witnessing of one's future in the mirror of genetic inheritance held up by a parent.[10] This is a trope that pervades writing on aging, one that is often accompanied by the daughter musing on photographs of herself and her mother, with the daughter, for example, now fifty, the same age as her mother in a photograph of the two of them together—but now the daughter is in the age-position of the mother.[11]

Growing older is presented in terms of the uncanny shock of recognition of one's aging as one is transformed into one's mother. This is a compelling model, to be sure, but it almost takes the form of presenting aging as a pathology, with the physical signs of aging serving as symptoms of the "disease." Here again aging is understood through the concept of identification—visual identification—with a member of one's family and one's mother at that, as though how we look were everything, as though maternal biology were absolute destiny. The model of recognizing one's own physical aging with a shock insists on aging as a crisis, one which does not accord with our gradual growing older over a long period of time.[12]

The point of view in this micro-narrative remains that of child in middle age. What if the point of view were reversed? In Penelope Lively's *Moon Tiger*, a novel written from the point of view of an older woman who is dying of stomach cancer, we have just such a reflective scene. Claudia, confined to the hospital, muses on the age of her daughter: "When I look at Lisa now I see the shadow of middle age on her face. This is disconcerting. One's child, after all, is forever young. A girl, perhaps, a young woman even—but that hardening of the features, that softening of the body, that hint that time past is levelling up with time ahead . . . dear me, no" (92–93). The hard-hearted Claudia, known for her caustic abruptness, here is revealed to not be thinking about herself (as is generally the case in the scene of the daughter witnessing her own aging in the mirror of her mother's face), but about her daughter, revealing a tenderness that catches even her unawares.

Finally, I turn to a model which for some reason is the most difficult for me to relinquish but which is one I cannot in all honesty continue to carry with me. In *Number Our Days* anthropologist Barbara Myerhoff writes about a community of elderly East European Jews—women and men in their eighties and nineties—who congregate around a senior center in Venice, California. She explicitly chose this group of people, she tells us, because for her they represented her heritage, a cultural legacy of sorts, as well as her future as "a little old Jewish lady." In the film of the same title made by Lynne Litmann which won the Academy Award for best documentary in 1976 (it is, I might note, dedicated to their grandmothers), Myerhoff explains that as an anthropologist she "tries to *feel* the inside of a native's head" but is painfully aware that she will never be able to truly inhabit that subjective space. "But I *will* be old. And I need to know that," she insists. "There's a validity in identifying with that. . . . I *will* be a little old Jewish lady." And she continues, "I look at my own gray hairs now with something akin to affection. And I think to myself, you know that those really signify coming into a different phase of life . . . a better one than the one that went before. I'm very fortunate and I am in the minority having models before me as to how to age well."

Number Our Days, both the book and the documentary, is heartfelt and inspiring, and I do not want to hold Barbara Myerhoff's untimely vanishing against her (she died of breast cancer when she was fifty-one). But I do want to insist that I do not think she would have been "a little old Jewish lady" in their reflection. And I do not think that, as Lynne Litmann put it, "we are all heirs of this small tribe."[13]

Myerhoff was keenly aware that the cultural formation of this group of people living in Venice, California was profoundly different from her own. Nonetheless, the model is, like the others I have mentioned, one of identification—either with the "idea" of an old person, a faceless image, as in Beauvoir, or with a member of one's family, whether extended, biological and nuclear, or cultural, as in Mead, Eiseley, and Myerhoff. It is largely detached from historical time. It takes its primary meaning from biological, developmental time. I do not want to be understood as wanting to forfeit the latter. What is important to me is the intersection of the two—biological time and historical time. But what I mean here by historical time is what model makes sense for us at this time.

Myerhoff, for example, was drawn to this altogether particular group of people in great part because for her they were survivors of the Holocaust, and she extended this metaphor of survival to old age itself. Simply to survive into what was seen as advanced or extreme old age in the decade of the 1970s when she did her research (she was then in her forties) was cast by Myerhoff as an act of heroic proportions, one demanding courage, resourcefulness, and independence as well as a passion for narration, especially storytelling, which in turn gave strength and vividness to life. I am not suggesting that this was not the case, or that these are not important skills for us at all points in our lives. I am insisting that historically, now, we are in the midst of a demographic revolution in longevity when living into our eighties and nineties and more is becoming a commonplace, not the result of special skills of survivorship. What is equally important to me in addition to this is a model not based in identification. And I should add again that perhaps "model" is too pretentious and too weighty a word.

Almost ten years ago, lesbian Baba Copper, reflecting on ageism within the women's movement, declared, "I am entering a time in which I have no models" (81). Others have echoed this complaint (Gloria Steinem is one of them). I think of this lack of models now as salutary, and perhaps this is why several small, small details from different kinds of literary narratives have persisted in my mind, have continued to speak to me, to generate a sense of generational connection, even though—perhaps precisely because—the nature of this connection is not specified at length. I think of these narrative gestures, for that is what they are (not themes, not plots), as inflections toward the future, as autobiography in the prospective, not retrospective mode.

Consider Jessamyn West's 1973 *Hide and Seek: A Continuing Journey*, written while she was spending a year by herself in an isolated spot in the American Southwest. The book is part journal, part memoir of her parents, part gesture toward the future. The future is represented for me by the figure of Lily, a woman who is simply part of the landscape, a neighbor who lives down the road in the nearest cabin. Lily is an eighty-six-year-old widow who became a painter in her sixties. That West does not romanticize Lily as a paragon of old age or present her as an anomalous phenomenon, an eccentric, is for me precisely the power of this figure of an older woman (she is some fifteen years older than West). Lily is neither invisible nor hypervisible. Lily is just there. West muses to herself that Lily "will live to be a hundred and ten. Why do painters and composers live for so long?" she asks. "Because they are joined in love with their subject matter" (217). West does not *identify* with Lily. She does not think of Lily in familial terms (as a mother, for example), although West does tell us that as a neighbor and an older woman Lily deserves her help and sympathy—in short, her respect.

What I find compelling, in other words, is the very ordinariness of Lily, a woman who reappears, as it were, sixteen years later in Margaret Drabble's novel *A Natural Curiosity*. Drabble's novelistic world is populated by middle-class, middle-aged women of means and character. About them I have forgotten everything except what is for me this wonderful detail: at the novel's end three of them—they are all in their fifties—set off to see a much older woman, a woman of wit and some wealth, a woman who lives alone, a woman who takes pleasure in the present. Unexpectedly, the novel, which is quite long and has introduced us to a panoramic world of characters of many ages, concludes by giving this woman the closing paragraphs, the last word, the final line of the narrative, one which promises a meeting of generations and offers the mood of expectation, not the expression of a Freudian pessimism.[14]

It is a simple sentence: "She is filled with pleasurable anticipation as she hears the wheels of the hired Renault [the car they had rented] crunch along the gravel drive" (309). Members of a younger generation of women are traveling to meet with an older woman. The assumption is that there are not just two generations, but many. In the world of the novel we come to see this is altogether in the natural course of things. At the same time the future is represented as open-ended, with generations of women loosely linked not through the trope of familial identification but rather through a curiosity akin to affection. Thus does Margaret Drabble delicately cast the narrative line of the novel in an altogether different direction, toward a present that is also a future, the present and the future bound together by anticipation. When I returned to the novel in preparation for writing these words of mine, reading the novel backward to see what I had forgotten, this is one of the passages I found a few pages before the end of the novel: one of the middle-aged women remarks, "'Odd, isn't it, the way new prospects continue to offer themselves? One turns the corner, one climbs a little hill, and there is a whole new vista'" (306). Instead of climbing the hill and finding themselves over it, they see a whole new landscape.

Some people take walks, finding new worlds. I read books, and musing on these women climbing hills I turned in my mind's eye to Marilyn Hacker's *Winter Numbers*, poems written under the pressure of the diagnosis of breast cancer and its treatment as well as the premature deaths of friends from AIDS. Several of her poems have become new talismans of mine, words that for me evoke the possibility of reminiscence that extends not into the past but into the future.[15] In "Letter to Julie in a New Decade," against what would seem all the odds, Hacker declares her friendship, as one declares one's love, projecting their epistolary closeness into the far future when they will be old women and they will be what they are today—feisty, dynamic women. These are the last lines of the poem:

> If I live long enough, my small ambition
> is, to be the next old lady on the third
> floor (blessed with indoor plumbing), in condition
> to send the next and next-to-the-last word
> to you, in some warm green place, with your grown-up
> granddaughter, and dogs, where it's not raining.
> I hope we won't be jailed, or veiled, or blown up
> and have the energy to keep complaining. (50)

This "old lady," who lives on the third floor in the building in Paris where Hacker also lives, is ninety-nine. She lives alone, yes, and her apartment does not have indoor plumbing, but she is not the object of either Beauvoirean contempt or sentimentality. On the contrary. She is long-lived and independent. (In "August Journal," the closing poem of *Winter Numbers*, we learn that Madame Mehling has died; she was 102 years old.)

What would this future be like? In "Dear Jool, I Miss You in Saint-Saturnin" in Hacker's *Collected Poems 1965–1990*, we see that it would be summery warm and clear, filled with desultory and ardent conversation. Hacker and an old friend are in a village in the south of France. That they are on a hilltop affording them the sight of a whole new vista is critical. It is as if they can see into the future, one where as older women they will talk together still:

> The air was gold
> with broom, and grape-leaf, plane-tree green, the air
>
> was blue blue blue July. With wine, we told
> each other that we'd be old ladies on
> a hill like this, where people still got old
>
> in housedresses and navy cardigans
> or patriotic azure *salopettes*. (219)

In these poems Hacker provides us with figures of generational continuity based not on the family but on the landscape of an everyday life, one that is inflected by the bonds of friendship and that can be cast into a potential future as one casts a lifeline.

Still, in all of these bits and pieces to which I have referred, the oldest woman does not play the central role. Unlike the commanding figure of a Louise Nevelson, to whom I refer in my introduction to this volume, they are not so much marginal as they are adjacent to the central figures, who are in midlife or in late middle age. However, more and more older women are writing the words of their experience of later years. I will mention only one such book here—Helen Bevington's *The Third Way*, a cross between a meditative journal and a book about women writers. Written over a period of some fifteen years (when the book was published Bevington was ninety years old), Bevington sets as her task the very challenge of finding a way to live her solitary life—her temperament has always been one of the solitary reader and writer—with independence and security. Her mind, she tells us at one point, "is full of trees" (174), not nostalgic trees from childhood but trees from a lifetime of learning, including the mulberry tree of Confucius. She closes the book with what I find to be a wonderful act. She goes to the store to purchase a large ficus (it is some five feet tall) for her house, a tree for her to sit under. In the very beginning of *The Third Way*, she had written:

> When I surveyed what ruins I might sit upon—my house and five acres, my typewriter, my Oldsmobile, my bank account—I could see that a smile of

undefeat would be bold but probably ironic. Besides, would it be possible to smile?

It was the idea of sitting alone on anything that baffled me. How do you accept aloneness, the kind without any reprieve? (4)

Instead of finding something to sit upon, she finds something to sit under. I imagine her sitting under that tree, one leafy and green in all seasons, reading and writing. What does she offer us in her meditations on aging? "To sit and write, I said. To stand alone. To keep the forked end down. To travel light, carrying the body along . . . because of its sentimental value" (115).

Patricia Meyer Spacks, in her essay "Stages of Self: Notes on Autobiography and the Life Cycle" published in 1977, makes the fascinating observation that every century has emphasized a certain stage of life. The twentieth century is the century of adolescence; the nineteenth century, of childhood; and the eighteenth century, of maturity, by which was meant middle adulthood. At the end of the twentieth century we find ourselves in an historical moment when we have the possibility of inventing the shape of our future as older women. Our historical situation is unprecedented. That few models exist to guide us is all to the good. This does not mean that there are no older women—there are— but that we have not before had a collective feminist historical consciousness of there being older women or of being older women. Historically we have not before had what I call generational consciousness of older women, which is being shaped for us today by what I have referred to, following Bollas, as "evocative objects," cultural texts that are helping us to imagine our possible futures. Thus we necessarily cannot reproduce the Freudian model of revolting against the previous generation.

It is fundamentally Freudian to imagine that we become particularly conscious of our own aging and thus our own mortality at midlife, when, as Bollas puts it, we become aware that when our mothers and fathers die we will be the last figures "in a generational triangle" (263). But my point is that if we take fifty as our midpoint, our lives will stretch to one hundred, and that there may be many women preceding us. As Patricia Mellencamp wonderfully asks in her essay in this book, an essay that stresses generational continuity and returns us to the family, "How many elders can one family have?" The answer is: many, many more than we had before thought possible. To which I want to add: my conviction is that as we grow older we invent fictive kin as well. Here I am reminded in fact that I owe a debt to the impressive older women I saw from afar when I had just finished my dissertation on the late poems of four of our gifted twentieth-century American writers and attended my first meeting of the Gerontological Society of America. It was my impression that there were many more vital older women involved in this professional association than in the Modern Language Association, and I made a kind of vow to affiliate myself with these women, inventing for myself, as it were, professional fictive kin.

NOTES

1. Sections from the first part of this essay are adapted from "Tribute to the Older Woman: Psychoanalysis, Feminism, and Ageism," published in *Images of Aging: Cultural Representations of Later Life*, edited by Mike Featherstone and Andrew Wernick. See that essay for an elaboration of the argument which is presented in condensed form here.

2. In *The Interpretation of Dreams* Freud refers explicitly to a woman of fifty as "elderly"; in this woman's dream, she herself figures her sexual desire as being received by men with a combination of embarrassment and admiration. Here are two specific examples of Freud's figuration of the older woman as an object of scorn. In "The Disposition to Obsessional Neurosis" (1913), he writes: "It is a well-known fact, and one that has given much ground for complaint, that after women have lost their genital function their character often undergoes a peculiar alteration. They become quarrelsome, vexatious and overbearing, petty and stingy; that is to say, they exhibit typically sadistic and anal-erotic traits which they did not possess earlier, during their period of womanliness. Writers of comedy and satirists have in all ages directed their invectives against the 'old dragon' into which the charming girl, the loving wife and the tender mother have been transformed" (SE 12: 323–24). In *Totem and Taboo* Freud discusses the ambivalent feelings aroused by a mother-in-law from the intensely negative point of view of the son-in-law this way: "she has many features which remind him of her daughter and yet lacks all the charms of youth, beauty, and spiritual freshness which endear his wife to him" (SE 13: 15).

See Maria Aldrich's "Lethal Brevity: Louise Bogan's Lyric Career" in which she argues that Bogan suffered from an invidious conjunction of social attitudes about age, gender, and genre—in particular from the Freudian view that menopause was a form of castration.

3. I have adopted the word "identity" here without being precise about exactly what I mean by it. "Identity" is often used in the sense of "wholeness," but I certainly do not wish it to carry that meaning here. "Identity" is also often opposed to "difference," and I do not want it to be construed in this sense either. Recent debates over identity politics and multiculturalism have placed a terrible strain on the notions of "identity" and "difference." It will suffice, I hope, to say that in the context of my essay "identity" does not preclude "difference." Indeed generational identity entails a difference based on a similarity that finds its expression in continuity.

4. See Mary Wilson Carpenter's excellent essay on what she calls "sexagism" in the academy, a combination of ageism and sexism; "it is the point in her 'reproductive cycle,'" Carpenter writes, "that determines the precise mechanism by which ageism will be brought to bear on the academic woman's career" (151). Carpenter is thinking here of ageism in relation to women in the academy not just in terms of aging and old age but also in terms of reproductive age.

I love the story the writer Nancy Mairs tells describing her doctoral work in English literature at the University of Arizona: "My 'good girl' voice was beginning to break up. I was laughing too hard to control it consistently. I was beginning to have too good a time. My sense of release must have been, in part, simply a function of age. Over forty, I knew that I had let the time for establishing myself as a reputable academic slip past. . . . I wasn't just growing old, of course. I was growing, well, odd" (34–35).

5. Through readings of essays by Elaine Showalter and Julia Kristeva, Roof explicitly takes up the question of the third generation. For her the third generation is the youngest generation of the three and the work of both Showalter and Kristeva expresses a fear of it. What would happen, I wonder, if we turned the numbering of generations around to accord with what appears to be people's subjective assessment of the importance of the production of their own generation? The younger generation, clearly feeling that they are not receiving their fair measure of attention, would be number one, and so on.

6. In his chapter "The Evocative Object," Bollas writes: "Objects . . . often arrive by chance, and these aleatory objects evoke psychic textures which do not reflect the valorizations of desire. We have not, as it were, selected the aleatory object to express an idiom of self. Instead, we are played upon by the inspiring arrival of the unselected, which often yields a very special type of pleasure—that of surprise. It opens us up, liberating an area like a key fitting a lock. In such moments we can say that objects use us, in respect of that inevitable two-way interplay between self and object world and between desire and surprise" (37).

7. The term "fictive kin," which I find wonderfully suggestive, is used in geronto-logical studies of housing, for example, to describe living arrangements of older people where those people literally close to them, but not related to them, adopt the responsibilities of family members. I am grateful to Sharon Keigher, a professor of gerontological social welfare at the University of Wisconsin-Milwaukee, for intro-ducing me to this term in a study group session at the Center for Twentieth Century Studies.

8. We learn in *Blackberry Winter* that Mead's paternal grandmother lived with her when she was growing up, and that Mead took her as a model for being a woman (in the sense of womanliness or femininity), a professional, and a parent. "She became my model when," Mead writes, "in later life, I tried to formulate a role for the modern parent who can no longer exact obedience merely by virtue of being a parent and yet must be able to get obedience when it is necessary" (45–46). She also notes that "it was my grandmother who gave me my ease in being a woman. She was unquestionably feminine—small and dainty and pretty and wholly without mascu-line protest or feminist aggrievement" (54). Interestingly enough, in *Blackberry Winter* Mead reflects not only on the important role her grandmother played in her early years but also on how she viewed her own role as a grandmother later in her life (see her chapter entitled "On Being a Grandmother").

9. I have only space here to introduce the figure of the grandmother in genera-tional relations, in feminism, and in age studies, a subject that requires sustained analysis. Beauvoir, for example, in *The Coming of Age*, suggests (I think bizarrely) that the role of the grandmother offers the older woman the pleasures of revenge against her daughter, a pleasure available to the grandfather as well: "For the old people the affection of the grandchildren is a revenge upon the generation in between, and the contact with their youth makes them feel younger" (475). She continues, with the implicit assumption that grandmothers are old: "The friendship

of the young is very valuable to old people" (475). Since Beauvoir's book was first published in French in 1970, our consciousness of age has changed dramatically. Hopefully, we would no longer automatically associate a grandmother with old age.

Activist Maggie Kuhn begins the story of her life with her grandmother. As she writes, "When I am asked to tell a little of my life story, I often start with my grandmother. Though I knew her for only the first five years of my life, I consider her a major influence" (6).

See also Mildred A. Hill's "The African-American Grandmother in Autobiographical Works by Frederick Douglass, Langston Hughes, and Maya Angelou."

10. I read Sylvia Plath's 1961 poem "Mirror" as portraying the process of aging as hideous through the visitation of her face as her mother's face in the mirror. Here are the last three lines of the poem:

> Each morning it is her face that replaces the darkness.
> In me she has drowned a young girl, and in me an old woman
> rises toward her day after day, like a terrible fish. (174)

11. Consider, for example, this passage from Simone de Beauvoir's *A Very Easy Death* in which Beauvoir, reflecting on the recent death of her mother and on the ways in which the lives of the two of them intertwined and diverged: "there are photographs of both of us, taken at about the same time: I am eighteen, she is nearly forty. Today I could almost be her mother and the grandmother of that sad-eyed girl" (120).

12. See my *Aging and Its Discontents* for a brief discussion of mirrors that do not produce the shock of aging (70–71).

13. Lynne Litman and Barbara Myerhoff, "Human Documentary," press release (March 15, 1976). Myerhoff is quoted in this document as saying, "In contacting them, I have found not only my childhood (I was raised by an Eastern European grandmother), but also my future, as an old lady. Our education, formal and informal, does not train us to cope with decrepitude and death. We are denied access to viable models of old people living among us. How then shall we rehearse and prepare for what is ahead? How shall we know the possibilities and limits of being old. . . . [We] are dehumanized and impoverished without our old people, for only by contact with them can we come to know ourselves, and only thus can we cease looking at 'them' as an alien remote people unconnected with ourselves." Here Myerhoff repeats the trope of Beauvoir.

14. Margaret Drabble writes of her character Liz Headland, who is a step-grandmother: "Liz is withering, the veins stand up on the back of her hands, and she is even developing dark freckly spots. She is putting on weight, but she is also withering. It is an interesting process, and she watches it with an amused fascination" (22). We learn early in the novel that Alix "does not find the company of old people easy" (43), yet we also learn at the same time that the poet Beaver, a "robust" man in his mid eighties, is experiencing the pleasures of having been rediscovered (45).

15. See my essay "Telling Stories" for a discussion of reminiscence, aging, and autobiography.

WORKS CITED

Abelin, Earnest A. "Triangulation, the Role of the Father and the Origins of Core Gender Identity during the Rapprochement Subphase." *Rapprochement: The Critical Subphase of Separation-Individuation.* Ed. Ruth F. Lax, Sheldon Bach, and J. Alexis Burland. New York: Aronson, 1980. 151–69.

Aldrich, Maria. "Lethal Brevity: Louise Bogan's Lyric Career." *Aging and Gender in Literature: Studies in Creativity.* Ed. Anne M. Wyatt-Brown and Janice Rossen. Charlottesville: UP of Virginia, 1993. 105–20.

Beauvoir, Simone de. *A Very Easy Death.* Trans. Patrick O'Brian. New York: Warner, 1973.

———. *The Coming of Age.* Trans. Patrick O'Brian. New York: Putnam's, 1972.

Bevington, Helen. *The Third Way: Reflections on Staying Alive.* Durham: Duke UP, 1996.

Bollas, Christopher. *Being a Character: Psychoanalysis and Self Experience.* New York: Hill, 1992.

Carpenter, Mary Wilson. "Female Grotesques in Academia." *Antifeminism in the Academy.* Ed. Veve Clark, Shirley Nelson Garner, Margaret Higonnet, and Ketu H. Katrak. New York: Routledge, 1996. 141–65.

Chodorow, Nancy. "Seventies Questions for Thirties Women: Gender and Generation in a Study of Early Women Psychoanalysts." *Feminism and Psychoanalytic Theory.* By Chodorow. New Haven: Yale UP, 1989.

Copper, Baba. *Over the Hill: Reflections on Ageism between Women.* Freedom: Crossing P, 1988.

Drabble, Margaret. *A Natural Curiosity.* New York: Viking, 1989.

Eiseley, Loren. *All the Strange Hours: The Excavation of a Life.* New York: Scribner's, 1975.

Freud, Sigmund. *The Standard Edition of the Complete Psychological Works of Sigmund Freud.* Ed. and trans. James Strachey. 24 vols. London: Hogarth and the Inst. of Psycho-Analysis, 1953–74.

———. "The Disposition to Obsessional Neurosis." 1913. SE 12: 317–26.

———. "A Disturbance of Memory on the Acropolis." 1936. SE 22: 239–48.

———. "Femininity." 1933. SE 22: 112–35.

———. *Interpretation of Dreams.* 1900. SE 4–5: xi–338, 339–627.

———. *Totem and Taboo.* 1913. SE 13: 1–162.

Friedan, Betty. *The Fountain of Age.* New York: Simon, 1993.

Gray, Francine du Plessix. "The Third Age." *The New Yorker* 26 Feb.–4 Mar. 1996: 186–92.

Hacker, Marilyn. *Selected Poems 1965–1990.* New York: Norton, 1994.

———. *Winter Numbers.* New York: Norton, 1994.

Hill, Mildred A. "The African-American Grandmother in Autobiographical Works by Frederick Douglass, Langston Hughes, and Maya Angelou." *International Journal of Aging and Human Development* 33.3 (1991): 173–85.

Hirsch, Marianne. *The Mother/Daughter Plot: Narrative, Psychoanalysis, Feminism.* Bloomington: Indiana UP, 1989.

Jardine, Alice. "Notes for Analysis." *Between Feminism and Psychoanalysis.* Ed. Teresa Brennan. London: Routledge, 1989. 73–85.

Kristeva, Julia. "Motherhood According to Giovanni Bellini" (1975). "Place Names" (1976). *Desire in Language: A Semiotic Approach to Literature and Art*. By Kristeva. Trans. Thomas Gora, Alice Jardine, and Leon S. Roudiez. New York: Columbia UP, 1980. 237–70. 271–94.

Kuhn, Maggie, with Christina Long and Laura Quinn. *No Stone Unturned: The Life and Times of Maggie Kuhn*. New York: Ballantine, 1991.

Litman, Lynne, and Barbara Myerhoff. "Human Documentary." Press Release. 15 Mar. 1976.

Lively, Penelope. *Moon Tiger*. Bath: Chivers, 1989.

Macdonald, Barbara, with Cynthia Rich. *Look Me in the Eye: Old Women, Aging and Ageism*. San Francisco: Spinster's Ink, 1983.

Mairs, Nancy. *Voice Lessons: On Becoming a (Woman) Writer*. Boston: Beacon P, 1994.

Mead, Margaret. *Blackberry Winter: My Earlier Years*. New York: Morrow, 1972.

Myerhoff, Barbara G. *Number Our Days*. New York: Simon, 1978.

Number Our Days. Dir. Lynne Litman. 1976.

Plath, Sylvia. *Collected Poems*. Ed. Ted Hughes. London: Faber, 1981.

Rich, Adrienne. *Of Woman Born: Motherhood as Experience and Institution*. New York: Norton, 1976.

Roof, Judith. "Generational Difficulties, or the Fear of a Barren History." *Feminisms and Generations*. Ed. E. Ann Kaplan and Devoney Looser. Minneapolis: U of Minnesota P, 1997. 69–87.

Spacks, Patricia Meyer. "Stages of Self: Notes on Autobiography and the Life Cycle." *Boston University Journal* 25.2 (1977): 7–18.

Steinem, Gloria. *Revolution from Within: A Book of Self-Esteem*. New York: Corgi, 1993.

"Talking Across." A Conversation between Jane Gallop and Elizabeth Francis. *Feminisms and Generations*. Ed. E. Ann Kaplan and Devoney Looser. Minneapolis: U of Minnesota P, 1997. 103–31.

West, Jessamyn. *Hide and Seek: A Continuing Journey*. New York: Harcourt, 1973.

Woodward, Kathleen. *Aging and Its Discontents: Freud and Other Fictions*. Bloomington: Indiana UP, 1991

———. "Telling Stories: Aging, Reminiscence, and the Life Review." *Journal of Aging and Identity* 2.3 (1997): 149–63.

VISUALIZING AGE, PERFORMING AGE

Trauma and Aging
Marlene Dietrich, Melanie Klein, and Marguerite Duras

E. Ann Kaplan

A man has every season while a woman only has
the right to spring. That disgusts me.

— Jane Fonda (1989)

Suicide is disproportionately common among
the elderly, as people face loneliness, infirmity,
and the prospect of a mental slide into oblivion.

— *New York Times* (1996)

A crumbling scaffold riddled with osteoporosis
probably is not an ideal one to go through nine
months of pregnancy.

— Dr. Healey (1995)

In this essay, I will first argue that, at least for western women, aging has been
and may yet be experienced as a kind of "trauma." Having worked this argument through, in Part II of this essay, I want to challenge the conception of aging
as trauma—not by disproving what I have already shown (I think aging IS a
trauma for some within modern ways of seeing and knowing)[1]—but by seeking
out new future (even millennial) paradigms for conceptualizing aging that may
begin to free women from dire humanist projections.

Working within modern paradigms in Part I, I focus on how discourses about aging, including cultural forms, are produced, circulated, used, and lived. There are three stages to this argument. I will show, first, that aging can be a trauma for all of us, existentially. Second, that aging need not *necessarily* be a trauma for women, but that western cultures may produce this result—particularly perhaps for white women—through prevailing gender constructs, and specifically the anxiety of (white) males about their own aging and their own death. And third and finally, that fears about global aging are a condensation of existential fears of aging (both male and female) and of patriarchal repulsion of the specificity of female aging. This repulsion emerges in current cultural and historical anxieties about a future world deprived of a generation of young people through which to negotiate denial of (white male) aging.

But first some general caveats and definitions. Scholars tend to use the term "aging" as an abstract developmental concept, and as if it connoted experiences common to all. While in what I have said above I may seem to fall into the same trap, I want to qualify my position now. For the specific contexts within which one ages clearly make a huge difference outside of the possibly general existential human predicament: I have in mind not only gender and race, but also one's culture, nationality, religion, and even geography.[2] In addition, scholars need to distinguish aging without severe health problems from aging *with* serious health problems. Too easily ill health in aging people is collapsed into the aging process itself. Another difference is the historical moment in which one is aging, since discourses about aging even within the same culture change with other historical and social changes. Like most human experiences, aging needs to be situated, and linked to gendered, raced, and cultural specificities.

Further, I recognize the dangers of collapsing widely differing uses of the term "trauma." Clearly the word used in relation to Holocaust victims or the victims of racism takes on quite different dimensions than when used in relation to aging. I have in mind ideologically and historically produced trauma rather than trauma produced through social institutions or through accident.

I also understand the danger of distinguishing men and women in regard to aging. But I am encouraged in my project by psychotherapist Laura S. Brown's essay in Cathy Caruth's edited volume, *Trauma: Explorations in Memory* (1995). Brown rehearses the Psychiatric Association's 1987 DSM III-R definition of trauma which states: "The person has experienced an event that is outside the range of human experience" (250). She argues that "human" here really means "male" and that the violence and abuse many women endure at the hands of men upon whom they depend within the private, interpersonal realm may represent a sufficient kind of damage to be named "trauma." It is a kind of trauma not often recognized in studies of trauma, and it may bear a similar *structure* to more dramatic and vast *public* damage usually the focus of such studies.

But how can I argue that *aging* is outside the range of "human experience"? And even if I persuade readers that aging itself is a trauma, how could I prove that it is more severe for women than for men? Indeed, I appropriate the phrase "trauma and aging" from another chapter in Cathy Caruth's pioneering anthology, but I use it in a different sense. Henry Krystal employs the phrase to discuss his important work with a specific aging group, namely, Holocaust survivors. He is interested in the impact of the trauma of the Holocaust on survivors as they age. While survivors of all ages are traumatized, what Krystal shows is how much worse it is for the aged survivors. "Old age poses a question of diminishing gratification, and, in this population, with serious to severe anhedonia being a common finding, we could expect special difficulty," he writes. "The progressive loss of gratification, support and distraction limits the choices to the two alternatives: integration of one's life or living in despair" (77).

We might say that these survivors experienced double trauma—that of the Holocaust and that which aging involves. Krystal argues that "integration of one's life" is part of aging successfully. For this specific group, that would mean being reconciled to the fact of the Holocaust—something impossible for most survivors. But the other trauma that many share is best expressed by Sartre's existentialist drama *Huis clos* (1947)—that life itself is a kind of prison, a hell, from which one cannot escape. The trauma of aging consists in being *in time* and unable to get out of it. One irrevocably *must* age; one must deal with the ravages of the aging body; and one must confront the fact that death is inevitable. All of which can be experienced as a trauma, which, though basic to human existence, is paradoxically also "outside human experience" in that no one returns from death.

With these caveats in mind, then, I argue that aging to an inevitable death on one level may itself be a kind of "trauma" for all humans. It is especially the increasing series of losses—of bodily function and appearance, of mental agility, of ideologies and values one grew up with, of friends and family—that may be traumatic for everyone in western culture. One may experience a kind of "loss" in the increasing gap between values and ideologies one carries with one from youth and the very different values in the culture within which one has aged. The loss is of a community of shared beliefs and world views.[3] These losses may apply to many, but here I want to explore the specificity of the trauma for select white women of European origin, living within certain locations and cultural/national contexts.[4]

In Part I, then, I provide examples of the trauma of aging through particularly poignant images that affected me powerfully as I was doing the research for this essay. All images are of twentieth-century women represented in narratives constructed by others and/or by themselves. There is first the image of an aging, and then aged Marlene Dietrich in Chris Hunt's documentary *Shadow and Light* (1993); second, the image of Melanie Klein in Nicholas Wright's play *Mrs. Klein* (1988); and finally, images of Marguerite Duras in a television interview and in her own narrative recording of herself aging in her diary-text, *C'est tout* (1995). The structure of the trauma is in each case different, because the historical era, national identity, and careers of the women differ. But there are some striking similarities. The fact that the women are white and European, and all (at least as adults) lived privileged lives, may be a common factor in their struggles with aging. It is possible that the *very privilege of white middle-class women prior to their aging* creates the trauma for them. Other people may not have the privilege of middle-class expectations either for a long life or for a life without suffering; this topic I will take up in future research.

I. THREE MODERNIST FEMALE AGING PARADIGMS

Aging and the Patriarchal Gaze: The Case of Marlene Dietrich

Within modernity, an aspect of aging as trauma that has distinguished men and women is women's social positioning as "to be gazed at." This gaze produces a specific *kind of female identity* (as much feminist research in the 1980s showed). Women's social positioning as "to be gazed at" may make aging especially traumatic in relation to the sheer external changes in the human body—even for those women who successfully negotiated prevailing female cultural mandates when young. As a woman's appearance begins to lose its youthfulness, there may be a crisis of identity: I am either good, beautiful, whole, and to be loved; or bad, ugly, fragmented, and unlovable, according to the degree to which my appearance fits into prevailing cultural discourses about "ideal" female beauty. Who am I if I am no longer a desirable object to be gazed at? Who am I if I do not like gazing at myself anymore because of unwelcome wrinkles and lines, sagging eyelids, and bags under the eyes?

My third epigraph shows that negative discourses about the postmenopausal female body—a body no longer amenable to being the object of the desiring male gaze—remain very much alive in American culture. Negativity about aging women's bodies is belied in the unhappy metaphor Dr. Healey chooses in her discussion of the implications of new reproductive medical technologies (specifically, removing a woman's ovaries before menopause and then replacing them after menopause when the woman may be fifty-five or more so as to allow her to give birth). Describing such a woman's body as a "crumbling scaffold, riddled with osteoporosis," Healey gives voice to her preconceptions about menopausal and postmenopausal women. She assumes that a woman this age is already "riddled with osteoporosis," something far from necessarily true. Relying on Darwinian notions of biological processes, Healey regards the procedure as clearly "against nature," and therefore offensive. In using an architectural metaphor for the body, Healey reworks ancient concepts: here the bones are the scaffold, the flesh the materials used to fill in the scaffold. The metaphor implies that once the infrastructure is ruined, as in the woman's bones (assumed to be damaged), the building is useless, and the woman by implication also useless. Here a postmenopausal woman who desires to prolong her reproductive (and by implication, sexual) life after menopause is stereotyped as monstrous. In this metaphor one can see how the medical establishment uses cultural discourses about female aging so as to render such ongoing research in reproductive technology pejorative, and possibly limit future research of this kind. The shocked reaction to the postmenopausal women in their fifties and sixties in England, Italy, and the United States who, with the aid of in vitro fertilization, recently gave birth to children, exemplifies the public and medical establishment's underlying disgust of the aging female body, a disgust that women internalize growing up in western cultures.

Given such powerful cultural discourses circulating in western cultures, it is not surprising that the dramatic changes in one's appearance that are associated with aging can be so traumatic for some women. Marlene Dietrich was particularly vulnerable to aging trauma because she was not only a successful Hollywood actress, used to being the object of the admiring male gaze, but was also intelligent, ambitious, and politically savvy (I am thinking of her outspoken disgust at Nazism and her participation in the war effort). The well-known crisis of aging female film stars and performers on the screen and in life exemplifies in the extreme the difficulties of aging for many women[5] (see Kaplan 1997). Marlene Dietrich is a particularly haunting example of a star who "lived" the cultural discourses in which being an object "to be gazed at"—a constant object of the admiring male gaze—had been conditioned in her and ultimately constituted much of her identity.

As a young German actress working in Germany in the era that spawned Hitler and Nazism, Dietrich was noticed by Josef von Sternberg and brought to the United States to act in his films. Her white, blonde, blue-eyed beauty was close to the ideal American form, but never quite achieved it—perhaps because her sharply etched high cheekbones, her coolly disdainful glance, her arched eyebrows, and her wide smile somehow never conveyed unalloyed or innocent pleasure. Dietrich knew how to present her body as a charged sexual object. Her long legs were evidently what first attracted von Sternberg, and her trademark svelte, tight-fitting dresses always revealed the elegance of her body's shape. Moreover, von Sternberg deliberately created for Dietrich an androgynous image that was challenging for its time. We might say that Dietrich symbolized the dark side of Marilyn Monroe, the side that Marilyn kept from public view. She was the all-knowing, sexually experienced woman to Monroe's precocious sexuality and innocence—the perfect mix for American male fantasy.[6] Dietrich's German accent further set her apart and prevented her finding the kind of adoration that Monroe obtained. As Richard Schickel put it at the time of Dietrich's death in 1992, quoting Kenneth Tynan, "She *knows* where all the flowers went," and, he added, "It is possible that she carried that instinctive knowledge in her soul long before she or anyone else recognized it."

This dark knowledge of aging as trauma is born out, I want to suggest, in two of the images we see of Dietrich in the documentary film *Shadow and Light*, images that are amplified by the information supplied by people interviewed

Figure 1. Marlene Dietrich. Everett Collection.

in the film. It does not matter for my purposes how "true" the events related in the film are: the language used by the interviewees provides evidence for the trauma of aging. I might note in passing that in the case of Dietrich (as will also be true of Melanie Klein), there is the particularly interesting twist to the experience of aging that has to do with each aging mother's relationship to her daughter. While mothers, daughters, and aging must be the topic of another essay, I will briefly address it in what follows.

Perhaps most striking in *Shadow and Light* is the role played by Dietrich's only daughter, Maria. The spectator must look between the lines, so to speak, and then speculate about Maria's resentment of her mother. But there is an abundance of evidence in Maria's facial expressions and gestures as she speaks, as well as in some of her barely audible asides. As a main interlocutor in the film, Maria, it is clear, has an investment in her mother having suffered aging trauma, for it was (arguably) only at that point that Maria could begin to reverse the power imbalance she had thus far had to endure all her life up to then. Whereas there may be a softening or "coming to terms" on the part of some mothers and daughters as they both grow older, evidently in the case of Marlene and Maria, this did not happen—something important and interesting in itself.

The documentary's frank rehearsing of quite intimate details of Dietrich's personal life allows one to infer what difficulties Maria might have had as the daughter of this lively, sexually vital, and engaging actress. Marlene had numerous lovers while still married to Maria's father, Rudy. Once Dietrich (at about thirty-eight years of age) became the highest-paid female actress in Hollywood through von Sternberg's efforts, she took long vacations on the French Riviera where these lovers joined her at various times—sometimes more than one at a time. Home-movie clips occasionally show Maria (perhaps a young teenager) bravely trying to get along with these lovers, or adopting poses on the rocks by the sea not unlike those Marlene is seen adopting. One wonders about the impact on a young girl of the life she witnessed. One wonders how she was cared for, what schooling she had. While the documentary tells us nothing about Maria directly, it's clear that Maria greatly resented—and after her mother's death still resented—Dietrich's many lovers and narcissistic life. One comment may reveal what has all along troubled Maria. When talking about the end of Dietrich's affair with von Sternberg, Maria (apparently identifying with von Sternberg's disillusionment in her mother, in particular his being closed out periodically) says, "If you do that a few times, and then she comes back to you, this wonderful enigma, and makes you love her, your mind is churned as in a laundry wringer, back and forth in this emotional see-saw." A bit later on, still discussing Dietrich's many lovers, Maria says in a barely audible aside, "if she ever knew how to love," here perhaps providing the clearest evidence of her own sense of being unloved, neglected, and unable to compete with all the lovers for Marlene's attention. It is not insignificant that throughout the interview Maria refers to her mother as "Dietrich," not "my mother." This puts a great distance between herself and her mother, a distance that reflects her unresolved emotions.

Meanwhile, while sympathizing with the child, the viewer can only speculate about the impact *on Dietrich* of Maria's sadistic witnessing of her mother's difficulties in losing her beauty. Keeping close to her mother, evidently, Maria describes preparing Dietrich for her cabaret performances when her mother was seventy or so and an alcoholic. Maria's description of bandaging her mother's leg between acts (the oozing wound beneath the shimmering dress would not heal because of her alcoholism) barely conceals her disgust which was, however, combined with a certain admiration for Dietrich's bravery as a "soldier on stage." Far less ambivalent is the touching, sympathetic portrayal the actress Glynis Johns provides of Dietrich plaiting her hair in tight little braids, linking them over her head so that the skin on her face was pulled tight, and then putting on a wig. (The spectator can only assume that Dietrich has this braided hair and wig on in one of the interviews in the film. Her mouth can barely move, so tightly stretched is her skin.) Johns seems admiring that Dietrich could endure this pain (Dietrich did undergo several facelifts, perhaps unbeknownst to her friends).

Several other people interviewed in the film testify to Dietrich's concern with her external appearance. Richard Todd notes that everyone knew she was careful, even "persnickety" about her external image, her looks. "She was well-preserved," Todd says, "and insisted on having her clothes designed by Dior." The narrator mentions that "Dietrich found it harder to sustain her image" as she neared fifty, and goes on to show how she suffered from the competition of Hollywood's latest discovery, Elizabeth Taylor, who married several of Marlene's former lovers. Dietrich struggled to keep up her image as a glamorous woman, performing way into her seventies. In the documentary we see her traveling all over the world, bravely performing, loving the attention, and trying to preserve the glistening beauty for which she had been so renowned.

When she was seventy-four years old, just after playing her final film role in *Just a Gigolo* (1978), Dietrich, we are informed dramatically by the narrator, "was driven to her Paris apartment," where she spent the last twelve years of her life in bed, "connected to the outside world by her telephone." Maria's revenge may have been the photo that she (possibly) took toward the very end of her mother's life. As Maria puts it, Dietrich did not become a recluse because she was afraid of age *per se*, but "because the legend could no longer be re-embellished." Maria further confides, "Anything degenerate, any decay of the Dietrich picture was abhorrent to her." The images from the end of the documentary that made me gasp, thus revealing my identification with Dietrich's trauma about her image, are ones that I cannot imagine anyone other than someone very close to Dietrich having had a chance to take. The first shot shows a surprised Dietrich, sitting up in bed, dressed all in white, with her hair pinned behind a bandana, revealing an ugly forehead and cheeks white with a facial (attesting to her continuing concern with her image, despite now being a recluse). Clearly Dietrich was not expecting to be photographed. Indeed, she is in the midst of protesting as the shot is taken. Too late! Posterity has the image she so feared—of a gaunt, aged face, trying to hide behind the windows of her Paris flat. Was Maria taking her revenge on her mother's narcissism that must have wounded her too much to forgive her, ever?

The second image is perhaps even more terrifying to me in relation to the trauma of aging. It is another still photograph from inside the flat—this time of an empty wheelchair, positioned at the tall glass windows. Presumably Dietrich (who so feared a gaze that would catch her wrinkled face) sat here in the afternoons and gazed out at the life going by in the street below, a life she had excluded herself from because of her own trauma of aging. She would control the gaze now—not because of the changes in her body *per se*, as we saw, but for fear of anyone *seeing* the changes.

These two photographs positioned at the end of the film speak volumes about Dietrich's incredible investment in her external image—in being the adored object of the male gaze and of the camera. They tell much about Maria as well, whose investment in ruining Dietrich's image is also clear (in the entire documentary, the only time that Maria speaks approvingly of her mother is when she describes Dietrich's participation in the war effort in 1943). Thus, in the case of Dietrich, the aging heroine is presented as devastated by the split between dramatic aging on the outside and the inner desire for continuing beauty and professional involvement. Once aging was out of her control, and her body could not be patched up, then she wanted to preserve her public and perfect image by not allowing anyone to see her as she now was, and thus imposed a prison sentence on herself. In Dietrich's case, her specific identity as a famous and beautiful Hollywood actress put particular pressures on her as she aged, articulated as a triangular struggle amongst her public image, her actual appearance, and her identity as tied up with the "perfect" screen and stage "picture."

Aging and the Intellectual Woman: The Case of Melanie Klein

My second example introduces a different arena—the trauma of aging in the intellectual sphere. If women are located so as to have an identity that is not confined to external appearance, they may avoid the distress of external physical signs of aging that obviously traumatized Dietrich. But they may still be unable to avoid prejudice and rejection. Here aging women come up against prejudices in regard to their continuing intellectual curiosity.

My example here is the representation of Melanie Klein in Nicholas Wright's play *Mrs. Klein*. Even before I saw the play, I had an image of Klein as a rather cantankerous, difficult psychoanalyst whose theories were viewed a bit askance, especially by some British Freudians. This ambivalence about Klein was produced, I knew, partly through debates and conflicts with Anna Freud in London, since Freud would not tolerate what she saw as deviations from her father's theory. From reading Phyllis Grosskurth's biography of Klein, I thought that perhaps negative reactions to Klein also arose partly from British anti-Semitism. But, after seeing Wright's play, I concluded that the hostility to Klein was not only that she was Jewish and refused to blindly follow Freud (she argued that her theories were merely extensions of Freud's in any case), but that, as an aging woman, she continued to be intellectually aggressive, brilliant, and innovative. Unlike aging male intellectuals, women are supposed to with-

Figure 2. Uta Hagen as Melanie in Mrs. Klein. *Photo: © Carol Rosegg.*

draw from the public sphere, cede to the young scholars upcoming, and rest on their laurels.

Set in 1934 London, Wright's play dramatizes a specific moment in Melanie Klein's menopausal life, when, at the age of fifty-two, she learns of the sudden death of her son Hans.[7] The intersection of intellect and emotion is particularly fascinating in Klein's case because her intellectual life and her career are involved in the theory and practice of a cure for emotional ills via a psychoanalyst/patient relationship. This relationship, *for the patient if also at times for the analyst*, deals specifically with emotions. Since her intellectual contribution to psychoanalysis was in the area of infant-mother relations, Wright has Klein's relations to her children (Hans and Melitta/Dr. Schmideberg) *mirror* her psychoanalytic theories. In so doing, Wright focuses on a little discussed, and fascinating, aspect of Klein's life.

I find Wright's representation of Klein particularly compelling because of the intergenerational competitiveness between mother and daughter which is similar to that I noted with Dietrich (it is also, of course, different). Wright links this competitiveness to Klein's psychoanalytic theories, which he interleaves with the play's narrative. That is, he shows Klein using her theories to defend against the jealousy and plotting on the part of the two younger women in the play, one of whom is her daughter, Melitta Schmideberg, herself already an analyst who is siding with colleagues opposing her mother's theories. But how far does the play show Klein as a victim of her own theories of the mother? It does so, I think, in the deliberate play on links between Klein's life and her psychoanalytic theories—between her intellect and her emotional life. Does the play intend us to believe Klein's theories have arisen unconsciously through her own needs to control and dominate? Is Klein to be understood as invading the unconscious of the child with her own unconscious knowledge of herself as a devouring, controlling mother, one narcissistically symbiotic with Melitta, insisting on keeping her close to her?

The answers depend on whether a spectator believes Melitta or Klein in their theoretical/emotional debates over the cause of Hans's death and over how Klein mothered her children. Central to the battle is Melitta's claim that Melanie neglected and damaged her children by turning them into psychoanalytic patients in order to develop her theories of child analysis. Melitta chooses a moment when Melanie is especially vulnerable due to the shock of Hans's sudden death—which Melitta claims was suicide, not a climbing accident as the play later affirms, because she wants to blame her mother for what happened to Hans as well as to her. Melitta insinuates that Hans had an arrested Oedipus complex vis-à-vis his mother, and that Klein was jealous of Hans's lovers.

A main fight in the play occurs over a letter Melitta has written to Melanie claiming that Hans committed suicide instead of being killed in some kind of climbing accident. At the start of the play, Melanie receives this letter but, intuitively fearing it, decides to delay opening it. Once Melitta raises the question of the letter, Klein opens it, but decides to tear it up, at which point Melitta delivers the letter's contents verbally. In theorizing Hans's suicidal state of mind—which Melitta links to his childhood analysis by his mother, as well as to her own analysis as a child—Melitta partly throws back her mother's theories at her, and partly challenges them. Klein's responses echo her theories of a split between the "real" mother and the "symbolic" mother. In telling Melitta that she must solve the problem of her mother with her analyst, Klein is being consistent. She argues that Melitta has not yet worked through her early dual mother fantasies to see the mother "whole."

Yet in the context of the play, Klein's reliance on theory (intellect) in the heat of their arguments seems as cruel to Melitta as Melitta's attempts to make her mother shoulder the guilt for Hans's death. It appears that Klein also uses theory as a defense against addressing her daughter's feelings. She pushes the feelings away, becomes the detached analyst asking Melitta to deal with her feelings within a transferential relationship with her analyst, not directly with her mother. Klein, in other words, refuses to answer the charges made by her daughter because her theory tells her they have to do with fantasy, not reality.

How are we to view this? As Klein's own inability to engage in one-on-one relating? Perhaps this is how Wright understands it, following Grosskurth.[8] But is this the only way to see it? Is Wright correct in presenting Klein's desperate need to control everyone, including (nay, principally) her daughter, as a main theme? It would seem that, in presenting Klein in this way, Wright is critiquing not only the intellectual woman (she is shown using her intellect to distance herself from her emotions which, in the feminine stereotype, she should value), but also psychoanalysis as practice and burgeoning institution.

In the written version of Mrs. Klein, when interacting with other characters, Klein mainly represents powerful intellect. However, in Uta Hagen's strong portrayal of Klein in the performance I saw of the play in New York in 1995, I saw emotion break through logical argument. Or, in reverse, almost as soon as emotion emerges, Klein begins to theorize what she's experiencing. For instance, in their long debate about the death of Hans, Melitta's older brother and Klein's second child (was it suicide? was it an accident?), there are several moments when Klein seems on the verge of emotionally breaking down, only to recover herself and continue the analysis of her relationships with both Melitta and Hans, while Melitta continues to try to convince her mother that Hans committed suicide. In this scene, Klein is made to summarize her theories regarding the baby's relation to the mother's breast—that it prevents the child from seeing the mother "whole," as both good and bad, loving and rejecting, and that understanding this signifies the cure to neurosis. Klein first accepts the suicide hypothesis, although it is terribly painful for her: "What none of us cares to ask is why a healthy, reasonably happy man of twenty-seven should. . . . You're too defensive. I'm too frightened. No I'm damn well not" (54). It's that spirited rebuttal of her fear that signals emotion being controlled by intellect and active mental curiosity about the problem at hand. She follows this soon with a detached analysis of Hans and his relation to the breast, which, of course, was her own. Here, her theory and her reality as mother coalesce in this extraordinary manner.

But she immediately turns cruelly on Melitta, in perhaps conscious revenge for Melitta's cruelty to her regarding Hans, and critiques Melitta's psychoanalytic techniques. The violence between them escalates until it erupts in physical action—Klein throwing wine at Melitta and cramming pieces of her torn letter into her mouth. But Wright again represents Klein as putting intellect over emotion: that is, we see how the force of Klein's intellect once again brings her to gain control over her violent emotion. This enables Melitta also to gain control and soon they are back to intellectual analyses of Klein's relations to her children.

Here, then, one sees how the play represents Klein as a kind of monster in defending herself, in refusing to capitulate to her daughter. It is her very intellectual agility as a menopausal woman that the play uses to produce her as monstrous, thus reinforcing stereotypes of the aging woman as "normal" only if she will "quiet down," so to speak. Perhaps even more important is the need to render the older intellectual woman as sexless—neither properly male nor female.

Trauma and Aging

Resisting Aging Categories: The Case of Marguerite Duras

Also white and European, Marguerite Duras had an upbringing quite different from both the previous two women. Born in Indochina, Duras never felt completely at home in France, where she lived and worked. From a young age, she was a rebel. Her love affair when she was fifteen with a Chinese man who was twelve years older, fictionalized so beautifully in her novel *L'Amant* (made into an exquisite film in 1993), violated the gender codes of her family and historical era. As a prolific and successful novelist, screenwriter, and playwright, Duras was always a loner: a feminist by nature, Duras marched to her own drummer—something that did not endear her to critics and scholars.[9]

In refusing the codes of her nation, situation, and gender, Duras avoided being a victim of those codes, as was Dietrich. While Klein did not internalize the codes that insisted she cede the intellectual terrain to younger women, she could not escape the conflicts, struggles, and endless contestations of an institution as vital and engaged as was psychoanalysis in its formative years. Duras, I suggest, only avoided being victimized by patriarchal codes by living as a kind of loner, living according to her own values and goals as a dedicated and prolific writer.

For many years, Duras seemed impervious to aging. Her brilliant film, *Le Camion* (1977), is basically an extended monologue by Duras, who herself acts the aging lady whom a truck driver (played by Gérard Depardieu) picks up. There is some dialogue between the protagonists, as the two face each other across a table in a darkened room—Duras deliberately casts aside the cinematic realism that would require the encounter to take place inside a truck. Duras has no apparent problem with her image as an aging woman in the film. As quoted by Mary Lydon, Duras noted, "I couldn't have made *Le Camion* if I had the slightest modesty. You have to be immodest to make *Le Camion*, but immodesty is humility perhaps" (164). According to Lydon, "It is Duras's dazzling originality to star, finally, in her own cinema, by virtue of what is most ordinary about her, what she shares with all other women, the eclipse of sexual identity, the invisibility conferred by advancing years" (165). (I assume Lydon alludes here to the aging discourse I have outlined earlier as *it* assigns these positions to aging women.) Lydon suggests that *Le Camion* forces spectators, paradoxically, to *see* the aging woman whom the truck driver would normally totally ignore and who in fact is shown to have zero interest in her during the film. Duras achieves *visibility* for aging women in this way, and is prepared to put her body on the line in the film to produce this visibility.

In her own life, Duras achieved something similar by continuing to have love affairs with younger men, defying cultural norms again, just as she had in loving an older man at fifteen. Unconsciously, perhaps, Duras was enacting her own concept of aging as "regression," which Lydon alludes to, and replaying her love for her younger brother who died prematurely.[10]

But perhaps to say Duras was *impervious* to her aging is to misstate the case. In some ways, Duras's entire corpus is about death. Unlike either of the two other women discussed here, Duras always foregrounded death, and thus she had already looked beyond aging to its inevitable result. She did not turn away from knowledge of death, but rather built this knowledge into her aesthetic forms and themes.

In the fascinating interview conducted in 1984 by Bernard Pivot for the television program *Apostrophes* in France, Duras sits very still, looking very small at one end of the table, facing Pivot. It seems that she cannot move her face too easily, since she speaks in a clipped way through a nearly closed mouth. Or perhaps this way of speaking is a strategy to keep a certain control over the interview, given Pivot's flamboyant, noisy style. It's only when she smiles that her face lights up. What particularly interests me in relation to aging are the photographs of Duras that are inserted periodically throughout the interview— indeed sometimes superimposed on our view of Duras in the present.[11] Most striking is the photograph of Duras as a very young woman—perhaps still a teenager, perhaps indeed at the time of the novel that is first featured in the interview, *L'Amant* (*The Lover*). The extraordinarily youthful and unusual beauty in this photograph—superimposed on that of the aging Duras—surely references the narrator's own discussion of aging in the opening pages of the novel. Just as the TV interview superimposes the aging and youthful Duras, so the narrator of *The Lover* juxtaposes herself aging and herself young through the stranger's comment: "Rather than your face as a young woman, I prefer your face as it is now. Ravaged" (3). The narrator goes on to say that she "grew old at eighteen," and continues: "My aging was very sudden. I saw it spread over my features one by one, changing the relationship between them. . . . I watched this process with the same sort of interest I might have taken in the reading of a book" (4). Perhaps most important of all is the narrator's sense that she has kept that new face, even if it is "scored with deep, dry wrinkles," and "the skin is cracked." But she ends with a less hopeful statement when she says of her face: "It's kept the same contours, but its substance has been laid waste. I have a face laid waste" (5). Interestingly, the script for the film later made into *The Lover* changes this last phrase to "I have a destroyed face."

Exactly what the narrator means by this is unclear. But the viewer cannot help but reflect on the contrasting images of the youthful image in the TV interview overlaid on the present live image of Duras, now seventy. Duras herself seems resigned, stoical, if not entirely accepting of the changes with the passing of time. We know that she remained intellectually and sexually active until near the end of her life, belying and defying cultural stereotypes just as she had courageously defied mainstream culture as a teenager when she ran off with the Chinese man more than ten years older than herself.

Yet, in the very last months of her life, Duras begins to articulate the trauma her characters had uttered long before her. In *C'est tout*, which consists of (imaginary?) dialogues between herself and her lover, Yann (presumably Yann Andrea Steiner, who was a frequent figure in Duras's works in the 1980s and 1990s), Duras confronts the void that death has to be for the non-religious. As a kind of diary of the last year of her life, *C'est tout* records even more graphically than her other works the experience of facing death. The first months of the diary describe Duras's inner state as a kind of emptiness: "Sometimes I am empty for a long time" ("Quelquefois je suis vide pendant très longtemps"), or as an absence of identity: "I have no identity. . . . I am a little removed from the place I speak from" (Je suis sans identité. . . . Un peu absente du lieu où je parle") (8). She still hopes to write a book, but is unsure if she can. When Yann asks if she is afraid of death, Duras is unable to say. The title for her next book, she says, is *The Book of Disappearing* (*Le Livre à disparaître*). She is preoccupied with writing, with love, and with death. With horror of love and fear of death.

By the "horror of love" she perhaps alludes to her constant preoccupation with the impossibility of desire and its object coming together, because the foundation of desire in the first place is the radical separateness of bodies and identities. As Leslie Hill puts it, "It is only ever when there is no possibility of relation between self and other that the other may be grasped as radically different, and thus genuinely desirable" (139). This, I think, is the "horror of love" for Duras: the most sexually desirable body is that which (like her Chinese lover), for social, political or cultural reasons, one cannot have.

It is only right at the end of the diary that there is any reference to the body. And just because it is the single instance of such a reference, it strikes the reader with great force. After a passage in which Duras declares that her life is ended, she states that she has become "completely terrifying" ("Je suis devenue complètement effrayante")—presumably to some spectator? to herself?[12] This is followed by these words: "I am falling apart. Come quickly. I no longer have a mouth, no longer a face" ("Je ne tiens plus ensemble. Viens vite. Je n'ai plus de bouche, plus de visage"). The shock to Duras of her fragmenting bodily schema is graphic in this powerful image. "No longer a face." It was this phrase that especially caught my eye since it seems that in western culture the face looms so large in the external appearance of a person.[13] I was struck that even for someone so sensitive to inner states as Duras, at the end the focus is on the look. And I was reminded of Kathleen Woodward's insights, building on Simone de Beauvoir and Sartre and in reference to Proust, that "to see, like Marcel, one's own aged body with a shock of recognition is to experience the uncanny" (63).

Duras's bravery and independence, however, allowed her to bring readers close to her experience of death and to represent herself to us, instead of being *represented*, as in the cases of Dietrich and Klein. Perhaps it was her defiance of mainstream culture that brought her this privilege.

II. FUTURE AGING PARADIGMS FOR A POSTMODERN AGE

Especially in the examples of Dietrich and Klein where the historical figures are represented by others, I have implicitly referenced three paradigms—one biological, one economic, and one psychological—that might explain the negative images of aging in western modern culture. The first is strictly biological and linked to survival of the species: in this Darwinian story, women's role in reproduction is central. Once a woman's childbearing years are completed, her role in the survival of the species is over and she can be discarded. (Men, of course, generally speaking, do not suffer this limitation.) Elements of this modernist biological determinist story circulate today in medical discourse (they are patently evident, for example, in Dr. Healey's words in my epigraph). The economic story has to do with notions of social efficiency and making the best use of the human body to produce material and intellectual goods. In this story, older people, who have made their contributions, should give way to those younger: the images of Melanie Klein in Wright's play seemed to adhere to this story.[14] The psychological developmental story is linked to this one: Erik Erikson's stage theory requires that older people either become generative, taking pleasure in supporting the young while stepping aside and preparing for death, or yield to despair.

I am dissatisfied with these major and pervasive modernist models of aging. Feminists need to develop new paradigms for conceptualizing aging as humans near the millennium, because it marks the development of new conceptions of aging partly produced through new scientific possibilities for delaying the effects of aging. As noted earlier, discourses—as much as biological realities—influence how individuals regard themselves as they age. In the nineteenth century, a woman of forty or fifty years was already considered "old," and most likely felt and acted as such. In our own period, women of this age are still considered relatively "young." New technologies change both what is possible and our thinking about what is possible.

Dire projections and ideas of the body in decay, typical of modern thinking, require challenging in light of medical and digital innovations. Women need to live aging differently, which means that they have to reconceptualize the very concept of growing old. Feminist psychoanalytic and postmodern/cyberage theories offer useful insights for challenging developmental models that make one a prisoner of one's developmental age. Chronological age is in one sense unavoidable (and therefore traumatic on the level I first talked about). But in the postmodern era of medical advances and digital technologies, age is being configured differently than before. It destabilizes the Darwinian discourse in beneficial ways if older women cannot be relied upon to fit their biological stages, and if women do not themselves view their lives as consisting of such pre-established and inevitable "stages."[15]

At the other extreme is the vision of cyberpunks. According to *Mondo 2000 User's Guide*, cyberpunks are deep into fantasies about the "extension of human possibilities by chemical and surgical intervention" (164). I mention this only to open up yet another theater of aging—that of preventing aging and death through increases in longevity. As *Mondo* puts it, "Self-experimentation seems logical. We'd better work with our own raw material: it's carrying an expiration date. . . . The obvious move is jiggering one's own biochemistry for personal fulfillment." The article on longevity goes on to discuss a "Transtime" laboratory where the science of "cryonics" (freezing the entire body or parts of a dead person, especially the brain, in the hopes of reanimating people in the future) is being carried out. In this vision, "the future will see a radical assault on aging in seven parts: cryonics, interventive gerontology (studying the aging process to do something about it), transplants, artificial organs, resuscitation, regeneration and cloning" (164).

In one sense, these are attractive fantasies: like many people, I fear death. So, it is gratifying to imagine ways of delaying the inevitable, to imagine living for many years more than I might expect. On the other hand, thinking less fantastically, I worry about efforts to radically alter the life course. Since I first began to work on this essay, cloning of humans has become a real scientific possibility in the wake of successful cloning of sheep, monkeys, and mice. The idea has spawned much media and collegial debate—something significant in itself. It's clear that having a clone of myself would not perpetuate "me." There would be another human with my genes, personality tendencies, and identical visual appearance. But "I" have been produced through my particular historical moment, relationships to siblings, specific parenting and child-rearing theories of the time, political and intellectual environment, and more. The clone would grow up a completely new person, so I would not in fact be perpetuated.

Living longer through the use of organs taken from other humans, however, does seem a technology I would make use of, one which offers interesting notions of bodies that are communal, in a sense. As the protagonist in Marlene Gorris's inspiring 1995 film *Antonia's Line* puts it, "Life wants to live." Like others, then, I am interested in exploring ways to prolong life as long as it is not at the expense of *living* (that is, being tied to a respirator and so on).

But there are other technologies that will preserve one's youthful image, and that might have enabled an actress like Dietrich to continue on film after her physical body aged. New digital technologies will enable aging actresses on film to look as they did at twenty. Further, we will be able to re-create famous actresses like Marilyn Monroe playing new roles, keeping her young and beautiful forever! The visual image can depart from the biological process. People will be split between two external images—one showing the aging process, the other keeping the body timeless, unchanging, and young on screen. While I am intrigued by such possibilities, one has to wonder what they will do to our understanding of time and of history. Will Monroe not be a star from a specific past, but a timeless star? Will cultures produce a timeless present that can include persons and objects from as far back in time as a specific culture began recording itself—perhaps thousands of years ago? What would this all mean?

I must defer following out the complex implications of new technologies with regard to aging to another time, and only note that the *Mondo* fantasies of aging require a certain privilege, money, and ability to "jigger one's own bio-chemisty for personal fulfillment"! As Woodward has shown, psychoanalytic theory provides a very different concept of inner/outer struggle,[16] and offers some insight into the threat that aging women may present in a still patriarchal culture. Implicit in Dietrich's struggles as portrayed in the documentary *Shadow and Light* was a conflict between a postulated inner self unchanged from her mature period and desiring to continue performing on film and stage, and an outer body that simply did not "look" as Dietrich wanted it to look. With the intellectual Klein, the psychoanalytic problem had more to do with mother-daughter jealousy in relation to the male authority of the institution of psycho-analysis, and with the patriarchal desire (which Melitta accepts for her own reasons) that the older woman cede to the younger. Even Duras finally suc-cumbs to her culture's notion of the aging face as a "destroyed face."

Kristeva's psychoanalytic concept of "abjection" helps us understand the way patriarchy deals with aging women. Such women are rendered abject. In Kristeva's powerful terms (although she does not explicitly refer to aging), old women are what we have to push away from both the social body and even the individual body in order for that body to remain clean, whole, pure. Dietrich and other "star" figures internalized this, and suffered painfully as a result. Klein and other intellectual women had to combat authoritarian male col-leagues, as well as younger women, who unconsciously believed aging women should abandon intellectual debates and creative activities. Only creative artists like Duras seem to resist patriarchal categorizing, but then the cost is a certain distance from the public sphere. In Duras's case, her desolate remark that she no longer has a face, a mouth, nonetheless suggests as well her anticipa-tion of the void that death holds out, and a welcome relief from final bodily dissolution.

Contrast these images of aging as decline, death, ruin, and the abject, with a typical ad, say from AT&T[17]—one showing a baby reaching out its arms and holding the world. "You want the whole world at your fingertips," the text says. "The possibilities are limitless." But only for the baby! It would make no sense to advertisers (although it would to me) to show an aging woman reaching out—other than to provide comfort to her from relatives in her decline (which AT&T ads frequently image). Only advertisements for Elder Hostels might extol the limitless possibilities of aging, and then such a discourse would already be clearly framed by the context of an address to the aging by institu-tions hoping to profit from their plight. Aging is yet one more industry, as I hope to explore in future research.

Trauma and Aging

The AT&T ad perfectly coincides with the sentiments in an article entitled "New Wrinkles for an Aging World" that appeared in the *New York Times* in September 1996. Worries about the graying of the world population as births decline and as older people live longer are on the increase. At stake here especially are male fears of aging in a world that can seem overpopulated with the "old." This creates a desire for more and more images of youth in order to push away—to deny—the aging that all unconsciously know is their fate.

But the worries are also economic. The economic concern that older people will weigh down the young—especially in regard to social security savings—feeds the growing battle of the generations that could, at some future point, turn ugly.[18] While there is some justice for attention to a globally growing group of older people, clearly both ageism and racism are at work here—racism, because it is *white* births that will be outnumbered by the year 2010;[19] ageism, because it is the largely white baby boomers who are beginning to complain about having to support their parents and who are worrying about increasing medical costs and whether there will be social security sufficient for their needs.

These fears are given visual force in a *Newsweek* image of a barely middle-aged white man staggering beneath the burden of his aging, helpless mother in a heavy wheelchair in the article on "mediscare" (*sic*) (see endnote 18); here again aging is collapsed with ill health. Why not assume that aging women have untold possibilities awaiting them? And that they will be in good health? Without going to the lengths of *Mondo's* article on longevity, do we not live in an era when the idea of the body has in fact changed? When the body is no longer reduced to a machine, or seen in architectural metaphors, but rather is imaged as plastic, open to change, even as "communal," in the sense of sharing organs through transplants? As the celebrated surgeon Christian Barnard has put it, "The body is no longer 'given' (meaning, traditionally, a gift of God); it is *plastic*, to be molded and selected at need or whim. . . . The body is not only plastic but bionic, with cardiac valves" (34).[20]

What position should I adopt toward these possibilities for change? In one sense, the new possibilities are part of the postmodern sense of multiple subjectivities and of the refusal of the negative story of age as decline. Still, the possibilities compel the question: in whose interest is the new plastic body? Is it really in the interest of an individual woman to have available the possibility that the performance artist, Orlan, has taken as her mission in life?[21] Are the potentialities of the new plastic body already overdetermined by the society in which the technologies are being developed, a global postmodern capitalism in which the only drive or engine for anything is the bottom line? Such a view complicates one's fascination with a postmodern feminist concept of the body as plastic and open to change, or of women as undertaking fleshly self-fashioning for their own ends.

The focus on changing the externals of the body displaces attention to what menopausal and postmenopausal women can contribute to society through their wisdom, deepened intelligence, and long and varied experiences. To focus on external appearance denies what is really important about people: their values, their capacities for human relating, their contributions to society and culture. To suggest that women can be *something* after being young and desirable to men, after childbearing and motherhood, or to suggest that one need not be chronologically young to be desirable or to have children—is to suggest that women can play a role that does not *per se* depend upon men, or in particular their voyeuristic gaze. It is in the interest of patriarchal culture to keep alive the myth that, after menopause, women have no particular function and therefore can be passed over for younger women who still depend on men. Much is at stake in aging, therefore, both for women experiencing age as "trauma," and for a culture fixated on youthfulness and so terrified of death that it erects defenses that are not, ultimately, in anyone's interest.

NOTES

1. What I wanted to indicate by using the term "modern" is the change from an era when religious systems still predominated in the West, to an era that begins with the Enlightenment. During the eras when strong religious systems defined people's world views, strong defenses against recognition of death were in place. You went to "heaven" (where you continued to "live" in bliss) or to "hell." While hell might be considered traumatic, in fact it is not because one has a choice as to whether to obey religious mandates and avoid hell, or to disregard them and risk going to hell. And it is precisely "choice" that is lacking with trauma. With World Wars I and II, and the later development of such new philosophies as existentialism, religious belief-systems had an even harder time retaining their power. It is when defenses against death wane that the possibility for death as trauma opens up.

I wanted to juxtapose this modern paradigm vis-à-vis death—essentially a humanist paradigm—with a postmodern paradigm, when things change yet again. Postmodern views emerge when in the West new concepts of the human body emerge—the cyborg, the plastic body, virtual reality, cyberspace. The trauma of death may be replaced by fantasies (again) of avoiding death. So in effect premodern religious systems and postmodern cyberage systems both fantasize overcoming death, but in vastly differing and interesting ways. In between is the era of humanist trauma around death, precisely because it is an era when fantasies of avoiding death seem at their weakest. Lacan's Real might be THE most powerful humanist formulation regarding death. For Lacan, the human requires the phantasmatic screen to avoid the horror of life—the Real—which is really the horror of death.

2. Indeed, of all these, religion may be the most important, and the one that challenges my argument about trauma: for most religions provide, for believers, the comfort of an afterlife that at least psychologically reduces the trauma I am talking about. But my main focus is on the predicaments of agnostics and atheists.

3. David Gutmann has argued that there are strengths that come from survival. It is possible that those who can work through the losses I mention here are indeed strengthened. I am arguing that a great deal depends on the discursive frameworks one brings to the aging process, and in that I am not far apart from Gutmann. But denying that there are real losses would not help.

4. In the longer version of this essay, I will include a fourth historical figure, Lena Horne. This will complicate the question of ethnicity, since the cultural formations, pressures, and anxieties about aging as an African-American actress and performer were certainly markedly different from those of the three women considered here. The fact that these three women were European and white certainly shaped their particular aging experiences, however contrasting the experiences are otherwise. Dietrich, of course, was a naturalized American; Klein, an Austrian, who later lived in England; and Duras, French. Important also, as will be clear, is the particular historical moment the women were living in as they aged.

5. As Jean Kozlowski points out, male stars' sexiness "can be stretched into a fantasy of ageless sexual potency" (8), while women stars are summarily dismissed from sexy roles on the screen after menopause. In Kozlowski's words, "Movies tend to give us only an abrupt shove from cute ingenue to weird old crone" (6). Hollywood occasionally addresses this issue, as in *Sunset Boulevard* (1950), where Gloria Swanson plays the aging star; or *Postcards from the Edge* (1990), with Shirley MacLaine, based on the life of Debbie Reynolds and her daughter, Carrie Fisher.

6. The best example of this Monroe image is, of course, *The Seven Year Itch* (1957). This film actually foregrounds and makes fun of American male fantasies of the sexy young woman whose very innocence permits her to respond to older men as if it were all child's play! This unknowing innocence evidently allays American male fears of the too sexually knowing woman. Such a woman quickly becomes the film noir *femme fatale*. Indeed, in one of Eddie McDowell's fantasies, he turns the innocent Monroe into a very *innocent* femme fatale! The best of all worlds for the American male, it seems.

7. Wright draws heavily on Phyllis Grosskurth's biography *Melanie Klein: Her World and Her Work*. Wright's play was published in 1988. The play was first performed in London at the National Theatre on August 10, 1988; its first production in the United States was the one starring Uta Hagen. Wright has written several other plays, and is Literary Manager at the National Theatre.

8. See my essay on *Mrs. Klein* for more details regarding these scenes.

9. In doing research for this paper, I came across several scholars who made unusually harsh statements about Duras. See especially Maurice Lemaître's *Marguerite Duras*. Far less offensive and self-serving is *Duras* by Frédérique Lebelley, who spends too much time detailing Duras's alcoholism and other illnesses for no apparent purpose.

10. Lydon quotes from Duras's "Texte de présentation" following the play version of *Le Camion*: "The woman of the truck is not bored any more. She is looking for no sense to her life. I discover in her a joy in existing without a quest for meaning. A true regression in progress, a fundamental one. The only recourse here being the definitive knowledge that recourse does not exist" (165).

11. I want first to thank Bethany Ladimer for enabling me to have a copy of this interview. Second, I refer readers to her paper, "Seductive at Seventy: The Aging

Face of Marguerite Duras," where Ladimer also discusses Duras's interview with Pivot and relevant Duras texts. In her paper, Ladimer comments on the insertion of photographs of a young Duras in the interview, if to make somewhat different points than I do.

12. Kathleen Woodward has written extensively on related issues to do with the aging body in her illuminating chapter, "Phantasms of the Aging Body," *Aging and Its Discontents* (167–91). See especially her discussion of a Duras novel in the section "The Immobile Body/The Companion Body," and on Sartre, in the section "The Empty Body." This section especially relates to what Duras writes in *C'est tout*.

13. For it is the FACE that always shows (except in Islamic cultures), since the rest of the body can be hidden, or its lapses easily shored up with undergarments (I wonder, do aging women feel better in Islamic cultures where their wrinkling skin is hidden behind the veil?).

14. We are seeing these arguments in the academy, particularly with new budget cuts and downsizing.

15. To his credit, the bioethicist Arthur Caplan, in an article by Gina Kolata in the *New York Times* in 1995 about new ovary procedures, is quoted as saying that when menopause is forestalled indefinitely, it changes our idea of the life cycle: "It may even mean that what we think of as a key sign of aging in women doesn't happen. We see ourselves very differently when fundamental biological clues don't happen. It forces us to rethink who we are and what we are in the life course." What is interesting is seeing these doctors struggling with the discursive medical formation regarding older women.

16. Woodward uses both existential philosophy and Freud in discussing the split between our inner experience and our outer body as perceived by another or ourselves. As Woodward puts it, "We may think of ourselves as young, but others will perceive us as old, perhaps even ancient." For Beauvoir and Sartre, old age belongs to the "unrealizables" (62). For Freud, his "mirror image of himself as elderly is that of the trespasser, of the interloper in the private domain of narcissism . . . the material of the unconscious rising through the open door into the unconscious" (64).

17. By "typical," I refer to the increasing use of the fetus or small baby in ads and articles of all kinds. Images of babies are increasingly used to symbolize the new, the future, the fresh, the upcoming. While the idea of the young child symbolizing the future is far from new, this heavy focus on fetal/baby *images* is new.

18. See, for example, the public attention already being focused on intergenerational conflict in articles like that by Howard Fineman in *Newsweek* titled "Mediscare: Young vs. Old: Who Will Carry the Burden?"

Anecdotally, let me cite the situation in a so-called "adult community" in Southern California. In this community, pressure is on to bring in more and more people at the younger ranges of the community, many between fifty-five and sixty-five years old. Such people are still able to drive safely and do not demand or need the services that people seventy-five to ninety might need and that cost the community more to provide. These kinds of problems are going to increase, as people in the lower age ranges resent having to pay for services they do not need (at the moment, at any rate!). It's interesting that there is no ability to think of the future—to realize that at some future time there will be people their ages providing for them, thus in a sense, evening things out. But this pertains to future parts of my research.

19. See Robert Samuelson's essay in *Newsweek* in 1995. A subtitle reads: "At last, Americans are really confronting costly entitlements for the elderly. As the first skirmish in the generational war begins, young and old get ready to get less." Later in the article, Samuelson notes that "the public costs of supporting the older generation, mainly through social security and Medicare, are becoming oppressive. They now constitute a third of federal spending, and by the time the baby boom hits 65 in 2011, they will be unaffordable in their present form." He adds, "To call this the onset of generational politics is not to predict generational war, though one could happen" (40–41).

20. To complete the quotation from Christian Barnard: "The body is not only plastic but bionic, with cardiac pacemakers, valves, titanium hips, polymer blood vessels, electronic eye and ear implants, collagen fibre and silicon rubber skins, and even polyurethane hearts" (34).

21. Performance artist Orlan has taken as her artistic mission to undergo frequent cosmetic surgery operations in which she has her face altered to look like one or another famous artist's model. She stages these operations as live performances to which spectators are invited so as to dramatize the plasticity of the body, and the changing nature of patriarchy's ideal "feminine."

WORKS CITED

Barnard, Christian. *The Body Machine*. New York: Crown, 1981.

Brown, Laura S. "Not Outside the Range: One Feminist Perspective on Psychic Trauma." Caruth 100–13.

Caruth, Cathy, ed. *Trauma: Explorations in Memory*. Baltimore: Johns Hopkins UP, 1995.

Duras, Marguerite. *C'est tout*. Paris: P.O.L., 1995.

———. *L'Amant*. Paris: Minuit, 1991.

———. *The Lover*. Trans. Barbara Bray. New York: Harper, 1986.

———. *Yann Andréa Steiner*. Ed. définitive. Paris: P.O.L., 1992.

———. *Yann Andréa Steiner*. Trans. Barbara Bray. New York: Scribner's, 1993.

Fineman, Howard. "Mediscare: Young vs. Old: Who Will Carry the Burden?" *Newsweek* 18 Sept. 1995: 38–44.

Fonda, Jane. *Daily Mail* 13 Sept. 1989.

Grosskurth, Phyllis. *Melanie Klein: Her World and Her Work*. Cambridge: Harvard UP, 1986.

Gutmann, David L. *Reclaimed Powers: Toward a New Psychology of Men and Women in Later Life*. New York: Basic, 1987.

Healey, Dr. Qtd. in Kolata.

Hill, Leslie. *Marguerite Duras: Apocalyptic Desires*. New York: Routledge, 1993.

Hunt, Chris, dir. *Shadow and Light: A Documentary*. American Movie Classics, 1993.

Kaplan, E. Ann. "Resisting Pathologies of Age and Race: Menopause and Cosmetic Surgery in Films by Rainer and Tom." *Reinterpreting the Menopause*. Ed. Philippa Rothfield and Paul Komorasoff. New York: Routledge, 1997. 100–26.

———. "Monster or Genius? Medea or Madame Curie? The Dilemma of the Post-

Menopausal Female Intellectual. A Review of Nicholas Wright's *Mrs. Klein*." *Psychoanalytic Review* 83.5 (1997): 787–92.

Kolata, Gina. "Surgery Preserves Parts of an Ovary for Reimplanting." *New York Times* 12 Dec. 1995: A1, C3.

Kozlowski, Jean. "Women, Film, and the Midlife Sophie's Choice: Sink or Sousatzka?" *Menopause: A Midlife Passage*. Ed. Jean C. Callahan. Bloomington: Indiana UP, 1993: 3–22.

Krystal, Henry. "Trauma and Aging: A Thirty-Year Follow-Up." Caruth 76–99.

Ladimer, Bethany. "Seductive at Seventy: The Aging Face of Marguerite Duras." Paper presented at the conference Women and Aging: Bodies, Cultures, Generations. Center for Twentieth Century Studies, University of Wisconsin-Milwaukee. 18–20 Apr. 1996.

Lebelley, Frédérique. *Duras, ou le poids d'une plume*. Paris: Grasset, 1994.

Lemaître, Maurice. *Marguerite Duras: Pour en finir avec cet escroc et plagiaire généralisé*. Paris: Centre de Créativité, 1979.

Lydon, Mary. "*L'Eden Cinema*: Aging and the Imagination in Marguerite Duras." *Memory and Desire: Aging—Literature—Psychoanalysis*. Ed. Kathleen Woodward and Murray M. Schwartz. Bloomington: Indiana UP, 1986. 154–67.

Mondo 2000: A User's Guide to the New Edge. Ed. Rudy Rucker, R. U. Sirius, and Queen Mu. New York: Harper, 1992.

"The New Wrinkles of an Aging World." *New York Times* 22 Sept. 1996: 1, 5.

Pivot, Bernard. *Apostrophes: Interview with Marguerite Duras*. Paris: Seuil, 1984.

Samuelson, Robert J. "Getting Serious." *Newsweek* 18 Sept. 1995: 40–44.

Schickel, Richard. "Remembrance: Marlene Dietrich 1901–1992. The Secret in Her Soul." *Time* 18 May 1992: 72.

Woodward, Kathleen. *Aging and Its Discontents: Freud and Other Fictions*. Bloomington: Indiana UP, 1991.

Wright, Nicholas. *Mrs. Klein*. London: Samuel French, 1988.

Not a Jealous Bone

(libretto from the videotape, 1987. 11 min.)

Cecelia Condit

NARRATOR

The hand of the Lord was upon them. And He set them down in the midst of the valley, which was full of bones. And, lo, they were very dry. And the Lord said to the bones, I will cause breath to enter into you and you shall live.

The magic bone knew that old people just want to live, and that young people just don't want to grow old.

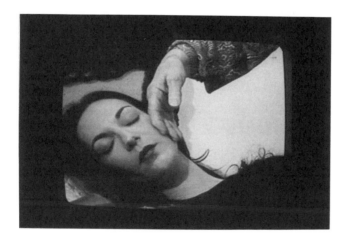

SONG

There's so little left to show
of what I looked like years ago.

Maybe when I'm 85
I will have a stroke and die.

Maybe when I'm 86
I will fall and break my hips.

Maybe when I'm 102
I'll have a lift and look like new.

Maybe when I'm 93
I'll do well to hold my pee.

If my mother could see me now
She wouldn't know me anyhow.

Summertime and girls and boys
Their bodies new like store bought toys.

It doesn't matter what you're told.
It's never you who will grow old.

Some things seem to never change.
They only pop up rearranged.

I'm the same at 82
as I was at 32 . . . .

> *NARRATOR*
>
> Having found the wishbone, Sophie thought she would live forever. She would go find her mother and perhaps they could share the bone. Then they could both live and no one young could take it from them.

SONG

Mother, Mother
I'm so lonely for you.
Mother, Mother
I'm afraid of dying.
How is dying, dying?
Mother, Mother
I need you now.

> *OLD WOMAN*
>
> I want to know what happened to my mother.
>
> *THERAPIST*
>
> Your mother's passed away.

OLD WOMAN

My mother still, thank God, is better than a lot of young people.

THERAPIST

We have to talk about REALITY. Mrs. Kessler we're going to find out what day it is.

OLD WOMAN

I'm looking for yesterday.

THERAPIST

Da Da Da. You're looking for yesterday?

OLD WOMAN

Yes, I'm looking for yesterday.

SONG

When I feel old the world's ice cold.
There's no drama, no action, no plot.
When I feel young, I find I become the bold
And daring young woman I'm not.

NARRATOR

Sophie had always shared good news with her mother. Now she would trust the bone to take her there.

SONG

Have you seen my mother?
I can't find her anywhere.
Have you seen my mother?
I'm so old I shouldn't care.

How are you doing today?
What's that you say?

Little crimes here and there.
Murders everywhere.
Life's a strange affair.
It takes one so unaware.

Have you seen my mother?
I can't find her anywhere.
Have you seen my mother?
I'm so old I shouldn't care.

THERAPIST

Do you want to stay living?

OLD WOMAN

Yes.

THERAPIST

You do want to be living?

OLD WOMAN

Oh, my God, and how!

NARRATOR

Sophie's mother had left a legacy of undying love and support.
But, there were others who wanted the bone. So as Sophie
searched for her mother, there were young jealous eyes on the
bone.

YOUNG PERSON

Give me the bone.

SONG

Bone, beautiful bone
Bone of the evening.
Slender and lean, gentle or mean.

All of the places I've been
Leave little traces of sin.
Skeleton, muscle, and skin.
Rickety, tickety tin.

Bone, beautiful bone.
Bone of the evening.

NARRATOR

Sophie had thought the legacy would protect her, but she knew
the will to live was bone deep.

SONG

Tough luck, Mom, poor Mom.
Tough luck, Mom, poor Mom.
I may be old, but you're dead.
Don't let being dead go to your head.
Did I miss something you said?
Cat got your tongue, poor Mom.
Shame you had to die so young!
You are dead, but I am still alive.
You are dead, but I am still alive.

Scary Women
Cinema, Surgery, and Special Effects

Vivian Sobchack

I once heard a man say to his gray-haired wife,
without rancor: "I only feel old when I look at you."

— Ann Gerike

"I'm prepared to die, but not to look lousy for the
next forty years."

— a woman qtd. in
Elissa Melamed's *Mirror, Mirror*

It's science now. It's no longer voodoo.

— an advertisement for medical equipment in
a trade journal for cosmetic surgeons

What follows is less an argument than a meditation on the dread of middle-aging as a woman in our culture, rejuvenation fantasies in the American cinema, and the wish-fulfilling "magic" and "quick fixes" of technologies of transformation and display. As might be expected of a woman with the privilege of self-reflection, at fifty-six, I am struggling with my own middle age. Indeed, I despair of ever being able to reconcile my overall sense of well-being, self-confidence, achievement, and pleasure in the richness of my present with the image I see in my mirror. Over the past several years, I have become aware not only of my mother's face frequently staring back at me from my own, but also of an increasing inability to see myself—with any objectivity—at all (as if, of course, I ever could). Within less than a single minute, I often go from utter dislocation and despair as I gaze at a face that seems too old for me, a face that I "have," to a certain satisfying recognition and pleasure at a face that looks "pretty good for my age," a face that "I am." I live now in heightened awareness of the instability of my image of myself. And this is a bad and a good thing. I think about cosmetic surgery a lot: getting my eyes done, removing the furrows in my forehead, smoothing out the lines around my mouth, and lifting the skin around my jaw. But there seems no point. I don't really believe it will make a difference. I know I will be disappointed. I know its effects wouldn't last. And so, while I don't avoid mirrors, I also don't seek them out. And I try very hard to locate myself less in my image than in my (how else to say it?) "comportment."

It is for this reason that I was particularly moved when I first read in *Entertainment Weekly* that Barbra Streisand (only a year younger than I am, a Brooklyn-born Jew, a persistent and passionate woman with a big mouth like me) was remaking and updating *The Mirror Has Two Faces*. According to Leonard Maltin, the original 1959 French film was about a housewife who "begins life anew after plastic surgery," but Barbra's update was to tell the story of "an ugly duckling professor and her quest for inner and outer beauty" (Wells 8). Obviously, this struck a major chord. Discussing the film's progress and performing its own surgery—a hatchet job to which I shall later return— *Entertainment Weekly* reported that the "biggest challenge faced by the 54-year-old" and "hyper-picky" Barbra (producer, director, and star),

> was how to present her character. In the original, the mousy housefrau undergoes her transformation via plastic surgery. But Streisand rejected that idea—perhaps because of the negative message—and went with attitude adjustment instead. Which might work for the character, but does it work for the star? "Certain wrinkles and gravitational forces seem to be causing Streisand concern," says one ex-crew member. "She doesn't want to look her age. She's fighting it." (Wells 9)

The Mirror—indeed—*Has Two Faces*. Except for the income and, of course, the ability to sing "People," Barbra and I have a lot in common.

Before actually seeing the film (eventually released in 1996), I wondered just what, as a substitute for surgery, "attitude adjustment" might mean. And how would that translate to the superficiality of an image—in the mirror, in the movies? Might it mean really good makeup for the middle-aged star? Soft focus? Other forms of special effects that do the work of cosmetic surgery?[1] And just how far can these take you—how long before really good makeup transforms you into a grotesque, before soft focus blurs you into invisibility, before special effects transform you into a vampire, witch, or monster? Perhaps this *is* the cinematic equivalent of "attitude adjustment." The alternative to cosmetic surgery in what passes for the verisimilitude of cinematic realism is a change in genre, a transformation of sensibility that takes us from the "real" world to the world of horror, science fiction, and fantasy.

Indeed, a few years ago, I published an essay on the terrors of female aging and several science-fiction/horror films made in the late 1950s and early 1960s that wove together objective analysis with expressions of my own uneasy contemplation of cosmetic surgery in the face of what seemed my unsuccessful "attitude adjustment" toward middle age. I was particularly interested in these critically neglected films because, working through genres deemed "fantastic," they were able to "displace" and "disguise" cultural anxieties about women and aging while simultaneously figuring them "in your face," so to speak. For example, in *Attack of the 50-Foot Woman* (1958), through a brief (and laughable) encounter with a giant space alien, wealthy, childless, middle-aged, and brunette Nancy (Allison Hayes) grows to a literal size, power, and youthful blondness her philandering husband can no longer ignore as she roams the countryside, wearing a bra and sarong made out of her bed linens, looking for him. In *The Wasp Woman* (1959), the fortyish head (Susan Cabot) of a similarly fading cosmetics empire can no longer serve as the model for her products ("Return to Youth with Janice Starlin!"), but finds that royal wasp jelly does royal bee jelly one better; it not only reduces but also reverses the aging process, although side effects regularly turn the once-again youthful cosmetics queen into a murderous insect-queen (in high heels and a sheath dress). And, in *The Leech Woman* (1960), blowzy, alcoholic, despised June (Coleen Gray) becomes her feckless endocrinologist husband's guinea pig and, taking a rejuvenation serum made from African orchid pollen mixed with male pituitary fluid (extraction of which kills its owners, one of them her husband), ultimately experiences, if only for a while, the simultaneous pleasures of youth, beauty, and revenge. In these low-budget films, scared middle-aged women are transformed—not through cosmetic surgery but through fantastical means, makeup, and "special effects"—into scary but rejuvenated women. Introduced as fading females still informed by—but an affront to—sexual desire, hovering on the brink of grotesquery and alcoholism, their flesh explicitly disgusting to the men in their lives, the women are figured as more horrible in—and more horrified by—their own middle-aged bodies than in or by the bodies of the "unnatural" and deadly monsters they become. Indeed, the films dramatize what one psychotherapist has described as the culture's "almost visceral disgust for the older woman as a physical being" and underscores "ageism" as "the last bastion of sexism" (Melamed 30).

Transformed, become suddenly young, beautiful, desirable, powerful, horrendous, monstrous, and deadly, each of these women plays out grand, if wacky, dramas of poetic justice. No plastic surgery here. Instead, through the technological "magic" of cinema, the irrational "magic" of fantasy, and a few cheesy low-budget effects, what we get is major "attitude adjustment"—of a scope that might even satisfy Barbra. The leech woman, wasp woman, and fifty-foot woman literalize, magnify, and enact hyperbolic displays of anger and desire, their youth and beauty now "lethal" as well as "fatal," their "unnatural" ascendance to power allowing them to avenge on a grand scale the wrongs done them for merely getting older. Yet, not surprisingly, these films also maintain the cultural *status quo*—even as they critique it. For what they figure as most grotesque and disgusting is not the monstrousness of the transformation, but the "unnatural" conjunction of middle-aged female flesh and still youthful desire. And—take heed, Barbra—the actresses who play these horrific and pathetic middle-aged women are young and beautiful from the start under the latex jowls and the makeup. Thus, what these fantasies of female rejuvenation give with one hand, they take back with the other. We are watching less a grand masquerade of resistance than a retrograde striptease that undermines the double-edged and very temporary narrative power these "transformed" and newly empowered middle-aged protagonists supposedly enjoy—that is, "getting their own back" before they eventually "get theirs." And, of course, as is the "natural" order of things in both patriarchal culture and genre films of this sort, they do "get theirs"—each narrative ending with the restoration of social (and ageist) order through the death of its eponymous heroine-monster. Attitude adjustment, indeed!

These low-budget films observe that middle-aged women—as much before as after their transformations and "attitude adjustments"—can be pretty scary. In *Attack of the 50-Foot Woman*, for example, as Nancy lies in her bedroom after her close encounter of the third kind but before she looms large on the horizon, her doctor explains away her "wild" story and strange behavior thus: "When women reach the age of maturity, Mother Nature sometimes overworks their frustration to a point of irrationalism." The screenwriter must have read Freud who, writing on obsessional neurosis in 1913, tells us: "It is well known, and has been a matter for much complaint, that women often alter strangely in character after they have abandoned their genital functions. They become quarrelsome, peevish, and argumentative, petty and miserly; in fact, they display sadistic and anal-erotic traits which were not theirs in the era of womanliness" (130). Which brings us again back to Barbra, whom it turns out we never really left at all. In language akin to Freud's "it is well known" and "a matter for much complaint," the article on the production woes of Barbra's film in *Entertainment Weekly* reported that Streisand was apparently more than a mere triple-threat as producer, director, and star. The "steep attrition rate" among her cast and crew and the extraordinarily protracted shooting schedule were attributed to, on the one side, her "hyper-picky" "perfectionism" and, on the other, to her being a "meddler." People, according to one source, were "dying to be let off this shoot" (Wells 8). We are also told: "Among the things she fretted over: the density of her panty hose, the bras she wore, and whether the trees would have falling leaves" (9). Barbra, though, did have some supporters. Former TriStar chairman and admirer Mike Medavoy "believes a stress-filled shoot is the price you pay to work with Streisand . . . a megastar," and coactor Pierce Brosnan "believes it's Streisand who has the true cross to bear. 'I've seen male directors throw tantrums and nobody says a peep'" (9). A leech woman, wasp woman, fifty-foot woman—in Freud's terms, an obsessional neurotic: peevish, argumentative, petty, sadistic, and anal-erotic—poor Barbra. She can't win for losing. Marauding the countryside in designer clothes and an "adjusted" attitude doesn't get her far from the fear or contempt that attaches to middle-aged women in our culture. Perhaps she—perhaps I—should reconsider cosmetic surgery.

Around ten years younger than Barbra and myself but anxious about the real source of her power, my best friend recently did, although I didn't see the results until long after her operation. Admittedly, I was afraid to—afraid she'd look bad (that is, not like herself or like she had surgery), afraid she'd look good (that is, good enough to make me want to do it). Whichever the case, separated by physical distance, I didn't have to confront—and judge—her "image" and so all I initially knew about her extensive facelift was from e-mail correspondence. (I have permission to use her words, but not her name.) Here, "in my face," so to speak, as well as hers (and now yours) were extraordinary convergences of actuality and wish, of surgery and cinema, of transformative technologies and the "magic" of "special effects," of despised flesh and malleable image (first "alienated" and later proudly "possessed")—all rendered intimately intelligible to us (whether we approve or not) in terms of mortal time and female gender. She wrote (in caps): "IT WORKED!" Her e-mail goes on:

> My eyes look larger than Audrey Hepburn's in her prime. . . . I am the proud owner of a fifteen-year-old neckline. Amazing—exactly the effect I'd hoped for. Still swollen . . . but that was all predicted. What this tendon-tightening lift did (not by any means purely "skin deep"—he actually. . . redraped the major neck and jaw infrastructure) was reverse the effects of gravity. Under the eyes—utterly smooth, many crow's feet eradicated. The jawline—every suspicion of jowl has been erased. Smooth and tight. Jesus, I look good. The neck—the Candice Bergen turkey neck is gone. The tendons that produce that stringy effect have been severed—for ever! OK—what price (besides the $7000) did I pay? Four hours on the operating table. One night of hell due to . . . a compression bandage that made me feel as if I were being choked. Mercifully (and thanks to Valium) I got through it. . . . Extremely tight from ear to ear—jaw with little range of motion—"ate" liquids, jello, soup, scrambled eggs for the first week. My sutures extend around eighty percent of my head. *Bride of Frankenstein* city. All (except for the exquisitely fine line under my eyes) are hidden in my hair. But baby I know they're there. Strange reverse-phantom limb sensation. I still have my ears, but I can't exactly feel them. . . . I . . . took Valium each evening the first week to counteract the tendency toward panic as I tried to fall asleep and realized that I could only move $1/4$ inch in any direction. Very minimal bruising—I'm told that's not the rule. . . . I still have a very faint chartreuse glow under one eye. With makeup, *voila!* I can't jut my chin out—can barely make my upper and lower teeth meet at the front. In a few more months, that will relax. And I can live with it. My hair, which was cut, shaved, and even removed (along with sections of

my scalp), has lost all semblance of structured style. But that too is transitory. The work that was done by the surgeon will last a good seven years. I plan to have my upper eyes done in about three years. This message is for your eyes only. I intend, if pressed, to reveal that I have had my eyes done. Period. Nothing more.[2]

But there's plenty more. And it foregrounds the confusion and conflation of surgery and cinema, of technology and "magic," of effort and ease, that so pervades our current "image" culture. Indeed, there is a bitter irony at work here that perversely reminds me of listening to several special computer effects guys from Industrial Light and Magic point to the incredible and "seamless" ping-pong match in *Forrest Gump* (1994) and bemoan the fact that no one could "see" all the time and labor they put into creating it. Having achieved a "seamless" face, my best friend has lost her voice. She cannot speak of the time and labor it took to transform her. The whole point is that, for the "magic" to work, the "seams"—both the lines traced by age and the scars traced by surgery —must not show. Thus, as Kathleen Woodward notes in her wonderful essay "Youthfulness as a Masquerade": "Unlike the hysterical body, whose surface is inscribed with symptoms, the objective of the surgically youthful body is to speak nothing" (133–34). But this is not the only irony at work here. At a more structural level, this very lack of disclosure, this silence and secrecy, is an *essential* element of a culture increasingly driven—both by desire and technology—to extreme extroversion, to utter disclosure. And it is here that cosmetic surgery and the "special effects" of the cinema converge, conflate, become phenomenologically reversible to what has become—particularly over the last decade—our "morphological imagination." Based in the belief that desire— through technology—can be given form, materialized, and made visible, the morphological imagination does a perverse—and precisely superficial—turn on Woodward's distinction between the hysterical body and the surgically youthful body. That is, symptoms and silence are confused and conflated as possibilities of the image of one's transformation and one's transformation of the image become phenomenologically reversible. Again, we can see these confusions and conflations most broadly—and literally—played out in the genre of fantasy where "plastic surgery" is now practiced through the seemingly effortless, "seamless," transformations of digital morphing.

In this regard, two relatively recent and gender-specific films come to mind, each not only making visible (and seemingly effortless) incredible alterations of an unprecedentedly plastic human body, but also rendering superficial and unprecedentedly literal human affective states. I am speaking here of *Death Becomes Her* (1992) and *The Mask* (1994)—both technologically dependent on digital morphing, both figuring the whole of human existence as superficial and plastic. *The Mask*, while about transformation, is not about rejuvenation—or, rather, if it is about rejuvenation it's about rejuvenation of the psyche and spirit, albeit significantly played out only on—and as—the surface of the body.

Paradoxically, when wimpy Stanley Ipkiss (Jim Carrey) is "magically" transformed by the plastic surgery of the "mask," there is no masquerade, no silence, since every desire, every psychic metaphor is materialized and made visible. His tongue "hangs out" and unrolls across the table toward the object of his desire. He literally "wears his heart on his sleeve" (or thereabouts). His destructive desires are extruded from his hands as smoking guns. And despite the fact that one might describe performer Jim Carrey as an "hysteric," how can one talk about the Mask's body in terms of hysterical "symptoms" when it all "hangs out." The Mask is simultaneously all superficial body and all extroverted id. Which makes it amusing as well as apposite, then, that one reviewer says of it: "The effects are show-stopping, but the film's hollowness makes the overall result curiously depressing" (Cinebooks).

Death Becomes Her functions in a similar manner—although, here, with women as the central figures, the narrative explicitly foregrounds a literal rejuvenation as its central thematic—youth and beauty the objects of female desire. Indeed, what's most interesting (although not necessarily funny) about *Death Becomes Her* is that plastic surgery operates in the film twice over. At the narrative level, its putative and also wimpy hero, Ernest Menville (Bruce Willis), is a famous plastic surgeon—seduced away from his fiancée Helen (Goldie Hawn) by middle-aging actress Madeline Ashton (Meryl Streep), whom we first see starring in a musical flop based on *Sweet Bird of Youth*. Thanks to Ernest's surgical skill (which we never actually see on the screen, a point I'll come back to), Madeline finds a whole new career as a movie star while Helen plots elaborate revenge.[3] Seven years into the marriage, however, hen-pecked, alcoholic Ernest has become plastic surgeon (and cosmetologist) to the stars— dead ones, that is—and he's no longer much use to Madeline. Told by her beautician that he—and cosmetic surgery—can no longer help her, the desperate woman seeks out a mysterious and incredibly beautiful "Beverly Hills cult priestess" (Isabella Rossellini), "from whom she obtains a youth serum with the Faustian side-effect of also granting eternal life, whatever the condition of the user's body" (Baseline). We are, of course, now in the second operation of plastic surgery which extends the narrative to the representational level—thus, the "magic" transformations of special computergraphic and cosmetic effects instantaneously nip and tuck Madeline's buttocks, smooth and lift her face and breasts with nary a twinge of discomfort, a trace of blood, or a trice of effort. (Rossellini's "priestess" describes the youth serum, but also might well be describing the cinematic effects, as: "A touch of magic in this world obsessed by science.") This literalization of desire and anxiety is carried further still—so that the repressed returns along with youth and beauty. When rejuvenated Madeline breaks her neck after being pushed down a flight of stairs, she lives on (though medically dead) with visible and hyperbolic variations of my friend's despised "Candice Bergen turkey neck." (Most certainly, her reference to "the tendons that produce that stringy effect have been severed—forever!" also resonates here.) And, after Madeline shoots Helen (who has also taken the serum), Helen walks around with a hole in her stomach—however rejuvenated and gorgeous, nonetheless a "blasted" woman, revealed as ultimately "hollow" ("I can see right through you," Madeline says). The rest of the film unites "Mad" and "Hel" in their increasingly unsuccessful attempts to maintain their peeling and literally "dead skin," to keep from "letting themselves go," from "falling apart"—which, in the film's very last shots, they quite literally do.

In both *The Mask* and *Death Becomes Her*, cinematic effects and plastic surgery become reversible operations—literalizing desire and promising instant and effortless transformation. Human bodily existence is foregrounded as a material surface amenable to endless manipulation and total visibility. As I indicated earlier, however, there is yet a great silence, a great *invisibility*, grounding these narratives of surface and extroversion. The labor and effort and time entailed by the "real" operations of "plastic surgery" (both cinematic and cosmetic) are ultimately disavowed. Instead, we are given a "screen image" (both psychoanalytic and literal) that attributes the laborious and costly and technologically based reality that underlies bodily transformation to the "magical" properties of, in the one instance, a primitive (ergo, non-technological) fetish and, in the other, a glowing potion ("a touch of magic in this world obsessed with science"). Of course, like all cases of disavowal, these fantasies turn round themselves like a Moebius strip to ultimately break the silence and reveal the repressed on the "same" side as the "screen image." That is, on the "screen side," the technological effects of these transformation fantasies are what we came for, what we want "in our face," so to speak. But we want these effects without wanting to see the technology itself, without wanting to acknowledge the cost and labor and time and effort of its operations—all of which might despoil our wonder at the ease and instantaneousness of transformation. Indeed, like my friend who wants the effects of her facelift to be seen but wants the fact of her costly, laborious, and lengthy operation to remain hidden, our pleasure comes precisely from this "appearance" of seamless, effortless, "magical" transformation. On the other repressed side (one that becomes the "same" side, however), we are fascinated by "the operation"—its very cost, difficulty, effortfulness. There are now magazines and videos devoted to "making visible" the specific operations of cinematic effects (and, no doubt, cosmetic surgery), their "magic" transformed into "aura" through a minute accounting of the technology involved, hours spent, effort spent, dollars spent. My friend, too, despite her desire to ultimately hide it, is fascinated by her operation and the visibility of her investment. Her numeracy extends from money to stitches, but is most poignant in its temporal lived-dimensions: four hours on the operating table, one night of hell, a week of limited jaw motion, time for her hair to grow back, a few months for her upper and lower jaws to "relax," three years before she will do her eyelids, seven years before the surgeon's work is undone again by time and gravity. The "magic" of plastic surgery (both cinematic and cosmetic)—at least when it's not screened—costs always an irrecoverable portion of a mortal life.

And a mortal life—at least when it's not screened—must *live through* its operations, not magically, instantaneously, but *in time*. It is both apposite and poignant that, offscreen, Isabella Rossellini, forever fixed as the eternal high priestess of youth and beauty in both *Death Becomes Her* and old Lancôme ads, joins the ranks of the on-screen "wasp woman," Janet Starlin: removed from her position as the cosmetic firm's "spokeswoman" and model because she became middle-aged. But unlike Janet who lives—and dies—only on the screen, Rossellini can't reverse the aging process nor is she likely to murder those who find her middle-aged flesh disgusting. It is also apposite and poignant that both physical and what has been called "discursive" surgery never quite match up to the effortless and "e-specially" effective plastic surgery of the cinema. Woodward, discussing the real facelift of a soap opera actress and its aftermath that is both televised and incorporated into the soap's narrative, cites Patricia Mellencamp's observation that "the viewer inspects the results and concludes that they are woefully disappointing" (134). This disappointment with the "real thing" could be heard in my friend's subsequent e-mail posts. Along with specific descriptions of her further healing, she wrote:

> Vivian, I'm going through an unsettling part of this surgical journey. . . . When I first got home, the effect was quite dramatic—I literally looked twenty years younger. Now what's happened: the swelling continues to go down. The outlines of the "new face" are still dramatically lifted . . . BUT the lines I've acquired through a lifetime of smiling, talking, being a highly expressive individual, are returning. Not all of them . . . but enough that the effect of the procedure is now quite natural . . . and I no longer look twenty years younger. Maybe ten max. . . . I'm experiencing a queasy depression. Imagining that the procedure didn't work. That in a few weeks I'll look like I did before the money and the lengthy discomfort. Now I scrutinize, I imagine, I am learning to hate the whole thing. Most of all, the heady sense of exhilaration and confidence is gone. In short, I have no idea any longer how the hell I look.

Which brings me back to myself before the mirror—and again to Barbra, both behind and in front of the camera. There is no way here for any of us to feel superior in sensibility to my friend. Whether we like it or not, we have all had "our eyes done." With or without medical surgery, we have been technologically altered, both "seeing" and "seeming" differently than we did in a time before either cinema or cosmetic surgery presented us with their reversible technological promises of immortality and figurations of "magical" self-transformation—that is, transformation without time, without effort, without cost. To a great extent, then, the bodily transformations of cinema and surgery inform each other. Cinema *is* cosmetic surgery—its fantasies, its "makeup," and its digital effects able to "fix" (in the doubled sense of repair and stasis) and to fetishize faces and time as both "unreel" before us. And, reversibly, cosmetic surgery *is* cinema, creating us as an image we not only learn to enact but also must—and never can—live up to. Through their technological "operations"—the work and cost both effectively hidden by the surface "magic" of their transitory effects—we have become subjectively "de-realized" as, paradoxically, these same operations have allowed us to objectively "realize" our flesh "in our own image."

Over e-mail, increments of my friend's ambiguous "recovery" from fantasies of transformation and rejuvenation seemed to be in direct proportion to the diminishing number of years young she felt she looked: "Vivian, I've calmed down, assessed the pluses and minuses and decided to just fucking go on with it. Life, that is. They call it a 'lift' for a reason. . . . The face doesn't look younger (oh, I guess I've shaved five to eight years off), but it looks better. OK. Fine. Now it's time to move on." But later fantasy reemerges—for the time being, at least, with real and sanguine consequences: "Vivian, the response has been terrific—everybody is dazzled, but they can't quite tell why. It must be the color I'm wearing, they say, or my hair, or that I am rested. At any rate, I feel empowered again."

In sum, I don't know how to end this—nor could I imagine at the time of my friend's rejuvenation how, *sans* cosmetic surgery, Barbra would end her version of *The Mirror Has Two Faces* or how, in our culture, "attitude adjustment" could ever substitute for "image adjustment." Thus, not only for herself, but also for the wasp woman, for my friend, for Isabella Rossellini, and for me, I hoped that Barbra—both on-screen and off—would survive her own cinematic production. Unfortunately, she did not. "Attitude adjustment" was overwhelmed by "image adjustment" in her finished film: to wit, a diet, furious exercise, good makeup, a new hairdo, and a Donna Karan little black dress. Despite all her dialogue, Barbra had nothing to say; instead, like my friend, she silenced and repressed her own middle-aging—first, reducing it to a generalized discourse on inner and outer beauty and then, displacing and replacing it on the face and in the voice of her bitter, jealous, once beautiful, and "much older" mother (played by the still spectacular Lauren Bacall). Barbra's attitude, then, hadn't "adjusted" at all.[4]

I finally did get to see my rejuvenated friend in the flesh. She looked pretty much the same to me. And, at the Academy Awards in 1997 (for which the song in her film and Lauren Bacall received the only nominations), Barbra was still being characterized by the press as "peevish" and "petty." I, in the meantime, have vowed to be kinder to my mirror image, to remind myself that it is thin and chimerical while I, on my side of it, am grounded in the thickness of a life, in the substance—not the surface—of endless transformation. Now, every time I start to fixate on a new line or wrinkle, on a graying hair, I try very hard to remember that, on my side of that face in the mirror, I am not so much aging as always becoming.

NOTES

I wish to thank the UCLA Center for the Study of Women for the mini-grant that helped support research for this essay.

1. It is of particular relevance here that recent developments in television technology have produced what is called a "skin contouring" camera which makes wrinkles disappear. In a *TV Guide* article rife with puns about "vanity video" and "video collagen," we are told of this "indispensable tool for TV personalities of a certain age" which "can give a soap opera ingenue a few extra years of playing an ingenue" but was first used "as a news division innovation" (among its beneficiaries: Dan Rather, sixty-four; Peter Jennings, fifty-eight; Tom Brokaw, fifty-six; and Barbara Walters, sixty-five). According to one NBC news director, "It can remove almost all of someone's wrinkles, without affecting their hair or eyes." However, as the article notes of these "top talents" who "get a little lift from the latest in special effects . . . the magic only lasts as long as the stars remain in front of the camera" (Robins 57).

2. An illuminating comparison might be made between my friend's detailing of her cosmetic surgery and its aftermath in this e-mail with J. G. Ballard's "Princess Margaret's Face Lift" in his revised and expanded *The Atrocity Exhibition*. Its opening paragraph reads: "As Princess Margaret reached middle age, the skin of both her cheeks and neck tended to sag from failure of the supporting structures. Her nasolabial folds deepened, and the soft tissues along her jaw fell forward. Her jowls tended to increase. In profile the creases of her neck lengthened and the chin-neck contour lost its youthful outline and became convex" (111).

3. In an apposite annotation to "Princess Margaret's Face Lift," Ballard writes: "In a TV interview . . . the wife of a famous Beverly Hills plastic surgeon revealed that throughout their marriage her husband had continually re-styled her face and body, pointing a breast here, tucking in a nostril there. She seemed supremely confident of her attractions. But as she said, 'He will never leave me, because he can always change me'" (111). *Death Becomes Her* plays out this fantasy as its initial premise but then goes on to exhaust the merely human powers of Madeline's plastic surgeon-husband and to avail itself of the rejuvenating power of "magic"—both through narrative and cinematic "special" morphological effects.

4. For a particularly devastating but accurate (and funny) send-up of *The Mirror Has Two Faces*, see the pseudonymous Libby Gelman-Waxner's "Pretty Is as Pretty Does." Reading the film's central thematic as asking and responding to Streisand's increasingly desperate question "Is Barbra pretty?," Gelman-Waxner also recognizes the displaced age issue—and, dealing with the confrontation scene between daughter and mother in which the latter reveals her jealousy and finally admits her daughter's beauty, she writes, "Watching a fifty-four-year-old movie star haranguing her mother onscreen is a very special moment; it's like seeing the perfect therapy payoff, where your mom writes a formal note of apology for your childhood and has it printed as a full-page ad in the *Times*" (38).

WORKS CITED

Attack of the 50-Foot Woman. Dir. Nathan Juran. Allied Artists, 1958.

Ballard, J. G. "Princess Margaret's Face Lift." *The Atrocity Exhibition.* Rev. ed. San Francisco: Re/Search, 1990. 111–12.

Baseline's Motion Picture Guide. Rev. of *Death Becomes Her. Cinemania 96.* CD-ROM. Redmond: Microsoft, 1992–95.

Cinebooks' Motion Picture Guide. Rev. of *The Mask. Cinemania 96.* CD-ROM. Redmond: Microsoft, 1992–95.

Death Becomes Her. Dir. Robert Zemeckis. Universal, 1992.

Forrest Gump. Dir. Robert Zemeckis. Paramount, 1994.

Freud, Sigmund. "The Predisposition to Obsessional Neurosis." *Collected Papers.* Ed. Ernest Jones. Trans. Joan Riviere. Vol. 1. London: Hogarth and the Inst. of Psycho-Analysis, 1950. 122–32.

Gelman-Waxner, Libby. "Pretty Is as Pretty Does." *Premiere* 10.6 (1996): 38–39.

Gerike, Ann E. "On Gray Hair and Oppressed Brains." *Women, Aging and Ageism.* Ed. Evelyn R. Rosenthal. New York: Haworth, 1990. 35–46.

The Leech Woman. Dir. Edward Dein. Universal, 1960.

Maltin, Leonard. Rev. of *The Mirror Has Two Faces* (Cayette, 1959). *Cinemania 96.* CD-ROM. Redmond: Microsoft, 1992–94.

The Mask. Dir. Chuck Russell. New Line Cinema, 1994.

Melamed, Elissa. *Mirror, Mirror: The Terror of Not Being Young.* New York: Linden, 1983.

The Mirror Has Two Faces. Dir. Barbra Streisand. 1996.

Robins, J. Max. "A New Wrinkle in Video Technology." *TV Guide* (Los Angeles Metropolitan Edition) 28 Sept.–4 Oct. 1996: 57.

Sobchack, Vivian. "Revenge of *The Leech Woman*: On the Dread of Aging in a Low-Budget Horror Film." *Uncontrollable Bodies: Testimonies of Identity and Culture.* Ed. Rodney Sappington and Tyler Stallings. Seattle: Bay P, 1994. 79–91.

The Wasp Woman. Dir. Roger Corman. The Film Group, 1959.

Wells, Jeffrey. "Mirror, Mirror." *Entertainment Weekly* 12 Apr. 1996: 8–9.

Woodward, Kathleen. "Youthfulness as a Masquerade." *Discourse* 11.1 (1988–89): 119–42.

Monster/Beauty
Midlife Bodybuilding as
Aesthetic Discipline

Joanna Frueh

I.

"She's an abomination," said the owner of a fashionable New York gym chain about a bodybuilder in her early forties. "I could love them all," wrote semiotician Marshall Blonsky about the twenty-seven bodybuilders in *Evolution F: A Surreal Spectacle of Female Muscle*, a performance staged in 1995 that included three women in their forties and one each in her fifties and sixties.[1] These two statements, both made in 1995, bracket the extremity of response to an aesthetic spectacle, one which is not just the female bodybuilder, but more complexly, her older incarnation.

A bodybuilder friend of mine also in her forties (she trains herself and others at this voguish gym and reported the owner's remark to me) told me she thinks the "abomination" was labeled so because of her stupendous shoulder and bicep development. A risky body such as hers and my friend's, a risk-taking soul-and-mind-inseparable-from-the-body, inspires hatred and disgust as well as stimulates erotic and aesthetic pleasure.

Monster/beauty provokes discomfort and lust through overarticulation. Whether the bodybuilder has created a sculpted form that merely exceeds a normative (relatively flaccid) appearance or one that is hypermuscular, the deliberately built older female body is an articulated physical presence that violates categories, one that is itself uncategorizable according to binary laws. Illicit and anomalous, the midlife bodybuilder speaks the paradox of pleasure that is monster/beauty. Her immoderate appearance ruins and increases visual pleasure. She is an erotic assault on the prevailing erotophobia regarding older women. She literally embodies supposed oppositions and dissonances: youth and age, the feminine and the masculine, touchability and dominatrix toughness. She is the sign and embodiment of confusions and dilemmas. A comic body based in hyperbole, she is a joke: on "feminine forever," because she crosses genders, anatomies, and generations; on the archetypal crone, the wise soul in a withered body; on sex-myth, which requires the respectable invisibility and matronly spread-and-shrivel of older women. The midlife bodybuilder is the return of the repressed—older women's erotic agency and urgency—and she is proof that an older woman can be the subject of erotogenesis.

Freud wrote, "Dirt is matter in the wrong place" (172–73). This describes the older female body in its conventional contemporary configuration of de-forming matter or of verging-on-formless matter: time has polluted the older female, and dirt manifests itself as sagging flesh, as atrophy. The myths of so-called graceful aging and acceptance of reality—submission to time and gravity—construct the older female body as more irregular than its younger counterpart, one which is also more chaotic and abnormal than a male body. Art historian Lynda Nead argues that "the formless female body has to be contained within boundaries, conventions and poses" (11) and that this has been the work of the female nude. In the West artists have idealized and romanticized women's bodies into predictable patterns in which youth and shapeliness signify allure and the decency of regularity, permitting viewers the relief of not having to literally or figuratively look at what culture assumes to be the natural state of defectiveness. Art historian Kenneth Clark, whose *The Nude* remains an inclusive consideration of the subject, asserts that the nude is art's answer to "the humiliating imperfection to which our species is usually condemned" (341). In effect he accepts the body as a death trap, as a loser's habitat. As Clark so bluntly puts it, "on the whole there are more women whose bodies look like a potato than like the Knidian Aphrodite. The shape to which the female body tends to return is one that emphasizes its biological functions" (93). According to Clark, in 350 B.C. Praxiteles' Knidia purified the "bulging statuettes from paleolithic caves," forms exemplifying tuberosity because their creators emphasized breasts, hips, and belly (71). Representing beauty, sex, and fertility to the Greeks, the Knidia became the model for the female nude. Most women, unable to compete with the classical goddess and her descendants, are reversions: and atavism, for Clark, is ugly. In his terms, the older female body could only be emphatically, and naturally, tuberous, with its presumably pendulous breasts and enlarged abdomen ironically stressing "biological functions" that may have ended.

Clark assumes the existence of natural bodies upon which natural events and forces operate. Calling this body potato-like or matronly doesn't make much difference. Within this system of values, the "natural" older body lacks proportion and harmony. The midlife body, an incarnation of the myth of the "natural" body that manifests itself in reality as self-fulfilling prophecy, is, like other conventional constructions of the female body, "easy to be intimate with."[2] Wrinkles, gray hair, and untoned muscle characterize the conventional figure of the grandmother, whose body welcomes familial embraces and provides nurturance and warmth safe from—because sterilized of—sex. Femaleness as an invitation to sex (whether loving or violent) and femaleness as a provider of emotional and physical nourishment are altogether familiar. But wrinkles, gray hair, and untoned muscle describe the hag as well as the grandmother. The hag is mean and hideous. Hers is not a body that supplies intimacy, yet it is as formulaic and as familiar as the body of the sexpot, the grandmother, and the midlife matron. The supposedly chaotic older body, with its erratic contours and unpredictable menopausal organs, keeps the order of formulaic fantasy writ as both expectation and reality.[3]

II.

Several years ago a longtime feminist artist then in her early sixties was wounded and astonished when, on two social occasions, groups of feminist artist friends of hers (they were in their forties, fifties, and sixties) verbally attacked her for not looking her age. The artist bodybuilds, and she told me, "I've worked hard to keep my body in shape, and women of my generation, and some younger, view me with suspicion, as if I've had massive plastic surgery or done something unnatural. They say, 'Oh, that's just the way you are—good genes.' They don't see my going to the gym as a discipline." The artist understands her bodybuilding as not solely a matter of appearance. Bodybuilding is the use of weight resistance to shape and strengthen the body—and the mind and soul. "They asked me," she said, "how I had so much energy, and as I continue to keep in shape, they can't move with as much flexibility. They have an obvious physical slowed-downness and self-consciousness—a feeling that they're losing their attractiveness. They seem to lack critical self-evaluation and knowledge of the connection between cause and effect. I love the experimentation with my body. Younger people today, who are thirty to forty-five, say, 'If you can do it, I can.'"[4]

Backstage at *Evolution F* I saw a competitive bodybuilder in her early thirties ask the artist her age. When she answered, "Sixty-three," the younger woman's eyes widened and she said, "I thought you were much younger."

We mistake attractiveness and energy—aesthetic vitality—for youthfulness. We are amazed by older women looking younger. Our vocabulary is wicked wrong; the notion of looking and feeling "young" undercuts the conscious creation of beauty and makes its possession possible only to younger people or, supposedly, their imitators. The feminist artist and other older bodybuilders who look beautiful, who incarnate monster/beauty through aesthetic discipline, do not imitate youth any more than do women who wear makeup. Imitation is useless because exact correspondence is impossible: youthful is not the same as young; youthful is the aesthete's halfway house; youthful is a sort-of state, not one of intriguing liminality; youthful is the matron's readjustment to society's age-dread, her redemption after falling into the wayward gracelessness of midlife. Beauty is not natural to anyone, for people create or negate their beauty by exercising—or not—aesthetic energy. This exercise can be conscious or unconscious. For the midlife bodybuilder, it is supremely conscious. Supreme aesthete/abomination, she is a model for women who desire the visibility that beauty brings.

For good reason, feminists have critiqued women's longing to be beautiful and to display themselves, because conventional female beauty is a symptom of patriarchal psychology.[5] We need to change the still monolithic feminist idea that women who want to be seen (as beautiful) are dupes of male desire. We have too easily constructed the older woman who works her body as being pathetic, as straining for youth, as fanatical.

"Bodybuilders are fanatics," said Deborah to me in the summer of 1995. A philosophy professor at the University of Nevada, Reno, Deborah is, like me, in her forties. I understood her comment as a critique of a midlife bodybuilder who had once been a faculty member at our institution and about whom Deborah had just been speaking. My friend Helen, another midlife woman and the director of the campus Women's Center, had known this bodybuilder, though I had not, and later that fall told me that she thought the bodybuilder looked sexy and great. "It's shameful for older women to feel and to be sexual," Helen said regretfully. We agreed that the older sexy body was an embarrassment, one stigmatized by hostility. Helen referred to Lillian Robinson commenting on her own "sexual isolation" as a fifty-three-year-old heterosexual in her review of two feminist studies of sex in the *Women's Review of Books*. "I am celibate and ashamed," Robinson wrote, "ashamed of my involuntary condition and ashamed that it is involuntary" (11).

The sexual isolation of older women is perpetuated by feminist ageism, as is altogether apparent in Lynne Segal's *Straight Sex*, one of the books Robinson reviewed positively, despite the uncomfortable feeling it gave her that "'real' heterosexual feminists—under fifty, under forty, maybe— . . . are the ones expected to be sexual objects," along with, perhaps, "some others still hanging in there (by our silver threads?), albeit potentially frustrated by the joint operation of sexism and ageism that is our personal problem" (12). As Robinson said, she feels "that the desire that inhabits me is a disease" (11). The desire expressed in an aesthetically shaped older body, one worked as a labor of love/play, is not fanaticism that takes the form of a desperate stalling of age. The bodybuilding fanatic *does* go beyond what is reasonable; she is unreasonably enthusiastic, unreasonably erotic, for she builds a body of pleasure, not desire. Muscle as shape and strength is attainable relatively easily, whereas the high-fashion height, slenderness, and flawless skin of the runway model or the sexpot curves and luxuriant hair of the porn icon are not. Both of these types symbolize youth itself and create longing: in addition, for the older woman, they represent loss. The midlife fanatic, who asserts her will against the expectation, even demand, that she become the formulaic matron, draws on the energy of the "tabooed logic" of eros and therefore appears unreasonable (Marcuse 185). We see this in Susan Bordo's words describing bodybuilding in *Unbearable Weight*, which Deborah had reminded me of: "adversarial relationship to the body," "compulsive," "perfection," "tightly managed," "disdain for material limits and the concomitant intoxication with freedom, change, and self-determination," "*control* . . . total mastery of the body" (151, 152, 211, 246, 301).

For most bodybuilders, pre-competition dieting is management-cum-punishment, comparable, they tell me, to anorexic starvation. Like many other women, many bodybuilders are not satisfied with their appearance all the time, so they obsess about control. Yet, Bordo's chiefly negative take on bodybuilding misses the important point of *aesthetic* control, which is a process and experience of sensuous embodiment and which is particularly beneficial for older women. Granted, I write about bodybuilding as a practitioner who perceives and interprets its best aspects, whereas Bordo—and Lynda Nead—present its worst features and write, to my knowledge, as non-practitioners. But neither Bordo nor Nead considers the midlife bodybuilder as embodying different needs and pleasures than her younger counterpart. Both posit the female bodybuilder as a contemporary icon of fit femininity who imposes imperatives of perfection upon herself and impossible achievements of appearance on others.

Beauty and perfection are not equivalents and beauty is creatable—and odd. Think of Frida Kahlo and Louise Nevelson. They styled themselves through the ornaments of clothing, jewelry, and makeup. The primary self-styling mode of the bodybuilder is the artist's basic, intuitive, and sensual shaping of matter into form. Bodybuilding has been described in such conventional terms as the modeling of the clay of the body and as the dexterous sculpting, chiseling, and whittling of the body, metaphors that trivialize the aesthetic process of bodybuilding as it has been exercised by the women I refer to in this essay. For them, these metaphors are either altogether inaccurate or imprecisely used. The bodybuilder as midlife monster/beauty is *bizarrerie*, a form of deviant content who, like all exercisers, has worked from the inside out. Molding and chiseling shape materials from the outside; the latter is a subtractive sculptural process. Resistance exercise as aesthetic practice is simultaneously additive and subtractive control that requires intuitive looseness as part of the discipline. My forty-eight-year-old bodybuilder friend Laurie Fierstein tells me as she trains me,

Laurie Fierstein, age 44. Photo: Mark Schaeffer, 1992.

"Don't count reps. Don't count sets. What does your body care about numbers? Eight? Ten? Use your intuition."[6]

The matron model assumes that women have no control over their bodies or that women cannot or will not assert it. Damning management, as Bordo and Nead do, dashes the fitness imperative model but also segues into acceptance of matronhood, whose loose flesh becomes the contrary of taut bodies built by the tight control of fear. Let us expand both models, and say that the matron may affirm the pleasures of literally and figuratively hanging loose, while the midlife bodybuilder may assert the necessary looseness of artistic process, which makes work fun and the aesthetic erotic.

Loose women lay bare flesh that once hesitated to love itself. Dimpled or solid, but never rock, they are bulkier than normal. They do not fit the excess-free zone.[7] They bulge into corners and across intersections. They project pleasure. Burly girls throw their weight around for the hell of it, in the buoyancy of eros.

III.

"There is not an erotics for older women. You're out of the game," an artist in her fifties whose work has been instrumental in the formulation of a feminist visual erotics said to me three years ago.[8] Personal shame, determined by cultural shame, is part of what redistributes, inhibits, and makes invisible older women's erotic flair and flesh. My bodybuilder friend, Laurie, in response to society's matronizing of women, has protested, "What are you supposed to do? Shrivel up and die?" Her body reads as pleasure to me—the opulent forms, the sweaty ecstasies of gym time, her telling me, "I feel horniest working out." Yet, shame also lives in powerfully erotic, beautifully powerful bodies. Many hyper-muscular female bodybuilders wear only large, body-obscuring sweat gear on the street because their bodies have frequently provoked verbal abuse. In the gym when she was training us, Laurie never removed her sweatshirt, and I could feel her self-consciousness when she took off her sweatpants and re-vealed her legs in tights. When she does reveal her body, her forearms rivet me with their shapely strength and severity. One day I watched her perform 315-pound squats, which moved me to tears. Another time her short legs, volup-tuously thighed and calved, elicited from me the passionate compliment, "Your legs are beautiful." I said that because I wished to acknowledge an erotic moment, and I said that to counter her shame.

I love her, this monster/beauty: how do I console or cajole her adequately when she tells me the following story whose quasi-humorous yet debasing content addresses her body as come-on, dare, and degradation, and provokes the public shame she feels that her physique brings her? "I was wearing tights, heeled boots, and a short, leather jacket, and was walking along Broadway late in the afternoon after an opening at Exit Art. A minivan slowed down and started following me. It was filled with teenage boys who were making comments about me. Then one stuck his head out the window and asked, 'Will you whip me?' I was angry. What a predictable response." Laurie's beauty is bizarre, and it always shows itself, whether she is in a state of more or less undress. Art historian Francette Pacteau writes in *The Symptom of Beauty*, a psychoanalytic study, that Baudelaire "spoke of *bizarrerie* as the condition of beauty, rhetorically asking: 'try to conceive of a beauty that would be commonplace!'" (138). However, Pacteau makes beauty a hopeless pursuit. She believes that women assume "that a sense of beauty in oneself can only ever be alien to oneself, can only be in an image: a 'beautiful work' formed in the gaze of another, and in the guise of another" (149). She argues that "the pleasure afforded by self-display arises from the subject's identification with the gaze of the other; the subject sees itself, as a picture" (186). Art critic Dave Hickey insists that beauty, as art, is a rhetoric, that it has an agenda. The bodybuilder's agenda is to show the bizarre—for it is "unbelievable"—spectacle of midlife eros.

The beauty of the bodybuilder, her eros, derives from bodily mastery and awareness. Foucault has explained the process this way:

> Mastery and awareness of one's own body can be acquired only through the effect of an investment of power in the body: gymnastics, exercises, muscle-building, nudism, glorification of the body beautiful. . . . But once power produces this effect, there inevitably emerge the responding claims and affirmations, those of one's own body against power . . . of pleasure against the moral norms of sexuality . . . decency. (56)

The body that lusts for itself does not lose itself, and refuses to be expelled from the terrain of eros. More prosaically, this body looks good naked. Consider an ad for a gym that contains no images, only words: "Look better naked." It may be taken as an admonishment to achieve something impossible, as an invitation to rejection, as an acknowledgment that everyone is embarrassed by their body or hates it, as a possible means to better sex—or as a suggestion that anyone can be a nude, clothed and confident in the beauty of her own skin, like Aphrodite.[9]

God knew better than Adam and Eve, who were beautiful in the garden, beautiful in their nakedness. But when they knew too much, they knew that they were naked, and God expelled them. Erotic shame and oblivion ensued. Today's bodybuilders know that they can look better naked. These words made flesh can reinstate the body in paradise.

The erotic requires connection, in which the gaze of another is essential, not alienating: I feel pleasure because you feel pleasure in my pleasure. You mirror my pleasure in myself. This does not separate a woman from herself, does not necessarily make her into an image, isolate her into a picture useful only as someone else's masturbatory tool. The erotic gaze derives from the mutually loving looks of mother and infant, a model of the freedom to look with love and pleasure at another human being and through that erotic interactivity, to look at oneself similarly.

Emilia Altomare. Photo: Sarah Van Ouwerkerk, 1995.

Older women are not supposed to show off their bodies, but the monster's purpose is to show and be shown. "Monster" derives from the Latin *monstrare*, to show, and within the western tradition monsters are meant to be visible warnings of all that is unreasonable. "Monster" also derives from the Latin *monstrum*, divine portent of misfortune. In her extravagant body, developed beyond the de-eroticized rationality of the body of the matron, the midlife bodybuilder is a prophetic vision not only of the body's power against the powers that be, but also of the horror of difference and the paradox of pleasure. Monster/beauty, doom to eros in the wrong body, doom to maturity as ripe, then rotten.

Just as nineteenth-century masculinism feared manly women and the unsexing of women achieved through purposive exercise and artmaking, so today women and men, many feminists included, derogate female bodybuilders for "looking like men." Bordo, for example, writes that the "new 'power look' of female body-building . . . encourages women to develop the same hulklike, triangular shape that has been the norm for male body-builders" (179). A hulk is large, heavy, clumsy, and slow, but many female bodybuilders, including Emilia Altomare—in her forties—and Linda Wood-Hoyte—in her fifties—are graceful, sleek, and flexible. The triangular shape of male bodybuilders replicates an ideal female form of large chest, small waist and hips, and round buttocks. In *Foreign Bodies*, a study of bodily pleasure, pain, and competencies, philosopher Alphonso Lingis writes of bodybuilders' "hermaphrodite muscles," an altogether accurate description of bodybuilders of both sexes

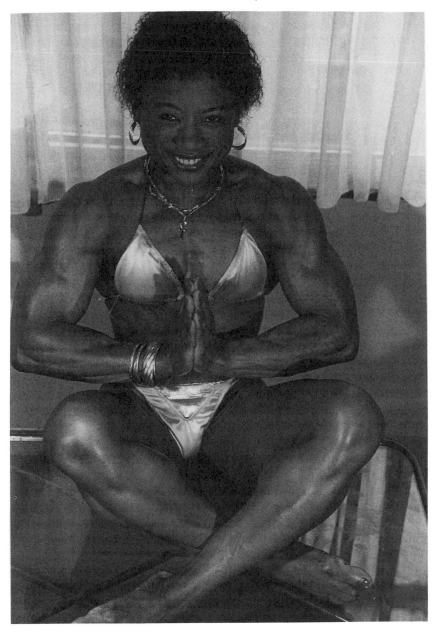

Linda Wood-Hoyte. Photo: Sarah Van Ouwerkerk, 1993.

(42). I would add that the hermaphroditic body is in excess of male and female; it is an unnamed sex, just as the midlife bodybuilder is, on sight, an undesignatable age.

Discrete muscle creates equivocation. Equivocation is erotic essence, part of the paradox of (aesthetic) pleasure. In *Libido*, Lingis asks, "Is it not the indecisive and equivocal carnality, rather than the splendor of proportions not yet disfigured by the fatigue of years, that makes youth troubling?" (62). Because she is bizarrely unfatigued in flesh, the midlife bodybuilder radiates a carnality whose sex and age seem vacillating and inconclusive. Her strong and shapely hypersexuality troubles time itself as the tyrant of reasonable aging.

The matron, a model of sedate inactivity, is the embodiment of the sedation of eros, having given in to the natural death trap of an aging body. The cultivation of the aesthetic of youthful prettiness in the midlife body, in contrast, neutralizes time, inhibits the living, acting, developing body. "Life Begins at Forty," *Playboy's* February 1995 cover story, features this surrender to prettiness, that of the "feminine subject" who, to quote Iris Marion Young, "posits her motion as the motion that is looked at," as "shape and flesh" to be enjoyed with someone else's purposes in mind "rather than as a living manifestation of action and intention" (150, 155). These youthful women in their forties exhibit inactivity more than capacity, which, ironically, corresponds to the matron's projection of body-experience. Unlike the midlife bodybuilders whose bodies represent intention, action, and, in the word of the artist to whom I referred earlier who bodybuilds in her mid-sixties, "experimentation," the bodies of these "fabulous" forty-year-olds lounge around—these women are aging "like wine, not vinegar"—and only time will tell the quality of their genes, gourmet good or otherwise ("Life Begins at Forty" 125).

All too often, contemporary cultural critics see the gym as a site of one-dimensional Foucauldian discipline, like a barracks, school, or prison. Gym as labor camp, producing the docile body desired by that desperate midlife youth-seeker. Wood-Hoyte, however, calls the gym "heaven," and Fierstein says that if working out isn't fun, it isn't creative.[10]

Training can be the same kind of experience that art making is. Time disappears and pleasure follows when one is living aesthetically. Marcuse calls the aesthetic attitude "purposiveness without purpose" and "lawfulness without law" (177). Today's sports audience expects muscle to perform—in a game, a competition, some display of prowess. In these terms, the bodybuilder's aesthetic expertise has no value: her muscles are gratuitous, dysfunctional, purposeless. In these terms, bodybuilding, purposive though it is, is a waste of time because it is non-productive, just as art is non-productive. But non-productivity—*being* as one trains, one's *being* as a body—distinguishes eros as it does the aesthetic. We are comfortable with the muscular body that does something, for it enacts the performance principle, whose laws are utility, acquisition, competitiveness, and domination, which, crushing pleasure, generates economically useful products rather than aesthetic/erotic citizens—narcissists, contemplators of beauty, and Aphrodites, agents of their own pleasure.

The midlife bodybuilders I interviewed began the discipline in their thirties and did so on their own. Women who take up bodybuilding in their early twenties often do so at the instigation of their bodybuilder boyfriends, who then become Pygmalions and Svengalis. For Altomare, Fierstein, and Wood-Hoyte, the gym has been and continues to be a pleasure zone that provides "challenge," "sensual transformation," strength, and development, and what bodybuilder and honored bodybuilding philosopher Al Thomas has called "bodies of content," in whose "sacrum[s] . . . thought has become living cells."[11] Thought, the concentration of Narcissus, made visible in the midlife body. Thought as physical education, educating the body in eros.

Writing about Ingres's *Grande Odalisque*, art historian Norman Bryson concludes that her body is "a radical disruption of the standard and homogeneous image of woman, in a self-dissolving and self-unraveling movement of what Barthes used to call *jouissance*" (137). A body that is sex-dissolving and sex-unraveling. An orgasmic body, hers and the midlife bodybuilder's, in which the undoing of discrete anatomies, the separated sexes, produces monster/beauty integrity. Orgasm as integrity, not as melting, not as dismemberment, parts felt separately from other parts. In *The Symptom of Beauty* Pacteau writes that "beauty resides in the *integrity* of the body"; she notes the derivation of integrity from the Latin *integer*, intact, and from the root *tangere*, to touch (85). The *Grande Odalisque* was a "body of content" (Thomas) for nineteenth-century critics, who saw her physique as pleasure and horror, as purest form and deformed, as sensually beautiful and as *bizarrerie*, as, according to art historian Carol Ockman in *Ingres's Eroticized Bodies*, destabilizing "the categorical distinctions between masculine and feminine" (91). Beauty is coming together, all parts organized for and resonant with erotic overarticulation, erotic leisure.

Counting reps is measuring productivity. Counting makes one tense, expectant, and takes her away from pleasure. A woman counting in the gym is like a man thinking about a golf game or a cold shower while fucking so that he will not come too fast. Protection from pleasure. Thought becomes the living cells of disengagement. A reason for being in the gym is to come and to come and come, to swell again and again. Orgasm, from the Greek *orgasmos*, to swell with lust.

I perform calf raises, seated rows, squats, and military presses more slowly than most people and sometimes linger, "wasting time," longer between sets than many experts recommend. This leisure is time to feel my muscles swelling. I love to swell like that, in a sacral joy that shapes intellectual and psychic as well as physical strutting. Swell and strut. The words "erection," "phallic," or "masculine" don't apply here.

Al Thomas writes that fulfillment "is not an idea," but is "in carnal thingness, in body," and that women's "complaint should be of de-objectification," for woman has been reduced to a "manipulatable abstraction" ("Some Notes" 4–5). Woman as object is an abstraction—the matron's flab, the midlife ingenue's flatteringly lit figure. The object is useful for sexual fantasy and fashion layouts, for deliberately political picturing, and for more intellectual mindplay. The object is a picture obviously lacking carnal thingness. Thingness for Thomas is not objectification, but rather an actual body's meaning created through thought made physical.

Visual pattern, force field, holy middle, flux of muscular transformations, viable vehicle of lust, écorché and Aphrodite, hair "dyed and fried" or going gray, the midlife bodybuilder is a creation not a picture, an abundance not a lack, a fulfillment ready to be more fulfilled.[12] She is: Emilia Altomare, Christa Bauch, Diana Dennis, Laurie Fierstein, Linda Wood-Hoyte.

NOTES

The research for this essay includes interviews with midlife bodybuilders Emilia Altomare, Laurie Fierstein, and Linda Wood-Hoyte, all of whom have competed, as well as interviews with younger bodybuilders and with the bodybuilding doyen Al Thomas.

1. The gym owner's statement was made in the autumn of 1995. Both the gym owner and the bodybuilder who heard what this gym owner said and repeated it to me must remain anonymous. I was one of the women in her forties who participated—speaking, not flexing—in *Evolution F.*

2. A student, Grady Schieve, made this comment about women's bodies in my course "Monster/Beauty" in the spring of 1995.

3. A mid-forties professor said to her introductory nutrition class of almost 200 students that because she was now in midlife she could look "like this, matronly." At least one student, twenty-three years old, heard her instructor's remark as an apologetic rationalization for becoming heavy and for apparently not putting to use a wealth of information that haunted and impressed the student. The student, who wishes to remain anonymous, heard this remark in the spring of 1996.

4. The artist, who wishes to remain anonymous, spoke with the author in a telephone conversation, March 21, 1996.

5. See Francette Pacteau's *The Symptom of Beauty* for an elaboration of this thesis. Within the sparse scholarly literature on female bodybuilding, feminists have analyzed women bodybuilders' investment in being conventionally sexy and beautiful. See Laurie Schulze's sharp critique of that position in Pamela L. Moore's *Building Bodies.* Moore's anthology is the first book to concentrate substantially and theoretically on female bodybuilding.

6. This conversation and numerous others from which I quote between Laurie Fierstein and myself took place in New York and on the telephone between May 1995 and April 1996.

7. Bordo uses the word "excess-free" (191).

8. The artist, who wishes to remain anonymous, said this to me in a telephone conversation, June 1993.

9. I saw this ad for a David Barton gym in the program for *Celebration of the Most Awesome Female Muscle in the World*, a 1993 bodybuilding performance.

10. Linda Wood-Hoyte, in conversation with me, New York, May 1995. Fierstein has also told me that the fun, the pleasure of the process, derives from the doing of it, whereas often the fun or pleasure of the result derives from others' reactions.

11. "Challenge" was used by Wood-Hoyte, "sensual transformation" by Fierstein, and "bodies of content" by Thomas, all in separate conversations with the author, May 1995. Thomas's second statement appears in his "Some Thoughts" (15).

12. "Dyed and fried" is Fierstein's phrase.

WORKS CITED

Blonsky, Marshall. "I Could Love Them All." Unpublished manuscript, 1996.

Bordo, Susan. *Unbearable Weight: Feminism, Western Culture, and the Body*. Berkeley: U of California P, 1993.

Bryson, Norman. *Tradition and Desire: From David to Delacroix*. New York: Cambridge UP, 1984.

Celebration of the Most Awesome Female Muscle in the World. Organized by Laurie Fierstein. Roseland, New York. Nov. 1993.

Clark, Kenneth. *The Nude: A Study in Ideal Form*. Princeton: Princeton UP, 1956.

Evolution F: A Surreal Spectacle of Female Muscle. Organized by Laurie Fierstein. Manhattan Center, New York. 11 Nov. 1995.

Foucault, Michel. *Power/Knowledge: Selected Interviews and Other Writings, 1972–1977*. Ed. Colin Gordon. Trans. Colin Gordon, Leo Marshall, John Mepham, and Kate Soper. New York: Pantheon, 1980.

Freud, Sigmund. "Character and Anal Erotism." 1908. *The Standard Edition of the Complete Psychological Works of Sigmund Freud*. Ed. and trans. James Strachey. 24 vols. London: Hogarth and Inst. of Psycho-Analysis, 1953–74. 9:169–75.

Hickey, David. *The Invisible Dragon: Four Essays on Beauty*. Los Angeles: Artissues, 1993.

"Life Begins at Forty." *Playboy* Feb. 1995: 125–35.

Lingis, Alphonso. *Foreign Bodies*. New York: Routledge, 1994.

———. *Libido: The French Existential Theories*. Bloomington: Indiana UP, 1985.

Marcuse, Herbert. *Eros and Civilization: A Philosophical Inquiry into Freud*. Boston: Beacon, 1955.

Moore, Pamela L., ed. *Building Bodies*. New Brunswick: Rutgers UP, 1997.

Nead, Lynda. *The Female Nude: Art, Obscenity and Sexuality*. New York: Routledge, 1992.

Ockman, Carol. *Ingres's Eroticized Bodies: Retracing the Serpentine Line*. New Haven: Yale UP, 1995.

Pacteau, Francette. *The Symptom of Beauty*. Cambridge: Harvard UP, 1994.

Robinson, Lillian S. "Doing What Comes Socio-culturally." *Women's Review of Books* 12.7 (1995): 11–12.

Schulze, Laurie. "On the Muscle." Moore 9–30.

Thomas, Al. "Some Notes Toward an Aesthetics of Body for the Modern Woman." *Compass* (Spring 1972): 3–10.

———. "Some Thoughts on Spirit: Its Source and 'Uses' in the Best of Games." *Iron Game History* 4.2 (1995): 14–19.

Young, Iris Marion. *Throwing Like a Girl and Other Essays in Feminist Philosophy and Social Theory*. Bloomington: Indiana UP, 1990.

Figure Model Series, 1991–1995

Jacqueline Hayden

On April 18, 1996 an exhibit of photographs from Jacqueline Hayden's Figure Model Series *opened at the UWM Art Museum, in conjunction with the conference on "Women and Aging: Bodies, Cultures, Generations" held at the Center for Twentieth Century Studies, University of Wisconsin-Milwaukee. The original photographs, from a series of over thirty, are unique silver gelatin prints approximately 84 × 52".*

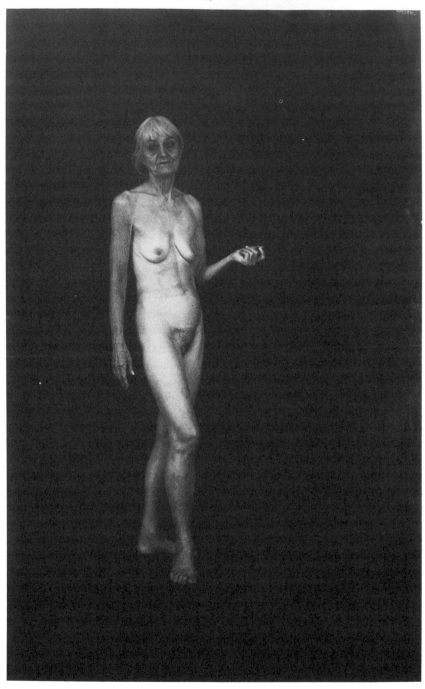

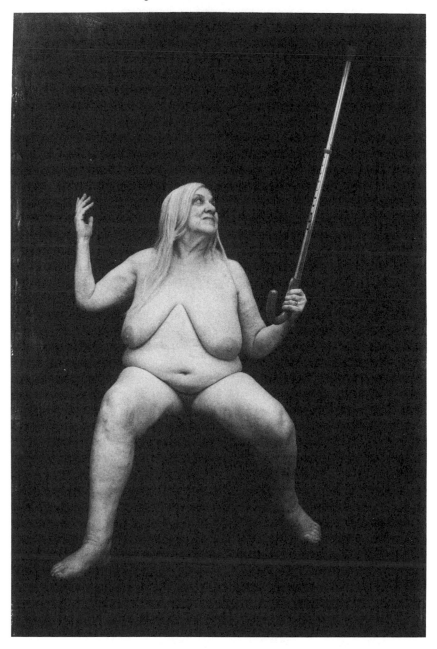

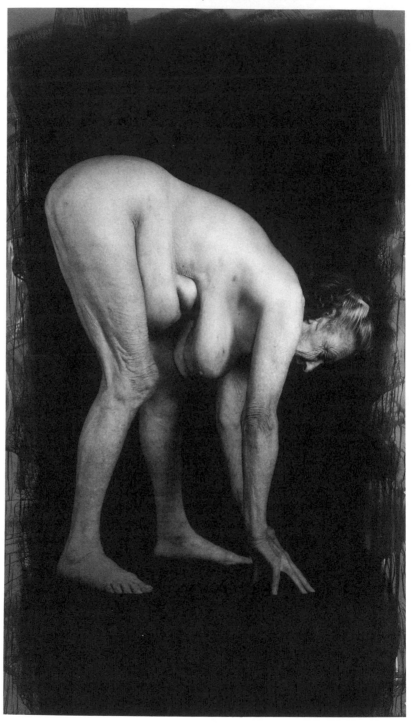

Performing Aging/ Performance Crisis

(for Norma Desmond, Baby Jane, Margo Channing, Sister George— and Myrtle)

Jodi Brooks

It took me donkey's till I saw the point but saw the point I did, eventually, though not until the other day, when we were watching *The Dream* again in Notting Hill, that time, couple of batty old tarts with their eyes glued on their own ghosts. *Then* I understood the thing I'd never grasped back in those days, when I was young, before I lived in history. When I was young, I'd wanted to be ephemeral, I'd wanted the moment, to live in the glorious moment, the rush of blood, the applause. Pluck the day, eat the peach. Tomorrow never comes. But, oh yes, tomorrow *does* come all right, and when it comes it lasts a bloody long time, I can tell you. But if you've put your past on celluloid, it keeps. You've stored it away, like jam, for winter. That kid came up and asked for our autographs. It made our day. I could have wished we'd done more pictures.

— Angela Carter

I.

In the 1950s and 1960s a new figure appeared in Hollywood film—the figure of the aging actress undergoing a crisis as she confronts her demise as a public star or celebrity. Produced as the studio system was at its end and the domestic introduction of television was well under way, these films—*Sunset Boulevard*

(Billy Wilder, 1950), *What Ever Happened to Baby Jane?* (Robert Aldrich, 1962), *All About Eve* (Joseph L. Mankiewicz, 1950), and *The Killing of Sister George* (Robert Aldrich, 1968)—narrate the passing of the old Hollywood through this figure of the aging actress. The central characters in these films are all thus marked by time twice over: as aging women they are marked as outside desire, and as aging stars, as image, they are both frozen and transitory. In these films we see them trying heroically to avoid being placed on this doubly defined trash heap of history (discarded older women and discarded moments of cinema and television), each of them attempting a grand performance either on- or offstage. If these films stage in different ways a crisis, it is predominantly one of confronting one's status *as* image—and as an image marked by its use-by date.

These women—Norma Desmond, (Baby) Jane Hudson, Margo Channing, and (Sister) George—are having a breakdown, a crisis which is not the "result" of aging, but of occupying the position of cultural refuse. If these women (who aren't after all that old) are staged in the moment of their redundancy, it is their refusal of this position that keeps us enthralled. Norma Desmond and Baby Jane seem to burn themselves into the celluloid as a blaze of white, delirious fury in their final moments of occupying a stage and finding an audience. Margo Channing finds a performance space offstage by relinquishing her career and taking on the bit part of the entertaining, smart-talking wife (but not without getting in a few good offstage performances first). And Sister George, who is subjected to more brutal humiliations than her earlier colleagues, at least gets to hold court during her character's wake, having refused the "killing" of her character by quite simply refusing to lie down and die; she will pretend to be asleep, she will pretend to be drunk, but she will *not* play dead. Of these four women, only George has no audience for her final moment. We last see her on the empty set of the TV show that she has, until recently, starred in. On the dimly lit set, she finds the coffin destined for her character and begins to smash it—and the set—to pieces. As the camera tracks back into a long shot from above, George begins to wail—or rather to let out a long, heart-wrenching "moo" (after losing her part as a motorbike-riding country nurse, her only job offer is doing the voice-over of a cow for an animated children's program).

The central characters in these films are played by major female stars, each of whom represented an earlier moment of cinema: Gloria Swanson in *Sunset Boulevard,* Bette Davis in both *All About Eve* and *What Ever Happened to Baby Jane?*, and Joan Crawford in *Baby Jane*. (Made in England and starring Beryl Reid, who had played the role in the earlier stage production, *Sister George* is the only one of these films which does not incorporate a major star.)[1] Both the actresses themselves (Swanson, Davis, Crawford) and the periods of cinema that they narratively represent function as souvenirs, souvenirs that are brought into a volatile juxtaposition with the present of the films. These women do not only figure as the discarded. They also stand as custodians and collectors of a discarded past of cinema, summoning and performing characters, stars, and scenes from other moments of cinema.[2] Norma does Chaplin and Merman in a private show for her younger (and reluctant) lover Joe (William Holden); George and her girlfriend Childie (Susannah York) do Laurel and Hardy at the local lesbian bar (though they are misrecognized as Abbott and Costello by an upmarket john visiting their prostitute neighbor); and Jane has no problems in mimicking Blanche's femme-screen-goddess number (and, we could add, Davis has no problems in performing Crawford as well).[3]

What happens to these "aging actresses" who themselves once represented the modern and the new? What happens when this "new" is discarded for another "new"—as the new always is? What happens when these women no longer represent the shock of the new, that is, the commodity fetish, but rather a different kind of shock, the shock of finding oneself discarded? The fascination of these films is primarily in the ways in which each of these characters resists being positioned as a figure of loss, a resistance which, not surprisingly, by and large fails, given their limited options. To refuse their status as what I call (following Walter Benjamin) discarded "transitory tyrants,"[4] they can, like Norma Desmond, attempt to freeze time (and their place in it) by trying to resurrect their status as fetish, which results in a psychic economy of narcissism. Or they can accept their place in the culture's gendered discourse of aging, one which will define them as "too late." Significantly, it is in their negotiation of these two options that we find something else altogether. While these characters may fail in terms of the outcome of the narrative, it is precisely in staging their crisis, one which is before all else an experience of time, that they articulate a different experience of time.

What these characters and their performances offer is a form of crisis in which time is loaded to the breaking point—the temporality of the commodity, the temporality of stardom for women, the temporality of woman as image. Both their refusal to leave the stage and the ways in which they negotiate their status as image take the form of *stretching time*, of re-pacing the temporality of spectacle, display, and performance. On the one hand, these women stand as dinosaurs, museum pieces, historical markers, and confront being left in the dead time of the museum. These women carry the burden of representing the forgotten and discarded: they are marked by and as loss without, it would seem, being able to represent their own experiences of loss. On the other hand (or at the same time), these characters' negotiation of their position as cultural refuse takes the form of summoning and displaying the discarded. Through the summoning of the forgotten into the present, they practice a form of remembering as a means of refusing their status as the discarded. Through this summoning of the forgotten, they charge the dead time in which they find themselves with anticipation: the discarded displays itself, demands attention. In *Sunset Boulevard*, for example, Norma's silent-screen melodramatic acting is set against the 1950s cool indifference and restraint of William Holden's Joe. The pacing of her performance slows down time, making it heady, while in *What Ever Happened to Baby Jane?*, Jane's wide-eyed expressions and gestures from pantomime and vaudeville drown out everything else in the frame. Through their pacing of performance, these characters stretch the temporal economy of spectacle, charging the image with a kind of rage.

Indeed, these films play out the temporal economy of the commodity fetish. These women, and the moments of cinema they represent, have functioned as commodity fetishes, both narratively and, through the use of stars in these films, extratextually. In the "now" of the films, however, they are the discarded. The ways in which these films mobilize star discourses is, of course, crucial here, and one of the fascinations of these films is the relation between the star/actress who has, in some sense, been discarded, and her performance of such a character. (The degree to which these stars are playing "themselves" and some of their previous characters is kept in the forefront, particularly through the use of footage from their earlier films.)[5] If we were to read these films through Walter Benjamin's work, we could say that these women stand at the intersection of the two axes that Susan Buck-Morss outlines in her reading of Benjamin's *Arcades Project*—petrified nature/transitory nature, and waking/dream. These two axes define four fields or "faces" of the commodity—ruin, fossil, fetish, and wish image.[6] For Benjamin, the commodity can become a ruin when its promise has not been fulfilled, and it has been cast off in favor of another commodity. As fossil, the commodity operates as a trace, a petrified imprint of "living history that can be read from the surfaces of the surviving objects" (Buck-Morss 56). The commodity, as the new, operates both as fetish (the new as the ever "always-the-same"), and as a wish image in that it contains a sort of promise and utopian potential (of happiness and fulfillment, for example). In these films, the aging actress is herself the site on which the various "faces" of the commodity are juxtaposed and brought into a tension. We find this most clearly in *Sunset Boulevard* and *What Ever Happened to Baby Jane?*, primarily because of the temporal distance the two films establish between the status of these women as fetish and wish image and their status as fossil and ruin, and because of the ways in which these two films explicitly draw on the discarded nature of their central players. But if the aging actress is the site on which the various faces of the commodity are brought into juxtaposition, she can also be seen as taking up particular relations *to* the commodity-image.[7]

What Ever Happened to Baby Jane? stages two types of relation to the commodity-image—what we could call a relation of longing and a relation of rage, each of which is based in an experience of proximity to the image. Blanche Hudson is the more familiar figure of the female spectator, the woman who is entranced by the image. When we are first introduced to Blanche (the adult Blanche, the Blanche of the now of the film), it is through her gaze at her own image. At her neighbors' house next door, a mother and daughter are watching a rerun on television of one of her films (it is, of course, an "old" Crawford film). Seemingly following the gaze of these two women, the camera moves in to the television screen until the whole frame is filled with the image of Blanche/Crawford, a closeup of a closeup of the star. As the camera draws back out, we find ourselves in Blanche's bedroom, and it is now Blanche who is seen to be captured by the image.[8] Enchanted, she smiles with that highly posed wide-eyed gaze we associate with Crawford.

If Blanche represents the female spectator caught in a relation of enchantment with the image, *her* image, Jane *displays* herself. The ways in which she does so have crucially to do with charging time—and charging herself into it. Jane certainly operates as an anachronism, a kind of cinema dinosaur, but at the same time that she is a figure arrested *in* time, she attempts to arrest time, to arrest the present and charge herself into it. Jane spends most of the film largely oblivious to the fact that she is no longer in the limelight and continues to operate as if she were. She seems to emanate her own stage lights, as if in her years as a child star she voraciously soaked up all the gazes upon her, hoarding them and adorning herself with them so that now they seem to beam out from within. With the slightest suggestion of an audience, she radiates.

Jane performs a particular kind of intoxication, one through which she attempts to animate herself as an image. Six years later, in *The Killing of Sister George*, Sister George will put on a rowdy drunken performance at her "farewell lunch" at the studio, much to her girlfriend's distaste. "*Appearing* to be drunk happens to be one of the easier ways of getting through life's most embarrassing situations," George tells her. Jane's attempts to resurrect her childhood act are a similar means of dealing with humiliation and redundancy, though she produces herself *as* a state of intoxication rather than simply feigning intoxication as does George. While all of these women are good drinkers, they practice forms of intoxication which extend well beyond their states of alcoholic inebriation. George may *appear* to be drunk at her wake to save face, but at other times George, Jane, Norma, and Margo perform a form of intoxication in relation to themselves as the image, an intoxication which is a cross between a desire to merge with that image ("they just didn't love you enough," Jane tells her "Baby Jane" doll) and a desire to blast the image apart and set it in circulation.

This charging of the image is produced in a number of ways, but most dramatically through the ways in which these characters are framed, figured as arrested and arresting image. Norma (Swanson), for instance, is often imaged as mummified, sitting on her "throne" like a wax figure. These shots, offered up as moments of horror, mark a different monstrosity to that which is defined narratively as monstrous in *Sunset Boulevard*, the "horror" of mutton dressed up as lamb. If these shots establish the obscenity of Norma, this obscenity does not have to do (or not only to do) with her refusal to perform a socially sanctioned version of the aging woman. Rather it is associated with the fact that she is economically—and indeed performatively—powerful over Joe and has no qualms in displaying it. It is shots such as these which are the souvenir "trademarks" of these films. The promotional stills tend to be shots of the aging actress figured as both arrested and arresting, as dinosaur and as medusa. But in the films themselves these shots are more complicated, for while these women may sometimes "forget" that they are seen as dinosaurs, they are well aware of the ways in which their very self-production as image carries the threat of freezing them in time. It is here—at the site of this tension—that they play out their struggle and stage their war.

These women attempt to (re)animate the image, to unleash what has congealed in it. Jane stands before the rehearsal mirror in the parlor, decked out in her "Baby Jane" costume and singing "I've Written a Letter to Daddy." Her performance is intoxicating, our gaze framed and held by her image in the mirror. The horrific whiteness of her presence seems to erode the surface of the film and burn into our eyes in the same way that early studio lights were said to burn out the eyes of the actors. But she is, of course, superb. She seems to stretch the temporality of performance and spectacle.[9] In these scenes it is only the return of the gaze which marks her as grotesque—the unwanted "intrusion" of the cut away from Jane to the look of distaste on her accompanist's face, or when, in her unaccompanied performance of this number, she screams and turns away from her own reflection before "recomposing" herself, slamming down the lid of the piano and leaving the room with a ballsy swagger. What is it that breaks the spell for her here? Is it her reflection, rendered grotesque by poor lighting? Or the persistent calling of Blanche's buzzer, summoning her back to the banality of her present? Jane, of course, does not need to be performing her "Letter to Daddy" number to distort the temporal logic of spectacle here. She does it just as well in the ways she occupies the frame, the ways she seems to make the shot wait for her, and then make it wait a bit longer.

These characters stage a particular relation to the image and to the temporality of the new. They summon themselves as an image, as the scene and site of a disappearance and a forgetting. While these women could certainly be seen as practicing a form of spectatorship characterized by an experience of proximity in relation to the image, here this proximity is summoned and infused with an explosive tension. Perhaps, in fact, we can see these films as soliciting a similar kind of gaze from the spectator—both now and at the time of their release. Each woman stages a kind of boredom and disinterest with the present in which she finds herself—a present which certainly excludes her. The 1950s pseudo-bohemian young Hollywood writers' scene in *Sunset Boulevard* is represented as vacuous. *All About Eve* heralds a new kind of 1950s star, one embodied in Eve (Anne Baxter) and Eve's own soon-to-be successor Phoebe. But this new "star" is in reality a figure who is formulaic and bland. Against this vapidness the tempestuousness, rage, and sheer presence of Margo (Bette Davis) can only stand as magnificent. And in those rare scenes in *What Ever Happened to Baby Jane?* when we leave the house of Jane and Blanche, the Californian culture of the late 1950s and early 1960s seems more arrested in an eternal, amnesiac present than do these two women seem caught in a past. If the present excludes these women, it does not seem to offer much worth claiming.

While these women do not, in the end, avoid the trash heap, they nevertheless stage something else—an experience of time and their place in it (as both historical markers and as discarded from the present) which is written through by shock and crisis. In their refusal to be allocated to the position of loss, these women, in a state of shock, produce a shock or arrest of the present, but in the end are left suspended there. Each of these films draws to a close with the aging actress staging (or restaging) her own disappearance in her very attempt to refuse it and to carve or burn her way into the present. As sole witnesses to their own disappearance, they have, it would seem, only one option—to reproduce that disappearance—now with an audience—through performing an excessive visibility. In the final scenes of *Sunset Boulevard* and *What Ever Happened to Baby Jane?*, Norma and Jane are both swallowed into whiteness, as if disappearing into and becoming one with the light of the projector. In *All About Eve* Margo (Bette Davis) avoids her disappearance by quietly leaving the public eye. But in her place we witness another disappearance. In the final shot, Eve's young fan Phoebe performs the disappearance which has already been marked as her future. Standing before a set of mirrors in Eve's apartment, her image is fractured across a million reflections, lost, once again, in a blaze of light. It is only George who is swamped in darkness.

II.

There are many films that address women's experience of crisis and depression, particularly in the histories of feminist filmmaking where it is frequently tied to experiences of time—and often through staging the contours of boredom (exemplary here would be the early films of Chantal Akerman and some of Marguerite Duras's films). I am particularly interested here, however, in John Cassavetes's *Opening Night* (1978), whose central female character offers an interesting reply to those in the films from the 1950s and 1960s I have just discussed. If in the earlier films the characters try to maintain or resurrect their status as image by burning themselves into the space of a spectacle, performing a kind of intoxication, a charging of time, in *Opening Night*, Myrtle (Gena Rowlands) mobilizes the shock of crisis as a means of rupturing both the dead time in which she finds herself immersed and the discourses of women's aging and depression in which she is implicated.

Myrtle is a fortyish actress who is to play a role which, she fears, will define her as "too late." The crisis which she undergoes results from her attempts to find a place for her character and for herself as aging women. In a state of shock, Myrtle tries to find a way of locating herself in relation to discourses of desire. In the process she must attempt to articulate loss (and to locate what this loss is) while not being defined by or as it. Myrtle is unable to communicate her experiences (she can hardly recognize them as her own), and she is constantly brought face to face with representations of herself which she doesn't understand. Her dilemma, then, is to find a way of producing an image of women and aging in which she can locate herself—and which doesn't send the middle-aged woman to the wings. She is, in short, in an impossible place. On the one hand, she is being incorporated into a narrative of women's aging in which she is marked as fading. On the other hand, she is experiencing her life as a collection of random, fragmentary, shock-like events. Both experiences of time threaten to annihilate her. It is only by bringing the force of shock of the rupturing instant up against this narrative of aging that she can both rupture and produce an image of gendered experience of growing older.

Myrtle is constantly trying to bring forth an image through which she can locate herself and make sense of the character she is to perform, a character that she says she feels nothing about, a character without hope. To do this she puts the very parameters of herself at risk—through intoxication, physical trauma, possession, and exorcism. What ultimately is produced is not only an image of an individual but also a rewriting of the dominant discourse of women, aging, loss, and depression, especially in relation to other films (notably *All About Eve*, which I will discuss later).

Myrtle summons states of shock and crisis as a means of rupturing both the present in which she finds herself and the image of her future with which she is confronted—a future marked by loss, regrets, and fading. The premise of the film is particularly apt: her task is to perform a character in a play, a character that she struggles against, a woman who is "past her prime," a woman for whom it is "too late for love" and who is coming into acceptance of this. "She'd like to fall in love but it's too late," Myrtle is told by the play's author, Sarah Goode (Joan Blondell), when she withdraws from the character, once again interrupting a rehearsal. In Myrtle's battle with her role, two figures emerge, both of which she has an ambivalent relation to: Virginia, the character she is to perform in the play entitled *The Second Woman*, and Nancy, a young woman who stands for her own youth, for what Myrtle thinks is lost or being killed off (some idea of passion and hope), and in relation to which she does not know whether she should be grieving or whether in fact this loss has even taken place.

"Virginia" regrets the choices she has made in her life. She revisits ex-husbands in an attempt to locate exactly what it is that has been lost and confronts her aging as the realization of lost opportunities. Nancy, a fan of Myrtle, becomes what we could call a casualty of the theater (early in the film she is knocked down by a passing car outside the theater as Myrtle and her colleagues are leaving). If this young woman's death is hardly noticed by those who witness it (Myrtle's cast and crew), her death crucially represents for Myrtle those things which she suspects are both being killed off in herself and defined as losses for the character that she is to perform. Myrtle "takes in" this young woman in the sense that she is possessed by her. If Myrtle feels, uncannily, that in the role of Virginia she is undertaking her own embalming (and participating in the laying out of the body of her character), Nancy at first seems to offer her a way of both giving form to this loss and disavowing it. From this point on, Nancy appears as a presence, a ghost, who increasingly threatens to consume Myrtle—and whom eventually Myrtle kills.

Thus both Virginia and Nancy threaten to define Myrtle as loss. Virginia threatens to define her both personally and professionally as outside desire, and, in relation to Nancy, Myrtle is an older woman, "afraid" and a "coward." Both these women (we could see them as the "first" and "second" woman, leaving Myrtle in the nowhere zone in between) have to be brought forth by Myrtle herself. Virginia exists on the page and in performance. Nancy exists as a ghost. Myrtle tries to recognize herself in these figures and these figures in herself, but to do so she must both take them in and keep them at a distance.[10]

Myrtle is thrown forwards and backwards throughout the film. The shocks she undergoes are the recognition of her own allocated disappearance, of her own no place, of her loss of identity. It is the very possibility of recognizing these experiences as her own that has her coming off the wall (and Myrtle spends much of the film up against walls—clambering them when she is too drunk to walk, throwing herself against them each time she exits the traumatic space of the stage). We could say that what she suspects is letting her down is perform-ance itself, and Myrtle is before all else a performer. The structuring of the film—the lines and relationships that cross from onstage to offstage (Myrtle's ex-lovers are her co-workers, playing her character's lovers and ex-lovers), the virtual impossibility of ever distinguishing between what is part of the play, what is improvisation, and what is taking place outside the play—means that performance occupies all of its parameters. It is not that the part she is to perform throws her forwards and backwards (we see early on in the film that the part she is to play, the way it "reads" her life, simply throws her into depression). It is the image of herself as loss and her inability to locate herself in relation to this figure of the aging woman that seems to pull the ground out from beneath her. "Does she win or does she lose?" is the question she asks about her character. What sets her spinning is the performance that she is trying to produce—a way of articulating women's experiences of aging which is not defined by the idea of being too late, or of being caught frozen in an image of narcissistic youth.

It is not that she finds a way of representing women's experiences of loss, desire, and aging (what would such a representation be?), but that she finds a way of *interrupting their narration*. Of course, she interrupts the narrative of *The Second Woman* repeatedly during the film—each time she leaves a rehearsal, and when she rewrites the part she is to perform. But these interruptions early on in *Opening Night* are read within the *same* narrative: Myrtle is having a breakdown, Myrtle refuses to recognize the reality of her aging, Myrtle is being a drama queen. To all this Myrtle can only respond, "I'm in trouble—I'm not acting." If in the end she finds a way of playing the part on opening night, it is because she has found a way of interrupting this narrative by embracing rather than refusing the stage. Barely arriving for the opening night performance, she turns up so drunk that she passes through the first two acts in a haze. Propped up on- and offstage, she collapses in shock with each exit. But by the final scene Myrtle has come into her own. We see her in a performance style unseen until now. In a mix of slapstick and 1930s vamp, she finds a way of both bracketing and embracing the part she is to perform. If in the final performance (it is, of course, opening night), she has found a way of performing the part, it is not by producing a unified character, subject, or body for Virginia. Rather it is through further fragmenting the image of the woman for whom it is "too late."

By the final performance another female character has taken on increasing visibility. For most of the film, Dorothy (Zohra Lambert), the wife of the play's director, has a barely articulated role in relation to Myrtle and her character (Myrtle rarely even addresses Dorothy throughout most of the film). Nonetheless, Dorothy's importance in the constellation of female characters whose gestures make up Myrtle's final performance is established relatively early in the film. In a remarkable scene, Dorothy and her husband Manny (Ben Gazarra), alone in their hotel room late at night, attempt to articulate their different experiences of time and loss, but their words circle each other without ever meeting. Manny asks Dorothy "what it's like to be alone as a woman": he needs to know for the play, he wants Dorothy to "fill Myrtle in" on herself. Manny complains about the rehearsals, saying that he is getting bored with things, with himself. Dorothy replies, "Manny, I'm dying. I know I'm dying because I'm getting tired. It's always the same—you talk, I sleep." Significantly, it is Dorothy's mute response to Manny's erasure of her which is taken up in Myrtle's final performance.

Later in this scene between Manny and Dorothy, Myrtle rings Manny to discuss a scene in the play where she is to be slapped by her lover. As Manny tries to reassure Myrtle about the slapping scene ("it's a tradition—actresses get slapped," he tells her), Dorothy fools around in the room, shadow boxing, playing at punching herself in the head, and collapsing on the bed. This too is incorporated by Myrtle in the final performance. Indeed, she has rewritten the play to the point where the slapping "episode" has disappeared, replaced by a form of shadow boxing where she hits toward the character who was to hit her. In the end, Dorothy is shown in the audience as Myrtle's *true* audience. The film's closing image is of these two women in an embrace.

If Myrtle's opening night performance is inflected by the gestures and desires of a number of female characters (Nancy, Virginia, Dorothy, and Myrtle "herself"), there is another figure that haunts this film—Margo Channing from *All About Eve*, perhaps the quintessential Hollywood film about women, performance, aging, and crisis. Unlike Nancy and Virginia, this figure doesn't have to be summoned, but rather seems to sit in the wings of *Opening Night* (and certainly haunts the film for the viewer). *Opening Night* is by no means simply a remake of *All About Eve*, although it does restage the earlier film, taking its central characters and its discourse of aging, femininity, and performance and refiguring them. What is brought into visibility in *Opening Night* is what was relegated to the "footnotes" in *All About Eve*—the breakdown of Margo Channing (Bette Davis).

Opening Night does the work of remembering for *All About Eve*. It unfolds *All About Eve* and interrupts it. Myrtle, like Margo Channing, is a successful actress. Like Margo, she is struggling against a gendered discourse of aging which threatens to make her disappear and in which she can no longer place herself. She is constantly being defined by roles of a "young girl, around twenty." But Margo at this point is forty years old. Standing in her kitchen, drunk, she spells it out to her producer and to us. "I'm forty," she says in her classic Davis drawl, "4-0." There are three choices available to Margo Channing in *All About Eve*. To continue to work, she can perform the role of a young woman, one she no longer seems that interested in. She can take up the position of the angry bitch, the drama queen who holds court (the deliberate camp that Sontag finds in this film). Or she can accept her culture's gendered discourse of aging which figures her as in her moment of fading. Margo ultimately chooses the latter option, accepting her position as one of loss. She decides to leave the stage, to marry her younger lover and colleague, and to hand over her next role to Eve (who has in fact already moved into it, with the complicity of Margo's friends and lover). She decides to leave one profession and to learn the "profession" that, as she says, "all women have in common, being a woman."

This resolution (if it can be called that) is only possible because we do not see Margo on the stage (except once from the wings via Eve's point of view as Margo is taking her bow at the end of a performance). If we know Margo as someone who takes pleasure in performing, it is less in terms of her work and more in terms of her histrionic performances offstage, for which she is both loved and punished. (This is what, after all, defines her as a "true star" in the film). Margo is reminded that "what is attractive onstage is not necessarily attractive offstage." But the resolution the film offers is both precarious and acceptable precisely because it is this histrionic form of performance, though muted, that we assume she will continue to produce, even if she leaves the stage. After the lengthy flashback that makes up the bulk of the film, we return to the scene of its opening sequence—the crowning of Eve as Margo's unworthy heir. We find Margo and her lover announcing their impending marriage to their "dearest and closest" friends in a double date at the "Cub Room." As she meets the toast of the film's male villain (Addison de Witt) with the raising and eating of a celery stick, it is clear that Margo has not in fact relinquished performing, but rather her profession.

If Margo produces a smaller stage for herself within the decorum of marriage, for Myrtle the distinction between onstage and offstage is less than certain. Her image and her gestures have become abstracted from her both on and off the stage. What has been lost—almost without her having noticed—is her ability to occupy her body. It is as if it has been erased by a narrative which is now rewriting it. Against this she embarks on a process of remembering, and without the ideal circumstances in which Proust, for example, undertook his project (his cork-lined room, and his cast and crew of supporting staff working offstage to produce and maintain the necessary environment). Worse, she has a deadline. She is not struggling so much against the temporality of aging as against a deadline she can neither avoid nor postpone—opening night.

Central to both *All About Eve* and *Opening Night* are a number of groupings of female characters—intergenerational "sets" of three. In *All About Eve* there are two such sets of characters, one of which could be seen as representing an axis of women's aging in terms of femininity, the other an axis of women's aging in terms of performance, the stage, and stardom. On the axis of aging in terms of femininity Eve is on the left, Margo in the middle (the Margo before her crisis), and on the right there is an open position, which is where Margo would be located if she were simply to remain on the stage, being "not a woman." This axis is demonstrated to be cyclical by the film's ending: Eve moves into the middle position, Margo avoids the last (but the film leaves it open as a sort of threat), and Eve's original position is occupied by the new young female actress and fan, Phoebe, seen in the closing shot of the film caught in a mirror maze of her own reflection. On the axis of women and the theater, Eve is on the left (entering the space of spectacle), Margo in the middle (about to leave the space of spectacle), and Margo's assistant, Birdie, the ex-vaudeville star, on the right (allocated to backstage and outside the space of spectacle). Both of these axes are marked by a movement toward disappearance.

In *Opening Night* these axes are both restaged and interrupted: on the axis of women and the theater, Nancy is on the left, Myrtle in the middle, and on the right, the play's author, Sarah Goode, played, of course, by ex-Busby Berkeley star, Joan Blondell. On the axis of women's aging in terms of femininity, Nancy is on the left (in the position of Eve), Myrtle in the middle, and Virginia, the character Myrtle is to perform, on the right—the space left ominously empty in *All About Eve*. In *Opening Night*'s restaging of *All About Eve* these axes no longer stand for a movement toward disappearance. It is not that Myrtle kills off the young woman and refuses the role of Virginia (the position on the right) so that she can retain her position in the middle. This position too is ruptured. Rather, in *Opening Night* these networks of characters are interwoven in such a way that the middle-aged woman is not confronting her disappearance *from* the present, but rather struggling for her appearance *in* it.

III.

In a letter to Adorno in 1935, Benjamin writes of the Grecian motto that he puts into practice in his work (it is central to his understanding of the temporal structuring of experience in modernity): "Seek to enlist time on your side in all things" ("Letter" 488). To enlist time on your side would not be to refuse aging (Benjamin's valuing of the process of aging in terms of the forms of remembrance it entails is a constant in his work). Rather it would be to grasp the temporal structuring of experience—to make it communicable and to use it as the basis of a form of transmissibility. In a photograph of Bette Davis taken in 1982, Davis is pictured sitting in what is presumably her loungeroom holding a cushion on which is embroidered "Old age ain't no place for sissies." None of the central female characters in these films could be seen as "sissies." Each is involved in a battle to articulate her experiences of time. Each stages the temporal structuring of experience in the age of the commodity-fetish—the relation between woman-as-image (star) and the commodity as the new-ever-always-the-same (and the soon to be discarded).

In the aging actress films of the 1950s and 1960s, the discarded female star attempts to refuse her status as the discarded by freezing time. These women are reluctant witnesses to their own disappearance. "To be traumatized is precisely to be possessed by an image or event," writes Cathy Caruth (4–5). "The historical power of the trauma is not just that the experience is repeated after its forgetting, but that it is only and through its inherent forgetting that it is first experienced at all" (8). Certainly *What Ever Happened to Baby Jane?* and *Sunset Boulevard* could be seen as staging the temporality of trauma, the repetition and belated experience of disappearance. Rather than producing the middle-aged or aging actress as arrested in a state of shock or crisis as she negotiates her demise, in *Opening Night* crisis—indeed, *performing crisis*—is precisely what enables Myrtle to articulate (and complicate) her position in a gendered discourse of aging. Myrtle attempts to both wrest herself from a narrative which she fears will mark her as loss, and also to find a way both of making crisis communicable and of coming through it. It is only by bringing the force of shock, of a rupturing instant, against this narrative of women's aging, that she can both rupture and produce an image of gendered experiences of aging.

NOTES

With thanks to Lesley Stern, Viki Dun, and Kathleen Woodward for their valuable comments on this paper.

1. While *The Killing of Sister George* differs from the other films in a number of respects, I have included it here for specific reasons. *Sister George* doesn't draw on Hollywood star discourses in the same ways that the earlier films do; the film is set in England rather than in Hollywood, and Beryl Reid, who plays George, is not a star of the order of Davis, Crawford, and Swanson (and hence there is not the same kind of play with a correlation or discrepancy between actor and role, except of course—in the publicity around the film—in terms of Reid's sexuality). Neverthe-

less *Sister George* revolves around the figure of an aging actress who is being dismissed from the visual sphere, and thus it stands as an interesting comparison to Aldrich's earlier film about an aging actress, *What Ever Happened to Baby Jane?*. As with all of these films (except *Sunset Boulevard*), *Sister George* focuses on a relationship between two women. As with *All About Eve* and *What Ever Happened to Baby Jane?* it involves (though more explicitly) a butch-femme dynamic.

2. For a discussion of the ways in which *What Ever Happened to Baby Jane?* can be seen as playing out a relation to Hollywood as lost object, see "Uses of Camp" by Andrew Ross.

3. In a promotion-review article in the *New York Times* titled "Rebirth of a Star," stills from *Sunset Boulevard* are set against portrait-style stills from some of Swanson's earlier films. What is most striking about this spread is how many of the characters Swanson had played are quoted in *Sunset Boulevard*: her Mack Sennett period (which Desmond performs for Joe), her "Sadie Thompson" character (which she often slips into), and most interestingly, a still from *Stage Struck*, where Swanson had parodied Chaplin (as she does for an unappreciative Joe in *Sunset Boulevard*).

4. Benjamin's term "transitory tyrants" is from Aragon's *Paris Peasant*, and refers to the endlessly usurped gods of modern existence. For Benjamin they are the "outmoded," "the objects that have begun to be extinct, grand pianos, the dresses of five years ago, fashionable restaurants when the vogue has begun to ebb from them" ("Surrealism" 181).

5. *Sunset Boulevard* is particularly noteworthy in this regard. The film is, in fact, populated by a number of discarded stars. Buster Keaton is in Desmond's bridge group, which is referred to by Joe Gillis (William Holden) as the "wax works," and Hedda Hopper appears in the final scene of the film as herself in her later life role as a gossip columnist. Interestingly, Swanson was to play out her "fading star" character in a different way in an episode of *The Beverly Hillbillies*, where, playing "herself," she is selling her house for charity. Granny hears of this, and thinking that Swanson is in desperate need of money, produces a film starring Swanson (with the rest of the family as the supporting cast) to save her from financial destitution. (Granny is also motivated by the fact that she believes that she and Swanson are twin sisters. The two women are, she claims, the spitting image of each other.) Granny "returns" Swanson to the *silent* screen, producing a silent melodrama which has its opening night in a barn in the family's hometown. It is worth adding that at the time of *Sunset Boulevard*'s release, Swanson had not exactly left the public eye: the year before she had started her own television program. For a discussion of *Sunset Boulevard* and its use of stars, see Lois Banner's *In Full Flower*.

6. "Each field of the coordinates," Buck-Morss writes, "can then be said to describe one aspect of the physiognomic appearance of the commodity, showing its contradictory 'faces': fetish and fossil; wish image and ruin" (211).

7. We can position the figure of the aging actress in these films alongside the social types Benjamin discusses. The ragpicker, the collector, the *flâneur*, and the whore can each be seen as staging a particular relation to the temporality of the commodity, and as embodying a particular aspect of the commodity. While the ragpicker and the collector are more concerned with the discarded commodity in its status as discarded, the whore and the *flâneur* are aligned with the commodity as fetish, as wish image. The ragpicker not only collects a culture's trash but is also allocated to the position of cultural trash; the collector is part of the collection; the

flâneur, like the commodity, is intoxicated by the crowd; and the whore is both commodity and seller in one. Like the collector, the central characters in these films both gather what has been discarded and have become part of their collections (they collect moments of cinema and reorder them, placing themselves in the collection as prize possession). Like the *flâneur*, they practice a form of intoxication in relation to the commodity-image, and like Benjamin's whore, these women (or their youth as stars) are both commodity and seller in one.

8. This is one of the most interesting edits in the film, not simply because of its "neatness," but also because it establishes the gaze at the closeup—one of the most familiar traits of the female spectator's alleged proximity to the image—as involving a mapping, a connecting of various gazes, producing a kind of web of various images of women, implicating them all ultimately in a discourse of aging.

9. As Jane does a slow spin, her dress swirls up and we see the considerably younger dancer's legs of Davis: thus, this body itself refuses classification. Discarded dream images return *en masse*—the performance style, the posture of her body, the stage lights around the mirror—and in doing so seem to take on a life of their own, returning like the uncanny.

10. Myrtle will go to great lengths to grasp that image in which both the character she is to perform and her own experiences of aging will make sense. She tries the dissolution-of-self-through-intoxication approach, drinking her way through much of the film. She tries to locate herself by revisiting a history of affairs and relationships (as her character does as well), but most dramatically, she will summon the figure of Nancy. Nancy is a way of giving form to and simultaneously disavowing the experiences of loss Myrtle is undergoing. Ultimately, however, the erotic charge between these two women that we find in the first part of the film is infused with terror, and Myrtle has to kill off Nancy because Nancy locates her in the discourse of women's aging ("you're an older woman, you're scared, and you're a coward") and because her affect-driven presence is tyrannical.

WORKS CITED

All About Eve. Dir. Joseph L. Mankiewicz. 1950.

Banner, Lois W. *In Full Flower: Aging Women, Power, and Sexuality*. New York: Knopf, 1992.

Benjamin, Walter. "Franz Kafka: On the Tenth Anniversary of His Death." *Illuminations*. Ed. Hannah Arendt. Trans. Harry Zohn. Suffolk: Fontana, 1973. 111–40.

———. "Letter to Adorno." 31 May 1935. *The Correspondence of Walter Benjamin: 1910–1940*. Ed. Gershom Scholem and Theodor W. Adorno. Trans. Manfred R. Jacobson and Evelyn M. Jacobson. Chicago: U of Chicago P, 1994. 488–91.

———. "Surrealism: The Last Snapshot of the European Intelligentsia." *Reflections*. Ed. Peter Demetz. Trans. Edmund Jephcott. New York: Schocken, 1986. 177–92.

Buck-Morss, Susan. *The Dialectics of Seeing: Walter Benjamin and the Arcades Project*. Cambridge: MIT P, 1989.

Carter, Angela. *Wise Children*. London: Vintage, 1991.

Caruth, Cathy. "Trauma and Experience: Introduction." *Trauma: Explorations in Memory*. Ed. Cathy Caruth. Baltimore: John Hopkins UP, 1995. 3–12.

Doane, Mary Ann. *The Desire to Desire: The Woman's Film of the 1940s*. Bloomington: Indiana UP, 1987.

The Killing of Sister George. Dir. Robert Aldrich. 1968.

Opening Act. Dir. John Cassavetes. 1978.

"Rebirth of a Star." *New York Times* 23 Apr. 1950, sec. 4: 26–27.

Ross, Andrew. "Uses of Camp." *No Respect: Intellectuals and Popular Culture*. New York: Routledge, 1989. 135–70.

Sontag, Susan. "Notes on 'Camp.'" *Against Interpretation*. New York: Farrar, 1966. 275–92.

Sunset Boulevard. Dir. Billy Wilder. 1950.

What Ever Happened to Baby Jane? Dir. Robert Aldrich. 1962.

Dolly Descending a Staircase
Stardom, Age, and Gender in Times Square

Anne Davis Basting

It was a bright November day in 1995 as I walked up Broadway toward Times Square with my ticket in hand to the sold-out production of *Hello, Dolly!* with Carol Channing. As I walked the city, I had an inexplicable feeling that I was making a pilgrimage to the source. In my research over the past five years on performing groups composed of older adults, I have witnessed and studied the transformative power of the theater for those people our society believes to be beyond growth or change. There was Brainerd, Minnesota's seventy-member vaudeville review with a cancan–tap dance line of women well into their eighties. There was the elegant and whimsical modern choreography of the formerly New York–based Marcus Dance Company in which the bare limbs of men and women in their seventies playfully poked out from behind red velvet screens. And there were the tentative first steps into theater for many of the thirteen women of Milwaukee's Artreach players, who, with script firmly in hand, shared their stories with an audience of severely developmentally disabled adults. With the exception of the vaudeville troupes, audiences for senior performances are usually fairly small, and their exposure limited to their immediate and largely supportive communities. These older performers often voice anxieties over memorizing their lines and falling on stage as commonly as they share their fierce pride and dedication to their craft. In many cases I have gone from observer to friend, enriched by the models they provide for coping with fears and uncertainties about aging.

My pilgrimage to *Dolly!* was born of a curiosity about the limits of the community-based model of senior theater. Would the possible transformative effects of community-based theater for actor and audience alike dissolve if their audiences grew? How is old age shaped in a performance on the level of international stardom? Is such stardom something that community-based performers might benefit from in some way? Or does stardom somehow catapult a performer beyond the mundane realm of the mortal to the realm of the timeless and ageless? Can an aged star act as role model for those who face, or will face, the challenges of aging in a culture in love with ideals of youthfulness, particularly older performers who internalize those ideals and who doubt their abilities to memorize their lines or to withstand the physical exertion of a three-hour show for days or even months on end?

Seventy-four in 1995, Channing was the toast of the town. Reviews, interviews, and advertisements had set the scene for the latest Broadway incarnation of *Dolly!* I expected jokes encrusted in glitz. Wrinkles, wobbles, and grace. Sentimentality and spectacle. It was Broadway after all. Before the show, I paused outside the theater to take in the scene. In Times Square flashing lights and enormous billboards vied for a consumer's glance. Among them, a sliver of an adolescent waif pouted in her Calvins kitty-corner to a nearly naked, Barbie-legged woman lounging like so much fruit cocktail in a champagne glass. Helen Hunt and Paul Reiser, then television's favorite happy yuppie couple, smiled down from a five-story, vertical banner. On that November day, Times Square was fast, young, gorgeous, and white. At least on the billboards. The consumers in the square—a rich blend of age, color, language, and gender—were worlds away from their two-dimensional counterparts.[1]

A red banner tethered across the width of the Lunt-Fontanne theater welcomed Carol Channing back home to Broadway. Elsewhere in New York on that day, actresses in their fifties, sixties, and seventies were reigning over the theater scene. A few blocks away, Betty Buckley starred in *Sunset Boulevard*; Zoe Caldwell in *Master Class*; and Carol Burnett in *Moon Over Buffalo*. Across the street at the Marriot Marquis, Julie Andrews played in *Victor/Victoria*. Down in the Village Uta Hagen played psychoanalyst Melanie Klein. *Having Our Say*, the story of the real-life centenarian Delany sisters, was finishing its run and preparing for a national tour. Essayists and reporters had picked up on the trend that countered the youthful face of Times Square. *Newsweek* columnist Jack Kroll attributed the return of the "divas" to a burgeoning gay culture ("Hello").[2] Invoking Wayne Koestenbaum, author of *The Queen's Throat*, Kroll suggested that the reemergence of divas on Broadway is a sign of maturity in American theater, not a sign of senility. This is a good thing. But older actresses are surely more than signs for consumption by gay male spectators. Critic John Simon suggested that the trend is predicated on rebuilding the reputation of Broadway. In a moment of bald boosterism, Simon happily proclaimed that Andrews and Channing are "still the grandest grandes dames on Broadway." Ironically, Kroll made no mention of the potential for an interest in aging as a cause for the appearance of older actresses. Nor did Simon take interest in the accomplishments of the male costars of Channing and Andrews. The appearance of older male actors on Broadway, it seems, is common enough to be unremarkable.

Still a "grande dame" of Broadway. As I took my seat in the last row at orchestra-level, I realized that I didn't have the slightest idea what this meant. Never a fan of the American musical, I was not yet born when Channing debuted *Dolly!* in 1964. From a bleary-eyed late night screening of *Thoroughly Modern Millie*, I barely remembered a hazy image of her. Instead, I more vividly remembered an imitation of Channing done in drag at the Baton Club in Chicago a few years back. Recently I had seen her on an entertainment news show. But to be honest, I didn't understand why she was considered news. Like many of my generation, the glory days of Broadway are empty rooms in my memory. As with *Phantom* or *Les Mis*, today it is the show, not the star, that rises to catch the public eye.

The heavy curtain swung open and Channing floated onstage with the momentum of the ensemble. I craned my neck left and right, bobbing around in the sea of craning and bobbing necks in front of me. As Channing took the stage as the character she had played more than 4,500 times, my thirty-year-old eyes locked on her seventy-four-year-old body. Three rows up, a man who looked to me as if he were in his seventies rose to his feet and loudly applauded her entrance. The rest of the intergenerational audience followed—including myself, a bit stunned. I had expected a courageous display of wrinkles. I had expected sentimentality. What I had not expected was the audience's frenzied approval of Channing's morphed body in what seemed a confusing display of yesterday and today—a face fallen and lifted, a body hidden and revealed, time frozen and flowing. I had made a pilgrimage to—and was participating in—a theatricalized display of Channing's simultaneously aged and un-aged body. As someone who works with older adults, often much older than Channing's "youthful" seventy-four years, I was saddened by the "inspirational" vision of old age the performance celebrated. Channing provided a symbolic alternative to what Margaret Gullette has called the "decline narrative" of old age. But Channing was also frighteningly static. Having repeated this role over 4,500 times, she was stuck playing a symbol of the past in a revival that obsessively isolated her age. This essay explores *Hello, Dolly!*'s spectacle of old age, the basis and limits of stardom for older women who act on stage, and my own questions as a much younger spectator.

I. GIVE ME STARDOM OR GIVE ME DEATH

Channing KO's Mortality

— Jack Kroll, *Newsweek*

My conflicted reactions to *Dolly!* are a microcosm of a larger scene of contradictions. I read the cultural event of the 1994 national tour and the 1995 Broadway production of *Hello, Dolly!* as generating conflicting images of older women, and as echoing the shifting and contradictory status of older women in American society today where, despite consistent living proof to the contrary, the narrative of aging as decline remains stubbornly persistent. This latest incarnation of Dolly Levi—a collaborative creation of Channing, the director of the production, the audience, and reviewers—soothes anxieties over individual journeys into old age. It eases concerns over the economic challenges marked by the coming of an aging society, one populated mainly by older women, by displaying the discipline and control of an older woman's body in a theatrical site, one that trembles with the unpredictability of live performance and that, as Herbert Blau writes, "stinks of mortality" (83). To celebrate Dolly (Channing) as spectacle, as the Broadway tradition of peppering performances with standing ovations encourages the audience to do, is for all generations to celebrate their distance from the cultural marker of "seventy-four." Yet even as *Dolly!* assuages anxieties about aging, it also marks a dangerous and unruly freedom that aging can bring.

The anxieties over aging—ones partially quelled by Channing's 1994–95 Dolly—manifest themselves not only in terms of individual aging, but also in the "aging" of Broadway. Laments over Broadway's decline are voiced in concerns over the unique status of theater stars as "authentic" in the age of multimedia pretenders. The yearning for authenticity here is a coded yearning for the seeming *realness* of youth. In Channing's case, this is middle age, since she debuted Dolly at age forty-three, at a time when talent/role/star merged.[3] Aging is imagined as mere repetition of that role, further and further from the moment of its utterance. The time trickery of repeating the same role over 4,500 times gives history an almost overwhelming stickiness, one that mirrors and feeds notions that people in their later years are merely distillations of their former selves, incapable of change or growth. The work of cultural theorist Michel de Certeau and philosopher Judith Butler counter this popular perception by suggesting that one performs one's self and creates one's identity through social acts across time. Although the stickiness of history informs our present performance of self, there is also newness and change in every utterance, every action and definition of self. Because Channing has played the same role so many times, she is in a way the ultimate test of performativity theories such as de Certeau's and Butler's. Reading the slippages of such an extreme example—Channing's use of her mask of a mask, and the newness that her age brings to the role—powerfully demonstrates the performative nature of the self across the life course, and calls into question romanticized notions of a stable, former, and most importantly, youthful self.

From its premiere in 1964 to its reopening on Broadway in October 1995, *Hello, Dolly!* has always been a show that knows it is a show. *Dolly!* is no mirror held up to nature, and it proclaims no urgent political message. For someone drawn to the dark side of theater, *Dolly!* is almost unbearably cheery. Its plot, based on Thornton Wilder's *Matchmaker*, turns on the manipulations of the charismatic widow Dolly Gallagher Levi, whose chutzpah is fueled by her strapped financial straits. Dolly can do anything it seems, but her forte is arranging marriages. By the play's end, she has contrived several pairs: herself with stodgy, wealthy dry goods dealer Horace Vandergelder from Yonkers; his young niece Ermagarde with the struggling artist Ambrose Kemper; and Vandergelder's enterprising head clerk Cornelius Hackl with the lovely Irene Molloy, owner of a hat shop. Set in turn-of-the-century New York, the costumes, painted flats, and set pieces attempt neither realism nor meaningful symbolism. In the first scene, a carriage rolls on stage drawn by two actors in a stiffly crafted horse costume, vaudeville style. In scene four, the ensemble sings "Put on Your Sunday Clothes," dancing about the Yonkers train platform in blinding, day-glo costumes, complete with matching chartreuse, magenta, and electric-blue parasols. *Dolly!* is wink wink nudge nudge American musical comedy, aiming solely for entertainment through larger-than-life depictions of people and a time that certainly never was. Hirschfeld's now famous caricature of Channing as Dolly, one that is plastered over playbills, posters, sweatshirts, coffee mugs, and souvenir programs at the stand in the back of the Lunt-Fontanne in 1995, is more than just a handy logo. It perfectly captures the pencil-thin lines of the show's plot and the director's vision.

Like *Gentlemen Prefer Blondes*, which propelled Channing to star status in 1950, *Hello, Dolly!* is a star vehicle whose plot and supporting roles are simply the trimmings on an elaborate costume designed for the title character. Winning ten Tony awards, the original *Dolly!* played for nearly seven years on Broadway. Publicity for the production that opened in 1995 refers to a January 1950 *Time* cover story on Channing's brilliant depiction of Lorelei Lee in *Gentlemen Prefer Blondes*: "On Broadway, an authentic new star is almost as rare a phenomenon as it is in the heavens. Perhaps once a decade, a nova explodes above the Great White way with enough brilliance to reillumine the whole gaudy legend of show business." It is the authenticity of the Broadway star that the 1995 production of *Dolly!* aims to replicate, an authenticity that reviewers both worry over and celebrate amidst the current wave of doomsday predictions for the death of Broadway. The structure of Broadway shows has shifted since 1950 from an emphasis on star vehicles toward ensemble shows and pop operas. In a January 1996 *New York Times* piece entitled "Quick, Name a Hot New Musical Star," Ethan Mordden first laments the lack of young stage stars today, but then finally poses this rhetorical question: "Do tourists really care who's playing Jean Valjean this week?" The answer is no, but they used to, that live theater, with no retakes or editing, was the proving ground for "real" acting talent, and remains, as Barry King suggests, "the yardstick against which to evaluate acting on screen" (167).[4]

Of the older women on Broadway during the 1995–96 season, Channing is the ideal representative of authentic stage star status. Unlike Julie Andrews and Carol Burnett, Channing's status as a star is largely contingent on the two roles she created on stage over thirty years ago, even though she has appeared in some films and on several television variety show specials.[5] Channing has publically mourned this fact, sharing her heartbreak when she was passed over for the film versions of both her famous roles. Marilyn Monroe came to the theater every night for three weeks to study Channing's Lorelei Lee, and Barbra Streisand took Dolly to the screen. The *Philadelphia Inquirer* quoted Channing on her reaction to discovering that the part had been given to Streisand: "I called up and said 'Is that true?' And everybody said yes. And I thought: 'All I have to do is open this window and jump out, and the pain will be gone. It will end it. You can take that sickness for just so long. Cancer is better. I mean, I can tell you—I've had it'" (Klein).

The 1995 production of *Dolly!*, along with the reviews of it, recreated Channing as an authentic theater star in several ways. First, critics repeatedly pointed to her unique status as a star of the stage. Jack Kroll described her variously as "one of those pure theater animals without whom there would be no theater at all" ("Exaltation") and as "the most indomitable theater animal in our history" ("Hello"). Praising Channing's return to the role after more than a ten-year absence, Octavio Roca of *The San Francisco Chronicle* wrote: "She belongs to the stage. Dolly's back, Channing's home, and the American musical is alive and beautiful." The production itself reestablished Channing's stardom by almost completely replicating the original show. Original costumes, blocking, set design, songs, and choreography were all recreated—and all were under the supervision of the original composer Jerry Herman, and the direction of Lee Roy Reams, an actor who played Cornelius Hackl to one of Channing's early Dollys.[6] Promotional materials proclaimed: "This 1995 *Hello, Dolly!* recreates all the Tony award-winning elements. The show features new sets and costumes—based on the award-winning designs—along with [Gower] Champion's inventive direction and choreography."[7] Everything is the same, it seems, except Channing is older.

By replicating the original, the *Dolly!* of 1995 isolated Channing's age as *the* difference between the first production and the new run, and as *the* challenge to her stardom. Will she fall? Will she look old? Will her voice crack? If the answers are no, Channing emerges a star. Enabled by her facelifts and her "well-preserved body" (which the reviews told us is due largely to a medically prescribed diet shaped by food allergies), Channing is an inspirational exception to an old age of decline. She promises us that with the right care and surgery we too can stave off time and walk into old age with energy and vigor. This positive model is clearly a large part of the show's success and the audience's generosity with standing ovations (mine included). But at what price inspiration?

For women, whom American culture ages socially more quickly than men, passing as a star has increased pressures. To prove stardom, older women have two primary choices: either play an older woman star lamenting the loss of stardom, or deny your age. In this regard, the 1995–96 New York theater season was typical. In *Master Class* Zoe Caldwell played Maria Callas at the end of her career, sharing stories of her golden past. In long monologues from which spill memories of her fame, Callas refers to herself in a distanced third person. In *Moon over Buffalo*, Carol Burnett played Charlotte Hay, a would-be diva in second-string touring productions of standard comedy classics. In the course of the play, her alcoholic acting partner and husband is offered a long-dreamed-of and too-late chance at stardom as a last minute stand-in in a Frank Capra film. *Sunset Boulevard*'s Norma Desmond (Betty Buckley) is arguably one of the most infamous theatrical has-beens, an actress particularly condemned for trying to play younger roles. If an older actress chooses to deny her age rather than lament missed opportunities or the loss of stardom, she must not only disguise the marks of age, but must also recreate the essence of youthful femininity which was, in many cases, the foundation of her stardom in the first place. Culturally, the older star's successful masquerade of youthful femininity functions to ease anxieties about the potential unruliness and economic drain of growing numbers of postmenopausal women freed from restrictive social roles and fallen away from standards of beauty set by young women.[8]

Amidst attempts to visually replicate the original, this latest incarnation of Dolly also differed from the original to offset Channing's age. Dolly is sexier now, as Channing was quick to point out in interviews.[9] But the triumph of the show and the proof of Channing's stardom rest in the negation of change. Does establishing the sexiness of an older woman create Dolly as a feminist icon? Or does the production reconstruct a certain type of femininity in order to re-root the older woman into premenopausal systems of value? Vincent Canby's comment was perhaps the most blatant in revealing the pressures on Channing to perform youthful or premenopausal femininity. "Unlike some other actresses of a certain age and unmistakable clout," Canby wrote, "Ms. Channing remains utterly, almost naively feminine, even as she is rearranging the universe. Celebrate her." Channing's display of (hetero)sexuality proves her feminine in a way that could be, and was, taken for granted during the 1960s, when she adopted the role of clown and eschewed the role of "sex symbol." But cultural anxieties around aging demand a shift away from her clownish stardom of the 1960s when she rejected her femininity from within it. In 1995, possessing a woman's body no longer culturally marked as feminine, Channing must first perform femininity before she can spin away from it.

As if to assist Channing in her illusion of stasis and her rebirth as feminine supernova, old age is exaggerated in both the reviews and in the show itself. Indeed several reviews bordered on ageism. Tom Shales wrote, "If Channing were the worse for wear, tottering or enfeebled, the current revival of *Hello, Dolly!* would, of course, not be the immense rewarding experience that it is." Pamela Sommers of the *Washington Post* concluded, "If you are wincing as you conjure up a wizened, enfeebled Channing tottering down the celebrated stairway, desperately trying to breathe life into the role of matchmaker Dolly Levi, you couldn't be more mistaken." In another particularly brutal description, Kroll wrote, "If *Hello, Dolly!* were a title fight, the septuagenarian Channing wouldn't be sanctioned by any athletic commission" ("Hello"). Shales, Sommers, and Kroll each exaggerate stereotypes of old age in order to recuperate a space in which they can praise Channing's performance.

Several moments within the 1995 production itself also hyperbolize old age as enfeebling, allowing the contrast between imagined decay and Channing's disciplined body to create an "ageless performance" and a triumph over time. In the final scene of the first act, Dolly, a longtime widow, stands before the Dry Goods Store of her dearly departed husband Ephraim. At the rear of the stage, an older woman—gray-haired and stooped as she pushes a cart—recognizes Dolly and asks after her. Even from my seat in the last row, I could see the makeup that denoted lines of age and pale skin, an effect that exaggerates old age and separated Channing from that image of decay, even though Channing is as old as, if not older than, the character at the back of the stage. As the scene progresses, Dolly closes the book on her past with Ephraim and rejects this phantom of her future embodied by the ghostly older woman at the rear of the stage. Before "the parade passes her by," Dolly turns to a life of love, companionship, and, mainly, financial support by setting her sights firmly on her marriage to Horace Vandergelder.[10]

Another telling instance of the use of exaggerated age makeup occurs in the courtroom scene in the second act in which a wizened judge attempts to sort out the facts behind the arrests of the previous scene's revelers at the Harmonia Gardens. The actor, wearing a comically large false nose and gray wig, feigns a wobbly voice and weak-backed posture. Like the phantom older woman, the hyperbolized representation of the judge as old distances Channing from old age, and helps reinforce her ageless star status.

My point is that Channing's performance of Dolly is no longer just about the antics of matchmaker Dolly Levi. In 1964, when Channing was forty-three, Dolly was in part a model of an independent, strong, middle-aged woman.[11] In 1994–95, the successful masking of Channing's seventy-four years assures audiences that the authenticity of stage stars is still intact and that old age among women can be controlled. Such masking also invites viewers to recreate their own idealized youth, which in fact several reviewers did—and with abandon. Canby, for example, found himself reduced to self-proclaimed "goon" status. "There I sat," he reported, "with some embarrassment as if chemically stimulated: helpless with pleasure and turned into a goon, wearing a dopey, ear-to-ear grin from the moment of her entrance through her pricelessly delivered remarks at the curtain call." Similarly, Ken Mandelbaum wrote, "There's little sense in feigning objectivity here—I was touched by the proceedings, marveling at the fact that something that was such a part of my youth was again available and still grand" (46). These two male spectators praise Channing's starpower and recreation of femininity as symbolic of their dream of youth. The happy journey Canby and Mandelbaum describe fixes what was undoubtedly a time of turmoil (the mid 1960s) as "grand" youth, the departure from which can only lead to a frightening decrepitude—both in the metaphor of the lifelessness of Broadway and in a personal narrative of decline.

But was there such a time? When stars were stars? When talent was somehow real—displayed and believed? From my generational location, I can not imagine a time like this. I can not journey back to the grandness of authenticity. I saw the sweet, mischief-making Danny Partridge become bitter, drug-addicted Danny Bonaducci, only to be reborn on national television as a seasoned-with-hindsight talk show host—*Danny!* I knew, and could not have cared less about, the sham of Milli Vanilli before the powers that be started talking about what a disgrace they were and took away their little award. I was not yet born when Channing debuted Dolly. Perhaps I've read much too much Baudrillard. I sat in the audience earnestly mystified each time the older man three rows up would shout "Yes!" or "Bravo" and clap (they were undeniable—heavy, lumbering, echoing claps). The nostalgic aspect of *Dolly!* in other words, flew high over my head, leaving me wondering what it was this man saw, what it was he remembered. Had he seen Channing's debut thirty years before? Had he witnessed its original fluffy optimism during a time of civil unrest, and felt comforted by the return of a symbol of that star power? Had he known that Channing was on Nixon's enemies list? Had he seen the revivals in the 1970s when Channing was playing merely her 3,000th show? Had he seen Ethel Merman or Pearl Bailey or Mary Martin play Dolly on Broadway, women whose talent reportedly outshone the machinations of the star industry?[12]

Some reviewers suggested that the production might be most effective for those who saw the original production, but the audience that stood and cheered when I was there was clearly intergenerational. Additionally, the view that reading Dolly as a happy journey back to the days of authenticity is solely generationally based overlooks older audience members who might not assume the theater to be an authenticating machine, or who might not subscribe to the inspirational model of Channing's attempts to erase age. What might the alternatives be? If the weight of authenticity and the burden of resurrecting an idealized individual and communal past are removed from stardom, if stage stardom is no longer predicated on the erasure and control of old age, what is left?

II. THE DANGER OF CHANGE

> World Beware: it's possible this woman is a
> substance that should be legally controlled.
>
> —Vincent Canby

Judith Butler's influential theories of performativity make a case for the coexistence of the momentum of history with the disruptiveness of the present. In this light, then, a body carries both its history of social relations and a potential for change.[13] It is ensnared in history that seeks to isolate and freeze it, and yet with every performative entrance to culture, it is also unlocatable. In

Dolly Descending a Staircase

1995 Channing paraded across a set design from 1964 in a costume from 1964. What emerged for me in the performance was not just the elaborate attempt to create stasis by conjuring up an authentic, youthful stage star. In fact, the time trickery in *Dolly!* was fairly easily dissolved. If magicians Penn and Teller had the chance, they might simply explain that Channing has excellent health care and a fabulous plastic surgeon. But Channing beat us to it. Several times. While Channing's performance erased the physical evidence of aging in order to celebrate it, the performance also pointed to the differences between the past and the present by marking her mask, and in turn, marking the performative aspect of *all phases* of the life course.

Channing created a *gestus*, a charged single image that accentuated the separation of the mask of stasis from her changing body and her craft as an actress. The scene is the Harmonia Gardens restaurant and dance hall. Dolly has finally cleared the field of suitors and sits to dine with Horace Vandergelder. Famished, she attacks her meal with ferocity. Clad in a long, red-sequined gown, Channing wears a choker with rhinestones around her neck, and white gloves that scale the length of her arms, nearly all the way up to the armpits. When she turns to eat, Channing takes off the gloves. The skin beneath her arms hangs loose, revealing her age in a way that up until this point had been nearly completely concealed. This moment of discovery is one Channing exploits. Cutting her food vigorously (Dolly has a voracious appetite), Channing wobbles the loose skin under her arms in a furious comic rhythm. The audience roared. Channing tells the joke and it is on her—and in turn on us. The punch line is the uncontrollability of aging, the control of which was the very thing the production set us up to desire. This moment of revealing comic excess challenges and rewrites the star pact by making hypervisible the mortal, aging body. It may have been a slip, it may not. Regardless of whether the moment was planned, Channing presents the contradictory images of fallen arms and lifted face and unsticks old age from being read solely as rigidity and stasis.

Channing's mask—her blonde wig, her Cheshire Cat smile, and her enormous eyes—also acts as a *gestus*. Her features are wider now with plastic surgery. The blonde wig, somehow believable at forty-three, is anachronistic at seventy-four. Our knowledge of Channing's age, and thus of the differences between her body then and now that the mask does not hide, serves to make the mask appear more stylized than before. It has become a mask of a mask. Tellingly, reviewers likened this production to Japanese Kabuki and Greek comedy.[14] One reviewer likened her to Rushmore and to Galatea (Stern). In terms of acting techniques, when she was a younger performer, Channing's mask could be naturalized and accepted as real. Now, at seventy-four and culturally defined as outside of femininity, her mask is "unnatural" and her clowning takes on a sense of danger. If one reads Channing's stardom as contingent on her remaining unchanged and on her erasure of age, Channing's clowning and mask of femininity prove her faded. If one reads her present and past in concert, her *mask of a mask* also becomes a mockery of the femininity that, being within it, was safer to parody in 1964.

Channing in 1964 (or 1974 or 1984) was no more Dolly Levi than she was in 1995 when I saw her perform. But naturalism in American acting on stage and screen is pervasive, and youthfulness is generally assumed to be *the* place to get off and linger as long as possible on the journey of life. Channing's early representations of Dolly are therefore assumed to equate Channing (Dolly) and youthfulness. Old age, the time when we suddenly *see* the writing of temporality on the body, is thought to be a mask of the former youthful self, automatically removing the possibility of naturalism in performance. "A garish exaggerated mask," writes Patricia Mellencamp, "hovers over as a reminder that we want to be someone we no longer are" (293). Channing's clowning with/of her exaggerated mask marks both the earnestness and the folly of such yearnings, making visible the mask of youthfulness and the performative, temporal quality of the self *at every age*.

Performativity, the idea that one performs one's self across the whole life course, can potentially open up a space for older performers developing their crafts to hope for, even achieve the recognition they deserve without adopting roles that lament the loss of stardom or erase their age. Performance critic and theorist Janelle Reinelt, however, astutely cautions against embracing performativity as an inherently subversive social act, and I agree. It is, of course, not just *that* we act, but *how* we act. *Hello, Dolly!* was and remains a celebration of predominantly white, middle-class values. *Dolly!* celebrates the loveless, financially convenient marriage of a galvanizing, independent widow to a grouchy, provincial, sexist (or at best, simply misguided) dealer of dry goods.[15] The dangerous newness in Channing's performance that Canby ironically suggests might need to be legally controlled, also speaks a certain flexibility that her whiteness and economic status allow. Still, in matters of age, recognizing the performances of older adults as more than mere shadows of former selves, and as destablizing youth as a privileged seat of subjecthood, no matter how fragmented, is a crucial first step.

III. DOLLY DESCENDING A STAIRCASE

The tension was building. I had never seen *Hello, Dolly!* before, but even I knew what was coming: the *triumphant descent*. Back where she belongs. The inverse of the decline narrative of aging. Like Duchamp's scandalous 1911 painting "Nude Descending a Staircase," Channing is both static and in motion. The young, handsome, all-male staff of the Harmonia Gardens restaurant has just completed its dance number. The staircase stands center stage. Long, narrow, empty—waiting.

Dolly Descending a Staircase

It is nearly time. Dolly appears through the curtains at the top of the stair. The red-sequined gown. The rhinestone and black velvet choker. The long white gloves. Exactly the same as in the photographs of the 1964 opening I had pored over at the New York Public Library of the Performing Arts. Exactly the same as in the publicity shots from 1978 when none of the highlights from reviewers used the word "still." Channing seems exactly the same. The orchestra begins the first few bars and I'm surprised that I know the song. Despite my ignorance of musicals, this song has seeped into my memory.

"Well, hello, Dolly."

She places a foot on the first step. The 1964 photos. Statuesque height, blonde curls, wide smile, runway model thin. Exactly the same. She takes another step.

"Yes, hello, Dolly."

Her foot wobbles just a bit. I suddenly become aware of how steep the stairs are and imagine the worst. I play the disastrous tumble over and over like a film loop in my mind. Her smile and outreached hands are like hardened concrete as she steadies. She takes yet another step.

"It's so nice to have you back where you belong."

Led by the older man three rows ahead of me, spectators of all ages begin to rise to their feet, clapping. He shouts "Bravo! Bravo!" so forcefully that I laugh out loud as I stand and clap along, caught up in the swell of giddy enthusiasm. As I clap, I notice the backs of my hands, blue veins beginning to rise from smooth skin. I see her difference. I see my changing body and apparitions of changes yet to come. She steps again. Her gown is heavy and extra material drapes around her feet. Worried, I watch them intensely. Her shoulders are bent slightly forward now, arms still reaching out. She seems to be embracing the crowd which cheers and encourages her progress.

"You're looking swell, Dolly."

She's nearing the bottom of the stairs now and I'm feeling the tension release. The waiters gaze up at her adoringly. Her confidence and charisma are comforting. The audience still stands, expressing what feels like a complex gratitude. For the mask *and* for the revelation of it. For the unchanging stillness *and* the newness. Set against the *trompe l'oeil* painted flats, Channing's Dolly steps down a precariously narrow staircase, entering a moment of radically contradictory and shifting images and meanings of old age—of both internalized hatred of one's mirror image, and of embracing the freedoms that falling out of social roles can bring.

The lights came up. "I am sorry, she has had at least seventeen facelifts," said a middle-aged woman scornfully. "She is not a day under eighty-five," said another. "I think she's doing okay for an old girl," said a man who appeared to be in his sixties. This age-talk showed both the instability of these categories (old age, middle age, youth) and the lingering biases against the visibility of time on the body, particularly for older women.

As I walked out, and back into the advertisers' battlefield of Times Square,

I looked up at Kate Moss in her Calvins. With eyes freshly trained to see the performance of and passage of time, I try to imagine her at seventy-four. I feel a strange relief. Moss, who is the other extreme of Channing's mask, is aging too. The intergenerational audience and the performance's hyperbolic attempts at stasis have given me an assurance of the certainty of change. Channing's mask, her wobble, her sexuality, are also glimmers that she *has* changed and that staying the same is really quite frightening. We *shouldn't* want it. Will the ground broken by the slight wobbles and the courage of Channing and Lee Roy Reams be enough? Coupled with the huge demographic changes to come, it is my hope that this and subsequent appearances of older women performers will lessen the pressure of stardom—and the pressure not to visibly age. Ideally, they will make it okay for Moss to appear on this same billboard forty years from now with breasts and cheeks no longer taut—but beautiful.

NOTES

Sincere thanks are due Lisa Bernd, Elinor Fuchs, and Carrie Sandahl for their generous reading and guidance of early versions of this essay. Thanks are also due Stacy Wolf for sharing with me her perceptive work on the intersections of queer theory and stardom in her essay on Mary Martin. Kathleen Woodward's insightful editing of this version, and her foresight in establishing the Rockefeller Fellowship in Age Studies at the Center for Twentieth Century Studies at UWM, with which I was graced, are beyond the reach of my ability to word thanks.

1. And Times Square is getting younger. The Times Square Business Improvement District has had surprising success in its cleaning up of sex shops, homeless people, and crime, and Disney has completed its renovation of the New Amsterdam Theater where *The Lion King* will play next to the neighboring production of *Beauty and the Beast*. I thank Mark Sussman for sharing with me his work on Times Square.

2. Kroll writes, "Why this sudden divandalizing of Broadway? Wayne Koesten-baum, author of *The Queen's Throat*, a study of opera and homosexuality, thinks the burgeoning gay culture has a lot to do with it. . . . 'Stars who meant a lot to me during my proto-gay youth are being brought back.' Koestenbaum calls this 'a beautiful moment'" ("Hello" 86).

3. I conflate middle age with youthfulness here with the understanding that these two, very generalized time periods are generationally constructed and consid-erably different. I include them together in this point on stardom because middle age is a transitional time period when one can still pass as youthful with the right economic, aesthetic (physical appearance), and social power. In "old age," however, one is beyond the point of passing.

4. Richard Dyer has written extensively about authenticity, stardom, and the use of the stage or unmediated venue in what he calls authenticating authenticity. In "*A Star Is Born* and the Construction of Authenticity," Dyer writes, "We must know that

her [Streisand's] star quality has nothing to do with recording techniques, with mechanical reproduction (even though what we are watching is perforce a recording), but is grounded in her own immediate (= not controlled), spontaneous (= unpremeditated) and essential (= private) self. That guarantees that her stardom is not a con, because an authenticated individual is acting as the guarantor of the truth of the discourse of her stardom" (139).

5. Both Julie Andrews and Carol Burnett started their careers on Broadway, but made the transition to film and television respectively. Like Channing, but to a lesser degree, Burnett is also "confined" by the vivid cultural memories of roles she created in her long-running television comedy series. Burnett's fellow actors acknowledge her confinement to television more than Burnett is willing to. Philip Bosco, her costar in Ken Ludwig's *Moon over Buffalo*, suggests that audiences "don't see her as an actress; they see her as this great comedienne, and that poses a different set of circumstances over which no one has any control. . . . The audience sometimes reacts to her as Carol Burnett, this larger-than-life figure, rather than as an actress doing what she does" (Purdum).

6. Reams, who met Jerry Herman through Channing, has performed with Herman throughout the years in a variety of venues from concerts to television specials.

7. New York–based public relations firm Boneau/Bryan-Brown sent me a press kit in November 1995. All references to promotional materials are taken from their press-release copy.

8. Emily Mann's adaptation of *Having Our Say* (1995), based on the auto/biography of the centenarian African-American Delany sisters, did not rely on stars to sell the show. Instead, the show, and the book upon which it was based, created "real-life" stars of the sisters themselves.

9. In a personal interview with the director Lee Roy Reams (November 1996), I learned that Channing was hesitant to diverge from the successful portrayal of Dolly in past revivals, and brought detailed notes of the original production to the first several rehearsals. Reams said that after a while he and Channing agreed on the importance of playing the role and directing the production for what it is today, rather than for what it was.

10. "Before the Parade Passes By" is one of the songs in *Hello, Dolly!*, one that reviewers who had seen the show in various revivals suggest has become more poignant as Channing has aged.

11. I thank Margaret Gullette for pointing out this reading of Channing's 1964 Dolly.

12. Tom Shales addresses this star power of days gone by most directly in his article "Curtains Rise, and Curtains Fall: *Dolly!* and Channing, Last of a Breed." Referring to the "communal orgasm" of *Hello, Dolly!* Tom Shales writes, "Such moments are rare, but in the musical theater, they were once more common. The great big stars who could fill the great big stages, as Channing does the Opera House's, had a magic beyond talent, and an audience got rewards beyond mere entertainment. It was a lot more than a good time" (G1).

13. Kathleen Woodward puts it another way: "We both are and are not identical to ourselves throughout our lives. It is as important to stress continuity as it is difference" (*Aging* 159).

14. Robert Sandia writes, "Always highly mannered (that's one of the things people like about her) she is as stylized in the current Dolly as a Kabuki actor" (98).

Similarly, Ken Mandelbaum writes, "What Channing does here can't precisely be described as acting, even if her work contains a number of beautifully judged moments of real emotion. This is, quite simply, star performing, the kind of thing we may have forgotten ever existed. Ritualized as Kabuki it may be . . ." (45).

15. In Act I, Horace Vandergelder leads the male ensemble in a chorus of "It Takes a Woman," a song that, with tongue in cheek, asserts the value of having a woman around the house.

WORKS CITED

Blau, Herbert. *Take Up the Bodies: Theater at the Vanishing Point*. Urbana: U of Illinois P, 1982.

Butler, Judith. "Performative Acts and Gender Constitution: An Essay in Phenomenology and Feminist Theory." *Theater Journal* 40.4 (1988): 519–31.

———. *Gender Trouble*. New York: Routledge, 1990.

———. *Bodies That Matter*. New York: Routledge, 1993.

Canby, Vincent. "Hello, Dolly!" *New York Times* 20 Oct. 1995: C1+.

Certeau, Michel de. *The Writing of History*. Trans. Tom Conley. New York: Columbia UP, 1988.

———. *The Practice of Everyday Life*. Trans. Steven Rendall. Berkeley: U of California P, 1984.

Dyer, Richard. "*A Star is Born* and the Construction of Authenticity." Gledhill 132–40.

Gledhill, Christine, ed. *Stardom: Industry of Desire*. London: Routledge, 1991.

Gullette, Margaret Morganroth. *Declining to Decline: Cultural Combat and the Politics of the Midlife*. Charlottesville: U of Virginia P, 1997.

King, Barry. "Articulating Stardom." Gledhill 167–82.

Klein, Julia M. "The Dolly Is Back Again." *Philadelphia Inquirer* 26 Feb. 1995: F1+.

Koestenbaum, Wayne. *The Queen's Throat: Opera, Homosexuality, and the Mystery of Desire*. New York: Vintage, 1994.

Kroll, Jack. "Hello, Dolly!" *Newsweek* 30 Oct. 1995: 78.

———. "Exaltation of Divas." *Newsweek* 18 Sept. 1995: 86.

Mandelbaum, Ken. "Musical Theater Review: 'Hello Dolly!'" *Theater Week* 6 Nov. 1995: 45–46.

Mellencamp, Patricia. *High Anxiety: Catastrophe, Scandal, Age, & Comedy*. Bloomington: Indiana UP, 1992.

Mordden, Ethan. "Quick: Name a Hot, New Musical Star." *New York Times* 28 Jan. 1995, sec. 2: 1+.

Purdum, Todd S. "Carol Burnett Comes Round to Where She Started From." *New York Times* 24 Sept. 1995, sec. 2: 4+.

Reams, Lee Roy. Personal interview. 7 Nov. 1996.

Reinelt, Janelle. "Staging the Invisible: The Crisis of Visibility in Theatrical Representations." *Text and Performance Quarterly* 14 (1994): 97–101.

Roca, Octavio. "Dolly's Back Where She Belongs." *San Francisco Chronicle* 5 May 1994: C1+.

Sandia, Robert. "Hello, Dolly!" *Dance Magazine* 70.1 (1996): 98.

Shales, Tom. "Curtains Rise, and Curtains Fall: 'Dolly!' and Channing, Last of a Breed." *Washington Post* 1 Oct. 1995: G1+.

Simon, John. "Hello, Dolly!" *New York* 6 Nov. 1995: 52.

Stern, Alan. "Look at the Old Girl Now! 'Dolly' as Classy as Ever." *Denver Post* 16 July 1994: E8.

Sussman, Mark. "New York's Facelift." Paper presented at the Association for Theater in Higher Education. New York, NY. 7–10 Aug. 1996.

Wolf, Stacy. "The Queer Pleasures of Mary Martin and Broadway: 'The Sound of Music' as a Lesbian Musical." *Modern Drama* 39.1 (1996): 51–64.

Woodward, Kathleen. *Aging and Its Discontents: Freud and Other Fictions*. Bloomington: Indiana UP, 1991.

Aging between the Ears

Rachel Rosenthal

*On April 18, 1996,
Rachel Rosenthal presented a
performance of "Aging
between the Ears," from
which the following is
excerpted, at the conference
on "Women and Aging:
Bodies, Cultures, Genera-
tions" held at the Center for
Twentieth Century Studies,
University of Wisconsin-
Milwaukee.*

Let's get down to business. I am sixty-nine—I will be seventy next November. When I was asked to come to this conference on women and aging, I didn't understand at first why I should be invited, and then I thought, yes, of course. I thought, in all these almost seventy years I've come to the conclusion that there is one thing I've learned—and that is how to apply makeup! (I also want you to know that I have watched the Academy Awards every year—not because of the movies, but because I wanted to see all those people getting older and older.)

Coming to Milwaukee is returning to the nest, so to speak, for the simple reason that I was here in 1986. I was turning sixty, and for the first time in my life it occurred to me that I was aging. It was very weird. There was something about that number, the roundness of it, the six with the zero, the six, a zero with a little tail. There was something scrumptious about that number. Up to that time I was a sort of Dorian Gray. I was eternally young, a mere *puer*. It never occurred to me that the years were going by. I wasn't aging. Suddenly in 1986 I realized I was SIXTY! It just hit me like a ton of bricks, and within moments I aged. I looked in the mirror and there was Old Woman!

I did a piece called *L.O.W. in Gaia*—I premiered it here in Milwaukee at Marquette—and in that piece I talked about aging, about turning sixty. I had a very nice sequence in the piece where I sat down and started to shave my head, as I dutifully do every morning. Rhythmical music accompanied the shaving, and so did photographs flashing on the screen—they were all big photographs of me, portraits in black and white beginning with my mother's pregnancy and then going back again. Because I've changed my looks so often, it was a continual metamorphosis throughout the years, and when the sequence of photographs went back to the beginning, what flashed on the screen was the baby—and I came out as a crone. This was the first time that The Crone surfaced in my work. I took a lipstick out of my pocket, and I wrote a red "60" on my head. Some years earlier I had shaved my head, and it suddenly occurred to me that this was me, that this was how I like to look. I felt absolutely right. This was the crowning moment for finding my own destiny because I felt now, ah! I look the way I should. I am . . . a million years of evolution! I identify with . . . me!

My life has been a continual effort to formulate for myself a life and a personhood that was different from what I had been given as a child. I remember the decades of my life as being periods of total metamorphosis. (I think I can probably empathize with insects who go through metamorphoses more than any other entity.) My life has been a process of orphaning myself, of becoming more and more tightly wound around a core that I have tried to find for myself, a core of truth and integrity inside my being, in the vague, watery, cloudy meteor that was the inside of my being.

The process of orphaning oneself is a process of growing up. It can take a very long time or a very short time, depending on the individual. Strangely enough, in my case it took decades. I was obsessed with demons that questioned my powers and my achievements, that questioned whether I was an artist. Then sometime in the past few years—I can't put my finger on just when it happened, I've racked my brain because I knew I was coming here to talk about aging— I realized that the haunting was over. I am no longer tortured by these demons. But when did it happen? It's driving me bananas. Such an important change, such a complete and full metamorphosis, such a final emerging of this poor little butterfly should have been marked by the pealing of bells and God knows what! But it was so sneaky, I never noticed it. One day I woke up and realized— oh, I'm a calm person. To be a good orphan means to take responsibility. I think I am finally getting the hang of it.

In my work I both teach and perform. I've had approximately three different careers, and I'm embarking now on a whole new one, which is making me very excited and very alive and very happy. I have a new company and we are creating new work which is based on the elimination of total fear. When we come to do a performance in front of an audience, we don't know at 8 P.M. what the evening is going to bring. We're just as surprised as the audience. I did this in the fifties and sixties but the audience wasn't ready for it. It took them thirty years to catch on. Now the audience really understands it, and we are off and running. This is my fourth career, happening right now.

I've thought about creative dying. I had a cat who showed me how to die ecstatically—she died in totally heavenly bliss. I hope that I will die just as high on something that is happening to me and that I won't know the end, just like at the end of *Star Trek: The Next Generation*, which I saw last night, they say, "To be continued." That's what I've decided. I'm very curious. After I die I'll come back as a ghost to see what's going on. To be or not to be. *To be continued.*

Touching Surfaces
Photography, Aging, and an
Aesthetics of Change

Anca Cristofovici

. . .
Just before rain it seemed the body
lingered transparent,

had carried one out under the firs, set
one free under the rotating spheres.
Now flesh was a constant breath
at one's ear, intoning

its litany of limitations. Yet how far the body
had to travel—when finally, after its shape
was fixed, and became one's signature
in the world of forms,

then faithlessly, like a ship tide-persuaded,
it drifted, abandoning what it sought
to become, the body in youth lingering
only a moment in its own folds.

— Ellen Hinsey, "The Body in Youth"

Photographs are strange creations. They are depictions of a moment that is always passing; after
the shutter closes, the subject moves out of frame
and begins to change outwardly or inwardly. One
changes. One shifts to a different state of consciousness. Subtle changes can take place in an
instant, perhaps one does not even feel them—
but they are perceptible to the camera.

— Susan Griffin

"The Body in Youth" by Ellen Hinsey, reprinted with permission of Yale University Press from Cities of Memory *(New Haven: Yale UP, 1996).*

By custom we conceive of aging as a separation over time—from youth and its attributes. Or, we think of aging, internally, as a split—between a younger self and another self, a stranger, new self, yet a self that is always getting older. But on the inner screen of aging, these shadows—memories of younger selves, anticipations of older selves—meet, conflict, interact. Separation *and* continuity are the source of a tension that helps us accommodate change. Incorporating previous states, we become the sum of what we have been. It is, paradoxically, a permanently inchoate process. As a rule loss and mourning accompany the discourse of aging. Yet loss's travel companion is accumulation—of imaginary selves, of psychic objects, of all the "baggage" of the past. How do we negotiate among what the psychoanalyst Christopher Bollas has called our "sequential self states" and "idiomatic dispositions" (29–30)? Here what concerns we might have about the accumulation of material stuff over time mirrors our worries in the psychic workshop of adult life.

Instead of thinking of old age as a discrete element in a linear narrative or in a hierarchy, I will focus in this essay on continuity, on the possibility of bridging our different age-selves, of creating a space of communication between one's own ages and between generations. While aging may encompass a "subtle continuum" of generations, in Kathleen Woodward's phrase (6), it is experienced precisely in the discontinuous flux of psychic images, in discrepancies between selves. Psychic space embraces the multiple transformations that make up the imaginary unity of the self. But the very multiplicity of these psychic images blurs our vision of this imaginary unity. Thus aging itself poses a particular challenge to the very possibility of its representability in visual terms. Yet in fact, does not the very indistinctness and indeterminacy of such blurred images—the elusive possibility of seizing the contours of the *state* of being old within the *process* of aging—seem more faithful to our actual perception and experience of aging? For at what age, actually, can we set up the borders of aging? Who decides the age of aging? As medicine has shown us, our body begins to age at infancy. Cellular tissues, the eye's crystalline, the nerve cells of the brain all diminish starting with the fifth year of life, as Paul Virilio reminds us in his *Aesthetics of Disappearance* (13–14). Even before our body has acquired a distinctive shape, it seems to start vanishing by virtue of a series of chemical transformations that appear at times to be alchemical. Aging equals change, everybody seems to agree, yet the ways of reading these changes and the direction of these changes are richly diverse.

Recent studies of aging have focused on the cultural stereotypes, ideological underpinnings, and theoretical deadlocks in which images of age have been confined. Our cultural tradition understands age in terms of a binary system. Old age is defined in relation to youth and thus essentially by what it lacks. In keeping with this negative definition, one of western culture's ways of dealing with old age has been to bring it into alignment with the model of youth. In an attempt to "combat" the aging process, contemporary practices such as cosmetic surgery and hyper-fitness regimes in fact contribute to the cultural denial of aging through an artificial aestheticization of the body designed to approximate the depersonalized canons of youthful beauty. We need, individually and culturally, appropriate images of aging just as crucially as we need ways of mourning, ways of dealing with loss. To deny aging results in psychic and cultural dysfunction, a kind of anesthesia of both the personal body and the body politic.

In the art world of the 1980s and 1990s photographic images appeared that challenge the artificial and frozen aesthetic of aging that has youth at its center. Recently aging has gained attention in cultural studies; work has focused primarily on the sociological and psychological dimensions of aging. But the aesthetics of aging—one of the most immediate ways in which we come into contact with the realities of aging—is still very much ignored. I would like to suggest that these visual works, several of which I will discuss in the following pages, may very well represent a decisive creation of new forms of expression similar to that which took place at the turn of the last century with the "esthétique du mal," one that integrates a conventionally negative value in a new vision. Here the question of aesthetics, then, is necessarily related to the question of ethics.

Given the double standard of aging for women, research on aging has focused mainly on the position, perception, and representation of older women. Here, however, I will focus on photographic images of older women and men made by both female and male photographers, images that disrupt that binary division between youth and age in an effort (more or less explicit, more intuitive than programmatic) to reverse the devaluation of aging. As I hope to show, these images foreground multiple visions of old age, exploring the rich potential of this period of human life, one that is in fact in the process of extending further and further into the future. The creative possibilities offered by these art photographs help make up for our culture's devastating lack of imagination in regard to this domain of our lives. It is important to note that all these photographers are younger than their models. Their images are, in a way, images of "the other" we feel growing in us as we grow old, explorations of what the French call "the gray continent." Yet they are also fictions of what we can hardly visualize: our own aging.

Photography is irremediably linked to the representation of personal identity and thus is central to the construction of our fables of identity. How, then, do these art photographs help us think differently about aging? Photography itself has to a large extent formed our perception of age. The photographic image accompanies us in mourning losses of so many different kinds. It fills in gaps in our memory, builds family narratives, and creates a continuum as we move through generations, one that functions as a mirror to our growing older. News photographs, family albums, and advertising photographs document—often in incompatible ways—our relation to time. Because of photography's strong adherence to the real, its images can express, as I hope to show, both idiosyncrasies related to age and also the possibility of changing them. In this essay, then, I will explore the ways in which photography can accommodate the tension between the state of being old and the process of growing old through its own techniques and metaphors. That we get old is a visually undeniable fact (although many do try to deny it). For the writer it is easier to create alternative spaces that account for the ambiguities and uncertainties we are faced with when we think of aging. But how does the photographer account not for the signs of aging (signs that are in one respect virtually invisible—the aging woman is an invisible woman in our culture), but rather for what is an inner reality and thus one that is necessarily relegated to the domain of the invisible? Rather than insist on old age as static, the authors of the photographs that inform my thinking here reflect precisely on the very contradictions and paradoxes of the *process* of physical and psychic change.

How does photography visualize aspects of aging that do not merely correspond in a documentary way to visible realities? How are such complex psychic structures as those related to aging translated into visual patterns? If accumulation of the stuff of one's own psychic life is as important as loss, what are the ways of dealing with such accumulation in the representation of identity? As Bollas suggests in *Being a Character*, we function in the waking part of our existence in accordance with the psychic mechanisms of condensation and displacement, of symbolization and overdetermination that Freud saw at work in the dream. We ourselves *"become a kind of dreaming."* "Although the internal world registers the multivalent factors of units of experience, rendered into textured condensations of percepts, introjects, objects of desire, memories, somatic registrations, and so forth," Bollas writes, *"in fact we become a kind of dreaming: overdetermined, condensed, displaced, symbolic"* (emphasis added; 52). Among these psychic processes, condensation and displacement are the most likely to represent movement and therefore to represent a psychic dynamic that allows for the imaginary exchange of psychic and physical bodies. Condensation and displacement are both psychic and aesthetic strategies that make the simultaneous existence or communication between ages within psychic space visually possible. Most of the works I discuss below create an intermediate area between reality and illusion, imaginatively exploiting the possibilities of the photographic medium not to delude but rather to construct visual analogues of psychic space and of inner experience. Situated at the intersection of the psychic and the corporeal, they utilize different techniques and tropes to approach aging. Mirroring psychic mechanisms, these photographs are also oblique responses to a culture that has rendered the realities of aging invisible, a theme that runs throughout the literature on women and aging.[1]

I. A HUGE BODY IN A SMALL FRAME

> . . . she is not an old lady but simultaneously a
> young girl and a child and all of them . . .
>
> — Czeslaw Milosz

> . . . people are not just their own age; they are
> to some extent every age, or no age . . .
>
> — D. W. Winnicott

In his photograph *The Giant* (1992), Canadian artist Jeff Wall boldly addresses the delicate subject of the female nude. Through a series of reversals of sizes that make up the illusionary space of this photograph, Wall suggests the psychic space that can simultaneously contain multiple ages. Puzzling elements contribute to the strange effect of the image. A naked woman on the landing of a library staircase is reading a scrap of paper while other readers go about their own business. The confusion in the perception of space, suggestive of Escher's drawings, is counterbalanced by the poised pose of the woman— modest yet unashamed. Another paradox results from the dimensions of the picture. Entitled *The Giant*, it is a small format photograph (15 × 18 ¾"), an unusual size for Wall's work. The relatively small size of the frame replicates metaphorically the boundaries and closures imposed upon the representations of the elder body. A huge body in a small frame. A visual pun as it were: a condensation of growing old, which is here figured as maturing (getting big) and getting old. But this is also the naked body of a woman in an open, public space. Size functions here as a visual metonymy for age. Magnified, overexposed, she is self-absorbed in her own private world, one that remains secret to us. Abstracted from all concrete data, she gains respect for the human body in its most genuine—and most vulnerable—appearance. The monumental architecture of her body defies the structure of the public space. The placement of the naked body within the space of the library suggests a syncopated overlap of the world of experience with the world of knowledge. In an uncanny way, this image bridges the large and the small, a sense of openness and a sense of confinement (and perhaps self-contentment), the geometry of rationalized space and the unpredictable habitations of the unconscious. Incidentally, in the exhibition at the Jeu de Paume Gallery in Paris where I first saw it, *The Giant* was placed in a corridor, a space of transition, surprising the viewers as they rounded the corner with its very discretion. And discretion is precisely what is so odd about this bold photograph, so unlike the inauthentic recent photographs of middle-aged female nudes in popular magazines.[2]

As in Lacan's reading of Poe's "The Purloined Letter," the mystery of *The Giant* lies in its very openness (as in many of Vermeer's paintings, the woman *is* actually reading a scrap of paper, a message of sorts). It is an openness that paradoxically suggests interior corridors, flights of stairs, meanderings and hidden corners of the psyche—knowledge contained between the covers of books and digested into the body. The multiple sources of light contribute to the dazzling effect of the photograph. Significantly, the photograph is not printed on paper, so fragile, skin-like, perishable. Printed on a transparency, the photograph is presented in a lightbox that intensifies the illusion of a third dimension. There is the light in the photograph itself, there is the impression of light that made the photograph possible, and there is the light coming from behind the image. Another space is thus created, one that radiates light from a hidden (inner) source. Physically and metaphorically, the photograph converts the unseen into (visible) matter. Yet at the same time, the image acquires a transparency that allows us, imaginarily, to see through the body—into another space, into another dimension. There, this older woman, The Giant, probably entertains a dialogue with the younger—smaller—figures in the picture. And in fact the geometric center of the composition is occupied by the small figure of a young woman situated on the same staircase landing, walking, as it were, in the direction of the figure of the older woman, an older woman whom she does not see. The accidental presences on the broken-angled staircase—two young women to the right going down, one to the left going up, an old man passing by on the upper level—disturb the hierarchy of the centuries-old pyramidal model of the ages of man and woman: our going up from childhood to maturity and from there on down to the grave. We might, then, read this image of an older woman's body framed by an irregular pattern as an ironic transcendence of age, for despite the unabashed display of the naked body, the composition of the work turns the viewer's attention toward the inside. Its syncopated visual rhythms echo the conflict between internal and external perceptions of age.

Wall uses the tools of computer manipulation to achieve the effects of displacement and condensation that result in *The Giant* in unsettling the convention of the nude, as well as traditional representations of the aging body. Like many art photographers today, he is known for discarding the predominantly documentary quality of photography. He has chosen, in the words of Vicki Goldberg, to "manufacture a reality that has the effrontery to look real" (32). For his *trompe-l'oeil* photographs in lightboxes, Wall uses actors who fake "real life" scenes. He intends to shock the convention-laden viewer by making use of the very conventions he attacks. Thus his method of composing a photograph explores the tenuous relation between reality and fiction as it is inflected by television, cinema, computer imagery, and the world of advertising. Where then can one psychically situate *The Giant*? In the realm of fantasy? Of desire? For its owner, the aging body is always a reality, always a fiction—a composite made up of past and prospective images, a portable set of generational images. Like the Rilkean angels alighting on the reading tables in a library in Wim Wenders's film *Wings of Desire*, the Giant is a powerful archetypal presence, one whose meaning, however, remains suspended in ambiguity. As Rilke wrote in a letter in 1915, "Everywhere space and vision came, as it were, together in the object, in every one of them a whole inner world was exhibited as though an angel, *in whom space was included, were blind and looking into himself*" (emphasis added; 16). Do we not sometimes notice in people who are older (our grandparents, friends, passersby) this sense of looking into oneself, of detachment and abstraction from the real that Freud associated with the death instinct?[3] With time, it's true, we seem to turn the world into ourselves. It is probably not (only) because of the possible limitations of our body that we tend to travel less, but (also) because of a self-containment that prompts us to pursue longer journeys within ourselves. Like giants in fairy tales or in myths, we contain so much space.

Most commentaries on Wall's *Giant* have in fact focused only on the mythic quality of the woman's body as a fixed image, thus rebuffing it as a potential vision of inner experience about the changing body over time. Discussing enigma in Wall's work, art historian Jean-François Chevrier, for instance, dismisses this otherwise quite enigmatic photograph as simply "allegorical" and "funny," thus voicing, probably unconsciously, the common attitude of keeping our eyes closed to the exposure of older shapes.[4] Aging can trick an eye trained in conventional readings for conventional signs. Even more reductive is Richard Vine's casually pejorative decoding of the mytho-poetic figure of *The Giant* as a "geriatric amazon" who "*though somewhat withered in her extremities*, retains a powerfully sexual torso and breasts, suggestive both of the physical losses that accrue with age and *of the erotic self-identity which may nevertheless stubbornly persist*" (emphasis added; 91). Vine interprets the relation between knowledge and experience in the photograph in consonance with a traditional linear narrative of age. He views pessimistically and, shall we say, dramatically, "the goddesslike idealization of the cultural pursuits that engage the surrounding students" as a representation of the futility of those pursuits that "will not save them from *time's insidious devastations of the flesh*" (91). Is not this reading of the nude as a mythical figure in contradiction with its being a sign of decaying flesh? For if the fear of one's *mortality* is what probably prevents the viewer from seeing that this nude is a beautiful, accomplished body, is it not also the fear of one's own *immortality* that makes it a visual impossibility and hence one rebuffed as possible vision? For eyes used to idealized representations of the naked body, is the openness of this image blinding?

Yet if classical art forms or modern advertising have made it possible to artificially fabricate such a natural phenomenon as youth, one could imagine the reverse paradox of fabricating—and marketing in the art world—the natural phenomenon of old age, and thus introduce it into the aesthetic circuit. In her article entitled "Photos that Lie—and Tell the Truth," Vicki Goldberg seizes on the productive nature of this paradox that confuses the relation between the natural and the artificial. "The most direct way to the visible," she writes, "is to make it up" (32). The strategies Wall uses to create a space of illusion place The Giant in an area that allows for new visions and reversible readings of one's own relation to changes in the physical and psychic body. Instead of aestheticizing the body, the technology used by Wall (the digital manipulation of images) exposes the body as it is—not as a youthful body, but as an accomplished shape, as significant form. Fiction documents a reality that sees beyond the visible. From this perspective, Wall's effort to challenge the limitations of his medium mirrors our struggle with the very limitations of our bodies.

II. LONG HAIR ON OLDER WOMEN

Paris, August 12, 1978
Suzanne
    The letter that I could write to you could be indecent: it would be a love letter.
    You seem to be talking to me, and I to you, we seem to communicate through these photographs much better than through words. With the same love that I wash your hair, depilate your chin or massage your tender muscles, my dream would be, of course, to photograph your body.
    Don't ever be afraid. If you turned blind, I would come to you and read to you. And when you feel yourself dying, call me, I will come to hold you in my arms.

    Hugs and kisses: Hervé

    — Hervé Guibert, *Suzanne et Louise* n. pag.

In her essay "Visible Difference: Women Artists and Aging," Joanna Frueh discusses the discrepancy between the formal norms established by the female nude in western art and popular culture and the real female body in terms of the opposition between the norm embedded in cultural icons and what appears as the shapeless reality of the body. "Aging women," she insists, "are excruciatingly aware of the visible changes in form that occur before their own and others' eyes, the 'shapelessness' that makes them, even more than young women, unable to be the incarnation of perfection" (212).[5] Recent important art shows such as "Feminin-masculin" and "Formlessness: A User's Guide" at the Centre Pompidou in Paris have explored this problematic in contemporary art, one in which shapelessness takes its place in the alphabet of forms. Of course a chain of diverse shapes informs the history of the nude from primitive Venuses to cubist figurations of the body. But the primary variable in the history of the nude is the binary fat/thin. If each period reinvents the feminine, the photographic images that explore the rich texture of the aging body will, perhaps, in time reshape the category of beauty.

This seems to be the intention of Jacqueline Hayden in her fascinating series entitled *Figure Model* (1991–95), a project involving photographing nude men and women. Ranging in age from sixty to eighty-four, they are portrayed in new versions of classical poses. The fact that her models have worked as professional models in art schools (all but one were still active at the time of this project) contributes to Hayden's purpose to challenge canons of beauty in western art that have informed our sensibilities for centuries, shaping what we see. As Hayden puts it, "Our public view of the body is much edited, whether conditioned by the ideals of classical sculpture or the images of modern advertising." Depicted in a lyric-dramatic mode and placed on a dark background, the nearly life-size black-and-white portraits of the *Figure Model Series* are denuded of any social context. The pictorial quality of the photographs (the result of the artist's direct intervention on the emulsion) foregrounds the shapes of the models' bodies and sustains the intense tactile quality of the photographs. A dripping effect cradles the body. The light Hayden uses softens (without effacing) the texture of the skin. It gives the flesh of the models the translucent quality of marble or alabaster. They are—as their size indicates—statuesque. But the effect is double. The soft light brings the surface of the skin closer to the eye. In their transparency we also read the frailty of these bodies. The subjects of the photographs are both art-like and life-like. That Hayden went to nursing school and worked in a hospital is relevant here. Her experience of holding, washing, and watching over the elderly shows in the gaze she projects on these images, a gaze that envelops her subjects and places them in a creative space. Where Wall uses distance as a form of modesty to protect the exposed body, Hayden uses closeness, a sensual approach that produces a space in which the models act out the realities of their bodies within the forms and fantasies of art history. I should add that these photographs are unframed, suggesting the precariousness of both the art image and the aging self. That they are unframed points to the human body's resistance to being framed by restrictive categories, to being immobilized into fixed forms. Sometimes the models are shown with canes and bandages, thus incorporating parts of a possible reality of the aging body into that of the art model.[6]

Hayden's choice to use models of both sexes is an implicit comment on the relation between gender and aging, one that echoes Woodward's provocative suggestion that "in advanced old age, age may assume more importance than any of the other differences which distinguish our bodies from others, including gender" (16). Makeup and costume discarded, the aging body is in a very real sense the same in men and women. Yet as the size of Hayden's photographs suggests, so is its potential monumental quality, a quality that redeems the diminishing that comes with time.[7] Images such as these are crucial to the visual integration of the realities of old age into an aesthetic circuit, especially because western art has mostly relegated images of old age to the domain of caricature. Real without being either cruel or sentimental (as documentary photographs of the elderly sometimes are) and fictive (set in an art studio context and on neutral, pictorial backgrounds) without being unfaithful, these art photographs offer an *aesthetics of expressivity* opposed to the *aesthetics of effacement* proposed by the "in shape" contemporary icons of aging that circulate in the media. Unlike these media clichés, in which both women and men are objectified, the nudes in Hayden's work and in Wall's are not idealized figures but rather representations of internal objects, each of them one among many "sequential self states" (Bollas) that negotiate the tensions between the actual and the internal and address in a complex way, in Hayden's words, "our sense of identity and our immortality." As photographs, they can function as transitional objects that accompany us in the rituals of passage from one age to another—for both the spectator and the models themselves. Her models are, Hayden has said, "professionals who are working to be *translated and transformed through the pictures*" (emphasis added; qtd. in Flynn).[8]

The effect these photographs is likely to produce is a moment of instant recognition—of the phantasmatic unitary self or of part of a generational code. If these figures can be looked upon as objects of desire, desire has a wide spectrum here. "The experienced body is deeply erotic," remarks Frueh, "for it wears its lusts and (ab)uses of living." But as Frueh also notes, the experienced female nude "contradicts the sex object status of most female nudes" (212). Frueh's inspiring understanding of this unconventional—or until recently, unrepresentable—form of desire is expressed in Hayden's photographs. "Perhaps the aged and aging female body," as Frueh puts it, "can become *an object of love, for the old(er) woman herself to have and to hold*" (emphasis added; 212). What is then seen conventionally as a sign of aging could be read as a sign of the woman's changing attitude toward herself—her self-esteem, her desire or, as Germaine Greer sees it, her coming to possess serenity and power (363–87).

Still, the association of eroticism, or of any form of desire with the old body, is indeed against the norm. The photographs of French photographer and writer Hervé Guibert—I'm thinking in particular of his portraits of his aunts Suzanne and Louise—have been interpreted as a form of perversion symmetrical with pedophilia (is gerontophilia, I wonder, a catalogued perversion?). Diagnosed with AIDS, Guibert created his works of fiction and his photographs with the awareness of the impending approach of his own early death. Used as characters in some of his novels and in the series of photographs reproduced in his book, *Suzanne et Louise: Roman-Photo* (1980), the two sisters—they are in their eighties—appear as an important affective and visual site of prospective identification very early in his work, even before the onslaught of his disease. A strange foreshadowing of his death to come.

Guibert's photographs are radically different in tone and intent from those of either Wall or Hayden. Different too is his highly charged emotional involvement with his photographic subjects, one from which he gains distance through a series of theatrical strategies. In both his fiction and in his essays, Guibert repeatedly insists on his love and affection for the people he photographed. Like "beauty" or "the aesthetic," it resists definition. For Guibert this vaguely defined form of love exists in a larger realm of creativity shared between aesthetics (as in love of beauty) and ethics (as in care for the other). Combining affectivity with sensuality, it saturates the artist's entire visual field, extending from people to objects and habitats. Paradoxically, it is this very attachment that allows the photographer distance from his subjects (most of them friends and family). For in turning them into "objects of vision" (thus, appropriating their shapes), Guibert is aware that the photographer always betrays them. His passion for photography originates, therefore, in his very resistance to it. What he documents is not a material reality but an affect. And bearing witness to his love for his subjects is, as he states it in the introduction to his collection of photographs *Le Seul visage* (1984), the aim of his entire activity. However diffuse or effusive this may seem theoretically, it is redeemed by his thin-edged gaze.

Guibert does not intend in his photographs to efface the signs of old age, but, on the contrary, to make them visible, even to enlarge them (Suzanne is pictured in one of the images holding a huge magnifying glass in front of one of her eyes). A daring project: to see both behind and beyond the signs of old age! One a widowed pharmacist, the other a former nun, Suzanne and Louise are Guibert's protagonists in his scenarios of aging. He has them pose in their domestic environment, one in which he stages, with affection and humor, an intermediary phantasmatic space where his own anxieties and fantasies liberate the two women's world of subdued desire. This is also a touching story of mutual love, one that unfurls the imaginations of the two sisters and engages them in the creation of poses. Like the active participation of Hayden's models in the composition of her photographs, this collaborative project documents the powerful creative potential of old age, one that awaits further exploration.

In imagining his own impossible aging by projecting it onto the two older women, Guibert also transcends sexual difference. The women pose not only as objects of his inquiry into the textures of old age, but also as mirror images of each other. As sisters, they are, as a simple matter of fact, likenesses of each other. One photograph actually depicts them together contemplating their own images in the frame of their bathroom mirror: one is pensive, the other inquisitive. Like Guibert's fiction, these images are a mixture of authenticity and reconstruction. They have a ceremonial aspect. They also have an ironic and playful aspect. Thus they hover wonderfully between reverence and daring. At the same time and in spite of their theatrical character, these photographs are also marked by a nakedness of style similar to Guibert's writing—a directness in the treatment of the image, a desire to spend it all, a passion for looking at the world as if the intensity of the gaze itself might coat the real in a thin film, one scarcely visible yet indelible.[9] His is an understanding of life as a framed picture in the interior of which the viewer can be—up to a point—a free traveler.

In contrast to the photographs of Suzanne and Louise, Guibert's photographs of young people—in *Le Seul visage*, for instance—are idealized; they adopt romanticized poses. Between the self-portraits or portraits of friends and the two old women there is a gap.[10] In his work, as in his own life, Guibert skips middle age. What is more alluring to him is the image in proximity to death even though what he seeks, as in the photographs of youth, is an enhanced sense of immortality. In following the two old women he loves into death, Guibert traces his own destiny as a human being and as an artist. A series of images actually stage Suzanne's death, casting her as the main actor. Unlike Hippolyte Bayard's famous 1840 photograph, *Self-Portrait as a Drowned Man*, Guibert displaces his own anxieties onto an other while frustrating the plot of photography as the conveyor of factual truth. We learn that Suzanne wants him to photograph what happens to her body at the medical school after her death, and in one of the short texts that accompany the pictures, he gives a long imaginary account of what happens. For Suzanne, accepting to pose for her nephew is to come to terms with death as possible reality. Yet in having Suzanne *perform* her own death, Guibert posits it as possible fiction. In the way she poses she seems to dream herself out of life. She enacts her death with a playful sense of complicity. It is a joke, a wink behind death's back. This is Guibert's signature of shamelessness and modesty, the same mix with which he recorded the last months of his life on the video piece, entitled significantly, *La Pudeur ou l'impudeur* (1991).

Modesty is not dictated by social norms but rather by a respect for privacy. It expresses a morality dominated by intuition rather than rule. One of the most stunning images in the series is the unbraiding of Louise's long, long hair. Liberated in 1945 from the Carmelite convent where she had spent eight years, Louise (not to be confused with French women whose heads were shaven for being suspected of having sinned with the enemy) had let her hair grow, decently coiled and pinned atop her head. By convention a sexual symbol, long hair is not part of the visual idiom of the older woman. It is seen as obscene because erotic, hence inappropriate, especially, to old age. Casually entitled *Une Transformation*, this sequence of elegantly unbridled portraits results in an actual transfiguration of Louise's gloomy face, one from which emerges the hypostasis of a new self, one that is also old (that is, reminiscent of the younger self). As in a fairy tale she suddenly turns into a resplendent woman. What happens when Louise looks in the mirror which these pictures represent? When she looks at these pictures of herself, she experiences a moment of de-realization. Deprived of her habitual image of herself, she thinks she sees *the other*, that is, her sister (this is an interesting dramatization of what is a common reaction to one's own aged image in the mirror—a fear of "the other within us"). As Guibert writes, "Isn't what happens on Louise's face at the moment I take the picture an actual transfiguration? When I show her the latest photographs of herself with her hair undone, her face relaxed, exceptionally beautiful, and having suddenly lost her age, Louise does not recognize herself, she first thinks she sees her sister: 'it is not I'" (*Suzanne et Louise* n. pag.).

Once "transfigured," once transformed into an art object, Louise is estranged from her own image of herself. Whom she sees instead is somebody familiar (her sister), not a stranger but not exactly her, either. Loss of age (of the conventional masks of age) can mean liberation. But it is a form of freedom that can be experienced as confusion, as a loss of identity—hence a form of death.[11] (Not long after these photographs were taken, Louise actually cut her hair short, "as if photography were a sacrificial practice," glosses Guibert.) Louise had, in fact, been deprived in another way of her own image—"separated from my image," as she puts it—during her years in the Carmel convent: "There was no mirror at Carmel, not even the right to suspend one's reflection in a window, or in the wash basin, in the morning. For eight years I did not see myself" (n. pag.). And she comments strangely, "But I do not regret anything. When I think of it, these eight years were the most beautiful of my life . . ." (n. pag.). There is an even larger gap in the two old women's images of themselves that comes from the common idea that, as Guibert puts it, "as we grow old we become ugly, old age is not showable." The two women had no photographs of themselves taken after the age of thirty. It is no surprise, then, as Guibert reports, that "they were surprised by this image of themselves that I was giving back to them, after a gap of forty, fifty years" (n. pag.).

Guibert's aesthetic reconstruction of the two women's femininity transforms the obscene (what is offensive to accepted standards of decency and modesty) into the erotic, *his* erotic (his love and desire for life which, paradoxically, he documents at the limits of death). A logic in which eros and thanatos are not in struggle with each other (as in Freud's scenario), but strangely intertwined and ultimately both absorbed into Guibert's aesthetic of love. By undoing an artifice—the braided crown—that had frozen the eighty-year-old woman into a portrait of a school girl, Guibert restores to Louise's chaste figure her sensuality. At the same time he grants himself something very important: an image of old age, one that in his later photographs he mourns, so aware is he of his imminent death. In the posthumously published volume, *La Piqûre d'amour*, several of Guibert's texts contain that possibility of anticipated mourning through which he paradoxically extended his own life by "stealing some years, some months to write against death not only the books of *his anticipated maturity* but also, like arrows, *the very slowly ripened books of his old age*" (qtd. in Bianciotti).

While Guibert looked gently and patiently both at and after the two sisters, while he thought of them as photographic images of another life, the very slowly ripened books of his old age were in the making. *Suzanne et Louise* was published in 1980. Hervé Guibert died at the age of thirty-six in December 1991.

In more than one way photography has always been linked to death, and, as Roland Barthes has theorized it, as an object of mourning. Also linked to our perception of aging, photography can trick time by effacing traces of aging through technical cosmetics. Yet the superb way in which Guibert associates love and eroticism with old age here renders these photographs not only enticing aesthetic objects but creative elements in the self's long work of preservation and reinvention.

III. IMAGES THAT MATTER

> She is looking at something visible, distant, but perhaps coming slowly closer.
>
> — Susan Griffin

The photographs I have discussed in the previous sections have in common an exploration of the phantasmatic realm of aging. They construct settings, stagings, and possible fictions that render the changing body visible while emphasizing its relation to dream, knowledge, experience, art, death. For them aesthetic strategies are used to explore—not to fake or to efface—the expressivity and the creativity of old age. The gaze of the photographers is gentle without being sentimental, the images pleasing without idealization. These photographs are alternatives to both artificial and negative portrayals of aging. Other art photographers address aging as *matter* and use enhanced artifice to incorporate realities and concurrent representations of old age into their work. They focus on the body, yet challenge it as the exclusive locus of cultural and discursive practices related to aging.

We have seen with Guibert that rendering old age in photographic works can place us imaginatively into spaces in future time. To accommodate the passing of time the subject has to project itself as a whole. Yet to the extent to which that sense of wholeness borders finitude, it is the fixity of form that we fear rather than shapelessness. Hence the necessity of disruption. Disjunctive images of the body are, then, not only enactments of the phantasms of fragmentation that accompany old age. Created by younger artists as reflective modes, these images also map out a matrix of freedom, ways of imaginarily eluding the body.[12]

In photography and film it is harder to fake old age than young age (although digital photography now makes possible any shift in time and space to give the illusion of a whole). In her series entitled *Homage to Käthe Kollwitz* (1992), Terry Pollack experiments with such reversible traveling from old to young age. In Pollack's remakes of some of Kollwitz's self-portraits (a process of introspection

Figure 1. Terry Pollack. Homage to Käthe Kollwitz. *1992. Courtesy Terry Pollack.*

and representation that spans Kollwitz's life in her drawings and etchings), it is highly significant that she uses younger models to play out a wide range of contradictory emotions related to aging. In this series about our tenuous relation to time outside of chronological conventions, aging is used both referentially and metaphorically. It constitutes the very matter of these images, all kallitypes printed on rice paper. Pollack uses alternative processes to integrate an element of time (of another time) in her space of representation—the aging of the paper, of the color itself. The images are evocative, nostalgic. Enacted by a younger phantom self (companion in our journey in time), the aging self in Kollwitz's originals is sublimated into a diffuse yet dominant presence in the photographs. The face takes refuge from the eye. The viewer's attention is displaced from the body to the background. We are projected into the future by going back in time. Individual aging is placed in the perspective of a larger framework of time. We are invited to step out of our bodies, into a costume, into a pose. Ironically, this thickly material reflection on aging is an idealization, one that reflects somehow Kollwitz's romantic frame of mind.

At the opposite pole are Cindy Sherman's photographic images of old age in her "history portraits" and her "sex pictures."[13] Her reconstruction of famous Renaissance portraits (1988–90)—some of which suggest the caricatural, exaggerating aging of the originals—challenges the idealization of beauty and the authority of models in a way different from Hayden's observant gaze at her models. As in the other impersonations she has created, Sherman uses makeup that transfigures her own face and false body parts to fake old age. The intention here is to imaginarily travel beyond layers of paint in search of the human beings who posed for the artist. Unlike Guibert, Sherman "unbraids" her models with a kind of childhood cruelty that undoes the toy to see what it is made of. She cunningly explores the creative potential within that destructive impulse. As in her sex series, she attacks taboos of representation and stages wild fantasies by expanding the limits of what photography can show. While deconstructing the western canon of beauty, Sherman's grotesque depictions of aging ironically refer to the clichés about visual representations of the elderly (the crone, the witch).[14] Yet by making use of these clichés, she also addresses some of our most visceral fears related to the visualization (that is, the materialization) of old age or of the body in pain.

In her more recent fashion series (1993), Sherman wonderfully incorporates the very materiality of age into her photographs by creating a subtle optical illusion, one at the limit of visibility. It is a "grain" effect she had used in her early *Untitled Film Stills* to enhance the suspense of the image. In one of her fashion photographs, the hands of Sherman/the model are foregrounded, touched by age spots. Given the large format of her photographs, the grain of the paper is thus extremely magnified and especially visible on the closeup of the hands. The age spots read as paper grain. Transposed on matter as fragile as the skin, they are not only preserved, but in a visually provocative way, celebrated. Here age provides the texture of Sherman's work as it provides the rich textures of our lives. Exploiting the becoming of the body is in fact only natural within the logic of Sherman's entire work, since over the years she has always used only her own body as a model. However, or precisely because of this travesty of the corporeal, her reflections on aging extend beyond a reflection on the body. The only time when Sherman uses non-Sherman and nonhuman models for her photographs (before she turned away entirely from her own body to use mannequins from medical supply catalogues) is in a series of relatively abstract compositions evoking decay and death (1985–87). Very pictorial, shot with dramatic lights and intense color filters, these images, ones that seem to dodge the body, represent in fact diverse rotting matter that Sherman had collected in her studio and studied as it changed, metamorphosing over time. What becomes of the material stuff of our lives? How is matter affected by the passage of time? How can we integrate such stuff into the psychic and material economy of our lives in the same way in which the residue of everyday life is incorporated into our dreams only to unravel deeper, hidden patterns? Called the "bulimic" series (or the "disgust" series), these images negotiate the unstable balance between lack and excess, between fascination and rejection relative to what eludes the form of our bodies. The great impact with which they play on that ambiguity strikes at the threshold of sensibility. The pictorial distribution of these elements in the photographs does not attempt to coat the real with a cosmetic layer but rather to shift our perspective on a common reality. Documenting the organic degradation of matter, Sherman reflects on the transformative possibilities inherent in that process—a cycle instead of a dead end. The fact that the shapeless parts of matter represented in her photographs are aestheticized does not necessarily make them more agreeable to the eye. Some viewers still consider them . . . disgusting, others (to the great surprise of the former) . . . engaging. It is a matter of taste, one could say. But it is mostly a matter of a point of view. To the realistic viewer (the one who believes in—or is tricked by—the mimetic power of photography), these "still lives" will appear as detritus. To the imaginative viewer, they will appeal as possibilities of life. In them time is incorporated, not denied.

Sherman has enjoyed great popularity in academia particularly because of her impersonations of conventional roles of women. What explains, however, Sherman's success as an artist is her very personal and daring use of the art of photography in ways that unsettle routine views of photography as a mimetic medium *par excellence*—and thus unsettle readings of the real. In her analysis of Sherman's "history portraits," Rosalind Krauss argues that Sherman's approach to images works precisely against "the sublimatory energy of Art" (174). In this sense, given the degree of entropy they entail, both the "bulimic" series and the "history portraits" series have a definite anti-aesthetic character. Yet Sherman creates disorder by forcing the very limits of her craft. In both subject and form, her series call on a wide range of modes of representation—cinema, painting, fashion, the fairy tale, history. She destabilizes the mimetic function of photography by staging entropy through a sophisticated system of aesthetic strategies borrowed from other modes of representation, from other regimes of visibility. In elaborating what Krauss calls "the field of a desublimatory," Sherman's subversion of the geometry of the beautiful bears witness to the fact "that behind the façade there lies not the transparency of Truth, of meaning, but the opacity of the body's matter, which is to say, the formless" (174).

It is, however, arguable that the strategies Sherman uses represent a "transgression *against* the form" (109). Her understanding of form is, I will argue, generative. Form as movable, dynamic, perishable: a perfect analogue to the art of photography itself. Like the process of aging that changes the body, her images disrupt conventional forms. They also explore the potential of form in disorder. Although her work presents figures, both the historical series and the sex series (the images of old age included) approach the non-figurative. Fragmentation and shapelessness are not the exclusive avatars of old age.

In ambiguous ways, Sherman denudes idealizations of the body and stereotypes of feminine mystique. At the same time, through the aesthetic codes she disrupts and reconfigures, her work also questions material reductions of the body. Laura Mulvey sees in what I call Sherman's "matter" series (what other critics call either the "disgust" or "bulimic" series), "a monstrous otherness behind the cosmetic façade" (148; see also Krauss 192–93). Yet I would suggest that what we find there is a part of the human that eludes discursivity, but not significance. Very few commentators of Sherman's work address its tactile sensibility and the aesthetic breakthrough her photographic thinking represents. While illuminating an important aspect of Sherman's complex project, most of the ideologically oriented readings of her work support, in a probably unconscious way, our culture's fear and anxiety related to matter, to some of the stuff we accumulate, to detritus, to a part of our humanity that is not framable by social discourse. Similarly, the image of "the sagging flesh," one recurrent in the discourse of aging, is a prime example of the poverty of metaphors our culture has for representing the transformations of the body.

IV. A SPACE TO HOLD THE GAZE

> I realized that, while I was writing about my childhood, about a certain year of my childhood, I was writing from everywhere, writing about my whole life, all years confounded, of this life, as I had never done before.
>
> — Marguerite Duras

In a composition entitled *Death Mask*, an 8 × 9½" Polaroid print, Terry Pollack superimposes her self-portrait on a projected slide of a portrait of her grandmother. Part of an installation piece that included a taped narrative of her grandmother's account of the loss of her first baby, this photograph creates an

Figure 2. Terry Pollack. Death Mask. *1987. 20 × 24 cm. Courtesy Terry Pollack.*

intricate pattern of identifications and projections that are made visible in simultaneity. The grandmother's wrinkles show on the young artist's face from behind her portrait, as it were. As in Pollack's construction of a generational simultaneity, we experience psychically the overlapping of generations, just as our old and new selves overlap or various places we have seen are superimposed in our mind to compensate for a lack of a sense of unity and continuity. As Bollas remarks, redefining D. W. Winnicott's notion of a true self (the vague site of a wholeness of being as opposed to fragmentary false selves), it is hard to conceive of the self as phenomenologically unified. The difficulty resides in the fact that "the true self is not an integrated phenomenon but only dynamic sets of idiomatic dispositions that come into being through problematic encounters with the object world" (30). Similarly, I would argue that there is no "true old self" or state but a permanently fluctuating relationship between a younger and an older self, perceived now as bracketing (hence the sense of closure, even of claustrophobia or of estrangement from one's chronological age), or as suspension (hence the sense of insecurity). These "different forms of being," also associated with different ages, are at times perceptible in a posture, a tone of the voice. In a short conversation with a friend my mother's age, for instance, I can see through her to others, as in sequences of different photographs projected rapidly on an imaginary screen. In her gestures and words I read visitations of my mother; in the impatient zigzagging of her hands, I see her daughter; in the undertones of her voice, her own mother. In such ways we are able to grasp our lives as a continuum, ways so different from the sense of hierarchy presupposed of old age (based on narrative or on the optical model of linear perspective).

As in the case of the cubist unfolding of the different sides and facets of an object not available to the eye, the photographer's conundrum is how to represent as a plausible (that is, visible) form of reality the "different forms of being" that inform our sense of identity. Our desire to see our lives as a whole, to see the histories of our bodies as an unfolded scroll meets, in the words of Jean-Pierre Nouhaud, the photographer's "renewal of the panoramic desire," his dream that the part of the real that is cut out in the photographic process is not a fragment, that what it shows equally contains what it conceals (26).[15] In making visible that "dynamic set of idiomatic dispositions," in Bollas's phrase, the photographer presents us with a new mode of visibility, and of relating to the real. The violation of rules of perspective results in a vision of time . . . of time passing.

Double exposure is a common photographic error. It is a visual reverse of a slip of the tongue that makes latent images surface unexpectedly. Consciously used, double exposure makes visible a physical impossibility: that of being in two places at once. Metaphorically, this physical limitation accounts for the many places we travel within ourselves, for the phantasmatic selves who inhabit us. We host within ourselves dormant images of aging, invisible prints on a film that awaits to be developed. Or, is it only a fiction that we preserve the various images of past ages as well as their potential?

In Pollack's intriguing composition of superimposed images, one form shows through another, as if by looking at a single image we could have access to many images, the familiar as well as the unseen, the conscious as well as the unconscious. This materialization of the condensation and displacement characteristic of dreams produces an uncanny feeling: the recognition of a form of thought that brings us to remote or to yet unknown facets of ourselves. It allows us to keep in touch with our younger selves, it gives us access to deeper and less well-known forms that our selves have taken on in time, some of them long since encoded in the unconscious, preserved there through shape, sound, and color.

In the photographic composition entitled *Blue Fear* (1990) by Canadian

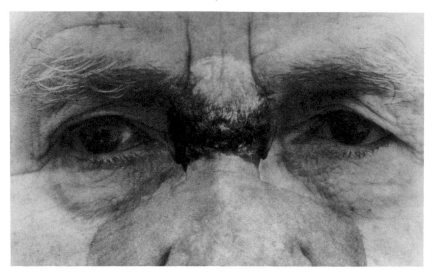

Figure 3. Geneviève Cadieux. Blue Fear. *1990. 185 × 292 cm.*
Courtesy Galerie René Blouin, Montréal. Photo: Louis Lussier.

photographer Geneviève Cadieux, the superimposition is not between two generations, as in Pollack's mask, nor is it between two age-selves. It is an altogether uncommon mirror image of old age. In this large format photograph on masonite (73 × 116"), the torso of an elderly man seen from the back is superimposed on a frontal close-up of his eyes. The image produces both repulsion and attraction, a pair of affects not unlike the dynamic of denial and desire in our relationship to our own aging or, sometimes, to old people themselves. The image is, as the title suggests, deeply disquieting. Blue fear—to be scared to death—is the fear of death.

Dipped in blue (the color of the man's eyes), the whole composition appears as an emanation of his vision, of his emotions in relation to his old age, to death. To the viewer's eye, this exorbitant surface of skin-cum-gaze appears as a disturbance in the boundaries between the physical and the psychic body. The photograph seems to dissolve under our gaze, like time that passes, like light eating into the paper, into the skin. The work expresses a fear stronger than that of the precarious image of our changing bodies—the fear of our very vanishing to which the blurred contours of the photograph allude. Recreated in this transparent photographic reality, however, fear is transformed into an indefinite and diffuse feeling. It is almost fear tamed, something soothing. This effect results from the paradoxical spectral area created within the image through the superimposition of two images. It is an analogue to that inner space Rilke describes, that of a blind angel looking into itself. (The project was initially entitled *Blind Faith*, and blindness is the intriguing subject of other visual works by Cadieux.) The image *includes space*. The photographed subject's gaze, one that uncannily mirrors that of the viewer, creates an interstice, an area filled up with air between the two simultaneous images of the same person, a buffer space to hold that metonymic body, to abide the crisis of aging.

To the extent to which we are open to the experience of such images of old age as aesthetic moments, they are not documents of old people but transformative holding objects for viewers of different ages. Photography, I would argue, creates an illusion of vision as a modification of the sense of touch in a more enhanced way than does painting. Larger than life, *Blue Fear*, with its dilated paper grain (like enormously dilated microscopic eyes), participates in this exacerbation of touch to create a powerful holding environment. The disturbances in outlines and conventions in this composition allow us to refigure new spaces of communication. Like Hayden's pictorial fields in which naked bodies are displaced from the usual habitat of images of the elderly, the confusing perspective of this work not only provokes but also sublimates the fears and anxieties related to aging by placing them in an aesthetic environment. For as they question classical or current public images of the elderly, these photographic works pose the problem of the representation of the body itself.

In his essay on Cindy Sherman, Norman Bryson reminds us that the understanding of the body as a social and historical construction faces its limit with the problem of pain. Perhaps even more so, an understanding of the aging body confronts that same limit, what Bryson calls "the boundary of the discursive empire" (219). This raises fundamental questions about representability and knowledge. If as psychic images, ages, like time, do not exist in isolation but rather simultaneously, so that we can read the younger woman through the older woman, the mother through the daughter, is it at all possible to isolate aging as a sign? How is it visually possible to symbolize the contradictory experiences of the changing body? Bryson articulates the conflict between discourse and the reality of the body this way: "the body is exactly the place where something *falls out* of the signifying order—or cannot get inside it. At once residue and resistance, it becomes that which cannot be symbolized: the site, in fact, of the real" (220).

The very de-figurations of the photographic reality that the images I have discussed here perform—be they grotesque (Sherman), lyrical (Cadieux) or, in a certain sense, parodic (Hayden), contribute, ironically, to setting the limits of representation. Through the very materials and aesthetic strategies she uses in her works, Cadieux makes a statement about physicality—and its sublimation. In the photographic works I have discussed, the artists do not figure the human body overtly mapped by social discourses with assigned meanings. Nor is their isolation of the subjects they represent from social contexts in any way essentialist. Instead, they capitalize on the metaphorical potential of a body on which *different inscriptions coexist in various degrees of visibility* (hence, for instance, the focus Cadieux places on "concepts of vision, both ocular and extraperceptible").

Consider this important detail in *Blue Fear*. We see the body of the man from above the shoulders. Part of his body has been left out of the frame. The viewer has to "restore a body to the vision," as Régis Durand has observed in connection with one of Cadieux's other works (124). The space that holds the blue gaze is symbolic for a gaze that holds the whole body. The poetic body. Inspired by these photographic works, I have come to think of the poetic body this way—as a form that ensures the connection between the physical and the psychic self, one that eludes the rationalizations of discourse or the hierarchies of narrative. In a single vision, it brings together imaginary age-selves, not with the constancy of the phantasm but as fleeting images, like photographs themselves. The poetic body makes it possible to keep in touch with one's different ages or different age-selves. As a shifting form that represents the subject's illusory unity, it brings order to multi-layered experience, it creates a generational continuum within the self. Yet the poetic body is elliptical. It contains and is comforted by loss. Volatile, it nonetheless has a particular inconsistent persistence. The retinal memory of the poetic body, like that of a person's aura, is now intense, then evanescent. It participates in a fiction necessary to the slow and often painful process of internalizing aging, a fiction that allows us to travel freely from one age space to another, to see our life as from everywhere in both space and time, a condensation of ages, as it were. From that privileged perspective, bridging past, present, and future, ages do not exist in isolation. We are not stuck in time. We ourselves create such metaphors of continuity, metaphors that provide a link between a larger past and a more extended (if not vanishing) future, as if these metaphors were, literally, vehicles that transport us from one age destination to another, now backward, then forward.

As I approach the end of this essay, an after-image persists in my visual field. It comes from E. J. Bellocq's 1912 photographs from Storyville, restored to paper form by Lee Friedlander from the original glass plates. The image is that of a young woman. Posing unsophisticatedly in front of a big wooden bed, she is nude except for her black stockings. As in some of Bellocq's other pictures, the face seems to have been erased by mysterious scratches. But in this picture an intricate network of cracks and scratches is superimposed on the image. A constellation of dark spots frames it. And where once the scratches were, the glass is now also cracked, broken. A dark cavity opens in place of the face. The image of the woman has come to us fragmented, deteriorated by various accidents. Attractive yet phantomatic. In its precariousness and fragility, the aged photograph rephotographed evokes what is most touching and most disturbing in our incapacity to envisage the shapes of our own aging. Enigmatically enclosed within it lies part of us that never grows old.

NOTES

All translations from the French are mine.

1. See Marilyn Pearsall's edited collection *The Other within Us* (1–16) for a discussion of this theme of invisibility.

2. See "Middle Age Is No Impediment in Posing Nude," an article that boasts the virtues of recent photographs of fifty-two-year-old Joey Heatherton and Nancy Sinatra by *Playboy*.

3. For a reassessment of this position, see Woodward 47–51.

4. Wall also comments about humor in this image in relation to the discrepancy of sizes. He considers *The Giant* and *Abundance*, one of his other images representing an old woman in the street, as "philosophical comedy" (*Jeff Wall* 21). In his own words, *The Giant* is an "imaginary monument" (21) expressing his intention to magnify "what has been made small and meagre, what has apparently lost its significance" (78).

5. In Lacan's description of the throat of Freud's patient, Irma, we are reminded that it might be, in fact, *the form* (as fixed, definitive, that is, not alive) that we might fear together with *the formless* (which, involving transformation, is life): "The flesh one never sees, the foundation of things, the other side of the head, of the face, the secretory glands par excellence, the flesh from which everything exudes, at the very heart of mystery, the flesh in as much as it is suffering, is formless, in as much *as form in itself is something which provokes anxiety*" (emphasis added; 154–55).

6. In his recent choreography, Merce Cunningham also wonderfully incorporates the incapacities of his body into the dance. Dancers such as Cunningham, Trisha Brown, Yvonne Rainer, and David Gordon have contributed significantly to the "exposure" of the older body.

7. I am reminded here of John Coplans's exceptional exploration of the traces of history on his own naked body and Richard Avedon's dramatic closeups of his suffering father's almost androgynous face.

8. Hayden continues her unconventional exploration of the aging of art canons and that of art models in a more recent project of digital photography (*Ancient Statuary Series*, 1997). Here she brings together photographs of elderly subjects with images of Roman and Greek statuary—a perfect computerized surgery that enlivens these ancient art modes that have been amputated by time with the imperfections of live models. An ironic inversion takes place in this series: the living grows into a prosthesis of the artistic and the residues of art are incorporated in new modes of representation (the size of these images itself is an ironic inversion, all being small dimension, 4×6"). An artifice itself, the aesthetic gaze drapes the body, protecting its vulnerability and veiling its nudity even while exposing it. If the postmodern proposition that what is real is the simulacrum has been applied to contemporary photography more than to any art form, the paradoxical displacements in these photographs suggest, however, that the reverse is also true. Fictions that inform the real are a form of the real.

9. This is a motif developed in his short fiction "Roman posthume," which was published posthumously in *La Piqûre d'amour et d'autres textes suivi de La chair fraîche*.

10. With the exception, perhaps, of two photographs of his parents, where the portrait of the middle-aged mother holding a picture of herself when young is an overt and parodic commentary on aging. See *Le Seul visage* (18).

11. This is very different from the kind of loss of identity that can be the result of cosmetic surgery, a change that does not reveal new layers of the self, as in the case of Louise. A friend of mine reports her encounter with the multiply lifted Cher in a Los Angeles store as follows: "She has had so much surgery it was impossible to tell how old she was—her face was so perfect like it was carved out of wax. And her body too. Neither young nor old, she was *beyond age*. And that was very scary. *Inhuman like nothing had ever happened to her*" (emphasis added; Owens). Indeed a lot had happened to her, but not in the shape of layered experience, as in Wall's *Giant*, but in the perfect shape of effacement, a perverted or deviant form of innocence.

12. For an analysis of the literary representations of the relationship between fragmentation and wholeness of the body in old age, see Woodward's "Phantasms of the Aging Body" (167–91).

13. Since all the photographs I refer to here are entitled *Untitled*, the titles of the series appear as in Rosalind Krauss's essay "Cindy Sherman: Untitled."

14. For a historical and sociological analysis of the origin of these representations, see Herbert Covey's *Images of the Elderly in Western Art and Society*.

15. David Hockney's photocollages, in their fragmentation of and then reconstruction of an illusorily linear perspective, also document that desire.

WORKS CITED

Bellocq, E. G. *Photographs from Storyville: The Red-Light District of New Orleans.* Reproduced from prints made by Lee Friedlander. Intro. Susan Sontag. Interviews edited by John Szarkowski. New York: Random, 1996.

Bianciotti, Hector. "Guibert, par-delà la mort." *Le Monde* 30 Sept. 1994: 3.

Bollas, Christopher. *Being a Character: Psychoanalysis and Self Experience.* New York: Hill, 1992.

Bryson, Norman. "House of Wax." Sherman 216–23.

Chevrier, Jean-François. Lecture at the Jeff Wall Exhibition. Jeu de Paume, Paris. 1995.

Covey, Herbert. *Images of the Elderly in Western Art and Society.* New York: Praeger, 1991.

Durand, Régis. *La Part d'ombre. Essais sur l'expérience photographique.* Paris: La Différence, 1990.

Duras, Marguerite. Interview. *Le Monde* 5 Mar. 1996: 3.

Flynn, Ann-Gerard. "Photographer Uncovers Beauty of Age." *Union News* 12 Dec. 1994: 12.

Frueh, Joanna. "Visible Difference: Women Artists and Aging." Pearsall 197–220.

Goldberg, Vicki. "Photos That Lie—And Tell the Truth." *New York Times* 16 Mar. 1977: 32+.

Greer, Germaine. *The Change: Women, Aging, and the Menopause.* New York: Knopf, 1992.

Griffin, Susan. *A Chorus of Stones: The Private Life of War.* New York: Doubleday, 1992.

Guibert, Hervé. *La Piqûre d'amour et d'autres textes suivi de La chair fraîche.* Paris: Gallimard, 1994.

———. *La Pudeur ou l'impudeur.* Videocassette. 1991.

———. *Le Seul visage.* Paris: Minuit, 1984.

———. *Suzanne et Louise (Roman-Photo).* Paris: Editions Libres, 1980.

Hayden, Jacqueline. Press Release. Center for Twentieth Century Studies, University of Wisconsin-Milwaukee. 10 Feb. 1996.

Hinsey, Ellen. *Cities of Memory.* New Haven: Yale UP, 1996.

Jeff Wall. Ed. Thierry de Duve, Arielle Pelenc, and Boris Groys. London: Phaidon, 1996.

Krauss, Rosalind. "Cindy Sherman: Untitled." Sherman 17–212.

Lacan, Jacques. *The Seminar of Jacques Lacan. Book II: The Ego in Freud's Theory and in the Technique of Psychoanalysis.* Cambridge: Cambridge UP, 1988.

"Middle Age Is No Impediment in Posing Nude." *Milwaukee Journal Sentinel* 20 Apr. 1997: 1+.

Milosz, Czeslaw. *The Separate Notebooks.* Trans. Robert Hass and Robert Pinsky. New York: Ecco, 1984.

Mulvey, Laura. "A Phantasmagoria of the Female Body: The Work of Cindy Sherman." *New Left Review* 188 (1991): 136–51.

Nouhaud, Jean-Pierre. *Blancs d'oubli: Onze photos de Suzanne Lafont.* Royaumont: Royaumont, 1987.

Owens, Ann. Letter to the author. April 1997.

Pearsal, Marilyn, ed. *The Other within Us: Feminist Explorations of Women and Aging.* New York: Westview, 1997.

Rilke, Rainer Maria. *Duino Elegies.* Trans. J. B. Leishman and Stephen Spender. New York: Norton, 1963.

Sherman, Cindy. *Cindy Sherman 1975–1993.* Text by Rosalind Krauss, with an essay by Norman Bryson. New York: Rizzoli, 1993.

Vine, Richard. "Wall's Wager." *Art in America* Apr. 1996: 86–93.

Virilio, Paul. *The Aesthetics of Disappearance.* Trans. Philip Beitchman. New York: Semiotext(e), 1991.

Winnicott, D. W. *Home Is Where We Start From: Essays by a Psychoanalyst.* London: Penguin, 1986.

Woodward, Kathleen. *Aging and Its Discontents: Freud and Other Fictions.* Bloomington: Indiana UP, 1991.

FAMILY
PORTRAITS

The Well of Wisdom
The Love of Older Women among French Lesbians

Marie-Claire Pasquier

I write as both a "native" and as an "anthropologist": as a native since my subject is older French women and as an amateur anthropologist since I have gathered some data which I attempt to interpret. First, a bit of background about myself. I consider myself fairly representative of both my generation and of my country. I was born in 1933, which means that I am the daughter of a generation of women who themselves were children at the outbreak of World War I. Like many women of her generation, my mother lost her father when she was very young and was raised by a war widow (her father was a pilot who was shot down by the Germans when she was seven; her mother later remarried). Schoolgirls of her generation in fact considered it shameful to have their fathers at home. Men were meant to fight in the war, and the only question raised was: what shall we do with them when they come back? Most of them did not come back, and families were reconstructed with what were understood to be lesser men, with the dead heroes being replaced by second husbands, who were stepfathers.

I should also say that I come from a family that played an important role in French Indochina and in French politics during the Third Republic. For the sake of telling a personal anecdote (and to boast a little), I have newspaper clippings at home which herald my birth, describing me as a healthy little girl with blue eyes and as the firstborn great-grandchild of President Paul Doumer (who had been shot just two years before). (If I was considered precocious early on, afterward I did everything a little late, or very late.) I should add too that I was a teacher in Algiers from 1958 to 1961 and thus was an eyewitness to the 1961 outbreak that preceded the independence of Algeria from France. When the student movement broke out in May 1968, I was an assistant professor at Nanterre, which was where it all started and where I participated as an active member of the teacher's union. During the feminism of the 1970s I was a single mother, which on the one hand made me a "pioneer" but on the other hand handicapped me a bit in terms of participating fully in the movement. I mention all this because I think that the relationships between women in France have been affected by the particular history of our country, including both world wars, two colonial wars and the loss of the colonies to France, the student movement of 1968, and the seventies of French feminism.

I.

My speculations are based on answers to a questionnaire I devised that was published in *Lesbia* Magazine in February of 1996. Addressed to younger women who were in a relationship with older women, it included such questions as the following. Do you share a home? Do you share expenses? Have your families met? Do you ever speak about the future? Who takes the initiative in making love? Does your lover resemble your mother? Do you love your mother? Who are your cult figures? Are you happy? My speculations are also based on personal interviews I conducted with friends and acquaintances as well as with several well-known figures in lesbian circles in France, including Michèle Causse and Geneviève Pastre, both of whom are writers in their late thirties. I draw as well on three in-depth "case studies" of women in their late thirties, each of whom (and for comparable reasons) has a history of regularly choosing an older woman as a "significant other." I call them Laura, Emily, and Beatrice. Orienting my reflections are the following questions. Is there something specific to lesbians in choosing someone older as the object of love (as opposed to, say, young women choosing an older man, one who might be termed a "father figure")? Is there something specific in this choice such that it is not based on the model of narcissism, on attraction to one's mirror image? In this regard, is there something historically and culturally specific to the choices French lesbians have made?[1]

Instead of referring monotonously to "the younger woman" and "the older woman," I have given these two composite portraits what I think are altogether suitable fictional names—Io and Salem. Io stands for "the younger woman." It reminds me of the Spanish "I" and of a version of Narcissa, only appropriate for a woman who prolongs adolescence into her adulthood. Io also recalls the young nymph loved by Zeus who was turned into a heifer by his wife Hera in a jealous rage and thus stands for clandestine love. In addition, Io has been identified with Isis and thus suggests a female ideal or an idol—in this case, the idol of Sapphic love. Salem stands for "the older woman." I thought first of the Bible's Methusala, then shortened it to Salem, which has the additional merit of being the name of place long associated with tradition (and witchcraft), a place which reminds us that the older woman in this couple often provides the younger one with a home away from home.

In opposition to the concept of aging as a slow process (of maturing or of decaying), the two terms "younger woman" and "older woman" represent a clear-cut polar distinction, a binary system of oppositions that is a dictate of the cultural mind. As we know, just how old an "old" woman is changes with historical periods and cultures. For Balzac, "la femme de trente ans" was clearly past her prime. For F. Scott Fitzgerald, a woman of twenty-seven was "faded but still lovely" (88). And for Eugene O'Neill, the forty-five-year-old Nina in his 1928 play *Strange Interlude* is definitely old: "Nina's hair has turned completely white. She is desperately trying to conceal the obvious inroads of time by an over-emphasis on make-up that defeats its end by drawing attention to what it would conceal. Her face is thin, her cheeks taut, her mouth drawn with forced smiling" (277).

Among lesbians, I would suggest, age barriers appear to be much more flexible. From the world of American lesbians who made their mark in Paris in the twenties, here is an excerpt from a letter written in 1968 by Natalie Barney (then ninety-two) to her friend Djuna Barnes (then seventy-six), who had been complaining of solitude: "Have you no 'mate' to torment and exalt you? Love is a better drug than drink. So I lift this glass of hope to you." Two years before, she had written to Djuna Barnes to say that she had "*une nouvelle petite amie*" (qtd. in Benstock 257).

Today in France the "watershed" or "continental divide" of age among lesbians seems to be thirty-five. In this regard a friend of mine told me, "No, I have never been a 'gerontophiliac,' but my ideal woman has always been the woman of thirty-five. When I was in my teens and early twenties, this was for me an older woman. Then I turned thirty and for a while my lovers were women my own age—from thirty to forty. As I grew older, I began to turn to thirty-five-year-old women as younger lovers. And as I keep growing older, the difference in age increases." I should add, too, that thirty-five is the watershed when one steps—or does not—into responsible adulthood (which includes financial autonomy and the responsibility of caring for others).

Is the love between Io and Salem nothing more than a reflection or a projection of themselves forward or backward, a reflection of what one used to be, a projection of what the other wants to become? If so, this would mean discarding the possibility that a "true relationship" would be possible between Salem and Io, that their relationship would necessarily be narcissistic, a mirage, an illusion based on a mirror image. My sense, however, based on personal observation and the other research I have done, is that Salem and Io may indeed be distinct individuals who recognize the other as such, that they give and take, share and exchange, drinking the same water from the well of wisdom and, importantly, playing role games together more in a spirit of fun than in order to follow stereotyped patterns.

During the conference on women and aging in Milwaukee, this question was raised: which part of us does not grow old? I suggest this answer: the playful part of us. Just as a child plays games in which she is alternately an adult and a baby, so a woman at any age can fancy herself in all kinds of ages and roles, provided she has a "playmate." I think, for example, of a friend of mine (she is sixty-seven and has "*une nouvelle petite amie*" who is seventy) who wrote this to me from her happy retreat in the south of France: "Often we feel, and sometimes, act, like little girls." Let me stress that both these women have had their share of responsibility in life. They have led successful professional careers— one as an academic and the other as a psychoanalyst (she in fact is still active professionally). One of them is a widow, the other has been married and divorced. Both are mothers and grandmothers.

How do we explain Io's choice of an older partner? (By older, I mean a difference of more than ten years.) The accepted explanation is that her choice is based on the mother-daughter relationship. I would like to suggest a different model, one that is nonetheless analogous and based on the nuclear family— that of the older sister–younger sister.[2] In France the eldest daughter is still given an important role as a substitute for the mother (this is especially the case in large families—the "*famille nombreuse*" is recognized legally and was the rule from the thirties to the fifties in this Catholic country of mine). Her mother's daughter, she is also her sisters' and brothers' "mother." A girl who has been in the position of the eldest sister may develop, I would suggest, the semi-erotic habit of liking to "have kids around"—kids to play with, to handle, to hug, to brutalize a little, to bully, to yell at, to comfort, to shelter from the parents or to give over to the parents' wrath. In a situation such as this there is a lot of physical contact, a lot of nurturing. The eldest sister is in a position of power, but it is a power that is only semi-legitimate, a power that is often characterized by some playful blackmailing ("don't you dare tell"). Might not this experience be one of the bases for liking to have a younger woman around, a substitute for a kid sister, someone preferably smaller, someone Salem can hug and kiss, can roughhouse with, someone whose hair she can pull? Remember *Emma*, by Jane Austen. When Emma thinks she will never marry and someone remarks to her that she will have a lonely old age, she responds, "I shall often have a niece with me" (75).

II.

I turn now to my three case studies.

The older of two sisters, Laura, born in 1958, was thus ten years old in 1968, a date crucial in recent French history. When she turned twelve or so, the situation in her family deteriorated, with her father drinking excessively and growing violent. When she was seventeen, she was sent to Australia for a year (in order to give her a rest from these family fights), and there she had her first sexual experience with a young man whose family she was staying with. She returned home to find her mother now separated from her father and involved with a series of lovers. Laura became her mother's confidante—she was there when her mother was alone or insomniac—and helped her raise her younger sister. Although she loved having her kid sister as her protégée, at the same time she disapproved of her mother's promiscuous life. Although she only saw her father once a year (at Christmas, and then reluctantly), she was devoted to her mother's mother, a Russian Jew (indeed the only Jew in the family), whom her mother had rejected as not being sufficiently assimilated to French culture, which is one of the reasons why Laura loved her (Laura's mother had married a non-Jewish Frenchman). Laura had a few Sapphic experiences with girls her own age, but when she was twenty-one, she fell in love with one of her professors, a woman of forty-five who in fact had a family of her own but did accept Laura first as her protégée and then finally took her as an intermittent lover (with the exceptions of brief vacations, Laura was seldom alone with her). For Laura this relationship was characterized by a mixture of an admiring and affectionate attachment to the older woman as the teacher, the model, and the homemaker, and of resentment against the adult woman who did not make enough room for her and who treated her more like a kid than a lover. Nonetheless, this relationship lasted for about ten years, at the end of which Laura, now an independent woman with a good job and an apartment of her own in Paris, cut loose. She now is involved with an older man, an intelligent scientist who is married and who is one of her supervisors where she works. She admires him enormously.

Born "out of wedlock" in 1960 to a young woman who only told her who her "real father" was when she was in her teens (she went once to meet him but nothing much came out of it), Emily was eight in 1968. She grew up with her mother and (for a time) stepfather and her four younger half-brothers, suffering (as did they all) at the hands of her depressive mother, who turned bitter and violent when her husband left her. Indeed violence was everywhere, escalating to the point of knife fights with her brothers. With her mother totally unreliable and the father of the family absent, Emily had the domestic chores of the household imposed upon her, a position of responsibility complicated by the fact that she was the "forbidden" sister in charge of a "clan" of united brothers. She developed an ambivalent relationship to violence both verbal and physical, turning violence into sexual fantasy, ready later on in the case of conflict to resort to violence in her relationships and demonstrating very little tolerance for any form of authority. Like Laura, Emily also loves her mother's mother, a caring, generous, and wealthy woman to whom she is very devoted and from whom her mother tried to separate her. In fact Emily says, half-jokingly, that her grandmother, who is now in her nineties, is in love with her. Not surprisingly, Emily left home early. She lived "off her charms" (she is exceptionally beautiful and she knows it), mostly with older women. But for a time she also did live with an older man who helped her complete her education. She left him to live with a woman twenty years older, and then left that woman for "another woman" fifteen years older. Her life is characterized by alternate periods of relative stability and fidelity and of "night life" (in one of which she learned geisha-like skills, including S&M). She works part-time, with her lovers and her grandmother taking care of the "extras." Presently she is involved with an intellectual woman in her fifties.

The eldest of four children (she has one sister), Beatrice was born in 1956 and was twelve in 1968. Beatrice's older brother—he was only two years older than she—"died on her" when she was seven. In a sense, he represented the masculine part of herself, and thus it is understandable that she was tempted to "replace" him symbolically or to keep him alive in herself, as it were, as one would a dead twin. Thus she found herself propelled into the position of the eldest daughter, whose younger sister imitated her and whom she protected and took along with her on her escapades. When she was twelve, she looked fifteen and pretended to the boys that she was seventeen. When she was thirteen, her father caught her necking with a boy and beat her up. She swore she would leave home the minute she was eighteen, and she did. Like Laura and Emily, she loved her mother's mother. She spent a lot of time at her grand-mother's place and, miserable after she died, had an affair with a schoolteacher, a woman who had a family of her own and only saw her on and off (in her "off" moments, Beatrice took to drinking). For six years she shared a home with a female lover ten years older than she was, after which she became the mistress of a married man who was thirty years her senior (during this time she had affairs with older women on the side). She developed a habit of having intermit-tent, casual relationships of about six months or less with older women (as a rule they were in their late fifties), who were less educated than she was (she had pursued her education while she worked for a living) and whom she met through the personals in gay magazines. She is now attached to a woman who is twenty years older than she is and who is culturally her equal.

In all three cases we find some form of violence in childhood and a maternal grandmother who represents an alternative home as a refuge. Salem represents not exactly the "good mother" but rather the fusion of the good mother and the good father, a source of warmth and comfort and security. At the same time she represents a younger, more glamorous grandmother, the mother's mother, as well as the older sister, a mentor, a guide, an educator. In all three cases, too, an experience with an older man is an alternative to Sapphic experiences. In all three cases the older man represents not only material but also educational and professional support without limitations of any consequence on Io's personal freedom. In Emily's case her male protector was not a Frenchman but a Swiss judge, and in the cases of both Laura and Beatrice, their male protectors were both Jewish men, who represent in France a "softer" kind of male domination. Why do I mention this? Because I suspect that one of the reasons why Io turns to Salem for shelter and sexual love is the fact that the ordinary French male remains to this day a misogynist. I should add that in my generation (not to mention the preceding generation), women were for the most part cut off from intellectual life. Those women who did "make it" did so as a rule some ten to fifteen years later than their male counterparts, and very often at the expense of a stable relationship with a man or a stable married life with children.

More importantly, in all three cases we find three elder or eldest sisters who were required to become adults too soon, girls who were never permitted to be the sheltered child, the baby in the family. My speculation is that these three women are making up in adulthood for the dependence on an older woman (the mother) that they never had in childhood, acting like kids and having the benefit of both age-worlds, enjoying the active sexual life that adulthood permits, and finding the protection, loving care, and relative irresponsibility offered by an older woman that is characteristic of childhood. And in fact, in their "private" relationship with an older woman, these three women all act younger than their age: Laura, by being passive-aggressive and sulky; Emily, by making scenes about little things; and Beatrice, by insisting on being "supported" in her daily expenses.

Who—Io or Salem—takes the initiative in sexual matters? Most of the women who answered this question more often than not responded that there were no clear-cut roles. But my own observations are these. Io, knowing that she is sexually attractive, has no fears of being rejected when she makes advances. Salem, considering herself "neutralized" by both her age and her social status (her "respectability") tends to be more reserved. Salem has a sense of her self-image (her dignity or her self-respect), but she also feels that she has no control over why Io might be attracted to her; in a sense, she has no confidence in her own appeal. Her attitude will be "wait and see," an attitude which paradoxically turns her, socially the dominant one, into the coy object of desire, waiting to be chosen by Io and sometimes not even suspecting that someone like Io might have an erotic interest in her. If chosen, Salem may respond in what might be described as a typically "feminine" or coquettish way, playing "hard to get." Thus courtship is probably initiated by Io, but neither Io nor Salem is fooled by this. Recently I heard that one Io, who had left one Salem after five years, announced with supreme cynicism: "Given her age, she should consider herself happy that I gave her these five years of happiness" (this Io had remained on good terms with Salem and there was no "other woman" in the picture). More typically, Io, considering herself (and rightly so) as rating higher in the erotic market, compensates for this by treating Salem as the "object of desire." But Io also uses her dominant position to assume the active male part, deciding, for example, when to have sex and in which style, taking the initiative and hence taking control.

What are the gratifications that Salem might expect from having a younger female partner in her bed and in her life? For Salem, the relationship is an elixir of youth, offering a fulfilling sexual life at an age when suitable male lovers are seldom available or interested. Salem is also bound to appreciate being a positive model for someone who seems to be aspiring to what she is and what she represents. If Salem enjoys the maternal role, she will take pleasure in having an extra child without having the full burden and responsibility that motherhood entails. For Salem there is also the pleasure of having a young adult for a companion (it is very charming to have a "niece" around, as Jane Austen reminds us in *Emma*). Io is someone Salem can boss around a little, someone who is helpful around the house, someone who can drive her places. Additionally, there is the opportunity to "play games" together on the social stage. Either people "know" or they don't even suspect. Io and Salem can invent a multitude of explanations and excuses that establish a delightful complicity between them without the fear of social rejection or of damaging gossip.

At a certain point, however (when, for example, Io is forty and Salem is sixty), Salem may find that she feels exploited, used for the goods she provides and having little control over Io who, if she now has a roof of her own, can "storm out" whenever she feels like it. Moreover, at this point in life Salem may no longer serve as a "model" for Io. What does she gain? Even if the answer is the gratification of an active sexual life and the theatricalization of what would otherwise be a humdrum life, she may nonetheless be tempted to ask: do I now have to pay for my sexual pleasures? Part of the gratification of sexual activity is in fact the sense of feeling attractive, perhaps even "young." To pay for sex means one no longer represents that attractiveness. It is not sex itself that is at stake, I would suggest, but rather what it brings with it—playing the games of love (if Salem and Io have been smart enough to make money itself part of the game all along, disguising its role, they may avoid this problem).

Are these relationships long lasting? Since in most cases Io is the one who will leave Salem, how long can Salem expect to "keep" Io? Many scenarios are possible, none of which, I suspect, have anything specifically "French" about them. Basically the relationship breaks apart when an important change occurs in Io's life, a change that is bound to happen. Laura, for example, remained with the same woman for ten years (this is longer than average); once she had a job, an apartment of her own, an older male suitor, and a better salary than her Salem, she left her.

Alternatively, why may there be a compulsion to repeat this same pattern— an Io choosing a Salem—when it is no longer adequate? As Djuna Barnes has written in *Nightwood*, "Love is death, come upon with passion; I know, that is why love is wisdom. I love her as one condemned to it" (137). The first object of sustained love is an older woman who provides both shelter and a sense of adventure, the pleasures of both the indoors (a second home, the warmth of a bed) and the outdoors (the excitement of transgression, of leaving the first home). Why repetition? Because sexual attraction is, we could say, in part triggered mechanically. If the first object of adolescent or adult love (sexual love) recalls the first object of love, which is the mother, then the third object will recall the second one, and so on ad infinitum. This may be how what we might call "gerontophilia" between women appears. Perhaps, as the French lesbian writer Geneviève Pastre suggests, we should not see in this pattern "repetition," but rather successive approximations: one keeps looking for an ideal, without ever finding it in reality. Gertrude Stein made an important distinction between repetition and insistence. For her, insistence is not far from intensity: one insists so that the sketch will become clearer, more intense.

Finally, why is Salem not looking for a daughter or even for a substitute daughter? Perhaps because she already has one, or perhaps because she has a sense of what it means to have a daughter. Chances are that Salem is a mother (she may have children still at home or they may have already left home). Having a substitute daughter means one more daughter. And I should add that the incest taboo is so strong that fantasies cannot be easily entertained.

III.

In France, the mothers of my generation were raised by strict, rigid mothers, women who gave little physical affection and who turned suffering into virtue. They were deprived by World War I of a sense of stability (and right they were, because by the time they were thirty they were going to have to go through World War II and the Occupation or, for some of them, the Resistance or concentration camps). Large families were the rule. Domestic life was full of chores with little time to give attention to the older children once they stopped being babies. The mothers relied on the eldest child. What characterized the childhoods of Laura, Emily, and Beatrice was true of theirs as well: the mothers of my generation had a childhood that was curtailed brutally. To this must be added a collective trauma, one I have often discussed with friends my age: for those of us who were not Jewish, there was the traumatic discovery of the extermination camps through albums of photographs that were distributed widely after the Liberation and which, when we were in our teens, we would peruse in secret for hours with a mixture of revulsion and fascination.

Among my lesbian friends in my generation, one had a Jewish mother who raised her as a Catholic and only told her she was in fact Jewish when she turned eighteen (up until then the girl had never understood why her grandmother, uncles, and cousins had suddenly vanished from her life). Another had a mother who, on her return to France from a camp (a camp from which her father never returned) would become so distracted that she would forget about her daughter on the subway, leaving her stranded at the age of seven, not knowing what to do. Another hid in the south of France throughout the entire war; her grandparents were assassinated by the Germans.

When we were growing up, my generation experienced a strong sense that the world was divided between victims and victimizers, a sense linked to the extermination of the Jews in World War II and to the colonial history of France. Among the lesbian couples of Io and Salem, there are couples mixed in terms of ethnicity. Salem is a Jewish woman who lives with Io, who is a German goy. Or Salem is French and Io is Vietnamese. Or Io is Algerian and Salem is French. Perhaps this pattern can be interpreted as one of atonement, of making amends, of compensating for the unforgivable. Perhaps, more simply, it is a fascination for the "other," a way of recapturing "heteroeroticism."

With 1968 and with feminism in the seventies in France, lesbianism became fashionable, "political," and I would venture to say that in the seventies, the pattern changed: couples formed, composed of women who were roughly the same age, women who wanted to live together and to raise a family together. But what of the young women who are in their thirties today, the young women (including Laura, Emily, and Béatrice) who are daughters of women from my generation, daughters who did not become lesbians? I have explained, I hope, why these lesbians emerged from these families. I should add too that the more liberal mores of the period extended the domain of choice. Those of us in my generation, whether straight or not, provide in fact no established model. The old-fashioned model of the family (as exemplified in Beatrice's family) is out-of-date. It is not that it is openly "fought," but rather that there is no invitation to adopt a similar path. Those of us in my generation do not provide a model for a secure future. Our mothers of my generation (the mother of, say, five children) provided a model either to follow devotedly or to run away from in horror. A mother of two or a mother of one represents not a model, but herself. Yet Beatrice and Emily both came from families of five. The old pattern does continue, overlapping historical periods, but it is the same with a difference.

I will now, tentatively, draw a few conclusions about these generations of women.

In my mother's generation, no woman became a lesbian unless she was ready to fit into the butch-femme pattern because the women of her generation were strong and self-reliant, raised, as I have said, in the absence of men. At the same time, these women were outwardly submissive; they gave in to the current ideology of society which was entirely male-dominated. There is not a contradiction here: dead heroes can be overpowering, and they left room in politics not for women but for younger men. My great-grandfather, who had a prominent political career, lost four of his sons in World War I, and some of his political enemies literally accused him of having thrived on this "heroic" posture. French women, it is astonishing to realize, did not have the right to vote until 1945. My own mother, Lucile Doumer, did not vote until she was thirty-four. If I wanted to be a little outrageous, I would say that these women were conditioned by the butch-femme pattern except that, for them, "butch" was a man.

In my generation, the daughters of these powerful "feminine women" were given a position of power within the family by virtue of being the eldest sisters of several children and thus started adult life with a certain advantage, the advantage of wanting to do something with their lives other than raise a family of five (in a sense they had already done that; it was behind them). When they reached a certain degree of recognition through a profession (albeit at a later age than their male counterparts), it was only natural that they should become models for younger women for whom they had paved the way and who could, through prospective identification, see what autonomy and relative success was open to them. In addition to serving as a model, Salem could also provide guidance and shelter; with no strings attached, she could offer what Io could not find in the Frenchmen of her own generation, men who had remained conservative in their preferences regarding women.[3] Today, now older herself, Io is too autonomous, independent, and self-reliant for such men; moreover, she no longer wants to pretend. Io does not claim independence; it is taken for granted. What she claims is the right to prolong the relative irresponsibility of adolescence. Even near forty, she shies away from the burden of making a home and raising children while following pursuits of her own. The double burden of professional life and domestic life—the double day—is heavy. Like a man, Io has become a professional; and in a sense, like a man, Io wants a wife at home, but she cannot afford one (I do know of a few Ios who have men at home, artists, for example, who, we could say, are femmes). Thus Io continues to choose an older woman who offers the best of both worlds, one who provides her with a home and one who protects her independence and, like a good parent, pushes her in life, encouraging her and praising her for her achievements.

What will come next? It is to be hoped that in the next generation young Frenchmen who have been raised by feminist mothers will in fact have learned how to cope with the needs of young and independent women. It is to be hoped that the new husbands (or the "new fathers," the "nouveaux pères" as the media have already dubbed them, probably more on the basis of anticipating the future than on direct observation) will have been trained to share the burdens and rewards of both domestic and professional life. This will be, however, a bad day for the Salems of tomorrow, who loved having Io at home: the Ios of tomorrow might indeed choose the sons of Salem in preference to Salem herself.

NOTES

1. Although I do not address this question directly, it is one we should keep in mind: is there something specific to lesbianism in the choice of an older partner that differentiates it from the gay male model of the Socratic model of master-disciple or of pederastic love? I suspect that the patterns of Sapphic love are less rigid and less stereotyped than these patterns.

2. In *Masculin/féminin: La Pensée de la différence*, Françoise Héritier-Augé, a structural anthropologist who holds the Lévi-Strauss chair at the Collège de France, offers some interesting observations that are relevant to this. She argues that there are three basic invariants on which all societies are founded: the preponderance of the masculine over the feminine, of parents over children, and of older brothers over younger brothers. The masculine does not necessarily correspond to men or the feminine to women. In some cultures, some women past the age of child-bearing are *men*, literally men, for all intents and purposes (some of them are even granted the right to have a wife). In another instance Héritier-Augé cites, names are given to children which do not necessarily correspond to their sex, with these little boys and girls then raised according to the gender suggested by the name (when, with puberty, the pattern may be reversed, it is apparently a painful experience for the individual child). In some cultures, there is literally no word to designate an elder sister because it would be an oxymoron, a contradiction in terms.

3. For a woman in France it is a mixed blessing to be young. A young woman is relegated to the position of *faire-valoir* for promising young men. While a promising young man is pushed forward in life by the expectations of his family or by the master-disciple relationship (an older writer supporting a younger writer, an older scholar supporting a younger scholar) or by the educational system embodied in the *grandes écoles* which were until recently institutions for men only, a young woman was still (also until very recently) only expected to study or work "before marriage." For her seductiveness a young woman may reap rewards, but she remains anonymous. Young and attractive women are interchangeable, replaceable. The result is that until recently and with only a few exceptions, it was only late in life that a woman in France was allowed a position of preeminence, of visibility. Simone de Beauvoir might be considered such an exception, but we must also note that she was largely figured as Jean-Paul Sartre's companion (besides, she had to choose between being an intellectual and having a family). Consider the writers Marguerite Yourcenar, Marguerite Duras, and Nathalie Sarraute: they only reached celebrity in their late fifties. The philosopher Simone Weil would also be a case in point as well as the writer Françoise Giroud, and Jacqueline de Romilly, a distinguished Greek scholar. As late as the early 1990s, all of the great women in France were over fifty.

WORKS CITED

Austen, Jane. *Emma*. New York: Oxford UP, 1946.

Barnes, Djuna. *Nightwood*. New York: Harcourt, 1949.

Benstock, Shari. *Women of the Left Bank*. Austin: U of Texas P, 1986.

Fitzgerald, F. Scott. *The Crack-Up*. New York: New Directions, 1956.

Héritier-Augé, Françoise. *Masculin/féminin: La Pensée de la différence*. Paris: O. Jacob, 1996.

O'Neill, Eugene. *Strange Interlude*. New York: Boni and Liveright, 1928.

From Anxiety to Equanimity
Crisis and Generational Continuity on TV, at the Movies, in Life, in Death

Patricia Mellencamp

I became an old woman suddenly, on February 15, 1996. I was walking my Cairn Terrier, Buster Keaton, through Lake Park, in Milwaukee. It was a sunny morning, and much colder than it looked. Then, without warning, I was no longer there. Like my dog's namesake, I had taken a pratfall and landed on my head, which received a deep gash. I was unconscious for some time in the snow, and faded in and out of consciousness for a week afterwards in the hospital. When I initially came to, the voice of a paramedic was concerned that I remember my name. I couldn't. (They would ID me from my dog's collar. My fingers were clenched on his leash.) Later, the voice of an emergency room MD asked me to lift my shoulders. I couldn't. Nor could I move any part of my body.

Fear began to coagulate in my cells, especially my knees. As the anxiety spread, I closed my eyes, focused on my breath, on inhalation, then exhalation. With this meditative ritual, my mind turned inward and grew calm. Fear receded, and never returned during the days in the hospital that followed. Through some amazing grace, I was not identified with my body—and the anxiety and fear that come with that identification retreated.

(Good thing, too, because I was not wearing makeup that morning and I had not washed my hair. This would be my unkempt state for six days. Being semi-conscious did have its advantages . . . I never go anywhere without makeup or hairspray! I was, however, perfectly dressed for a fall in subzero weather, wearing a thick headband and hood which cushioned my head. My heavy parka and silk long johns protected the rest of my body from the cold.)

I was *in* my body, but I was not my body. I was peering out of my eyes, watching, as though I were looking through the face mask of a deep-sea diver. No matter what happened on the outside, a parameter which now included the immobile shell or shield of my physical body, I was safe inside. My body was a space suit, or a self-propelling vehicle now broken. While my friends were both curious and upset about the events of the fall and the medical diagnosis, what fascinated me was my inner state of being a witness to outer events. I was involved, and in some pain . . . but detached.

What does this story have to do with being old? After ambulancing me to the hospital, the rescue squad had taken my dog to the humane society for safe-keeping. When my sister, Nancy, picked him up, she was given a manila envelope containing his sweater. She gave me the envelope six weeks later, when she decided I was sufficiently recovered. On it was written, "elderly owner in hospital." My nameless body had been given an identity. Although "elderly" was a new adjective for me, my first thought—truly—was of the wisdom and status accorded elders in Native American cultures.

My second thoughts were less noble. How could I be elderly? Not only was my eighty-two-year-old mother still giving daily counsel, but so was her mother, my grandmother, still alert at the age of 104. Although I was a mother, with children in their mid twenties, I was also a dutiful daughter and grand-daughter. How many elders can one family have? Our place in this familial time line, along with our bodies, faces, and organs, delineates age, an archeology as much as a chronology, an ethnography as much as a geography, a physiogony (generation of nature) as much as a physiognomy (knowing one's nature).

One minute I was a middle-aged professor, taking a walk, the next I was elderly, unable to move. This split-second transition was an effortless passage from one state of awareness to another. In each state, something within remains the same, what Germaine Greer calls our "inner landscape," Kathleen Wood-ward through Freud calls "psychic space," and Sanskrit scriptures call the inner self.[1] This inner space was vast, tranquil, and still. (Was this a sneak preview of death? If so, death was not to be feared.) It has taken me years to achieve this experience of inner tranquillity. I had changed the way I thought—not for noble reasons, or in a spiritual quest, but out of panic that made my nerves, and my heart, raw.

I. CRISIS AND ANXIETY

It began as a mother's nightmare. In 1988 my brilliant son, Rob, was diag-nosed with myocardiopathy, a degeneration of the heart muscle. There was no explanation and no cure other than an eventual heart transplant. While Rob's life had been an ongoing series of medical crises, with thirty-one broken bones and various emergency surgeries, this was primordial. God had upped the ante to life or death (or so I thought). I can still recall the pounding terror I felt when I walked down the hospital corridor to his room each day. At night I would sit bolt upright in bed, awakened by fear.

My anxiety was exacerbated by the lack of diagnosis and prognosis. This was a story without origin, without linear progress (improvement or cure), without cause-effect logic, without closure, and without a future. This long-term crisis had no time frame—it could be weeks, years, even decades. It was a continuous, indeterminate crisis, a contradiction in terms. Paralyzed by fear, I counted on my mind, ironically enough, to get me through.[2]

I read Freud, Walter Benjamin, and René Thom on anxiety, shock, and catastrophe. It all made perfect sense. My life resembled Thom's words: "Our everyday . . . may be a tissue of ordinary catastrophes, but our death is a generalized catastrophe" (251). In fact, my reaction to Rob's initial diagnosis was textbook Freud. As the doctor spoke, I began to feel panic, a hyperstate of anxiety. Anxiety is very physical. I remember visually receding. Sound became barely audible. My body was separated from reality as if encased in thick glass. Only my eyes allowed the real in, and if I closed them, I was shielded from bombardment. It was like floating in an air-proof bubble. Fear and anxiety, which were almost unbearable, had for the moment been physically mediated. A shield, like a cellophane membrane, distanced me from the world and from my own senses. Then it blanketed me in exhaustion. I slept for two days, afraid to wake up. If I didn't open my eyes, this painful trauma would go away.

As Freud puts it in *Inhibitions, Symptoms and Anxiety*, I had "two reactions" to what was "real danger," not neurotic danger. The first was "an affective reaction, an outbreak of anxiety" (165). For Freud anxiety is a physical response to danger, real or remembered, factual or fictive. The amount of anxiety rises to an unpleasurable level without being mastered or discharged. Anxiety is a situation of helplessness predicated on "missing someone who is loved and longed for" (136). Longing turns into anxiety. The second reaction was "a protective action" (165). Or as Samuel Weber writes, the shield, which is porous, has a "double function": it "transmits excitation from the outside to the inside," but it also protects us "against excess excitation" (143).

This experience (or figure) of being encased in an outer covering was comparable to my experience of falling in the park eight years later—but without self-awareness or understanding. I had not yet discovered Greer's inner landscape. "I" was hollow. There was no comfort or safety inside, or anywhere. Fear and danger were the only signals coming from everywhere. Thus, the shield was not only a form of protection. It was also my problem—an outer crust where all my fear, attachments, identifications, addictions, and obsessions had accumulated. It bombarded me with danger. Ultimately, it could not protect me from my own mind. Wolfgang Schivelbusch has astutely observed that the Freudian shield is in fact the "outer world . . . absorbed and interiorized" by the subject (167). "I" was a shell of inherited fear about to crack.

To relieve my anxiety about my son, I sought further information. I did research on heart transplants and talked with medical specialists. But science offered no hope or solution. Because I couldn't escape or quiet my thoughts, I sublimated, displaced, avoided, whatever: I began to write a book about catastrophic logic, analyzing electronic culture (television in particular), as both shock and shield. Although I included a cancer scare in the first pages,

High Anxiety: Catastrophe, Scandal, Age, and Comedy, as I called it, ignores the true crisis which is at its core. To be honest, I don't think I saw the connection until the manuscript was finished two years later. In retrospect, what intrigues me is this denial of the personal experience of a crisis (the thread that runs through this essay). These small thoughts (small because personal, even intimate) are what Weber calls an "aftereffect" which repeats and alters events, rendering them "psychically real" (147). For Freud, this process of disfiguration is stoppable only by myth and eros, or what Weber calls "the death drive as another name for a story" (145). I will return to this later. For I now agree that the death drive is inspirational, and that love can turn life into legend. But I am getting ahead of myself.

For most of my life, both intellectual and intimate, I have valued crisis and discontinuity (along with the rational assurances of science). The celebrated events of history, politics, art, and my daily life came from the exceptional, the extraordinary, and the upsetting, not the reassuring and the everyday. Crises made life more exciting. I created drama, even chaos, in personal affairs. Like so many visual culture critics whose aesthetic was influenced by events that rocked universities in the 1960s, an era of social causes and political movements forged in crises, I had taken my academic cue in 1968 from Walter Benjamin (along with Sergei Eisenstein's films and writings). Like Benjamin, I wanted history to change—particularly for women, white and of color. And shock and discontinuity were central to his determination of changing history.

Significantly, when Benjamin wrote about the technological culture of modernity in the 1920s and 1930s he looked to Freud, particularly *Inhibitions, Symptoms and Anxiety*. If Freud described a psychic process of anxiety, fear, and danger, Benjamin provided the social context which fueled this mental logic. For both of these theorists of crisis, the danger situation came from the modern world—from war, crowds, communication technologies, and industrial production. Technological and social change was the key for Benjamin, who looked to public spaces. For Freud, looking at private, familial dramas, along with the victims of World War I, the personal experience of loss was central.

In *High Anxiety*, drawing on Freud, Benjamin, and Thom, I initially applied my theoretical model to catastrophe coverage on television. I saw television as a tautological catastrophe machine (Thom's term), bringing fear, anxiety, disaster, and death into private homes. But TV is more complex than this. Television both delivers and then ameliorates the effects of images of death, administering and discharging anxiety, producing shock and therapy, even mourning—strategies which call for more time spent watching TV. For the viewer, TV is both the shock and the shield, assaulting us with repetition, then soothing us with "information." Perhaps in fact the huge success in 1995 of NBC's serial medical drama, *ER*, suggests that life is seen by many of us as a series of emergencies or traumas between lulls, with relationships viewed as equivalent crises. The rapidly edited style of continual camera movement, the cuts to unexpected or unwanted bloody closeups, and the focus on the constant movement of characters (all of whom are speed walking) installs a scenario of unpredictability, creating anxious expectation. For Freud the primary mechanism of our defense against danger is repetition, the "compulsion to repeat," one virtually embodied by television.

It wasn't, in other words, just my personal trauma that produced my heightened fear of loss, the anxiety of not being in control. If television was a catastrophe technology, history had prepared me for it. Like other early boomers born to Cold War logic and nuclear fear, I had been taught to think catastrophically—both globally and personally. Later, as a good consumer, I had also learned obsessive thought, a logic of more; the same was not good enough. The point is that the cultural production of anxiety has imploded. The logic of crisis can now apply to virtually anything—a war, an earthquake, a faculty meeting, being late, being overweight, being forty, and growing old. We have been trained to think anxiously and compulsively as the norm, not the exception. This is the way many women in our culture view the process of aging—as a crisis, as a process of loss which triggers anxiety.

For Freud, anxiety is related to perception. As we read in *Inhibitions, Symptoms and Anxiety*, "the first determinant of anxiety, which the ego itself introduces, is loss of perception of the object (which is equated with loss of the object itself)" (170). In our culture, youth is imagined or represented as a lost object, rather than as a subjective process or a passage through time. Our face in the mirror can grow unfamiliar to us, causing anxiety and even fear. The modeling of self as an object defined by the physical body, the process of aging portrayed as a series of losses rather than achievements or successes for women, says much about the anxious logic of enduring multiple plastic surgeries. We imagine that we have or will become the "forsaken object," to borrow Freud's phrase in "Mourning and Melancholia" (249).[3]

"It is precisely in women," Freud asserts in *Inhibitions*, "that the danger-situation of loss of object seems to have remained the most effective" (143). Thus women's "loss" of youth as if it were a tangible object, measured by our faces and bodies, is a culturally produced fear that verges on a national obsession-compulsion. Obsession, based on reproaches, guilt, sexuality, and shame, is applicable to the aging body. Physical changes linked to sexuality become the locus of anxiety and fear that drive the marketing of age remedies. This nexus of personal fears locates our identity in our bodily image, in our appearance, and in our relation to the material world. Marketing turns obsession into normality by concealing the cultural as the natural. As Margaret Gullette astutely points out, aging is a cultural process. "We think we age by nature; we are insistently and precociously being aged by culture. But *how* we are aged by culture—*that* we need to know more about" (6–7). As she forcibly puts it, aging is a culturally produced narrative of decline, and "age is still at the stage where gender and race used to be: hidden by its supposed foundation in 'the body'" (202).

I will never know whether my personal anxiety triggered my fear of aging or vice versa. But as I worried about my son's heart, I began to focus on the bags under my eyes. Which I would compare to the eyes of others. I had reduced my identity to a small area of skin. Which was ridiculous until I calculated the astronomical profits made on this single square inch by the cosmetics and plastic surgery industries. The anxious workings of my mind and the obsessive logic of consumer culture coalesced into a logic of contradiction—eat/diet, spend/save, be old/look young. Obsession, and how it was culturally constructed, became intellectually crystal clear.

Everything from the stock market, the *Wall Street Journal*, drugs, and gossip, to plastic surgery, lingerie, funerals, Clinton's rhetoric, and aging fit my model. In fact, there was *nothing* in popular culture my model of obsession could not explain. All went into *High Anxiety*, published in 1992, a fat little text indeed.

Good for me, thought I. I've mastered fear, and *all* the cultural world, through intellect. While my analysis of television's logic still stands, I failed to see how my thoughts, now in overdrive, to say nothing of my outsized ego, were still my problem. Furthermore, reading the book produced anxiety! I had mimicked TV's logic too well. Although I had analyzed my emotional state, nothing had changed. My anxiety level was high. While Freud always plots an intriguing situation, his conclusions can be crashing letdowns. Other than blaming the past (especially family members for one's childhood), Freud's causal interpretations (infantile sexuality, particularly fear of castration) are of little help in changing anything in the present. How could I live with any tranquillity, or happiness? I longed for equanimity and serenity (both as experiences and as qualities), but saw them beyond my life's reach.

Then I had a simple and startling insight. I realized that my son's heart condition was not my greatest problem. Rather it was my fear for him, and my anxiety magnified his worry. In addition, my desire for a cure to the crisis made acceptance impossible. This was my turning point, the pivotal moment when my life began to change. I imagined myself on a journey through anxiety which began with facing death. But my fear was so deep and archaic that my mind couldn't touch it. (Besides, my noisy, restless mind was part of the problem.) In 1990, I went to India, to a small village outside Bombay, called Ganeshpuri, where a brilliant woman became my spiritual teacher. Fortified with ancient texts and the practice of meditation, I began to detach myself from fear, and eventually from logics of duality, difference, and separation. Like Germaine Greer in *The Change*, I was learning to shift my attention away from my body ego toward the soul. Greer couldn't find any role models. There were, she insisted, "no signposts to show the way" (12). I found wisdom everywhere. According to the *Tao Te Ching*, "If you realize that all things change, there is nothing you will try and hold on to. If you aren't afraid of dying, there is nothing you cannot achieve" (#74).

II. CONTINUITY AND GENERATION

If television privileges catastrophe, television's flux also profits from an economics of continuity, normalcy, and regularity, a view of history as incremental change that overrides and incorporates crisis. Like the days of our lives, TV flows in gradual increments, sometimes interrupted or momentarily derailed by crises. Television can be counted on, at all times, to be there. Soap texts in particular are measured by the decade, which for the audience might be one generation or several. Thus the structure of TV is all about aging, not just as the shock of crisis but also as a process of gradual change and familiarity through generations and history.

Quite different from cinema, television is a medium of extended families and generational families. The extended families of daytime soaps depict three or even four generations, with parents and grandparents living nearby. Yet while everyone loves the great-grandmothers (Alice Horton of *Days of Our Lives* and Lilah Quartermain of *General Hospital*), their roles, like those of aging middle-aged characters, are small. As characters age on soaps (with the exception of Victoria Lord and Dorian Lord on *One Life*), entering another generation, they move to the margins of the story, appearing in fewer and fewer segments until, like Dr. Tom Horton on *Days*, Erica Kane's mother on *As the World Turns*, and Steve Hardy on *General Hospital*, the characters die when the actors die, are mourned, and then remembered on holiday episodes. Dead soap characters are grieved for their loss to the fiction, which, as we know in these three instances, is also true of life. Still, television's predilection for extended families, along with its preference for medium shots over closeups, accounts for the preeminent place of middle-aged women, so rarely seen starring in movies after the age of thirty. Since its inception in the late 1940s, television has been the stomping ground for middle-aged women, particularly on situation comedy. Consider *I Love Lucy*.[4] The series has been on the air now for forty-five years, shown in every country in the world. I was impressed when I discovered that Lucy was in her forties when the CBS show went on the air in 1951. A forty-year-old woman performing such agile physical comedy was an extraordinary achievement. But: she played twenty-nine. The famous German expressionist Karl Freund is credited as the cinematographer. He lit the stage evenly and diffusely so that Lucy could move around the set in uniform light, thereby not gaining wrinkles and sags by moving out of her light. Ethel, her generation-older friend, was in fact a year younger. Her age was represented by her frumpy housedresses and her weight (which she contracted to maintain), but particularly by her husband, Fred, who was sixty-four. Ethel, like most best friends on TV, also was not a mother, while Lucy had "little Ricky" and her own mother as generational characters.

Chronology disavowal—women can now be forty or fifty but they must look thirty—is a double-whammy logic with which women are all too familiar. In *Inhibitions, Symptoms and Anxiety*, Freud labels this "diphasic," "the power of ambivalence" (113). He explains, "one action is canceled out by a second, so that it is as though neither action had taken place, whereas, in reality, both have" (119). In many ways, Lucy exemplified this contradiction. Each week she tried to escape domesticity and get a job in show business, and each week she resigned herself to stay happily at home, serving both big and little Ricky. We didn't notice the feminist strains, only her zaniness.

Another of Freud's stories—one about a woman "no longer young" re-counted in his lecture on "Anxiety and Instinctual Life" in his *New Introductory Lectures on Psycho-Analysis*—could be a synopsis of *I Love Lucy*: "I once suc-ceeded in freeing an unmarried woman, no longer young, from the complex of symptoms which . . . had excluded her from any participation in life. She . . . plunged into eager activity, in order to develop her by no means small talent and to snatch a little recognition, enjoyment, and success, late though the moment was. But every one of her attempts ended either with people letting her know or with herself recognizing that she was too old to accomplish anything in that field" (108). The phrase, "too old," like "no longer young," is telling. It is a disclaimer, a prohibition due to what Gullette calls "cultural aging," a field of hierarchy and power comparable to patriarchy or colonialism. Freud's story is a "narrative of aging as decline," a "story of losing what we have, never of gaining," that mistakes the cultural for the natural, or biological. Thus, social conditions are mistaken for symptoms, as Freud continues his tale. Rather than having a relapse which according to Freud "would have been the obvious thing" (108), "the woman no longer young" instead had continual accidents "till at last she made up her mind to resign her attempts and the whole agitation came to an end" (109). Her resignation is, for Freud, the happy ending. Why did the "woman no longer young" have accidents? According to Freud, there is "no doubt about the origin of the unconscious need for punishment" (109). He labels it "guilt," but the real obstacles are sexism and ageism.

I think of Lucy's *physical* struggle to escape 1950s policies of containment of women in marriage and domesticity, and her decision, each week, to stop trying. However, unlike the other "woman no longer young," Lucy never resigned herself to domesticity. Not only did she begin her quest for fame anew each week, but eventually Lucille Ball owned one of the largest studios in Hollywood. She regularly returned in new series, reaping tributes and acco-lades until her death in 1989.

What Freud didn't know was that the "unmarried woman no longer young" had an accomplice, an Ethel who believed in her talents. While the difference between the 1950s and the 1990s is, of course, enormous, friendship between middle-aged women has survived intact as a staple of situation comedy. Al-though the language is tougher, and their transgressions against feminine propriety raunchier, Lucy and Ethel are regularly reincarnated. This is another form of continuity on TV. The most outrageous couple is Edwina and Patsy in the British comedy, *Absolutely Fabulous*, shown on the comedy channel. Ed-wina and Patsy are wealthy, divorced, and knee-walking drunks, which they play for laughs. They party, drink, shop, drink, and live trends, full time. Although both have jobs, it's impossible to distinguish work from leisure, or life from fashion.

Along with booze, the other everlasting value is the latest high style, including clothing, architecture, food, and self-help therapies. (For Patsy, uninvolved sex with young, anonymous men is important.) Edwina buys flashy French designer styles in wild prints (often leather or spandex) by Versace or Lacroix that are too youthful, too tight, too short, and too loud. She has an outfit for every activity. Her clothes are a size too small because of the weight she is constantly promising, and struggling, to lose. Patsy, a version of Ivana Trump, wears more tailored, muted, *tasteful* designer styles. Edwina is a sacrilegious mother to her more mature, plain, studious daughter, forgetting such a sacred duty as her daughter's birthday and lying to her about going to the Betty Ford Center. Along with turning her maternal crimes into comedy, she commits the greatest sin of all—she refuses to feel guilty toward either her mother or her daughter, although she will feign it. Edwina and Patsy are shameless.

On *Cybill*, Cybill Shepherd plays an aspiring actress who is a grandmother, twice divorced, with a teenaged daughter still living at home, which is a spectacular house with a view of Los Angeles. Money is not really a problem, and the difficulty of a middle-aged actress getting good roles is turned into comedy. Cybill's best friend, the filthy rich Marianne, is a divorcée and constant drinker who, like Patsy on *Ab Fab*, has no children and wears designer fashion. It would seem that children would place limits on the availability and devotion of the best friend who is somehow more important to the star, to the story, and to the comedy than the biological, three-generational family.

These best friends are never afraid of making spectacles of themselves. They perform physical comedy, they go on capers, they plot and scheme together. They are unfailingly loyal to each other. Not even their biological families can come between them. Cybill will cancel family holiday dinners to help out Marianne, although unlike Edwina, Cybill is a concerned mother. *Ab Fab*'s Edwina and Patsy unconditionally endorse everything about each other, no matter how appalling.

But there are major ancestral differences. While Lucy and Ethel always had to ask Ricky and Fred for money, constantly scheming for their shopping trips, the outrageous middle-aged women of the 1990s have money of their own and are not economically subservient to men. They have economic independence and careers (at least they pretend to professionalism). Unlike Lucy and Ethel, all of these women work, or at least pretend to work, outside the home in professions connected to popular culture, to leisure and entertainment (thus subtly suggesting that women's work is simply fun). Characters move back and forth between home and work, having fun in both spaces, neither of which is middle class.

Episodes of *Cybill* often begin with her current acting job in B movies. Marianne lives off alimony from her rich husband, Dick the doctor, the source of many jokes. Patsy and Edwina work in the fashion and publishing industries. Or rather they posture as working, going to Edwina's office for wine and zany encounters with her eccentric assistant. For them, what counts as work are the accoutrements—an office, a telephone, a FAX, a computer, a schedule book, and an assistant. It's enough just to manage these trappings. Patsy and Edwina don't spend money, they squander it, as they do with time and responsibility.

Space, or decor, is upscale, a luxurious world where money is neither an object nor a problem. Perhaps the greatest change in addition to money, however, is that these new comic heroines are all divorced (Cybill, twice), using their ex-husbands as secondary characters or jokes (Edwina's ex is gay). Sex, a frequent topic and behavior, matters more than marriage. Although the setting still remains the family and domesticity, marriage is not the dominant institution (as on *Roseanne*). Neither is work or career (like *Mary Tyler Moore* or *Ellen*). Most important are female friendship (like *Kate and Allie* and *Designing Women*, unlike *Murphy Brown*) and fashion (unlike *Kate and Allie* and like *Murphy Brown*), along with fun.

Television's affinity for generational return and "the family" is more than its regularity and repetition *through* time. TV personalities are not the same as celebrities in cinema's star system. They become imprinted as memories of specific scenes, of an earlier family. TV stars carry their context, their relations with other players, their TV family, with them. TV history is mixed up with the comfort and reassurance of personal history and personal memory, which is often generational and familial. TV personalities have become markers of our generational history. We watch them change over time. We remember and welcome them back, like members of the family or old friends at a high school reunion.

As Kathleen Woodward has written, we are not *divided* by generations, but "somehow *connected* by them." "Generational identity entails . . . *similarity* that finds its temporal expression in *continuity*."[5] This is what CBS is counting on in its appeal to an older audience, a generationally bound audience. Its strategy for the 1996–97 season was to bring high-powered stars of former TV series, now a decade or more older, to reprise their characters in new series. In the fall of 1996, Don Johnson, Rhea Perlman, Scott Bakula, Ted Danson, Bill Cosby, and Felicia Rashad were all back (presumably older and wiser), in the same formats as their previous series.

In what follows I will expand on continuity, a word rich in meanings, and emphasize the continuity of generations, turning from television to a recent film, *Antonia's Line* (1995). The law of continuity posits that nothing passes from one state to another without passing through all the intermediate states. If rupture and discontinuity blur into the speeding up of time, which is increasingly a cultural phenomenon, continuity means to persist, to persevere, to carry further. Continuity joins, unites, holds things together. Continuity brings coherence and establishes value. In logic, a "continuative" is a figure for duration. The sentence "Rome remains to this day" includes at least two propositions: Rome was, and Rome is. Similarly, we were, and we are. We embody and inhabit our own history, which we call our age. Generational continuity is another way of thinking through time which includes lifetimes ahead and behind.[6] Or as Samuel Weber puts it, the death drive is a process stoppable only by love (145).

Antonia's Line, directed by the Dutch filmmaker Marleen Gorris, opens with the day of Antonia's death and then retraces events of her life which is composed of the loving connections among four generations of women. The great love is that between mother and daughter, portrayed through intercut looks between them, granting strength and self-sufficiency. It is a love between women that is compassionate and tolerant enough to include others. In a series of lovely outdoor feasts, the family table expands, eventually including a family of men. Then, with age and death, it begins to grow smaller. The film which begins on the day of death also ends on the moment of death. Death inspires the film. Death, coming to the end of it, is the culmination.

The film opens on a mirror shot (we only realize this retroactively) of a middle-aged woman in bed beneath a blue blanket. A female voice-over tells us, "She knew that this would be her last day. Antonia knew when enough was enough. She would summon the family and inform them of her death." As the voice-over continues to relate Antonia's interior thoughts, including the details of the funeral ceremony, Antonia gets up and walks toward the camera (the mirror). In the close shot, she "thinks of her granddaughter," and says, "It's time to die." The camera dollies back, revealing the mirror shot. "She got out of bed to begin the last day of her life." The film's end returns to finish this day, and to complete this opening scene.

After this prologue come the film's credits. The camera accompanies Antonia through the rooms of her farmhouse, moving outside to give us a sense of this place. The film will fill this home with memories, with Antonia's family of four generations. As Antonia makes her tea, she looks out the kitchen window. Cut to a frontal shot of her face. Dissolve to her past, the story of her life, which, as we will discover, is a story of her relationships with her daughter, granddaughter, and great-granddaughter. *Antonia's Line* is a story of lineage itself, of the continuity of generations, of women's relationships of caring, reciprocity, and mutuality. While there are tragedies, crises, and dramas in the film, continuity enfolds these catastrophes within the embrace of time, the passing seasons, and within maternal and familial love. *Antonia's Line* is a film about the cycle of life and death, in which death is a part of life.

This story of the past begins when Antonia and her daughter, Danielle, arrive on a bus and walk to the home in a country village that Antonia left twenty years ago. We notice immediately the strong and sensual way Antonia strides, head held high. She is a powerful and sensuous force, and we can feel the closeness and admiration between mother and daughter. They are one, connected by intercut looks of mutual understanding. As it turns out, Antonia has come home to bury her bald—and ribald—mother, who, to their surprise, comes to life to make a last rude criticism and some lewd remarks. Later Danielle will see her spirit in church, awakening from her coffin in a grotesquely surreal rendition of "My Blue Heaven" (a scene reminiscent of Dennis Potter's musical interludes in his productions for the British Broadcasting Company). This, and other surreal moments, parody the hypocrisy and intolerance of the Protestant church.

As Antonia and Danielle stroll confidently through the village, we are introduced to an extended family consisting of eccentrics and outcasts. The characters take on allegorical dimensions, as the familial is taken fancifully into the realm of myth and eros. Gorris has created a world that represents Antonia's expansive energy, her powers of invention and inclusion, her wisdom and compassion. Crooked Finger is a grizzled intellectual who lives in a dark room, closed off from the outside and from light, immersed in books and philosophy professing the meaningless horror of life. Mad Madonna is a middle-aged woman who also lives alone and bays at the moon in sadness. Her religion (she is a Catholic) has kept her from her lover (he is a Protestant) who lives beneath her. Olga owns a cafe where the men drink, and where the villagers gather.

The voice of the narrator—we will hear it throughout the film and ultimately understand that it is the voice of Sarah, Antonia's great-granddaughter—says, "And so Antonia and her daughter returned. . . . The women settled into their house." The seasons pass in glorious shots of the farm and the countryside as Antonia and Danielle work, painting, plowing, milking, and planting. The film's spaces are connected by Antonia and Danielle, working side by side, looking at each other, walking arm in arm. What is compelling about these women, from four generations (five, if we count Antonia's mother), is how very different they are—in mind, body, and spirit. Their differences are not sources of conflict but pleasures, traits to be admired. (Yet along with religious intolerance, there is domestic violence and even evil in this small town.) Danielle goes to art school and becomes a painter, as more seasons pass, or, as the narrator tells us, "Weeks turned into years."

The love between Antonia and Danielle is a magnet, attracting Farmer Bas and his five sons. Bas inquires about marriage to Antonia saying, as if it were an incentive: "My sons need a mother." Antonia replies with great logic: "But I don't need your sons." Bas: "Don't you want a husband either?" Antonia: "What for?" So in friendship only, bringing food, Bas and his sons join the family feasts. Danielle wants a baby, but not a husband. Antonia helps her find "the services of a man" in another town, and in due time Danielle gives birth to Therese, who grows up to be beautiful and a genius. "And so the years passed," says the narrator. "Time gave birth again and again, and in contentment reproduced itself." The table of the family feasts grows even longer. Lara (Therese's teacher) and Danielle fall in love. "And then love bursts out everywhere," says the narrator, introducing a sexual montage of consummation scenes among various couples. But after this climax, the cycle of life passes into a cycle of death, one that is broken, if only for a moment, when Therese, now a brilliant mathematician, becomes pregnant, comes home, and gives birth to the beautiful, red-headed Sarah. Danielle, Therese, and Sarah live and work with Antonia on the farm.

Sarah, the great-granddaughter, is a lovely and curious child of around six or seven, who carries around a notebook, asking the adults about death and writing stories. "Time flowed," we hear, "season after season, wanting to end the exhausting round of life and death." Sarah talks about death with her great-grandmother, and she consoles her mother. At a family feast, Sarah watches everyone, including ghosts from the past, as they subtly and almost imperceptibly become their younger selves, and dance. It is a joyous moment of life's summation before death.

The film returns to the day of the opening scene. Antonia tells Sarah, "I'm going to die today."[7] The family gathers around Antonia's bed. The voice-over adopts the first person "I," now clearly connected to Sarah, the great-granddaughter with the strawberry-blonde hair. "I wouldn't leave because I wanted to be there," she says. After Antonia dies, the following words are printed on the screen: "And as this my chronicle concludes, nothing has come to an end."

As the seasons pass, so do generations, our daughters becoming women with minds and souls of their own. As with Antonia, it has been a great joy of my life, one made possible by my age, to have been—to be—a part of this process. *Antonia's Line* remembered for me my grandmother's country life of faith, family, and physical work, and the eccentric and disabled characters who populated the Wisconsin town of Cadott. It is not that I identified with the women characters in the film, all of whom, even the actress who plays Antonia as a great-grandmother, are young enough to preclude that investment. But the moving portrayal of the passage of time and the close relations between women does resonate with my own experience. For this story, one from another continent and a director I have never met, is remarkably similar to my own. *Antonia's Line* is a distant cousin to Rose Sedlacek's line.

Like Antonia, my grandmother, Rose Sedlacek, lived and worked on a farm near a small town. Disabled characters with strange names, tormented by the farmboy bullies, became local legend. During the summer harvest, outdoor tables were piled high with food. Family dinners meant twenty to forty people and often more. Like Danielle, my mother had an artistic and serious nature, along with dark hair. Like Therese, I never felt as if I fit in. As a teenager, I loved ideas, particularly existentialism, thought about death, and eventually would have blonde hair (not natural). Like Therese, I was awkward with motherhood, never knowing quite what to do in the maternal role. But the most uncanny resemblance between art and life is between the gorgeous child Sarah, and my daughter Dae, who has strawberry-blonde hair, porcelain skin, and a beautiful face of light and happiness. As a young girl, Dae, like Sarah, would observe life around her. Dae was born with a wise soul. She inherited my grandmother's red hair and her joyous laugh.

Last year, when Rose Sedlacek was 104, my mother and I made our "last" (the fifth of now eight) pilgrimage to Cadott where my grandmother has lived all of her life. Not a single building has changed on Main Street in forty-five years, the time of my memory.

Although delicate of stature, Rose was an independent woman, self-sufficiently living in her own home until she was ninety-eight. With red hair down to the small of her back, she bore and raised ten children on a large dairy farm which had been built by her father, a German immigrant. My mother was born first, in 1915. After morning prayers at 4 A.M., Rose worked until evening prayers at 7:30, canning, baking, cleaning, sewing, milking, and gardening.

Her Catholic faith gave her sublime purpose, her family provided great joy, and the discipline that came from hard work was her salvation. Self-reliance was a given. Rose bequeathed all these qualities to her ten children. As the oldest of Rose's sixty-six grandchildren (yes—it's true), I was the first to inherit this mixed blessing of spiritual faith and worldly determination. My identity, which stems in great part from my place in this lineage of women, is, to draw on the words of Woodward, "at base *generational* identity," which links me to "generations ahead and behind through the relation of caring" (*Aging and Its Discontents* 99). If its traits are reciprocity, mutuality, and continuity, generational identity also took the shape of homemade bread, jam, chicken soup, poppyseed cake, and pies—hundreds, even thousands, of homemade pies in chocolate, apple, and rhubarb.

It was a gray, overcast day as my mother and I walked into the hospital. We entered my grandmother's room, and I saw a skeleton, shrunken with age, gaunt with time. The eyes in the skull were vacant, unseeing. The teeth were on the nightstand. "We must be in the wrong room," I whispered to my mother. But she walked to the bed, leaned over and said, "Mom, it's Margaret." The eyes opened and saw my mother. The face of a stranger was suddenly transformed into the familiar expression of my beautiful grandmother. She smiled radiantly and clasped my mother's hands to her heart with extraordinary force, as if to let go would be to lose each other forever. "Margaret, oh Margaret, you're here." Light poured into the room. How strange, I thought. There is no sun outside. I watched my grandmother's spirit come to life and reinhabit her body upon the sight of her eldest daughter.

I was fascinated by the simultaneity of my vision with my memory, the timelessness of sight leavened by love for these two women. I was seeing my 104-year-old grandmother and my eighty-one-year-old mother as they were now *and* as the way I saw them when I was a child. It's true, then, I thought. The spirit never ages, only the body ages. Something eternal and ageless was animating my grandmother's almost unseeing eyes. If I could not exactly see it, I could experience it and feel it. It was energy, it was bright, it was illuminating.

As I looked at my mother, her back weakened and bent awkwardly by cancerous tumors and radiation, leaning over to embrace her mother, now just skin and bones and far too frail to walk, I felt the power of generational love. Each was brought to life by the other. I suspect that their mutual desires to care for each other, daughter for mother and mother for daughter, animate their very souls. As we read in Amy Tan's *Joy Luck Club,* "You must peel off your skin, and that of your mother, and her mother before her" (48). Our mothers are in our bones. Or as Woodward has written, "in psychic space our bodies can lose their boundaries. . . . At stake is generational identity, which is bound up with two wishes—to be taken care of by the mother and to care for the child. But if years before the differences were clear, now they are indistinct. . . . In age, who is the mother? And who is the daughter?" (*Aging* 100). How different my experience was that day last year from the bleak scenario Germaine Greer paints. For her, "it is a bitter irony" that caring for aged parents is done by "menopausal daughters" whose "world seems all loss and death," a world of depression, exhaustion, and grief (277).

For Tan, it is only when the daughter comes to understand her mother, often in adversity, that she can know her own strength and wisdom. To achieve this, the daughter has to hear her mother's story, granting her the authority that comes with history and through generation. As Margaret Gullette so rightly cautions us, point of view matters, for there is much at stake. The objectifying gaze of someone young, or *younger,* "can erase the idea of old age as 'normal,'" along with appropriating the material of older women's lives and deaths. "If ailing parents told their own stories," Gullette writes, "we might learn how burdensome the loving gaze of the survivor can feel" (210).

Coincident with the appearance six years ago of my mother's first tumor in her upper spine, I developed acute pain in my neck which didn't subside until her tumors receded. Although it was attributed to rheumatoid arthritis, I have always known the true origin of my pain. It came from the ancient bond so strikingly portrayed by Tan. An old mother is dying. The granddaughter is the privileged viewer, witnessing a scene of private devotion, just as I did in Cadott. Her mother is making soup in an ancient Chinese tradition to help nourish her mother. She cuts a piece of meat from her arm, adds it to the soup, and then gives it to her dying mother. The granddaughter, observing this act of love and sacrifice, understands. "I could see the pain of the flesh and the worth of the pain. . . . The pain of the flesh is nothing. . . . Because sometimes that is the only way to remember what is in your bones. You must peel off your skin, and that of your mother, and her mother before her. Until there is nothing. No scar, no skin, no flesh." She concludes, "Here is how I came to love my mother" (48).

I want to return to the figure of Freud's protective shield, seeing it now through my vision of my grandmother—and through her, of my mother's struggle with cancer. We can see the shield as the physical body, which changes and decomposes in time, becoming stiff, leaky, dry, eventually dead. As Weber has written, musing on Freud's distinction between the death instincts and the life instincts, this "crust" serves as a shield "against powerful energies which would 'slaughter' it," losing "the structure proper to living matter, becoming inorganic" (142). "The outer layers die to save the inner ones," he writes; "the envelope sacrifices itself for the core" (145).

The core, then, would be the inner self, the spirit that is changeless, the radiant energy that animated my grandmother's shrunken body, stiff with 105 years of life. It would be my mother's luminous courage, generosity, and love for her family which have become more apparent with each onslaught of pain. The distinction between the "crust" and the "core" also comes close to the experience of my falling in the park with which I opened this essay. I experienced an inner world, one encased in an outer covering. Is this the way, I wonder, my grandmother saw my mother that gray day? Does my grandmother dwell in an interior space of freedom? If my mother found this place, could she go beyond pain? This is what I have been told is possible.

As I did with my grandmother, I can see the widening discrepancy between my mother's body collapsed from bone cancer and her indomitable spirit which grows more valiant as her body weakens. Because I look like my mother who looks like her mother, Rose, it's like living Edward Albee's play, *Three Tall Women*. Three actresses play three different stages of a woman's life—twenty-six, fifty-two, and ninety years old—remembering and, in the last act, contemplating which age was the best. In this final scene, the old woman's comatose body is lying in bed, stage left, close to death. Her character, her energetic spirit, takes center stage and concludes the drama with the following: "The happiest moment of all? Coming to the end of it, when all the waves cause the greatest woes to subside, leaving breathing space, time to concentrate on . . . the end of it. There's a difference between knowing you're going to *die* and *knowing* you're going to die. The second is better; it moves away from the theoretical. . . . Coming to the end of it, yes. . . . That's the happiest moment. When it's all done. When we can stop" (109).[8]

I *knew* the simple truth of these words. All *movement* onstage and within the audience came to rest in a poignant conclusion of stillness. The play's passage through three generations, three ages of being, is one of becoming, becoming old, a process of generational *knowing*. The most interesting and powerful woman is the old woman. She is the summation of all the life that comes with old age. This knowledge, this history, this *story* of achievement is what I see in my mother. I hope this is what my daughter, Dae, who looks like me, will see in me. For in many ways, we are all one and the same.

FAMILY PORTRAITS

NOTES

1. Greer 39; Woodward, *Aging* 100, 105, 169. Woodward's thoughts have deeply influenced mine. I am grateful to her for orchestrating a year at the Center for Twentieth Century Studies devoted to aging, a year of knowing fellowship which included the brilliance of Elinor Fuchs and the artistry of Cecelia Condit, among my other fine colleagues in residence. I am in addition *forever* grateful to Kathleen for her genius editing which gracefully took this essay down from more than sixty pages. Friendship with this talented woman has been a great boon in my life, personally and professionally.

2. I had just returned from the Betty Ford Center in Palm Springs and treatment for a grudgingly admitted addiction to Valium. Seventeen years earlier, my gynecologist had prescribed this tranquilizer for my difficulty in sleeping. I was a single parent, with little money, two children (one chronically ill with osteogenesis imperfecta), a fulltime job, and no daycare. No wonder I had trouble sleeping! Over time, Valium became a problem, not a solution, resulting in blackouts and suicidal thoughts. Then came the recovery years of skin-crawling anxiety.

3. Women as "forsaken objects," abandoned for younger versions, is the premise of *The First Wives' Club* (directed by Hugh Wilson, 1996). Goldie Hawn, Diane Keaton, and Bette Midler, "acting their age," the mid forties, reunite at the funeral of a college friend who committed suicide. Her husband had left her for a young woman, and the same fate has befallen her three friends. But these women join together and uncover information that they use to extract "justice" from their former husbands. They take Ivana Trump literally: they don't get mad, or even, they get everything! And they are very funny along the way, all three being/acting the comic personae they perfected in previous films. The delight of the film is watching these three powerful women, who have become producers and directors with real influence in Hollywood, talking about the double standards of age.

4. See my chapter in *High Anxiety* for an extended discussion.

5. Woodward, "Tribute" 91, 98. Taken together, discontinuity and continuity can be simultaneous and sequential. But neither term can exist without the other, although our focus, our outlook, can be selective.

6. *How to Make an American Quilt* (1995), directed by the Australian filmmaker Jocelyn Moorhouse, has a scene of community comparable to the outdoor feasts of Antonia. Women, now grandmothers, who have been together for generations, make quilts which tell the story of their lives. Together, they have grown older, wiser, funnier. They have survived romance, loss, death, and betrayal, and can embrace life with equanimity. Age represents gains as much as losses. The older women are beautiful; plastic surgery has not erased the expressions on these actresses' faces.

Ditto a Canadian film directed by Cynthia Scott. *Strangers in Good Company* (1991) is about a group of older women, without any elements of masquerade, stranded when their bus breaks down in a beautiful countryside landscape. They have to spend the night in a deserted farmhouse. Nothing happens, except the stuff of ordinary life. No one panics, but they accept events and don't treat things like a crisis. They wait, survive, and remain calm, together. They rescue themselves, take care of themselves, and get to know each other. The ordinary, on second thought, is extraordinary indeed.

7. Antonia embraces death, as does A, in Edward Albee's play *Three Tall Women* (1992/1994). Another fictive character, Patrice Umphelby, a terrible name, in Amanda Cross's (aka Carolyn Heilbrun) mystery, *Sweet Death, Kind Death* (a title taken from a poem by Stevie Smith), loves death. Patrice is a scholar who "fell in love with death sometime in her early fifties," and who had "knowledge of how death gave intensity to middle age as passion and hope gave intensity to youth" (28). In her journals, discovered after her mysterious death, Patrice wrote some observations worthy of a famous literary scholar. "Whenever I read the story or autobiography of an older woman . . . I find that though it is written by a woman in her fifties or beyond, she writes only to go back to her youth; she abandons age, experience, wisdom, to search the past, usually for romance. . . . I am an intelligent woman of fifty-five, and all the story I have is in the present. . . . For me, stories of youth are tired stories. But the story of age, of maturity before infirmity . . . has never been told" (25). Women, like Gorris, are telling the story of age, of maturity.

8. The American premiere opened on July 30, 1992 in Woodstock, New York; the same cast opened at the Vineyard Theatre in New York City on January 27, 1994.

WORKS CITED

Albee, Edward. *Three Tall Women*. New York: Penguin, 1994.

Benjamin, Walter. *Illuminations*. Ed. Hannah Arendt. Trans. Harry Zohn. New York: Schocken, 1968.

———. "On Some Motifs in Baudelaire." *Illuminations* 155–200.

———. "Theses on the Philosophy of History." *Illuminations* 253–64.

Cross, Amanda. *Sweet Death, Kind Death*. New York: Dutton, 1984.

Freud, Sigmund. *The Standard Edition of the Complete Psychological Works of Sigmund Freud*. Trans. and ed. James Strachey. London: Hogarth and the Inst. Of Psycho-Analysis, 1953–74. 24 vols.

———. "Anxiety and Instinctual Life." *New Introductory Lectures on Psycho-Analysis*. 1933. SE 22: 81–111.

———. *Inhibitions, Symptoms and Anxiety*. 1926. SE 20: 77–175.

———. "Mourning and Melancholia." 1939. SE 14: 239–58.

Gorris, Marleen, dir. *Antonia's Line*. 1995.

Greer, Germaine. *The Change: Women, Aging, and the Menopause*. New York: Fawcett, 1991.

Gullette, Margaret Morganroth. *Declining to Decline: Cultural Combat and the Politics of the Midlife*. Charlottesville: UP of Virginia, 1997.

Mellencamp, Patricia. *High Anxiety: Catastrophe, Scandal, Age, and Comedy*. Bloomington: Indiana UP, 1992.

Schivelbusch, Wolfgang. *The Railway Journey: The Industrialization of Time and Space in the Nineteenth Century*. Trans. Anselm Hollo. Berkeley: U of California P, 1986.

Tan, Amy. *The Joy Luck Club*. New York: Putnam's, 1989.

Tao Te Ching. Trans. Stephen Mitchell. New York: Harper, 1992.

Thom, René. *Structural Stability and Morphogenesis: An Outline of a General Theory of Models*. Trans. D. H. Fowler. Reading: Benjamin, 1975.

Weber, Samuel. *The Legend of Freud*. Minneapolis: U of Minnesota P, 1982.

Woodward, Kathleen. *Aging and Its Discontents: Freud and Other Fictions*. Bloomington: Indiana UP, 1991.

———. "Tribute to the Older Woman: Psychoanalytic Geometry, Gender, and the Emotions." *Psychoanalysis, Feminism, and the Future of Gender*. Ed. Joseph H. Smith and Afat M. Mafouz. Baltimore: Johns Hopkins UP, 1994. 91–108.

Genealogy

Joanne M. Braxton

MISS MAIME: *An old Colored woman whose picture*
I take out at three o'clock in the morning
between calculus and Brecht

No straight lines but drooping shoulders
And old hands chewed a red-brick brown
Hands that healed my bee stings
With three different kinds of leaves and love
Offset by two skinny yellow bowed legs
Knotted with brown spots
Where the veins were ripped out
When she was refusing to die
And I was afraid and crying
These are hands that prayed well
"The Lord is my light and my salvation. . . ."
And followed well
When she ran me down with switches
In my youth

You always seem surprised when I come home
Would you think I'd forget you
You made me such
Gingerbread woman topped by crown of snow

FAMILY PORTRAITS

POEM ON TURNING AROUND

for a Fanti queen of Sonoma

between 3 and 4 o'clock
in the morning
she wakes to see the brightest star
shaded by a crescent moon

until the morning bursts
a belly of swollen light

in this world of images
where we live and die

a wrinkled old woman speaks
out to her mother
in the voice of a baby
the listener calls her grandmom
not daughter
and cannot recognize the birthmark
the image of one she has never seen
as manifest in walnut face
the smile the hands of youth

seasons pass
risings and fallings
that crescendo with each new birth
each passing festival
of juba, boogey and bop

washboard symphonies
and country crucifixions
where they spill our blood

who will survive America?

Genealogy

who will survive neo-colonialism
who will survive default
          urban renewal
          unemployment
          police violence
          piss poor education
          and smack?

In America, who will survive?
Who will hold the dream
    the vision of the King?

Who will unite the consciousness of the people
              as it makes war against itself?

Who will show America
       which way to go
as generations are born
and returned to the soil
in singing sadness
our desperate hope:
the trial of staying alive in this white America
to survive with humor
        dignity
        and style

FAMILY PORTRAITS

FOR SUGAR

when she called me her shy colt
i did not know that little girl
whose family belonged to
the joe louis beach club in ontario
"where all the black people were"
and where she kept a pony
that ate sugar from her hand

i could not have known
that on sundays her mother made
fried chicken sandwiches on buttered bread
and wrapped them in wax paper
kept warm in a neat picnic basket
while her daddy
(who loved her and hated her)
drove the no doubt too big
buick across the boundaries
of race and nations

when she told me not to bolt
i could not see
the proper young lady
astride her mount
the one she had tamed all by herself

when she rode me all spurs and sweat
silencing me with her "be quiet"
i did not know the younger rider
trained from infancy
to command me in bed

and when i came to her hand
because she had called me
called me out of myself
i thought it was for my own pleasure
i did not know that this bed
was my red and clovered pasture
that i had come, like her pony
for sugar

GENEALOGY
(for Mycah)

i cannot give you
a father
with bourbon laughter
and a salt and pepper moustache
a family crest
no name—other than my own

you were conceived too perfect
immaculate
like a diamond
in the molten bowels
of the earth

it was a saturday
in november
we had chosen
the gene stuff
swam in the pool
imagined you

(the first time i saw you
in a dream
you were 12 years old
with a ponytail
and you did become
golden)

no manners
no manners at all
mooned us on ultrasound
before you were born
already a cut up
before you were born
sure 'nuff a Braxton behind
before you were born

before you were born
we sang to you, your song
and you were born
knowing your name

FAMILY PORTRAITS

wide set eyes
pot belly baby laugh
newt faced baby

are you human?
are you mine?
or merely some little visitor
here for a time?

to eat ticks
and call them raisins
play in the potty
when I'm not looking

demand deep water
over my head
laughing as I kick back
and paddle
trying not to drown us
both

in everything
all of it
the wonder of us
you
me
and
your mother

yes, we
exiles
like Ishmael
his hand raised

pariah
of the white
and the black
and the gay
and the straight

Genealogy

what kind of a world
have we created for you?

will my ancestors
recognize your face
and your sweet and gold spun hair?

will you love me
despite my selfish act?

making you
my child
my diamond?

© 1993 Joanne M. Braxton.

Missing Alice
In Search of a Mother's Voice

Susan Letzler Cole

My mother's voice is one of the voices we're losing in the world. Vanishing ahead of us is a generation of women who came of age during the Depression, gave birth during the last world war, will not greet the millennium with their children. Most of them are uncelebrated, undocumented, hardly remarked upon as they pass from our view. These women made a life out of certain values that contribute much to the world we have known. We need to listen to more of them: old voices, sick voices, quiet voices.

Alice's voice is musical and well-modulated with intelligently varied patterns of stresses and rhythm. Recognizably feminine, it is a voice of many colors and "lights." There is, surprisingly, no trace of her native New York in her accent. It is a voice in the medium range, sometimes falling into the lower range. Except when tired or nervous or saddened by a particular memory, her voice carries with it a sense of pleasure in all the sounds of every word it knows. There is in its emphases a hint that the sounds of a voice in conversation can be as musically precise as those of poetry. Saying "fifty-three," the voice takes pleasure in the strong "r" of "three"; "snow" is stressed in the phrase "in the snow," and "deep" in the phrase "in this deep snow." Always distinct, never loud, never shrill, Alice's voice generally avoids the contemporary rising inflection at the ends of sentences and phrases. There is nothing lazy or inattentive in the wordsounds it "sings" in normal conversation or in its flawless command of grammar and syntax. This voice is not in the least showy. Only those attentive to the music of speech would recognize its quality.

Alice's voice was my earliest connection with her. It is what I miss most. Photographs won't return it; dreams can't reproduce it. My aural memories require a reappearance of sound and now there is only silence. None of us can be counted on to be always fully present in the voice. But she was, with me. In the sounds of our voices we didn't hide or withdraw from the other. Voice was our most intimate emotional, intellectual, and spiritual meeting place. My mother was fully alive, uniquely present, in her voice. I have never heard anything like it.

Alice Parson Letzler died of colon cancer in the late summer of 1990 at the age of seventy-eight, and I began to write letters to her in the summer of 1993. After a time the silence in this one-way dialogue became unbearable. The year before my mother died she and I, at my urging, had made three tapes of an unfinished "oral history" of her life. My desire to hear her absent voice led me to listen to and then transcribe those tapes. But this was not the end of my search for Alice's voice.

Marianne Hirsch in *The Mother/Daughter Plot* has said, "The woman who is a mother was a subject as a daughter." In August of 1994, I unexpectedly found in the bottom of a file cabinet in my brother's basement a small notebook covered in brown wrapping paper. It said: "Property of Alice Parson. Private." On the second page were the words, "Diary: Memoirs, Comments, Incidents." After an hour of hesitation I began reading.

Alice's diary was written in July and August of 1926 when she was fourteen and her own mother had suddenly and mysteriously fallen ill, though she does recover. It contains a voice I never heard—very young, dutiful, at times bewildered, always hopeful. But the diary is opaque, the diarist hidden in her diary. Once again I write letters to a missing Alice, a fourteen-year-old diarist, the mother who isn't there yet.

What are the narrative strategies appropriate to the project of telling a life? The obvious way to tell a life is a chronological account, with a beginning, middle, and end. My way is nothing like that. I begin by writing to my mother, not about her. Through writing to and about my mother I meet her again. Now I am the older woman and she grows younger. Death has brought no closure to our relationship: we are both changing.

June 5, 1996

Dear Alice Parson,

As I begin my sixth motherless summer, what can I say to you? How can I tell you what it's like to lose the mother you became?

I wrote letters to her; I listened to her voice; I came to the end of my resources. Then I found a trove of words I didn't even know existed. But they are your words, Alice Parson, not my mother's. And so my dialogue continues but with another Alice.

You, the subject I write about, write on the very subject I write about: the absence of the mother, though death is deferred. We are co-writers, a woman and a young girl, dealing with the difficulties of losing a maternal presence. Your diary is a kind of adolescent rehearsal of my adult experience.

In your diary you do not acknowledge the possibility of your mother's death; my letters written to my mother after her death are, by their very existence, a profound denial of absolute loss. You write to yourself; I wrote to the self you will become. You call your daily recordings of what you observe and experience a diary; mine I called letters, or echolocations, but they are a kind of diary eventually opened up to public view, like yours. You write to yourself in the summer season, the summer of 1926, and now I write to you, seventy summers later.

You write before the loss: I write the loss.

June 8, 1996

Dear Alice Parson,

I am reading your diary over again today. I thought I would feel joy in the simple act of rereading.

For a moment you rise up, quite alive, in your excited opening sentence. Then I am alone, my solitude merely deepened by the return as reader to what the writer has left behind.

June 13, 1996

Dear Alice Parson,

Now I cannot stop writing you and I cannot write letters to anyone else. I try to pack up what I have written and hide it away. I walk out of the room, but it follows me. Late at night, first thing in the morning, it cries: You aren't through with me!

June 17, 1996
New York City

Dear Alice Parson,

In *Aging and Its Discontents*, Kathleen Woodward suggests that the "'essence' of a memory of someone . . . [might] have to be that which we could *not* remember, never having known it." The daughters I search, you and me, are not remembered: they exist for me only in their self-constructions, only in their own texts, the diaries which I reread. Past selves exist for me as writing.

I write to you, Alice Parson, in order to remember what I never have known.

I write (to paraphrase Sor Juana) into a silence that is filled with voices. The texts in which I seek comfort are forms of absence. I write to the lost voice of nightly telephone conversations and to the taped voice of an old woman dying and to the voice of a fourteen-year-old diarist. I even write to my own adolescent voice.

I write in response to overheard remarks, casual questions, changes in weather. I write of night dreams and images that rise up before me as I awaken in the morning.

All that I write, Alice, I would destroy in a minute if I could hear for one minute the voice I seek.

July 2, 1996

Dear Alice Parson,

In *Through the Looking-Glass*, the White Queen says to Alice: "living backwards . . . always makes one a little giddy . . . but there's one great advantage in it, that one's memory works both ways." I am able to find in my own diaries a generic 1950's adolescent. With you it is different, not because I know less about you than I do about myself but because I know more. Octavio Paz writes, in *The Labyrinth of Solitude*, "Our deaths illuminate our lives. . . . Tell me how you die and I will tell you who you are." I know you, Alice. I was there as your life was illuminated. My memory works both ways.

July 6, 1996

Dear Alice Parson,

Two years ago in a dream my mother said to me: "You should say goodbye at the boundary." I didn't know what she meant but I wrote down the words and the date, February 21, 1994.

A few moments after my mother's death the young woman from Sierra Leone whom I had just hired to take care of her said, "Your mother will make a way." I didn't know what she meant but I wrote down the words.

No one speaks for you and you do not appear in my dreams. I have just met you. I don't know how to say goodbye. I haven't found the boundary.

The references for the citations in the letters are: Lewis Carroll, *Alice's Adventures in Wonderland and Through the Looking Glass* (New York: New American Library, 1960) 172; Marianne Hirsch, *The Mother/Daughter Plot: Narrative, Psychoanalysis, Feminism* (Bloomington: Indiana UP, 1989) 170; Octavio Paz, *The Labyrinth of Solitude: Life and Thought in Mexico* (New York: Grove P, 1961) 54; and Kathleen Woodward, *Aging and Its Discontents: Freud and Other Fictions* (Bloomington: Indiana UP, 1991) 119.

Making an Exit

Elinor Fuchs

Journal entry, like many others. Seven years into the emergency: I arrive to find that mother has staged a riot earlier in the day, when she was supposed to have her hair trimmed. It was noon and the little salon was full of patrons under dryers. Betty came forward with a plastic apron, and—WHOOP!—mother is defending herself against an ax murderer. On the loose! She screams, shouts for help, hurls insults, tears, bites. People run to help from the lobby, the nurse's office, and housekeeping. Patrons are disgusted and wish mother would move out. "She's impossible," says Betty, who runs the one-room shop in the retirement residence. "I feel sorry for her. I feel sorry for *you*."

I didn't tell Betty: mother was always impossible. She was not impossible because she was cruel or cold. She was impossible because there was so much of her. You could admire her, enjoy her—as indeed she did herself—but you couldn't really love her. Once, when I was a newlywed, she tried to buy me a sex manual in a Provincetown bookstore, like the ones buried in her underwear drawer when I was growing up that showed the best positions. "I'd rather read a love manual," I murmur, pushing her out of my bed. "Love?" She sounds incredulous. Love was one of the creepy words, like "God," "soul," and maybe "woman."

With her booming voice, her high energy, her drive for financial success, her buoyant self-promotion, her contempt for stupidity, especially right-wing stupidity, her confidence daring itself out over the concrete pools without water that were not only the chances she took, but also the dry, unwatered places within . . . in any given room, mother took up all the room there was.

My grandmother, my mother's mother, encouraged mother in this self-expansion. Indeed it was for her that it was fundamentally performed. She skipped her brilliant daughter two whole grades, listened raptly to her powers of oratory as the first woman president of the Glenville High debate team, and proudly sent her off to college at sixteen. My grandmother was thus somewhat compensated for the tragic waste of her own high intelligence, thwarted when my great-grandfather forced her into a cigar factory after sixth grade to help support the younger siblings.

Let not the child stand in the way of opportunity! my grandmother counseled mother, when the offer came to direct a statewide federal program one hundred miles away in the state capital. My glamorous mother, with her cornflower blue eyes, infectious haw-haw laugh, and perhaps too authoritative voice at thirty-one, would never snag another husband, her mother thought, if her family situation were on display. And if the husband didn't work out, at least Lil would be the first female senator from the state of Ohio or something equally meteoric. The child stayed "at home," in a swirling depression-style household—half the rent paid by absent mother—that included my bankrupt grandfather now reduced to selling men's jackets on the road like Willy Loman, my mother's younger sister and her husband, their two toddler daughters, my mother's brother Ed, going through medical school on the end of the family shoestring, and my embattled cat Blackie, whom I tenaciously defended against the indifference of relatives who had already managed to lose a wirehaired terrier puppy through sheer distraction.

Four years later, not yet a senator or a wife, mother had advanced from state capital to national capital. She sent for me after I wrote a postcard to protest her flirtation with a twelve-month position in Brazil. "Washington will have to do for the time being," I sniffed, in round, childish letters. Slipping the knot of generations, like young career girls now, we shared a small one-bedroom apartment in the overcrowded wartime capital, all she could afford.

Every morning mother and I would see each other off to our respective jobs, in office or in fifth grade. It was my task to supervise my mother's appearance. "How do I look?" she would ask, rotating like a fashion model. I would study her, in her brown and blue knit tunic suit and her suede platform shoes with the double straps that showed off her slim ankles. "Your belt is twisted," I observe. "Thank you!" she sings. "Are my seams straight?" I study the stockings critically. "Yup, they're O.K." Then off we'd go, she putting a hatpin through some "smart" confection on her head and carrying a briefcase, me already three inches taller than my mother, just a little overweight, and somewhat awkward in my new Buster Brown lace-up shoes with the arch supports.

It was in these improbable quarters that mother began her career as hostess. How mother loved a party! Parties were her coming-out ball, her platform, her stage, her launching pad, her natural environment. Against a wall of that apartment we had an upright Mason & Hamlin piano on which I worked at my two-part inventions. At parties, mother sat at the keyboard before the anthology of old American songs she coedited—it had been published by Doubleday, Dorn, & Co. a few years earlier—and played Civil War songs like "Just Before the Battle, Mother." These peak moments, when the buffet had been cleared, and the last of the demitasse was scattered around the room, were always introduced with rolling arpeggios, and then a highly dramatic version of "The Anniversary Waltz," played with the teetering dynamics of the waltz from

Rosenkavalier. Mother also loved to dance. Without notice at these parties, she would suddenly be advancing rhythmically across the living room, running her hands down her body in some combination of Isadora Duncan and Carmen Miranda, or lifting her narrow skirt above her knees, tossing her head over first one lifted shoulder, then the other. I almost died.

After the war, mother went into business. The idea was inspired by the vast amount of American equipment littering the globe from Brazil to Burma. The military purchasing missions attached to the embassies lining Massachusetts Avenue would have an endless need for American automotive parts. She would be the "middleman" and supply them. Committed early to what I took to be the higher calling of a life in art in solidarity with my absent father, I persuaded myself that I despised my mother's values. So boring, this attraction to business; so irritating, the related passion for clothes, for parties, and later, for caterers for parties, for interior decorators for larger apartments, needed for parties.

I went to college, graduated, married at once. Mother had said, "For God's sake, don't end up like me—marry him!" Then mother went off to Pakistan and India, to Iran, South Korea, and Japan, selling spare parts, machine tools, roadbuilding equipment, electronic components, and paramilitary gear, and coming home like Marco Polo with ten of whatever there was to buy, one for each of her employees. I wrote in my attic and raised babies. Sitting in my suburban kitchen, mother read the manuscript of the large documentary play I had worked on for three years, and tossed it on my desk. "Well, it's interesting, but it's not a play. I don't know what it is, but it's not a play."

She said this in the voice of objective certitude that sometimes won her praise for having a mind just like a man. The nerve! She didn't even know me! I kept my distance, at first by moody instinct, then by advice and design. "Vot?" my eccentric Berlin-trained analyst asked me in New York, "You vould have your mother stay viss you in your house? Vot is ziss? Scrrrambled eggs? Are you crrrazy?" Each to her own shell. In truth I kept my distance not just because I scorned the business life, though I was entirely innocent of what it meant for a woman born in 1908 to do what mother did, but because my mother's body put me into acute, if suppressed, discomfort. In a photo of myself at three, wearing a smocked dress and a hairbow, I sit next to my pretty mother on a studio couch. Our bodies do not touch. I am looking at her tentatively: who is this stranger?

Later, my puritanical child's modesty was frightened by the exposed female bodies that populated my mother's family. I prayed that God would spare me what I took to be the certain consequence of age, my stout grandmother's flap of a belly, which hung over her pubic triangle like an immense third mammary. Then there was my mother's plump and cheerful sister, who would always say "Come in" when you knocked on her bedroom door, even if she was in bed with my uncle wearing nothing at all. Why did people sleep that way?

In our small apartment, to my inward shudders and reluctant fascination, mother paraded her naked body like a costume, but beneath the carnival she was in fact her body's stern and driving master. She smoked two packs of cigarettes a day, stayed up all night when bids on parts lists had to be submitted, ate marbled beef for recreation, and didn't believe in illness. Illness was a moral failure or a mental error. She never indulged it. When the heart attack came at sixty-three she threw away the cigarettes and kept on going.

"Keep on going!" was her mantra, uttered optimistically well into Alzheimer's disease, with a triumphant fist raised in the air, but that was later. Two years after the heart attack she researched, then ignored, the diagnosis of ductile carcinoma in situ in her right breast. "It's *in situ*," she explained, of this invisible granule, "Only one out of ten will actually spread." After she tumbled into Alzheimer's in her early seventies, mother took to calling the prosthesis for this breast (which was excised, along with several lymph nodes, when the granule became a golf ball) her "baby," and would tuck it tenderly into her specially constructed brassiere. I, on the other hand, became her "mother," as she often called me when she needed a name for our relationship.

My ten-year career as mother, as caretaker of the body that was once my childhood problem—as inhabitant almost of the same skin, so acutely could I anticipate her needs—was forecast here, at the moment of this mastectomy. We are in the hospital, a few days after the operation, preparing to go home. Mother's chest wall is protected by white gauze and a large ace bandage. "Mother, have you looked at it?" I ask. "No," she says, with snap-shut denial. I see what must be done. "Well," I say, drawing a deep breath, "Let's do it together then." She raises her arms. I unwind the dressings. Slowly we turn, as if posing for a family photograph, and gaze in the mirror at the long, jagged scar.

"I'm afraid the home care system you have in mind can't be worked out in this area," says a District of Columbia geriatric social worker after there is no escape from the diagnosis of Alzheimer's, and I explain that I am looking for a part-time companion for my mother. I want someone who is intelligent, imaginative, fun!, someone *not* in a white uniform, someone with a car. "There are no agencies that supply such people," she tells me. I am impatient with this advice. *I* work in the theater. There are *always* people who are fun, etc.—and of course I find them. But the decline is precipitous, and I am running, running, to catch up. We go from fifteen hours to thirty, from five days to seven, from half-days to whole days, and then to nights. Mother's apartment does not permit a full-time companion living in. She fills up every inch of it. Young professional women and willing grad students rotate on the sleeping sofa, attracted to ads in community newspapers that read, "Earn Money While You Sleep."

In monthly visits from wherever I am—now New York, now Atlanta—to Washington, and for the early hours of every day on the telephone or in correspondence, I perform my mother's life. I am the link to her caregivers of course, and to her doctors, her lawyer, her bank manager, her accountant, her insurance agent, her landlord, the IRS, the Social Security Administration, the man who bought her business. I am her traditional son: acquiring some of the business skills I had earlier scorned in her, I study her money, learn how to produce an income. I am her traditional daughter: I sew on buttons, shore up hems, reheel shoes, repair the television set, stake up the begonias in the flowerpot, change the light bulbs, scrub the carpet, spray for roaches. I know her medications, her diet, the potassium, the salt, the fat. I do mother's body for her. Her toenails need cutting or they will be ingrown. The cortisone for the psoriasis is thinning away the skin. Try tar. Mother has false teeth, dentures so natural I had almost forgotten their existence. She no longer remembers to clean them. She no longer remembers them at all. I reach into the back of her mouth—she won't bite me as she does the other helpers—and pull on the little hook that releases the upper plate.

Then I realize that mother wears, *oh my God* a pessary! So that's what happened when she was too busy to bother with an operation for her sagging uterus and bladder. And now it seems that mother has mild osteoporosis. Ruth, mother's companion-in-charge, telephones: she has broken her collarbone, and is in bed, sporting a sling. I go down to Washington. Mother is wearing diapers for the first time. That night, the two of us alone, and with a fresh horror which would mitigate through practice, I learn to change my mother's diaper.

I have become a crustacean of memory, my mother's carapace, her protective shell. She drags within me, this still flamboyant drag queen. I am engorged with every aspect of my mother's life. Indeed I am sick from excess memory. I need twenty-four hours after every visit to pass back through the membrane of emergency—the nail polish mistaken for lipstick and painted on the lips ("See how gorgeous?" she preens), the hair combed with toothpaste, the feces dropped distractedly in a trail leading from the bathroom, the screams that one helper or another is trying to kill her, the sentences forgetting their direction in the middle and wagging helplessly like severed dogs—I need twenty-four hours before I can stop gasping and choking, losing words and thoughts, and falling asleep standing up. And beyond even that I live in a state of perpetual affright at death. I am aging and dying axiomatically. Like a little service boat grappled to a barge, there is no way I can resist the journey. I am too young to see all this, I moan inwardly. I dream I am standing head down in a black stagnant pool, I dream of great black and white birds of death crashing through my windows.

But if I am overstuffed with memory and memory-sick, in the ironic ecology of dementia, mother is lightening like a helium balloon and better than well. When she is fresh and clean and not in a suspicious patch and smiling in that lit-up way of hers and sailing forth in her red Castleberry suit, she carries everyone she encounters into a realm of high spirits new even to her, though that was after we made the move.

Some six years into the emergency, she stopped dead in the hall outside her livingroom one afternoon and stammered to me, in surprising lucidity and sequentiality, of boredom. "I don't know how many times before they've . . . they've . . . created this situation, getting people to . . . to express themselves in this . . . this *boring* way. I—I have an intelligence that is being overlooked," she almost wept, "It's so far beneath me it's . . . it's . . . " Soon after this, reluctantly incinerating most of a one-term academic leave, I closed mother's home of thirty years, and moved her to a retirement residence, known in the trade as an assisted living facility.

For mother, this somewhat conservative, southern place with its well-bred ladies enjoying its gracious small apartments, pink-linened dining room, daily cocktail hour, "stimulating" exercise classes, and quiet lobby with the player piano plugged in on major holidays, now became the social and intellectual equivalent of just having gotten into Radcliffe. Better, it was a perpetual party. For at least a few hours of each day now mother was in love with everything and everyone. Entering the dining room she exclaims, "I just love this! It's really marvelous!" She gusts through the corridors loudly calling out, "I love you! Something great! Something gruchious! Something above us! Something loves us!" To a passing nurse she booms, "Hallo, sweetie!" and to another, "Hi, my sweetheart!" Each oncoming Jamaican lady in a white uniform is a potential dancing partner. "Chachacha!" she calls out on approach, and soon Chacha has become her nickname. "How is my little Chachacha today?" they greet her, stroking her cheek, and mother responds "Chachacha!" on cue, beaming like a beloved three-year-old, with a delighted little shimmy of the hips.

In this setting I think of mother not so much as ill, but as an Original, inventing a fractured language that reminds me of Lucky's speech in *Godot*, or perhaps Marinetti's futurist ideal of words floating deliriously free of syntax, *parole-in-libertà*. On the telephone, we have delicious little conversation-simulacra:

Elinor: Hello, mother!
Mother: Elinor! Did you get the—the group?—the inspection? Have there been any Stalins at all?
Elinor: Not many.
Mother: They've been girding a lot. That, plus the infinity. There was a lot of starting at the beginning.
Elinor: Oh, this is marvelous!
           (Peals of laughter, both sides.)
Mother (darkly):   It's such bad athols here. It's all over the place. There's a lot of whiting going on, a lot of whiting and riting.

"Uh*huh*. Can you do it, too?," I ask, not knowing whether to understand the intimate sounds we are exchanging in the discourse of orthography: writing; or religious ritual: riting; or ethics: righting; or shipbuilding . . . etc., etc. Each choice summons its own zany perspective.

FAMILY PORTRAITS

We have conversations at the dinner table:

Elinor: How's life treating you, mother?
Mother: Panasonic. I started out with the Serb people from the upper lakes.
Elinor: From the upper lakes?
Mother: So I had to take those in.
Elinor: Um-hummm.
Mother: Although not exactly, because I'm sitting at the other place having darts downstairs, so I didn't know. In other words, we didn't have a predelexis shookel.
Elinor (incredulous tone):   *Shookel*? (We collapse in laughter.)

And again on the telephone:

Elinor: Hello, mother.
Mother: Hello! my mother, duther, wrubber, brother, dear, dear lovely, dovey—
Attendant: She's your daughter, Lillian.
Mother: My lovey daughter (merriness and hilarity).
Elinor: You're in a festive mood.
Mother: That I am, and I most certainly will be to the very end!

The word "love" regularly crossed mother's lips now. My daughters would exclaim, "Mom, Alzheimer's has been *good* for Grandma!"——But writing this, I begin to sense the tug of Narrative. Let me guard against the triumph of redemptive suffering. In many ways, the "very end" was an obscenity.

After eighteen months at the retirement home, where mother's advancing regress more and more isolated her in her little cell of round-the-clock helpers, the opportunity came to move her one last time, now to the best Alzheimer's unit of any nursing home in our community. She had been on the waiting list for many months "just in case," we said, and might have to wait several more if we did not seize the opening now. She qualified for this honor by scoring less than five on the mini-mental test (failing questions like "Can you say bureau, ball, dog?"), a test on which she had received a none too stellar twenty-seven five years earlier when she was already quite impaired.

"No!" cried Ruth, "She's not ready!" Mother's brother Ed, a psychoanalyst, urged me to go ahead. "It's the right move, and at the right time, while she can still make positive social efforts," he urged. "She can be with people there right up to the end." I was thinking both of mother and of myself, I must confess. I had put nearly a decade of my life into the emergency, a decade in which my daughters in college could have done with more attention, in which my work was retarded, in which my last best years to remarry (at least actuarially speaking) had expired—a decade in which I had suddenly grown old. The nursing home would for the first time relieve me of day-to-day decisions. And then there was the money. The nursing home would cost only somewhat more than, instead of more than twice, her annual income.

On her first day there, mother gazed at the pines and the locust tree outside the window of her room. She looked right past the yellow cotton curtains drooping at a depressing angle on a broken wall bracket, and exclaimed, "It's beautiful!, just *beautiful*!" "I've witnessed a miracle!" Ed exclaimed in turn, his voice choked with love and wonder. I wasn't so sure: maybe "beautiful" was just the word of the day. And at the moment, the place wasn't beautiful to me. The babble, shrieking, shuffling, and wandering of the patients seemed a scene from hell.

Several nurses surrounded mother to do an intake examination. Stripping her, they turned her slowly, like a dummy, taking written note of every discoloration and abnormality. They spoke kindly, mother laughed gaily, but tears were streaming down her face. A half hour later, however, we watched as she bobbed out upon this world of the crazies, enthusiastic for new experience. She seemed genuinely glad to have shaken off the constant attendant at her elbow.

In the bright central space where everything but sleep occurred, mother encountered all the residents of the Special Care Unit many times a day, each time delighting in a new set of fellow sufferers. Mr. Blue, one of two male dementees in the unit, fell in love with mother. One day, in an affectionate confusion, mother was found wearing Mr. Blue's dentures. Once a week a movement teacher came for the entire home. Mother joined her on the stage and danced, I was told, like Isadora Duncan.

In her ninth month at the Washington Home and Hospice, on the Saturday when I was there to celebrate her eighty-fifth birthday, mother, enjoying her new independence of movement, fell on the hard floors that had no rugs because rugs are not safe for older people with dementia, and broke her hip. Some weeks later, despite the physical therapy, her legs were sticks. There was food under her cracked fingernails. Her hair was scraggly. She wore white elastic stockings up to her thighs for circulation. Her teeth were lost, her lips sunken. She sat for long hours with her eyes closed. But now she opens them and greets me with a whoop of recognition. "Is that . . . is that . . . the one I love?" she cries hoarsely, picking up my hand and covering it with kisses. "Is that the . . . the . . . bbbaby?" "I LOVE you!"

Going home on the train a few days later, I write an entry in my journal:

> Sitting here drenched in tears. Thinking of mother, dying. Feeling the horrible loneliness of being separated from my mother—a real, and a mythical, being. Oh mother what grief, what terrible grief. I'm sitting here with my eyes closed, just like you, weeping and weeping for you and for myself. Oh little bones! Little lamb! It hardly matters now which of us is mother and which the daughter. Taking care of, as good as being taken care of. My task: to keep the little spirit in the world.

"Never give up" mother always said, and we did not. When the physical therapist gave up on mother's twice-weekly sessions, I hired extra people to walk her. The walking came back in part. The eyes opened once again. One day, in her old businesswoman's voice she even boomed, "Well, I'll have to stop dying." But on a Saturday morning a few months later she had a sudden heart attack and was gone within a minute or two.

I have been asked by friends, searching for the thing to say, "Did your mother know you?" They assume of course I knew my mother. In truth, I knew her better when I loved her less. We had shared decades of dis-knowing, before that the early times of never-having-known. The last ten years: they were our best.

NOTES ON CONTRIBUTORS

ANNE DAVIS BASTING teaches playwriting and cultural studies in the English Department at the University of Wisconsin-Oshkosh. Her scholarly and creative work focuses on memory, generations, and aging across the life course. She is the author of *The Stages of Age: Performing Age in Contemporary American Culture* (1998) and the award-winning plays *The Last Dinosaur* and *Memory Box*. Basting is currently creating intergenerational storytelling workshops with people with Alzheimer's disease.

TERESA BRENNAN is the author of *History after Lacan* (1993) and *The Interpretation of the Flesh: Freud and Femininity* (1992), the editor of *Between Feminism and Psychoanalysis* (1989), and the coeditor, with Martin Jay, of *Vision in Context* (1995). In addition, two books are in press: *Consciousness and Social Consciousness* and *Beyond Hubris: Elements for a New Economy*. She has been Visiting Professor at Cornell, Brandeis, and Harvard and is currently Schmidt Distinguished Professor of Philosophy and Sociology at Florida Atlantic University.

JOANNE M. BRAXTON is Professor of English and Frances L. and Edwin L. Cummings Professor of American Studies and English at the College of William and Mary. She is the author of a collection of poetry entitled *Sometimes I Think of Maryland* (1977) as well as the genre study *Black Women Writing Autobiography: A Tradition within a Tradition* (1989). She has also edited *The Collected Poems of Paul Laurence Dunbar* (1993) and coedited, with Andree N. McLaughlin, *Wild Women in the Whirlwind: The Renaissance in Contemporary Afra-American Writing* (1990).

JODI BROOKS, formerly Lecturer in Cultural Studies in the English Department at Melbourne University, now teaches in the School of Theatre and Film at the University of New South Wales. She is the author of essays in *Art & Text*, *Continuum*, and the collection *Kiss Me Deadly: Feminism and Cinema for the Moment* (1995).

SUSAN LETZLER COLE is the author of *Directors in Rehearsal* (1992), *The Absent One: Mourning Ritual, Tragedy, and the Performance of Ambivalence* (1985), and *Playwrights in Rehearsal* (forthcoming from Routledge). Cole is Professor of English and Director of the Drama Concentration at Albertus Magnus College in New Haven.

CECELIA CONDIT is Professor of Video and Film at the University of Wisconsin-Milwaukee. Her videos include *Suburbs of Eden* (1992), for which she received a Guggenheim Fellowship, *Not a Jealous Bone* (1987), *Possibly in Michigan* (1983), *Dressing Up and Down* (1982), and *Beneath the Skin* (1981). Her most recent work is *Oh, Rapunzel* (in collaboration with Dick Blau, 1996).

ANCA CRISTOFOVICI is Associate Professor of American Cultural Studies at the University of Caen, France. She is the author of essays on contemporary American fiction and photography, in addition to a book entitled *John Hawkes: L'Enfant & le cannibale* (1997). She is working on a book on representations of aging in recent literary texts and art photography.

JOANNA FRUEH is an art critic, art historian, and performance artist. She is author of *Erotic Faculties* (1996), a collection of her critical and performance art writings, and *Hannah Wilke: A Retrospective* (1989). Frueh is the coeditor, with Cassandra Langer and Arlene Raven, of *New Feminist Criticism: Art, Identity, Action* (1994) and *Feminist Art Criticism: An Anthology* (1991), both of which contain essays by her. She is Professor of Art History at the University of Nevada, Reno.

ELINOR FUCHS teaches at Columbia University and the Yale School of Drama. Her articles and essays on theater have appeared in *The Village Voice*, *American Theatre*, and numerous journals and anthologies. Her books include *The Death of Character: Perspectives on Theater after Modernism* (1996), *Plays of the Holocaust: An International Anthology* (1987), and the documentary play *Year One of the Empire*.

MARGARET MORGANROTH GULLETTE is the author of *Declining to Decline: Cultural Combat and the Politics of the Midlife* (1997). She has also written *Safe at Last in the Middle Years: The Invention of the Midlife Progress Novel* (1988) and many scholarly essays and popular articles on the history and ideology of the middle years of life. Her work has been recognized by a Bunting Fellowship and fellowships from the ACLS and the NEH. She is a Research Associate in Women's Studies at Brandeis University.

JACQUELINE HAYDEN is Associate Professor of Film and Photography at Hampshire College. She is the recipient of two fellowships from the National Endowment for the Arts as well as a fellowship from the Guggenheim Foundation for *Figure Model Series*, her work with elderly models. Recently she has been an artist-in-residence at the Banff Center for the Arts, Canada, and at the American Academy in Rome, Italy.

E. ANN KAPLAN is Professor of English and Comparative Studies at SUNY Stony Brook, where she also founded and directs the Humanities Institute. Her books include *Looking for the Other: Feminism, Film and the Imperial Gaze* (1997), *Motherhood and Representation: The Mother in Popular Culture and Melodrama* (1992), and *Rocking Around the Clock: Music Television, Postmodernism and Consumer Culture* (1987). She is currently working on a book on trauma, aging, and ethnicity.

STEPHEN KATZ, Associate Professor of Sociology at Trent University in Ontario, Canada, is the author of *Disciplining Old Age: The Formation of Gerontological Knowledge* (1996). He has contributed to *Images of Aging: Cultural Representations of Later Life* (1995). His essays have appeared in *Journal of Women and Aging*, *Journal of Aging Studies*, *Political Studies*, and *Australian Cultural History*.

TERESA MANGUM is Associate Professor of English at the University of Iowa. She is the author of *Married, Middle-brow, and Militant: Sarah Grand and the New Woman Novel* (1996) and is currently writing a book on Victorian conceptions of aging. Her work on aging has been published in the *Blackwell Companion to Victorian Literature and Culture* and will appear in *The Handbook of the Humanities and Aging* (2nd ed.).

PATRICIA MELLENCAMP is Distinguished Professor of Art History at the University of Wisconsin-Milwaukee, where she teaches film, video, and the electronic arts. She is the author of *A Fine Romance: Five Ages of Film Feminism* (1996), *High Anxiety: Catastrophe, Scandal, Age & Comedy* (1992), and *Indiscretions: Avant-garde Film and Video* (1990). She is the editor of *Logics of Television: Essays in Cultural Criticism* (1990).

NANCY K. MILLER is Distinguished Professor of English at the Graduate School and Lehman College, CUNY. Her most recent books are *Bequest and Betrayal: Memoirs of a Parent's Death* (1996), *French Dressing: Women, Men and Ancien Régime Fiction* (1995), and *Getting Personal: Feminist Occasions and Other Autobiographical Acts* (1991). She is currently working on a project about young women and the culture of the 1950s in New York.

MARIE-CLAIRE PASQUIER is Professor of American Literature at Paris X-Nanterre and the author of two books on American and British theater. Pasquier has translated Virginia Woolf's *Mrs. Dalloway* as well as works by William Kennedy and Norman Maclean into French.

RACHEL ROSENTHAL is a performance artist based in Los Angeles whose work explicitly engages ecological and feminist concerns. Rosenthal is a recipient of two fellowships from the National Endowment for the Arts and a Genesis Award. Her recent works include *Zone* (1994), *filename: FUTURFAX* (1992), and *Pangaean Dreams* (1990).

MARY RUSSO is Professor of Literature and Critical Theory and Dean of the School of Humanities and Arts at Hampshire College. She is the author of *The Female Grotesque: Risk, Excess and Modernity* (1994) and the coeditor, with Beverly Allen, of *Revisioning Italy: National Identity and Global Culture* (1997) and *Nationalism and Sexualities*, with Andrew Parker, Doris Sommer, and Patricia Yaeger (1992). Her essays have appeared in the collections *Women and Spatiality* (1997) and *Comparative Literature in the Age of Multiculturalism* (1995).

VIVIAN SOBCHACK is Associate Dean and Professor of Film and Television Studies at the UCLA School of Theater, Film and Television. Her books include *Screening Space: The American Science Fiction Film* (1997), *The Address of the Eye: A Phenomenology of Film Experience* (1993), and an edited anthology, *The Persistence of History: Cinema, Television and the Modern Event* (1996). A collection of her own essays, *Carnal Thoughts: Bodies, Texts, Scenes and Screens*, is forthcoming from Univ. of California Press.

SUSAN SQUIER is Julia Gregg Brill Professor of English and Women's Studies at the Pennsylvania State University. A Faculty Affiliate of the Penn State Gerontology Center, she is the author of *Babies in Bottles: Twentieth-Century Visions of Reproductive Technology* (1994) and *Virginia Woolf and London: The Sexual Politics of the City* (1985). She is the coeditor of *Arms and the Woman: War, Gender and Literary Representation*, with Helen Cooper and Adrienne Munich (1989), and the editor of *Women Writers in the City: Essays in Feminist Literary Criticism* (1984).

KATHLEEN WOODWARD, Director of the Center for Twentieth Century Studies and Professor of English at the University of Wisconsin-Milwaukee, is the author of *Aging and Its Discontents: Freud and Other Fictions* (1991), as well as *At Last, the Real Distinguished Thing: The Late Poems of Eliot, Pound, Stevens, and Williams* (1980). She is the editor of *The Myths of Information: Technology and Postindustrial Culture* (1980) and the coeditor, with Murray M. Schwartz, of *Memory and Desire: Aging—Literature—Psychoanalysis* (1986).

INDEX

Index

Index

Index

Index

Index

Index

Index

WITHDRAWN